Milan 4th July
2018

To Gary
with best regards

Alberto

Companywide Quality Management

Companywide Quality Management

Alberto Galgano

Publisher's Message by Norman Bodek

Productivity Press

PORTLAND, OREGON

Address all inquiries to:

Productivity Press
P.O. Box 13390
Portland, OR 97213-0390
United States of America
Telephone: (503) 235-0600
Telefax: (503) 235-0909

Cover design by Abrams + La Brecque Design, Cambridge, Mass.
Printed and bound by the Maple-Vail Book Manufacturing Group
Printed in the United States of America

Library of Congress Cataloging-in-Publication Data

Galgano, Alberto.
[Qualità totale. English]
Companywide quality management / Alberto Galgano ; publisher's message by Norman Bodek.
p. cm.
Translation of: La qualità totale.
Includes bibliographical references.
ISBN 1-56327-038-2
1. Total quality management. 2. Quality control. I. Title.
HD62.15.G3513 1994
658.5'62--dc20 93-39945
CIP

98 97 96 95 94 10 9 8 7 6 5 4 3 2 1

Contents

Publisher's Message

It's a great pleasure for me to publish books by authors from all over the world. Alberto Galgano is the head of a very large consulting and training company in Italy. In a way he is a competitor of mine, but he is also a friend with a story deserving to be told, one of value that I am glad to be sharing with all our readers. *Companywide Quality Management* is the quality story of the decades since World War II, told in a fascinating way. As the reader, you will learn just as Galgano learned. You will enjoy the story within the story, the adventure of Ichiro, a Japanese manager struggling to survive forty years ago — how he learned and used quality as the driving force to lift his company to international competitiveness. It is a story American managers should have read years ago, but I believe it is never too late.

Mr. Galgano is a perpetual student, a wonderful observer who has helped hundreds of companies install total quality. He gives the information and the guidance for senior managers to create a long-term strategy using quality as the driving force for success. Total quality is an issue that everyone in an organization can buy into: managers, workers, customers, suppliers, even your bank and insurance company. Everyone has something to gain as you improve the quality of your products, your processes, your services, and the very quality of the work environment.

The book is divided into five parts. Part One gives an overview of the whole system of CWQM and its basic definitions. As total quality is fundamentally a set of strategies that are implemented through techniques and processes, Galgano devotes the three central parts of the book to these basic elements.

The eight chapters of Part Two describe in detail the strategies that CWQM entails, beginning with understanding and coming to "love" the customer. *Companywide Quality Management* further requires new ways of thinking about a company's human assets, its relationships with suppliers, and its product development mechanism. It requires a new orientation toward improving the *process* rather than focusing only on *results* — an orientation that means continuous improvement at all levels, not just intermittent breakthroughs. Galgano devotes a chapter to each of these revolutionary strategic approaches.

Part Three is equally significant in describing the techniques required to make CWQM succeed as a companywide endeavor. The initial chapter covers the seven statistical tools (seven QC tools) that are the heart of the quality revolution, telling how all employees can apply a scientific, data-oriented approach to workplace quality problems. Galgano also covers the seven management tools (sometimes known as the seven "new" tools) — important vehicles for making sense of valuable qualitative information. Quality function deployment is covered in this part, as is Ryuji Fukuda's CEDAC approach.

Galgano's Part Four covers CWQM processes as they involve the executive leadership of an organization. Here you will learn about hoshin management — a system for deploying top management policy throughout the company — and its complementary management element, daily routine work. Chapters also describe how quality circles and teams work, what education is required for optimum companywide involvement, and the role of top executive leadership in carrying out the President's Diagnosis.

Part Five offers helpful insights into what it takes to introduce CWQM, with unique information on Japanese and European quality efforts.

Finally, an international bibliography offers appropriate further reading for the main topics covered in the text.

This book presents the tools and techniques of quality, the methodology and the new language of quality. It is easy to read and full of the wisdom necessary to bring the quality concept to life throughout your organization. Have fun reading it, and great success putting it to work.

I wish to thank Alberto Galgano for bringing his book to Productivity Press to translate and publish. Special thanks also go to those who helped to produce the book: Speakeasy for the translation; Karen Jones and Diane Asay for editorial resources; Christine Carvajal for copyediting; Elizabeth Sutherland for proofreading; Mary Junewick for word processing; Bill Stanton for book design; Caroline Kutil, Michele Saar, and Karla Tolbert for art creation; Gayle Asmus for page composition; and Abrams + La Brecque Design for cover design.

Norman Bodek
CEO, Productivity Press

Preface

The contents of this book represent an attempt at explaining the meaning and the impact of a new way of managing a business, or, speaking more broadly, any organization, be it in the public or private sector. The term used to refer to this new management system is *total quality* (TQ), or *companywide quality management* (CWQM).* *Total quality* is the better known of the two, although in the text itself we will always refer to it as CWQM. There are specific reasons for this decision. The term *total quality* was created in the United States but remained devoid of meaning there until just a few years ago. The Japanese, on the other hand, adopted it as one of the pillars of their industrial rebirth, and, in 1968, they decided to call their version of this approach *companywide quality management,* specifically to emphasize its difference from the American approach.

CWQM involves a series of considerable innovations in the area of business management, innovations that started with control of product quality. The most significant aspects of such innovations were perfected in Japan between 1950 and 1965, and they represent one of the main factors behind that country's great economic development.

---

* The term used in Japan is "Company-wide Quality Control."

In 1980 this approach began to spread to industries in the United States and Europe, and we can now say that all leading companies in the main industrialized nations have introduced CWQM programs.

In recent years, both in the United States and in Europe, this approach has also been applied in the services sector and in government.

Often business scholars apply and speak of CWQM without giving proper credit to those who perfected it. They do not seem to remember that Western countries failed to understand how innovative this approach was until twenty years after its development. It is not easy to admit that in the past thirty years the Western world has achieved few valuable breakthroughs in the field of management. During that same time, Japan was witnessing a true revolution, one that has made that country the world leader in the industrial sector.

The Meaning of Companywide Quality Management

The expression *companywide quality management* indicates that the concept and techniques behind quality control are broad ones, and that they are to be applied to all sectors of a company. This is the main significance of the new approach. This book will attempt to show the powerful consequences of extending the quality control concepts to an entire business.

Professor Tetsuchi Asaka, one of the four professors who created CWQM[1], attributes the success of quality control in Japan to a mistake in translation. In 1950, the word *kanri* ("management"), instead of *jishego* ("control") was used to translate "control"; thus, quality *management,* rather than quality *control,* began to be implemented. Playing an important role was the Quality Control Research Group, created in 1949

[1] The other three professors are Kaoru Ishikawa, Masao Kogure, and Shigeru Mizuno.

within the Union of Japanese Scientists and Engineers (JUSE). One of the group's most influential members was Professor Kaoru Ishikawa, who served for many years as general secretary of that association.

The first companies to begin applying quality management techniques quickly realized the following:

- These techniques could be extended to all company activities.
- To be truly effective, these techniques had to be applied by the entire workforce, not only by quality specialists.

The word *quality,* which had been kept outside of management vocabulary, was now entering it with full honors. Its entrance was a truly revolutionary event, and something that explains the West's great difficulty in getting into the CWQM spirit. Western management vocabulary makes great use of words such as *productivity, costs, profits, marketing, market share,* and *ROI,* while the word *quality* is hardly present. In the past, quality was considered the exclusive domain of specialists. With CWQM, however, the word *quality* becomes the most important term in management, even more important than *profit.* In a way, quality management comes to represent the essence of business management.

Companywide Quality Management as a New Management System

The basic premise guiding this book is that CWQM is a truly new management system. Its concepts lead to radical changes in

- management values and priorities
- company culture
- management of company operations
- management and decision-making processes

- techniques and methods used by employees
- company climate, or people's perceptions regarding the company's relationships, organizational mechanisms, personnel policies, and environment

The management system deriving from these elements can be seen as a reference model that must first of all be understood. Japanese experts sometimes call this model the "constitution" of a company, and they say that CWQM represents a radical modification of the traditional constitution.

The chapters of this book are like pieces in a mosaic, each one representing one part of the theory under discussion.

Companywide Quality Management as a Strategic Tool

CWQM represented a survival tool for the Japanese until the end of the 1970s. It came into being as a means for overcoming the enormous difficulties encountered by industry in the postwar period, and its role was further strengthened during the oil crises of 1973 and 1979. After 1980, as the business "constitution" grew strong through the application of CWQM, Japanese businessmen realized that such an approach could become a powerful instrument to carry out a company's strategies.

My friend Masaaki Imai holds seminars around the world to spread a message that has been widely accepted in Japan: no other management system has been able to mobilize a company's human resources and focus them on few strategic goals as successfully as has the new total quality approach. This was confirmed by a study carried out by four researchers at the Massachusetts Institute of Technology, which focused on the automobile industry. Results of the study were published in a book whose title, *The Machine That Changed the World*, explains it fully.

The above study, published in October 1990, took five years and cost six million dollars. It offers convincing evidence that the Japanese model can be applied to Western business.

Among the study's striking findings are the fact that the only Western factory (in Europe) with higher quality than the Japanese needs four times as many workers to achieve it.

The Role and Limitations of CWQM in Management

The role of CWQM in managing a company should be neither understated nor exaggerated. CWQM is not simply a means of reducing defects and improving morale in certain departments, but rather it is a tool for improving a company's constitution and effecting radical attitude changes among employees. Yet it is an exaggeration to say that it will automatically increase sales and profits, and thus insure the company's success.

In its context, CWQM is necessary, but not sufficient in itself. A company cannot be managed through CWQM alone. Markets and technologies are now evolving so rapidly that no amount of improvement to existing conditions can guarantee competitiveness and success. Rather, companies must move beyond analytical processes to a constant search for innovation, creativity, and entrepreneurship.

For this reason, success will be neither assured nor lasting for companies that are not able to bring about constant innovations in strategic areas such as technology, production systems, products, materials, and communications systems. However, CWQM plays an essential role in innovation, as well. The reasons for this are the following:

1. Innovation always creates problems, and if the company's structure wastes too much time in trying to solve them, it limits the benefits of the innovation while delaying its further developments. CWQM favors progressive innovation.
2. Applying CWQM encourages innovation because it increases sensitivity to problems and improves the ability to act. Through its problem-solving

activities, CWQM improves the ability to make things happen; therefore it improves the ability to bring about innovation.

3. Whereas innovation is a specific event, CWQM is an all-encompassing approach. Since innovation requires the involvement of all company employees, CWQM is essential for achieving this end.
4. The application of CWQM requires a courageous attitude and a radical change in personnel's views, combined with a rational approach to problem solving. Such an approach also fosters innovation. Therefore, as CWQM is global, innovation itself becomes global, and well rooted in the company.

The dynamic nature of innovation in Japanese industry testifies to its involvement with CWQM.

The Universality of the CWQM Message

Italo Calvino, in his *Lezioni americane,* suggested six literary values to preserve for the next millennium. These values were intended as the subject of six lectures he was to give at Harvard University, as part of the Charles Eliot Norton Poetry Lectures. The six ideas he proposed bear surprising resemblance to the basic concepts of CWQM.

Lightness. Nothing is lighter than a company without inventory, or than an electronic instrument, such as a VCR, that has been reduced from the size of a large room to that of a box.

Speed. With CWQM, orders can be filled within a short time — in most cases, a few days or even a few hours. In the same way, the development time for new products is normally cut to less than half of that required by Western models.

Precision. CWQM increases precision in the production processes to the extent that defects in these processes are measured in parts per million, and in some cases, in parts per billion.

Visibility. A visual control system is one of the most advanced techniques for managing a company's operations.

Multiplicity. Managing the variety of products from one department or one line is the strong advantage of Japanese factories, and this is achieved at lower cost.

Consistency. The entire CWQM structure rests on a few concepts that are essential to success.

How I Discovered CWQM

It took me a long time to understand the extent and true significance of CWQM — about fifteen years, to be exact. This is common to many business executives who find it difficult to assimilate new messages.

My being one of the first to divulge this new business approach in Italy is due to the lucky circumstance of a very early exposure to it, at the beginning of the 1970s. For this, I must thank a Dutch colleague, Hans Enters, from Wan de Bunt, a Dutch consulting firm with which we were associated for many years. In 1969 Enters, an expert in quality management, spent time in Japan studying Japanese business management systems, and he brought back much information concerning the new approach to quality.

In 1972, Galgano & Associati signed an important consulting contract with a company then known as SNIA Viscosa, for a quality project. The program included a six-day seminar for top executives of that company, which we organized with Enters' assistance. During the seminar, we discussed total quality at length, using the terminology Enters had acquired. At the time I understood precious little about this new approach, but the seed had been planted in my mind, and fortunately, it began to grow. It took me another five or six years to understand its revolutionary importance. A milestone was reached when we fully realized that quality was the path to reducing costs and increasing productivity.

At that point we decided to commit ourselves seriously to promoting in Italy this new approach to quality. Our effort was aided when another colleague appeared on the scene: Masaaki Imai, author of the book *Kaizen,* which we later published in Italy (Edizioni del Sole 24 Ore). It was Imai who, during my visit to Japan in 1980, introduced me to the Union of Japanese Scientists and Engineers (JUSE), the group that had promoted and led the introduction of CWQM in Japan after 1950. And it was Imai who later introduced me to Ryuji Fukuda, one of the leading Japanese experts in the field of quality and production.

From 1981 on, Galgano & Associati became strongly committed to introducing the new approach to total quality in Italy. The first years of our activity were difficult ones, both because of our imperfect preparation and because of great skepticism about the Japanese model we were proposing. Over the years, however, our greater experience, as well as the phenomenal success achieved by Japanese industry worldwide, made our job less difficult. Today Galgano & Associati, along with a group of over eighty consultants, is considered to be one of the world's leading experts in CWQM.

The Book's Structure

The book includes an introduction and five parts.

The introduction explains that between the 1970s and the 1980s Western companies discovered the importance of quality for a business. It also analyzes those aspects of the Western approach to quality management that need to be changed.

The first part of the book provides an overall view of CWQM, in an attempt to present the forest before analyzing its trees. Chapter 1 presents the basic choices of CWQM, while Chapter 2 illustrates the system's main parts. Both chapters present an original view, the result of years of study, and attempt to explain the real significance of CWQM to businesses. Chapter 3 traces the development of CWQM in Japan. The second part of the book illustrates the basic strategies underlying CWQM. Each represents a radical change in the management of a company.

The third part of the book covers the techniques and the tools widely used by the employees of a company geared to CWQM, with one chapter showing the attitude employees must acquire if CWQM is to be successfully applied. Indeed, the development of a new company mentality and the widespread use of powerful techniques and tools represent two of the main strengths of CWQM.

The fourth part of the book describes five of the six basic processes of CWQM. A chapter is dedicated to each. These processes constitute the operational core of CWQM. They give rise to tangible operations and procedures. Only one of the processes, that concerning the management of products or services, is not analyzed here. To do so would require a whole separate book. The last chapter in this section, Chapter 23, is dedicated to the "engine" that moves this new approach: the chief executive's leadership ability.

The fifth part of the book treats the introduction of CWQM into a company. One chapter deals with its introduction in Japan, while two other chapters focus on its introduction in Western companies.

Acknowledgments

This book is nothing more than the setting forth of what we at Galgano & Associati have learned, especially through our many contacts with the Japanese business world, over the last ten years. Our contacts during the same period with American companies and experts, as well as with European colleagues, have also been extremely useful.

Our largest debt of gratitude is owed to JUSE, and to its executive director, Junji Noguchi. This association has assisted us throughout the years by making available to us its consultants and by organizing many visits to Japanese factories, both for our own experts and clients and for many other Italian companies.

It is difficult to find words to express the sense of gratitude that all of us at Galgano & Associati feel toward Ichiro Miyauchi, also of JUSE, who from 1981 to 1989 followed without interruption our trek along the arduous path toward CWQM, a goal that we have not yet fully attained.

Further thanks are owed to the professors who, again through JUSE, came to Italy to open up for us the great views of CWQM: to Yoji Akao of Tamagawa University, for the applications of quality deployment and quality function deployment, and to Ryuichi Kobayashi of Rikkyo University (Tokyo), for advanced statistical applications. We also owe posthumous thanks to Professor Kaoru Ishikawa of the Musashi Institute. Perhaps the greatest Japanese expert in CWQM, he came to Italy on behalf of Galgano & Associati to hold seminars, and he provided precious advice during the development of our professional activities.

In 1989, two months after the death of Professor Ishikawa, another great teacher of CWQM died. This was Professor Shigeru Mizuno, who gave us much valuable advice and whose profound book constituted an important source in our struggle to understand the new approach to quality. We also thank Professor Hitoshi Kume, the heir to Ishikawa's chair at the University of Tokyo, especially for the many seminars that he holds in Italy on behalf of Galgano & Associati.

Other Japanese firms and experts have helped us during the past years; I must mention, first of all, Masaaki Imai, chairman of the Cambridge Corporation in Tokyo, who introduced me into the Japanese world, and who assisted me and my colleagues by allowing us to participate in the interesting visits and seminars he has organized in Japan over the years. We owe to Imai the long collaboration that we began in 1984 with Ryuji Fukuda, whom we must thank for our success which we have worked in the areas of total manufacturing management, just-in-time, and product reliability.

I must also mention Masao Kogure, professor emeritus at the Tokyo Institute of Technology, and Yoshio Kondo, professor emeritus at the University of Kyoto, who provided excellent suggestions and advice.

The United States also proved a considerable source of material pertaining to quality. I would particularly like to thank Dorian Shainin, a member of the International Academy of Quality and one of the primary experts in statistics as applied to quality in the United States, for the seminars he has held regularly in Italy since 1985. I also want to thank Frank Caplan, for the seminars on quality that he has held in Italy in recent years.

I cannot neglect my European colleagues from Coopers & Lybrand, and in particular Bob Millar, as well as our friends and consultants Attila Oess of IMT (Instituts für Management Training) in Cologne and Philippe Goillandeau of Euro-Symbiose, in Nantes. My sincere thanks go, too, to the many clients with whom we have worked over the past ten years. I would like to mention them all, but the list would be too long.

Finally, I must mention those colleagues with whom I have a longstanding professional association. When there is great unity, and when the same values are held in common, it is hard to determine where a particular individual's contribution ends and someone else's begins. Whatever is good about this book is certainly the product of such a collaboration. In particular, I would like to mention my partners in the Galgano Group: Franco D'Egidio, Emilio Di Cristofaro, Marco Diotalevi, Giorgio Merli, PierPaolo Momo, Giancarlo Pagliughi, and Riccardo Varriale, to whom I owe much, as we have together assimilated the great innovations contained in the Japanese model.

This book would never have been completed without the cooperation of my assistant, Maurizio Sala, to whom I express my heartfelt thanks. Bruno Susio also collaborated in the research activities.

Last, but not least, I would like to thank my dear friend and colleague Renato Comai for the great help he provided in setting CWQM in a management framework, and Mr. Elia Martini for the great support he has given me, both with the small problems and the large, during so many years of my professional activity.

Concluding Remarks

I am proud of the active role Galgano & Associati has taken in bringing CWQM into Italian business, even though I realize that much still remains to be done.

CWQM is an endless process, and this book represents simply an attempt at presenting to executives and managers, as well as to scholars of management, what I have learned in an area that is strategic for both private and public companies, with the hope that others may improve upon it.

Alberto Galgano

Companywide Quality Management

PART ONE

Companywide Quality Management: A Summary

As I mentioned in the preface, it is not easy to understand the meaning of companywide quality management (CWQM). The clearest indication of this fact can be found in the difficulties companies encounter, first, in understanding its importance, and second, in understanding its mechanisms and processes.

In this part of the book I attempt to present an overall view of CWQM, from two angles. The aim is to give a sense of the whole before analyzing each part. In order to do this I will present the

- managerial decisions implied by CWQM
- elements constituting the general framework of CWQM

They are very different perspectives, yet complementary. It is a rather original elaboration, the result of years of experience in both theory and practice. Before describing the two angles, I will say a few words about the concept of quality, which assumes a highly innovative meaning within CWQM.

CHAPTER ONE

The Meaning of Quality

Introduction

The introduction of CWQM within a company endows the word quality with a new significance in that company, a significance not embraced by the traditional approach.

Ever since the Western world discovered the importance of quality, a debate has raged over the meaning of this word. David Garvin of Harvard University dedicated three chapters of his book Managing Quality to this matter, but no definition of quality is as simple and concrete as that espoused by CWQM. In CWQM quality becomes a comprehensive and unifying concept, concerning mainly the internal structure of the company. Besides this, quality can assume an operational meaning, which is projected toward the outside world and represents a pillar of the CWQM structure. Quality can have a negative or a positive meaning. Further, the concept of latent quality is fundamental for a company's primary activity — the development of new products. Two more points are fundamental to an understanding of quality:

- Quality is a function of time.
- The variability rate of this function increases constantly.

To some extent these points explain the skepticism of Japanese experts regarding the relevance of national and international standards. They believe that a stationary quality level is incompatible with the demand of a dynamic market for ever-rising quality levels.

Comprehensive Meaning

In CWQM the word *quality* becomes both a reference point and a goal for all activities undertaken within a company.

No limited reference point or goal (such as productivity) can be approached separately without the risk of neglecting other important reference points or goals.

The customer (whether internal or external) always demands a comprehensive performance (the mix of price, quality, delivery, service, safety) and for this reason, no single factor should be made the sole object of attention. Pursuit of such a limited objective may jeopardize a customer's satisfaction as a whole.

Making quality the reference point carries no such risks. *Quality* embraces and unifies every element contributing to excellence, which is the fundamental goal of every company. Quality, therefore, includes the following:

- competitiveness
- delivery
- cost
- morale
- productivity
- profit
- product quality
- quantity or volume
- performance
- service
- safety

- concern for the environment
- the stockholders' interest

The all-embracing dimension of *quality* is particularly important at the operational level of a company. Here the ability to combine all these factors is fundamental. It is in fact at this level that planned actions and predicted results should take place. Therefore the activities implemented must be well balanced in all aspects related to excellence.

Quality not only has a unifying dimension, but it also can be viewed as an enlarged concept. For example, when talking about quality one may refer to all of the following aspects:

- quality of a company's performance (in terms of costs, quality, delivery, service, safety)
- quality of individual performance
- quality of the organization
- quality of the company's image in the marketplace and worldwide
- quality of the working environment
- quality of relationships among employees

Operational Meaning

The operational meaning of quality is the very essence of the concept, and it represents a revolutionary break with the past. Such an operational concept can be examined from two vantage points:

Quality as customer satisfaction. Considering quality in light of the customer vastly improves upon the traditional concept. Quality thus acquires a "warm" meaning, which goes beyond numbers and technical details. Indeed, customers cannot be limited by any framework and always have the last word. Once the word quality embraces customers it becomes comprehensive and objective rather than parochial, partial, and subjective.

This definition also discourages excuses based on technical factors ("I was following specifications!"), since the last word always belongs to the customer. If the customer is not satisfied, no degree of compliance with specifications or standards can help. The only thing that counts is the level of customer satisfaction achieved.

In handing out the Malcolm Baldrige Award in November 1989, President Bush gave a perfect definition of quality, "In business, there is only one definition of quality: that given by the customer."

Quality as output. The second point of view is just as important as the first. Each individual and each organizational unit within a company finds its justification in the production of a specific output that, in turn, is used by other units or individuals. The output represents the individual's or unit's quality. The parts produced by a manufacturing department represent the department's quality just as a report or a budget represents the quality of the budget department.

Output is quality, and quality is output. If the terms are indeed synonymous, then everyone has to pursue quality in their output. This further unifies company objectives. The person in charge of accounting must be as committed to quality as the machine operator. The quality of the general manager is just as important as the quality of the warehouse manager.

Characteristics of each output may differ according to the process but the following remain constant:

- the output itself
- the output's goal of providing customer satisfaction

Negative Quality and Positive Quality

Negative quality refers to any gap (in a negative sense) between actual results and established or expected results: non-compliance with delivery schedules, excessively high defect level, machine efficiency below expected standards. To eliminate these negative gaps one must first identify them, and that means tackling problems related to negative quality.

In the sense that this kind of approach represents a response to a negative situation, we also refer to it as *reactive quality.*

Companies are fast catching on to the enormous potential involved, and to the pressing need to act to reduce negative quality.

The idea behind *positive quality* is that it is not enough simply to eliminate negative gaps. The products that result in this case do not necessarily meet customers' requirements. In any case, every company must aim to provide something that will increase the level of customer satisfaction. Therefore CWQM gives great attention to positive quality. This is certainly more difficult to address than negative quality, but the effort is also more stimulating. It requires a much more active approach, which is why it is also called *active quality.*

Latent Quality

Latent quality is quality that surmounts what is required or expected. *Required quality* is what the customer asks for when listing the characteristics and specifications of the desired product or service. *Expected quality* reflects those aspects of quality that are taken for granted by the customer, who is not even aware of them. Required and expected characteristics however, go only so far in satisfying a customer. Countless requirements are left unspecified, and it is up to the company to discover them.

Latent quality becomes evident when a customer receives something unexpected, although potentially needed (see also Chapter 4). Latent quality is also referred to as *exciting quality,* since its appearance is always unexpected. A company's survival depends on its ability to fulfill latent expectations, since customers always look for something new.

CHAPTER TWO

CWQM: Basic Decisions

Introduction

In 1981, when Galgano & Associati began promoting consultancy services in the field of companywide quality management, our biggest challenge was in finding a way to effectively present the new Japanese approach to quality.

At that time quality was not yet perceived as a managerial problem. Furthermore, promoting a "Japanese approach" would elicit negative reactions, since that country's culture is so different from Western culture. After a few false starts, I decided to present the new model through a fictional story about the brave decisions made by a Japanese businessman named Ikiro.

The key elements of the new model regard decisions, priorities, and values.

Decisions. Managing is a company's most important function. Its aim is to choose the right direction, in other words, to make the right decisions. Therefore, a fundamental knowledge of CWQM requires an understanding of the managerial decision implied by this approach. This might seem a somewhat detached way of considering CWQM, yet it is the most complete and precise.

Decisions are aseptic items, having no relation to age, gender, environment, or culture. When a businessperson decides to invest an amount equivalent to 5 percent of the company's payroll in training and education activities, it makes no difference whether that person is Argentinean or Korean. Of course, because of environmental factors, as well as incentives provided by government or by culture, the Korean is the one more likely to make such a decision. On the other hand, it is also true that many Korean businesspeople from the same culture wouldn't dream of making that decision.

Priorities. Decisions are made on the basis of set priorities. Setting priorities is another essential element of managing. Priorities are useful reference points, guidelines" for decision making. Indeed, one cannot make decisions without referring to priorities, since decisions are by nature indications of priorities.

This notion of priority is one of the most important concepts governing company management. Like decisions, priorities are a neutral entity in the environment or organization.

Values. The last step concerns the criteria used to establish priorities. Such criteria can be defined as values. Setting values represents the highest task of management, particularly in regard to human resources.

Since the analysis of values embraced by CWQM would lead me into philosophical considerations, I centered Ikiro's story on the priorities and decisions that characterize the CWQM model. The story thus allowed me to present the core essence of CWQM.

Companywide quality management is innovative and revolutionary precisely because it is based on priorities and decisions that differ radically from those of the Western pattern. Eight years after inventing this story, I had the pleasure of having my theory of CWQM as a "managerial choice" confirmed by Hitoshi Kume, who succeeded Kaoru Ishikawa at Tokyo

University. Kume was quoted in one of the most popular Italian newspapers (*La Repubblica,* July 20, 1990) as saying that "quality is not simply the result of culture, nor of technology: it is a choice."

Ikiro: The Story of a Japanese Entrepreneur

To effectively present the fundamental aspects of this new model, I will rely on your imagination, and make use of a rather original method.

Let's pretend that we are in Japan in 1950.

A Japanese executive named Ikiro is trying to find out what the basic conditions are for his company's success. Forty or so years later, he has succeeded. How did he do it?

In 1950 our hero is effectively dressed in rags. The Japanese population is in a terrible state, just emerging from a bitter defeat. Japan is a small country: Its surface is only 20 percent larger than Italy's, yet in 1950 its population touches the 90 million mark. Most of its inhabitants are concentrated in small areas of land, since the rest of the country is mainly covered by forests and mountains.

The entire industrial system has more or less been destroyed. Because of its concentration in just a few small areas, it was an easy mark for American bombers. Besides, the country is almost entirely lacking in natural resources. As is the case in Italy, much has to be imported from abroad.

In a country with scarce food resources, Ikiro is hungry. He does, however, have at least one strength: the will and ability to implement the three basic strategies required for success. These three strategies are essential to success in all fields, from war and politics to the arts and sciences, as well as in the industrial world. In every success story we can find some combination of these three basic strategies.

To summarize, Ikiro lacks material resources but possesses a wealth of moral and spiritual resources.

The Three Basic Strategies for Success

A digression is in order, so that I may explain what the three strategies for success are. They can be stated as:

1. Make use of reference models.
2. Apply the universal law of priorities.
3. Make maximum use of available resources.

Use of Reference Models

People are always making use of reference models. To cite some examples:

- Parents serve as reference models to children.
- The great Italian Renaissance painter Giotto had Cimabue as a reference model.
- Dante took Virgil as a reference model for his poetry.
- Napoleon studied and applied battle models of important generals such as Alexander the Great, Julius Caesar, and Frederick II of Prussia.
- Karl Marx used the philosophical model developed by Hegel.
- Picasso took African art as a reference model to bring great innovation to painting.

In other words, some of our best minds seek reference models. As I mentioned, doing so is a fundamental strategy for success.

To quote Isaac Newton: "If I have seen further, it is by standing upon the shoulders of Giants." Humans cannot achieve anything important without reference models.

Application of the Universal Law of Priorities

That a universal law of priorities exists may be demonstrated by two examples.

The solar system includes the Sun and many planets. There are, in fact, thousands of these planets, although in school we learn only about nine of them, one of them being Earth. The other planets we call "asteroids." Yet within this immense system two planets — Jupiter and Saturn — account for 80 percent of the total planetary mass. So we can say that there are two priority components within the solar system.

Let's now move to a more humdrum item, the telephone book. I will take the Milan edition, but the same thing exists in any city telephone book. The Milan telephone book has over 2,100 pages, divided according to the 26 letters of the alphabet. However, only 6 letters, that is, less than 25 percent of the alphabet, cover about 60 percent of all the pages. Those 6 letters have far greater weight than the remaining 20.

This universal law can be spotted just as well in any other field. If, for example, we consider Italian rivers, we see that the flow rate of only a few of them makes up a considerable portion of the total flow of Italian rivers. If we consider sugar beet, we find that 2 of the 20 Italian regions produce 60 percent of all the sugar beet in Italy.

In business this universal law is known as the "80-20" law, or the "ABC" law. We know that 80 percent of turnover derives from 20 percent of all customers, that 20 percent of sales employees bring in 80 percent of new customers, and that 20 percent of all employees account for 80 percent of absences.

This law plays a major role in the context of quality: In rough terms, 20 percent of defective items corresponds to 80 percent of all defects.

At this point you may be asking yourself why this law is so important. This is why: Given that in every situation the important factors are few and the unimportant ones many, anyone who wishes to achieve success must concentrate on the few items that really matter, without wasting effort on the ones that don't.

The existence of this law is fortunate for us humans, because if the myriad of factors affecting any situation were all equivalent in importance, our efforts would lead to far more modest results than thus far achieved.

Maximum Use of Available Resources

The third law is the simplest to describe, yet the hardest to implement. In order to succeed, we must make the best use of available resources.

The most important resources are of course human resources. Therefore this last fundamental strategy consists of knowing how to make best use of human resources. The Japanese say that the brain is their only available resource, as nature and Providence have not given them much else. With a rainfall five times greater than in Italy, Japan has an abundance of water, but no minerals or oil, and a scarcity of land for growing food. So the brain becomes all the more important as a resource; indeed, it is limitless, and Ikiro is conscious of this fact.

We shall now see how Ikiro makes use of such strategies.

The Customer as a Priority

Bearing in mind these three fundamental laws for success, Ikiro starts setting up his company. It is quite easy to imagine his simple start.

The first question he asks himself relates to the universal law of priorities: What is the most important factor in business? What one thing should guide all of my decisions, whatever their nature? In other words, what is the priority factor? Ikiro knows that if he can identify this factor and focus his resources on it, he will have laid down the foundations of success.

To answer this question, Ikiro applies the first law of success, that of the reference model. Therefore, he sets out to find the priority for the most successful model.

It is now 1950. America has won the war, and the Japanese have been brought to their knees. Ikiro will try to discover which priority factor guides all decisions made by American business. In fact, he is known as a great copier, someone who knows how to carry out research in a meticulous and careful way. He quickly discovers that profit is the priority factor for

American companies. At the top levels of a business organization, nothing is more important than profit when a decision is being considered or made.

In the United States (and I am referring here especially to large universities such as Harvard and Stanford) the word profit is not used. Indeed, people speak of the *bottom line.* The *bottom line,* in Western business, is the top priority.

Having applied the first basic strategy for success, and having examined the American model, Ikiro falls back on his own resource, brainpower. He does not believe that profit should be the first and foremost priority of business. He does not dispute that profit is a business's ultimate aim, for he knows that without profit a company cannot survive.

Nevertheless, it is not the absolute priority. To Ikiro, profit is only a consequence of the prioritary decision, a prize for his contribution to the economic system. No, the true priority for Ikiro's business is the customer. The customer stands above any question of choice. Can you imagine a business without customers? Such a thing happened in Monza, a small town near Milan, during the 1930s. Men suddenly decided to stop wearing hats, instantly putting hundreds of small, artisanal hatmaking establishments out of business for lack of customers. Customers are the real priority, as it is customers who fuel a company's activities.

To refine this priority, Ikiro identifies "customer satisfaction" as the top priority. He knows that in order to acquire and maintain customers, he must satisfy them, and he do it better than his competitors. If customers have the option to choose, that is, if Ikiro does not possess a monopoly on his product, then they will clearly choose the business that gives them the greatest satisfaction. So Ikiro establishes "customer satisfaction" as the top priority for his business.

Thus customer satisfaction guides all decisions made at all levels.

At this point Ikiro asks himself, what does a customer want in order to be satisfied? The answer to this question is easy: The customer wants only three things:

- quality (includes safety)
- price
- service (includes delivery)

The Choice of Quality

Ikiro must in turn establish priorities among the aforementioned satisfaction factors. There are several elements that produce customer satisfaction, and he must decide which of these takes precedence. After brief reflection, he determines that quality is the primary factor for satisfaction: that is, in order to satisfy a customer, Ikiro must give priority to the quality of the product or service he provides.

Remember that this is only a model. Our decision might be different from Ikiro's, yet quality is the priority factor he has chosen.

To understand the difference between quality and service, let's consider the following example: You have just bought a new car, made by a particular automobile manufacturer, because you are very enthusiastic about the service offered by this company. Its service stations operate throughout Italy and abroad, are open on Christmas and New Year's day, and on Saturdays and Sundays. What fabulous service! Yet, having bought the car, you then discover it has one problem after another. How much satisfaction are you going to derive from that stellar service? The car will need constant attention and will inevitably become a source of dissatisfaction.

Remember that the customer is buying quality before anything else.

Let us return to our gentleman's thoughts. Ikiro asks himself, now that I've opted for quality, what next? What must I do

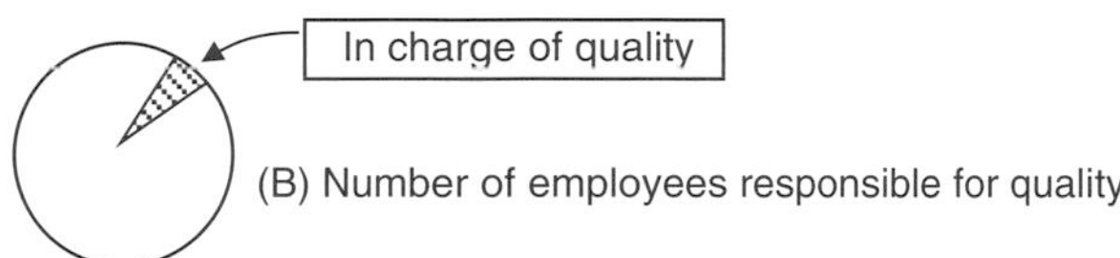

Figure 2-1. Quality as the Responsibility of a Few

for the sake of quality? He decides that the time has come to leave off simply theorizing and take concrete steps.

He returns to the first strategy for success, re-examining the American approach to quality. Having examined the Western model, he finds that if he represents a company's employees as a circle, the segment in charge of quality is very limited (Figure 2-1). This comes as a great surprise to Ikiro. He cannot see where the third strategy for success is being applied. Resources are not being used to their maximum potential in the pursuit of basic priorities.

Ikiro takes a different approach, based on the following fundamental considerations: *If it is true that quality is the dominant factor, I must ensure that all employees working for my company are concerned with quality. Besides, if quality holds top priority, it must permeate the entire business. This means that the entire organization should be centered on quality.*

Only the customer can establish the basis for such an approach. Putting a few people on the job of "quality" will definitely not suffice. If quality is to come first, *it must be the fundamental process underlying all aspects of the business.*

A Broader Meaning of Quality

Thus does the word quality take on broader meaning. It is not simply defined in the traditional terms of rejects and defects on the production line. In fact, every mistake occurring in any part of the business impacts quality as a whole. For example, quality defects occur in the following areas:

- Accounting
  - delays in the submission of statements and reports
  - erroneous data entered into computers
  - errors in statements and in reports
  - erroneous invoices
- Design
  - variations due to errors
  - mistakes in design
  - delays in the issue of specifications
- Data processing
  - computer downtime due to errors
  - reprocessing
- Sales
  - errors in drawing up a contract
  - wrong description on production orders
  - schedule badly planned
- Purchasing
  - variation to orders due to errors
  - delays in the receipt of materials
  - incomplete description of materials

To achieve quality no mistakes should be made in any part of the company. According to Ikiro's point of view, quality should permeate every operation, not only those strictly connected with production. Here Ikiro makes an important decision, one that will strongly affect his model.

To guarantee quality in all company operations, he establishes that *each person within the organization must be responsible for the quality of his or her work.*

The Operational Priority Essential for Quality

At this stage, on considering his efforts thus far, Ikiro ought to be fairly satisfied. In planning how to set up his company, he has already made some decisions that break tradition with his reference point, the American business model. He believes that his decisions will give him a great advantage, because he senses that they are the better ones. Yet despite his conviction that the priority given to the customer and the involvement of all employees in quality issues are winning strategies, he is far from being satisfied.

Until modern times, the prevailing culture in Japan was that of the samurai. A samurai is a warrior, a fighter, and there are few things more "operational" than fighting. Fighting is action, and it involves effort.

The Japanese view their culture as being in opposition to the Chinese mandarin culture. A mandarin is a man of letters, a philosopher, a man of thought, a man who shuns action and sweat. A mandarin believes that action is to be assigned to men of action, and he does not consider practical activities to be the highest form of action.

In accordance with his samurai culture, at this point Ikiro feels the need to tackle concrete matters, and, in his view, anything concrete involves activity. So he asks himself the following basic question: *If quality is to be my highest priority, then what is the most practical activity for each person in the company to carry out in the interest of quality?*

To clarify the meaning of this question, Ikiro ponders the following analogy: Historically, humans have embraced religion, its form depending on period and geographic location. People have always worshipped gods or divine beings, but the ways in which they do so vary greatly. African natives may worship their gods through singing and dancing. Singing and dancing are practical activities, that is, action. Muslims carry out the action of bowing toward Mecca five times a day. Ancient pagans would take an ox or a lamb to the altar and slit its throat. (Killing an animal is certainly an active manifestation.) Christians engage in various operations, such as receiving Communion, saying prayers, taking part in processions. Each type of worship is different, yet each a valid way of actively serving one's god. The basic question, then, for Ikiro is the following: As there are many different ways to serve quality, *which operational activity should receive priority within my company?* If Ikiro can determine the nature of such an activity, and then concentrate the entire work force upon it, he will obtain a business model far more effective than the American one. The question is, therefore, one of capital importance.

In applying the first law of success, Ikiro sees that, in the matter of quality, the American model attributes top priority to "control." Let us not forget that this is 1950. The entire organization pertaining to quality is based on control and inspection. The office in charge of quality is called the quality control office.

Ikiro is doubtful of this approach. Should quality control really take priority over all others? Control is indeed important (the lack of it it would be dangerous), but it certainly isn't the most important activity. To find the one that is, Ikiro refers to the original priorities that he has established to guide all decisions.

If the company's highest priority is customer satisfaction, then all Ikiro needs to do is further deploy this concept. He begins by analyzing the expression *customer satisfaction,* noting that it consists of two parts, *customer* and *satisfaction.*

Ikiro turns his attention to the customer. Who is this customer? He or she is, first and foremost, a human being. Even for someone selling dog food, the customer is a human being, certainly not a dog. When someone sells something to a company, the customer is not the company itself, which is an abstract concept. Selling to a company is, in fact, selling to human beings, and it is these human beings, not the company, who must be satisfied. Thus Ikiro determines that his top priority is to satisfy human beings.

What are the basic characteristics of human satisfaction? Ikiro knows that pure and lasting satisfaction does not exist, for as soon as a certain level of satisfaction is achieved, a higher level is sought, in a process that continues indefinitely.

So, things being what they are, Ikiro can only conclude that among operations, that of *improvement quality* should take top priority. To constantly coddle the customers and improve the product or service is essential, in order to prevent their going over to the competition, which might be able to provide greater satisfaction. Keeping the customer satisfied is, as explained above, an endless task.

Ikiro understands that this decision is central to his entire model. The company must take the approach of *continous quality improvement.* Quality improvement should not, however, be limited to products; rather, it should be aimed at improving the quality of all operations carried out by the company.

Other Practical Decisions

Here again Ikiro might well be pleased about the decisions made. Yet he is deeply frustrated. He is aware that he has chosen an objective with vast implications, and wonders how he is ever going to achieve it. It is as if he had set himself the task of climbing Mount Everest. The goal of climbing 8,000 meters is an ambitious one indeed, requiring the proper instruments, skills, and knowledge. Ikiro feels that he is in a similar kind of situation.

What instruments should the company adopt to actively pursue constant improvement? What is the equipment needed, what are the methods and techniques? Again, Ikiro goes back to his reference model strategy, to see if the tools he needed for quality improvement could be found in the American business model. Here, Ikiro is pleasantly surprised. Up until this moment he had not found a satisfactory answer in the American model. But in this case he finds just what he needs. In 1950 the Americans have already perfected some superlative techniques for quality control, based on a statistical approach to problems. Such techniques provide Ikiro with the necessary tools and methods for the pursuit of constant quality improvement.

Ikiro decides to make such techniques the top priority for his company. Any action undertaken within the company must be improved by means of such techniques.

To achieve this goal, he makes another decision, one based on the third strategy for success. Given Ikiro's limited resources and the state of Japanese industry in 1950, this decision is extremely brave. Ikiro decides to invest in a massive training program in which the entire work force of the company is given the tools and knowledge to carry out continuous quality improvement.

Ikiro also senses that the training must somehow effect a complete change in the mentality of all employees. Such a change must have all the characteristics of an ideological revolution.

He now makes the final decision, the one needed to complete the new model. He decides that, in order to bring about such a revolution in attitudes, management must take an active role in the leadership of quality-related activities within the company. This is a new idea, since until this time management had always viewed quality as a technical matter best left to specialists, a detail pertaining to products.

For management to take a leadership role, *it has to establish the quality goals, and then guide the entire company in the direction of these goals.* At the same time, decisions pertaining to quality must be strategic, that is, dealing with the long term.

The End of the Story

Ikiro's story is practically finished. As I mentioned at the beginning, the purpose of telling this story is to highlight the reasoning behind the choices observed in the Japanese model: CWQM. The most significant points of the story form a strategy that can be summarized in these terms:

- The customer is the top priority factor guiding every decision.
- Satisfying the customer is the true priority.
- Of the three elements that determine customer satisfaction — quality, price, and delivery — quality takes precedence, becoming synonymous with customer satisfaction.
- The concept of quality is extended to the entire range of a company's operations, and everyone within the company becomes involved in quality according to the following criterion: each person is responsible for the quality of his or her own work.
- The concern for quality is made evident by the constant effort to improve it. Constant improvement represents the central pillar of the entire CWQM system, and thus it is the most important task of every employee.
- To bring about constant improvement, a company must adopt quality control techniques, which then become primary.
- The company's entire workforce must be trained in the techniques of quality control, so that they may adequately participate in quality improvement activities. Intensive and continued training is an essential component of CWQM.
- Training must be directed toward producing a deep change in employee attitudes. Without such a change, CWQM would remain a utopian idea.
- For such a change in attitudes to take place, management must assume leadership in quality-related matters within the company.

Everyone within a company should have absorbed these concepts before CWQM is implemented. Table 2-1 gives a concise synthesis of the above items. This, in summary, is the message contained in Ikiro's story.

Table 2-1. Fundamental Tenets of the CWQM Model

1. The customer has given up top priority; thus "customer satisfaction" is the goal.
2. Quality is the most important factor governing customer satisfaction.
3. The meaning of quality is enlarged.
4. Responsibility for quality extends to all employees in a company.
5. "Continuous improvement" of quality is the company's priority objective.
6. Every individual is personally responsible for quality improvement.
7. Quality control techniques are the principal tools for managing the company and the quality of its product.
8. All employees receive education and training in quality control techniques.
9. Training is aimed at effecting a radical change of mindset.
10. Top management champions quality.

A Small Tragedy and a Great Success

Ikiro's story comes to a rather dramatic end. After all his intense mental labor, and having made decisions that are meant to be the foundation of a new model, poor Ikiro collapses under an overwhelming sense of frustration and a destructive sense of uncertainty.

Why did this happen? It seems that while studying American quality techniques, Ikiro encountered a diagram that left him thoroughly dispirited. This diagram is among the first things shown to anyone wishing to learn quality-related techniques. Neophytes are taught about the relationship between cost and quality: If, on a Cartesian plane, we place quality along the abscissa and cost along the ordinates, we can represent the cost of defects with a curve (Figure 2-2).

As quality increases, a decrease in the number of defects takes place, as well as a decrease in cost. However, in order for this goal to be achieved, other costs must be borne, such as those related to prevention, employee training, and the quality-related structure. Hence, we have the second curve, as seen in Figure 2-3.

The curve resulting from the two (Figure 2-4) follows a parabolic trajectory, and, in parabolic fashion, it has a minimum cost point at a particular level of quality.

It is this parabolic cost trajectory that drives Ikiro to despair. His goal of constantly improving quality will lead to exorbitant costs and, in the final analysis, to failure. If Ikiro insists on pursuing his course, his actions will be those of a madman.

There have been, however, some successful "madmen." One example is Christopher Columbus. The experts of his day considered him ignorant or crazy, because, by traveling westward, to reach India he would have to cover 20,000 kilometers (the Greeks had already calculated the earth's radius). Given the small size of the boats at his disposal, he would certainly perish before reaching his destination.

Another so-called madman who succeeded was Guglielmo Marconi. In 1903 Marconi was preparing to broadcast over the airwaves between England and Canada. Scientists at that time believed such an undertaking to be impossible, as the Hertzian waves he intended to use for such a broadcast travel only along straight lines. In order to broadcast from England to Canada, Marconi would have had to build an antenna 300 kilometers high.

As we know, Columbus did not die during his trip, but instead found America while en route, about 6,000 kilometers away. We also know that Marconi did not fail in his attempt, because, although it is true that Hertzian waves travel along straight lines, they are reflected by the ionosphere, which acts like a mirror.

Ikiro too was lucky. His discovery was of a different kind, not as grand as Marconi's or Columbus's, but a fundamental one for business: The quest for quality leads to better productivity and lower costs.

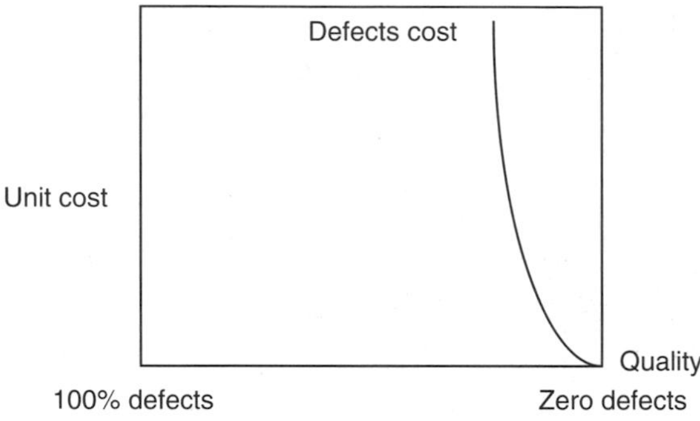

Figure 2-2. Defects Cost Curve

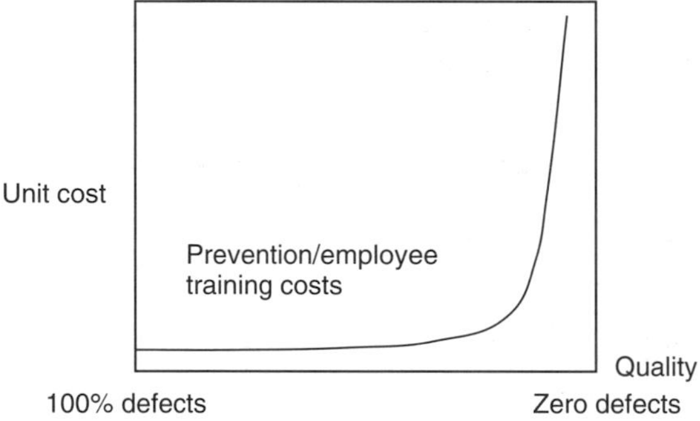

Figure 2-3. Prevention, Employee Training, and Related Cost Curve

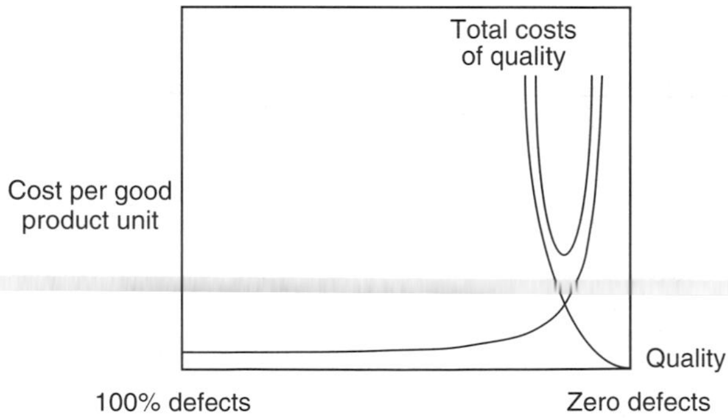

Figure 2-4. Total Costs Curve

It is this discovery that really displaced us in the Western world. The Japanese suddenly appeared on the international market with high quality products and competitive prices. At first we chalked it up to low labor costs, and dumping practices. The real reason, of course, was the perfecting of a new business model, more effective and dynamic than ours. It is through this model that a company can:

- improve product quality
- increase flexibility
- increase product diversification
- decrease costs and inventory

It was the Japanese who brought about the revolution.

CHAPTER THREE

CWQM: The System

Introduction

In the introduction to Chapter 2, I showed how we initially solved the problem of explaining the new approach to quality. We next encountered the problem of presenting companywide quality management in a complete yet concise manner to someone totally unfamiliar with it. How were we to provide an organic and comprehensive picture of the new approach?

This proved to be a difficult hurdle for us at Galgano & Associati, as the Japanese experts provided only partial help in the matter.

The only two existing English-language texts on CWQM were written by the foremost experts in the field: Kaoru Ishikawa and Shigeru Mizuno (both of whom died in 1989). Both are excellent and extremely useful volumes, but they do not provide a full and organic view of CWQM.

The picture outlined in this chapter represents our contribution to the building of a comprehensive view of CWQM, and it summarizes all the knowledge we have acquired up to 1990. Most likely, this picture will be further improved and enriched over the next few years, as CWQM has been, and still is, a constant source of discovery for us at Galgano & Associati.

A Comprehensive View of CWQM

Figure 3-1 illustrates this comprehensive view of CWQM.

There are four building blocks to companywide quality management:

- basic assumptions
- quality culture
- basic processes
- top-management leadership

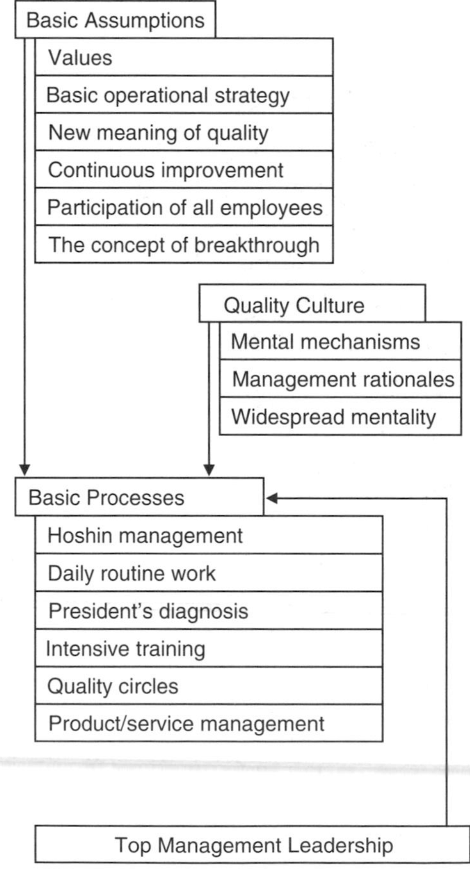

Figure 3-1. The Total Quality System

The basic assumptions constitute the foundation of CWQM. Assumptions precede everything else, and strongly permeate the new approach.

By *quality culture* we mean the way a company approaches problems and decisions, and the attitudes held by employees toward situations or toward others at all levels in the company. The term *culture* is thus used in the narrow sense of company attitudes.

The basic processes of CWQM form the operational core of this new approach, and its most visible aspect.

Basic assumptions and quality culture are intangible elements, albeit essential ones. Processes, however, lead to operations and procedures that are very tangible. Without correct application of the basic assumptions, CWQM is not possible. Top-management leadership is the engine that keeps CWQM moving. Top executives exert this leadership by periodically setting policy and by remaining actively involved in the improvement programs launched each year.

In this chapter we briefly describe the four building blocks in order to better explain the whole.

Basic Assumptions

As we have said, the basic assumptions are the foundation of CWQM. They comprise six elements:

1. basic values
2. basic operational strategy
3. the new meaning of quality
4. continuous improvement
5. involvement of all employees
6. the concept of *breakthrough*

Basic Values

Values are those things that a person considers important. Values are rooted more deeply than attitudes within a person's beliefs. They are far fewer in number, more involving, and more permanent.

As we saw in Chapter 2, values play a fundamental role in a management system because they set the priorities and thus guide any decisions made within a company.

The basic values of CWQM pertain to the three groups of people that play a fundamental role in business:

- customers
- employees
- suppliers

A company's goals must tend to enhance the role of these three groups. Due importance must also be given to stockholders and to the outside world, of course, but within a company these three groups carry the greatest weight.

Customers

Everything done within a company must be done in reference to the customer, and all employees must understand that the customer represents an essential value, the very lifeblood of a company.

Employees

A company's main job is to ensure the jobs of its members. Thus company survival should come before everything else. It is obvious that if employees feel confident that management holds the security of their work position as its primary objective, they will be more inclined to commit themselves to the company. They will also exhibit the same respect for human beings in their working relationships that they see in management.

Suppliers

Suppliers constitute another important value. This is because both suppliers of material goods and suppliers of services provide an essential contribution to the satisfaction of the ultimate client, and, therefore, to a company's competitiveness. Thus a solid partnership between company and supplier ultimately benefits the final customer.

Notice that although profit is certainly a basic goal for any company, it is not a basic value. With CWQM, profit becomes secondary in the short term, although it is maximized in the long term, as a company applies the three values and improves its ability to develop its resources. Indeed, the misplaced emphasis on profit as the absolute value in Western industries allowed Japanese industry to take the lead more easily.

Thus *human* value is more important than *profit* value, and in the end, it leads to greater profit.

The Basic Operational Strategy

An entire section of this book is dedicated to examining the basic strategies of CWQM. By introducing what I call a *basic operational strategy,* I do not wish to generate confusion. The strategy I refer to here represents the basic criterion necessary to coherently carry out any activity or make any decision.

I introduce it here because it holds priority over all others, and because it involves each individual. Such a strategy can be simply stated as *quality comes first,* a valid suggestion in every situation. It provides any person working in the company with powerful guidelines for every situation. It applies in major decisions such as investments and the choice of products and markets, as well as in minor decisions such as those made by machine operators. This operational strategy even gives the assembly-line operator the right to stop the line if something is amiss in the quality of the process.

In applying this strategy, no compromises are allowed. It cannot be forgotten under any circumstances or at any times. The greater the responsibility one holds, the broader will be the impact of not following such a strategy, since from then on employees at lower levels feel authorized to discard the rule, which leads to dangerous compromises. It is only by applying this strategy rigorously that one can gradually achieve the basic conditions for "doing things right the first time."

The New Meaning of Quality

As explained in Chapter 1, introducing CWQM requires a company to give quality a new meaning, a significance that doesn't exist in traditional models.

Quality therefore acquires

1. an all-encompassing meaning
2. broader meaning
3. practical or operational meaning regarding
   - customer satisfaction
   - output
4. a positive and negative feature
5. a latent feature

Continuous Improvement

Through CWQM, continuous improvement is sought in every activity of the company. This is the great innovation that was put to work in the Japanese business model. Such an invention, which led to a radical change in international competition, is founded on two assumptions:

- This kind of improvement can always be attained. That is, people possess the resources to achieve it, and these resources are unlimited.
- Improvement occurs not just by means of innovation, but also through a myriad of small improvements, carried out by the entire workforce.

Thus we discover a new dimension in improvement: the *small-step approach to improvement.*

Employee Involvement

Employee involvement is perhaps the most difficult component in the cultural changes brought about by CWQM. Yet it is also the most critical. Many Japanese companies recognize it as the essence of innovation and productivity.

Involving all employees means transforming each individual into a "problem solver" who is constantly seeking new improvements. That is, everyone should have two tasks: performing one's own work and improving the work process. This requires a firm trust on the part of managers in the abilities of all employees, and in their desire to improve.

Alas, many managers are unequal to the task and thus miss the chance to improve a company's structure and management. Perhaps they do not clearly understand that a company's commitment depends on the employees' commitment to quality.

The Concept of Breakthrough

The concept of *breakthrough,* which is part of CWQM, was introduced by American quality expert Joseph M. Juran. This concept refers to the achievement of a considerable improvement in a particular level of performance. Figure 3-2 shows a schematic view of such improvements.

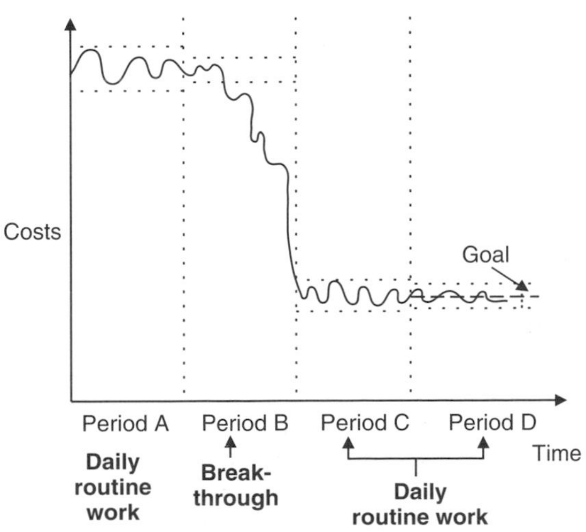

Figure 3-2. Breakthrough Diagram

The concept of breakthrough is based on the belief that human creativity and commitment, combined with a powerful method, can bring about important and positive change in any kind of process. The opposite of breakthrough is *status quo.*

Breakthrough goals are not necessarily limited to processes for which it is easy to obtain numerical data. For example, it is possible to set breakthrough goals for a training program, for the reorganization of a particular sector, or for a reporting system.

The most strategic application of breakthrough can be found in the main process of CWQM: hoshin management.

Culture

The quality culture basically covers three items:

- mental mechanisms
- management rationales
- companywide mentality

Mental Mechanisms

To understand the meaning of mental mechanisms within the framework of CWQM, we must ask ourselves the following question: Can every employee within a company learn, on his or her own, the mental mechanisms that lead to excellence in business activities? The answer, of course, is no.

We have seen that it is not sufficient to involve just a few employees in the pursuit of excellence. It is therefore necessary to make the most effective mental mechanisms available to everyone. These mechanisms should be:

- powerful
- easy to use
- easy to learn

According to those requirements the main mental mechanisms fostered by CWQM are the following:

- cause-and-effect relationships
- the seven statistical tools (seven QC tools)
- the five W's and one H (5W and 1H)
- the plan-do-check-act cycle (PDCA)
- the seven management tools

Such mental mechanisms, except for the 5W and 1H, are shown in Part 3 of this book. Here we stress a few important concepts related to them.

Cause-and-Effect Relationships

We might say that to master this relationship is the essence of business management. In fact, excellence can be attained only when maximum control is exercised over such relationships. This is because the company must constantly pursue increasingly ambitious goals, a task that involves anyone who forms a part of it. But after all, what is a goal, if not an effect?

Once people have acquired the mental mechanism that makes them sensitive to the importance of the cause-and-effect relationship, and can analyze the "effect" in a methodical and intelligent fashion, the company acquires an enormous thrust toward the achievement of ambitious goals, or "effect."

To master and exert maximum control over this relationship, a company must be able to seek and identify the real causes that lead to certain effects. It is this ability that characterizes the scientific method. Companies that do not apply CWQM carry out the search for critical causes in an empirical, improvised way, often affected by prejudice. The lack of a scientific approach in turn leads to the following consequences:

- Effects are often mistaken for causes.
- No attempt is made to clearly establish the real causes.
- Remedies are undertaken in a superficial way.

The lack of this mental mechanism becomes apparent when a problem occurs. When a problem occurs, the first question usually is, who did it? (concentrating on the effect), while what one should be asking is, why did it happen? (seeking its causes).

According to Professor Ishikawa, the correct application of this mental mechanism occurs when, in facing a problem, we ask ourselves *why* at least four times. Once the first *why* has been answered, we must search for the cause of the first cause, and so on. In some cases it is necessary to go a further four times. By fostering the application of such mental mechanisms, a company develops its operators' ability to perceive the so-called weak signals transmitted by machines and processes before a breakdown occurs.

Application of the mental mechanism of cause-and-effect relationships lays down a new foundation to the approach to work: one that is entirely focused on causes rather than effects, and one that uses the scientific method.

The 5W and 1H

The expression *5W and 1H,* refers to the English words *who, what, where, when, why,* and *how,* which constitute the six points to be considered in relation to any kind of problem or situation. Only the systematic and continuous application of these six reference points to any problem constitutes the concrete acquisition of this mental mechanism.

PDCA

If the essence of business management lies in mastery of the cause-and-effect relationship, then *plan-do-check-act* (PDCA) is the process by which such management takes shape.

Professor Ishikawa stated that the essence of CWQM lies in repeated applications of the PDCA process, until a goal has been reached. Masayoshi Ozawa, a former top executive in the

NEC Corporation, states in one of his books that "nothing in this world is impossible if the PDCA process is applied repeatedly." The four stages of PDCA, shown in Figure 3-3, represent the mental path that must be followed constantly to achieve one's goals (see Chapter 12).

Focusing on the cause-and-effect relationships and constantly applying PDCA are the basic mechanisms at work in employee attitudes toward problem solving and continuous improvement of their performance levels.

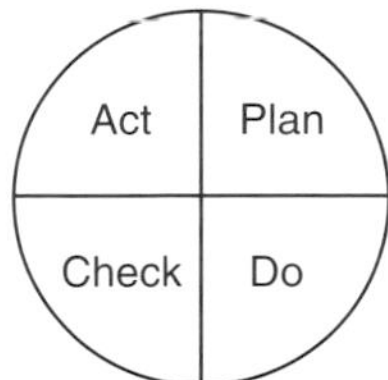

Figure 3-3. The Four Stages of the PDCA Process

Management Rationales

With the expression *management rationales* I refer to the criteria, or guidelines, that constantly drive management activities during CWQM implementation. These are concrete operational criteria similar to the aforementioned mechanisms, except that they are applied only at the managerial level. The most important management rationales are the following:

- industrialization of the improvement process
- focus on processes
- recognition of employees' efforts
- upstream and downstream quality
- quality as integration
- visual control system

Industrialization of the Improvement Process

As said before, continuous improvement represents for CWQM a company's core activity; therefore it must involve all employees. Depending on the size of a company, it involves dozens, hundreds, even thousands of people.

Improvement-related activities cannot be carried out in an artisanal form, that is, with different approaches and after long training periods. Such activities must be carried out in an industrial fashion; that is, they must be

- easy to reproduce
- standardized
- easy to learn

We have seen that the above-mentioned mental mechanisms subscribe to these criteria. Management rationales must also refer to these principles so that improvement-related activities become widespread and industrialized.

Focus on Processes

The second management rationale is the focus on processes rather than on results. As we explain in Chapter 7, process is the heart of any organized unit, and thus represents the first priority for the unit itself.

This focus on process stands in contrast to the focus on results that characterizes Western management rationales. The latter focus leads to an emphasis on quantity over quality, which largely accounts for the loss of competitiveness among Western companies.

By focusing on processes in analyzing a problem, management tends to concentrate on the left-hand side of the cause/effect diagram, alternately known as the Ishikawa, or fishbone, diagram (see Chapter 12) — that is, on causes. We know that by focusing on results we can tend to find solutions that are only temporary, because they do not address causes. The radical move toward focusing on processes was nothing less than revolutionary. The parameters adopted are completely different: it is like grabbing the bull by the horns, instead of by the tail.

Masaaki Imai, in his book *Kaizen,* speaks of P (process-oriented) criteria and R (results-oriented) criteria. The diagram in Figure 3-4 points out such differences.

Focus on processes leads to the setting of control points, in addition to checkpoints.

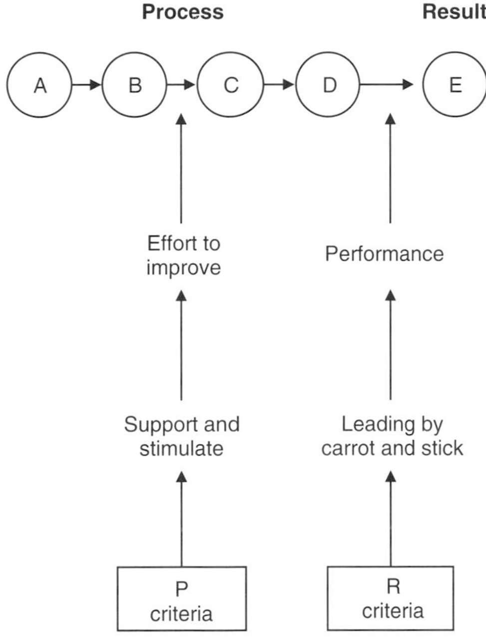

Figure 3-4. Process-oriented Criteria and Results-oriented Criteria

Rewarding Employees' Efforts

The abilities of employees will continuously develop only if their efforts — not just their results — are rewarded. By adhering to this principle, top managers support employees, generate confidence, create a positive environment, and regard mistakes as an unavoidable by-product of the learning process. Employees must feel the full support of their supervisors to grow in the company.

The foundations of this approach will be fully examined in Chapter 5. To apply such a rationale, management must

- have implicit faith in people's potential for growth
- be persevering, and thus able to be patient and supportive until the desired results are achieved.

Upstream and Downstream Quality

This rationale reckons that excellence cannot be achieved unless each of the many processes leading to the end product or service are strongly linked and integrated, both upstream and downstream. It applies both inside and outside the company, to the suppliers and intermediaries through whom the final customer is reached, and can be interpreted from two points of view:

- Narrow range: Each person considers the upstream office a supplier, and the downstream one a customer. The basic goal of each unit is to optimize quality for the downstream customer.
- Broad range: All processes outside the company are linked with internal ones and have an impact on the satisfaction of the intermediate or final customer.

Quality as Integration

We have seen how quality, by ranging upstream and downstream, applies to vertical processes, such as production lines. It also applies, however, to organizational units that are connected horizontally by any particular process. Processes that cut across organizational units include:

- new product development
- order filling
- material management

A company's functional division, as well as the units that make up the company itself, are the vertical boundaries determined by a company's size, specializations, and employee skill levels. To achieve a high level of quality, there must be strong integration among all organizational units in terms of the three parameters affecting customer satisfaction:

- quality
- cost
- delivery

The people who make up the structure must keep such integration in mind at all times in carrying out their tasks.

Visual Control System

With visual control the information needed for management of operations is located directly on site of the operations. Such information is made available through the use of visual aids providing immediate notification of any problem. The system is based on the simple assumption that in order to solve a problem, one must be able to see it.

Through this system, any irregularity is highlighted in real time, so that it can be solved in a quick and effective way, and so that similar problems can be prevented. The kanban system, as well as the CEDAC diagram, are typical examples of visual control systems.

CWQM reaches the most advanced levels of application when visual controls underlie the entire management system.

Companywide Mentality

Companywide mentality refers to the beliefs held in common by employees of CWQM companies. Such beliefs are the following:

- Respect employees as human beings.
- Put quality first.

- Focus on the market (market-in).
- The downstream process is your customer.
- Analyze facts and speak through data.
- Concentrate on a few important things.
- Control within the process (*in-process control*).
- Control the upstream (*upstream control*).
- Do not attribute fault to others.

These beliefs are described in Chapter 17.

Basic Processes

The first two building blocks to CWQM considered, the basic assumptions and the quality culture, are the intangible aspects of CWQM. Nonetheless, they must permeate the entire company.

Processes, on the other hand, are the visible aspects of CWQM, and as such they must generate specific activities, as well as clearly defined procedures and flows. All but one of these activities are discussed in Part 4. The product/service management process is so vast a subject that an explanation of it would require a separate book. Mizuno's book, which we already mentioned, covers many of the pertinent themes.

Hoshin Management

Hoshin management is a tool for improvement, and as such represents the heart of CWQM. It is an organic management activity that

- has as its purpose the implementation of an annual policy set on the basis of the company creed and management philosophy, as well as on medium- and long-term planning
- requires that each level, by matching its policies with those of others, formulates, develops, and implements them in a coordinated fashion

- analyzes results and undertakes those actions that prove to be necessary

Within the context of this management activity, the word *policy* indicates:

- a course of action, by which is meant a theme or direction (such as cost reduction)
- a quantitative goal to achieve within the chosen course of action (to pursue the example mentioned above: a 10 percent reduction)
- the choice of a course of action, that is, *how* to reach the goal (again, to pursue the above example: by acting upon the logistic system).

Hoshin management involves all the executives and the managers of a company. Under normal circumstances, operators and their immediate supervisors are not directly involved.

The basic criterion followed in applying hoshin management is the concept of *breakthrough,* whereby each year a company concentrates on a very limited number of priorities.

Daily Routine Work

It is impossible to improve if one's actions do not rely upon levels of process performance that remain constant.

The literal interpretation of *daily routine work* does not capture its real scope in CWQM. It is a management tool both for maintaining current performance in organizational units and for carrying out improvement-related activities not specified in annual policies.

The primary purpose of daily routine work is to guarantee a stable performance, which always responds to the requirement at hand. For this to be achieved, it is necessary to identify processes, parameters for measuring output, and output goals, as well as to define the daily check system. Three concepts underlie daily routine work:

- working with the internal customer in mind
- doing things right the first time
- standardizing activities

Figure 3-5 shows the link between hoshin management (HM) and daily routine work (DRW).

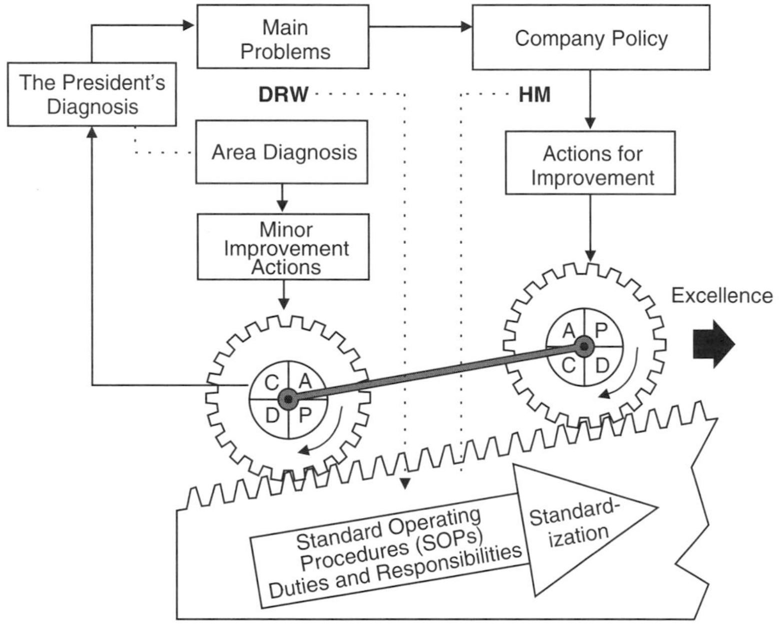

Figure 3-5. The Hoshin Management-Daily Routine Work Link

Intensive Training

The power of a company resides in the strength of its employees, which in turn is closely linked to its training activities, just as an athlete's power is linked to the intensity with which he or she trains.

CWQM requires very intense training, of a kind never imagined for the Western business model. Training activities must be seen as

- a real investment (perhaps one of the most profitable a company can make)
- based on a 10-year plan (a shorter period does not allow for the establishment of good programs for employee development)
- strictly related to the career development plan of every manager in the company

Channeling the flow of communications inside the company forms a considerable portion of the training process.

Quality Circles

Quality circles constitute the principal tool for involving operators in improvement activities, and they generate a rich *bottom-up* flow of information, suggestions, and ideas.

Through quality circles, top executives and managers become acutely aware of the operations and processes themselves, as well as of any problems encountered. At the same time, frontline employees acquire a greater understanding of the processes they are involved in and of how to keep them under control.

Product/Service Management

Product/service management comprises a series of subprocesses that are connected in complex ways. In order to function, it requires many techniques, some of which are new, while others were developed in the West but are being applied in a new fashion.

Figure 3-6 provides an overview of the techniques that compose this process. As we have already said, we are not analyzing them in this volume, which focuses on managerial, rather than technical issues.

The President's Diagnosis

The application of CWQM requires systematic verification by upper management. Such verification must be carried out by

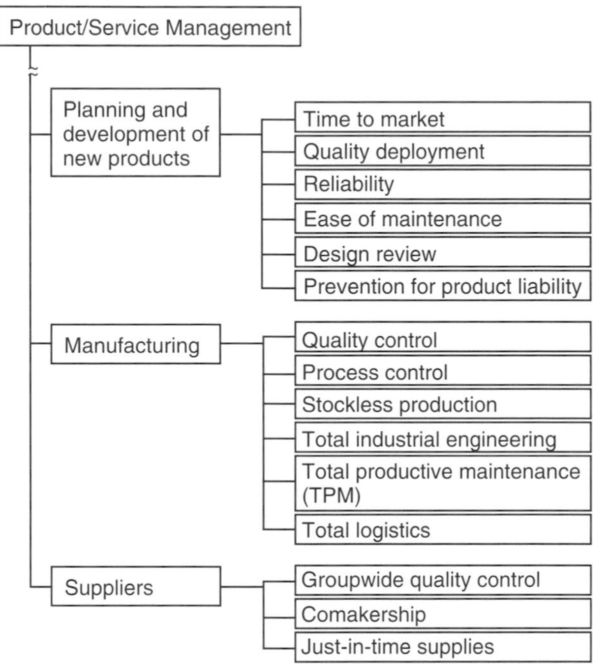

Figure 3-6. Some Product/Service Management Techniques

the chief executive officer, and it is thus called the "president's diagnosis." The term *diagnosis* was chosen, rather than the term *audit,* because it better describes the activity, which is not limited to a simple verification.

Such a diagnosis constitutes the formal moment when a company's top management checks the coherence and progress of each section in the practical application of CWQM concepts. The main purpose of such a diagnosis is not to criticize the results obtained by workers, but rather to highlight and comment on the processes leading to those results. This helps the workers to recognize any deficiency in their activities, and provides them with valuable support and guidance.

Such verification is also applied by lower levels of management. For example, division managers or functional managers, perform a diagnosis of the units they are responsible for at least once a year (more often twice).

Top Management Leadership

The leadership of the chief executive officer is the real engine behind CWQM. A revolution within the management system cannot take place without the will and constant support of a company's highest authority.

As we explained in Chapter 2, the president must assume the leadership role with regard to quality: he or she must set the goals to be reached and then guide the company toward those goals. To this end, the president is invested with a great variety of responsibilities. Here we shall mention three of them:

- The president is directly responsible for setting policies concerning quality.
- The president must implement training activities that support a program based on medium- and long-term planning.
- The president must establish his or her own responsibilities in ensuring quality, and approve the system required.

PART TWO

CWQM Strategies

In Part Two we examine the fundamental strategies of companywide quality management. Such strategies constitute the greatest innovation in modern industry after World War II. In the Western world we have not yet completely grasped the importance of these strategies which, when taken together, represent a true revolution in management. I have isolated nine such strategies. The first three involve a reconceptualization of the three great players in the business system:

- customers
- company employees
- suppliers

Since all three of these players are human beings, the strategies that involve them focus on human qualities.

Customers

The *customer strategy* replaces the traditional Western emphasis on profit with an emphasis on the customer. Therefore, customer satisfaction becomes the basic value guiding a company's activities. Within such a framework, product or service quality takes first place in providing customer satisfaction, so that *quality equals customer satisfaction.*

Company Employees

The *company employee strategy* recasts employees as valuable resources for the company rather than tools. Unlike other resources, they have unlimited potential, and so managing them consists largely in educating them.

The strategy of managing employees through education is based on the idea that *needs* fuel the great human "engine." Through this strategy, resource-scarce and under developed Japan became one of the richest countries on earth.

Suppliers

The *supplier strategy* puts suppliers in roles not previously considered — those of partners in the pursuit of excellence and contributors to the development of increasingly innovative products. As suppliers too are human, their resources are limitless.

Process

The *focus on process strategy* redirects the focus of operational activities from results to process. Accordingly, the priority for management shifts from effects to causes. Analyzing cause-and-effect relationships in all sectors becomes the basis for all activities. As Professor Mizuno says, true management is the prevention and elimination of the causes of disturbance.

Quality Control in Management

The fifth strategy applies quality control concepts to company management. Although quality control was originally applied to production activities, the Japanese soon realized that the same approach could be applied to managerial activities, with impressive results. Through this strategy, a Cinderella among business techniques became a real princess, with a primary role among all other quality control techniques and approaches. It is now widely recognized that good management requires a comprehensive use of quality control concepts.

Continuous Improvement (Kaizen)

The sixth strategy assumes that improvement activities are ongoing and unceasing. The concept of continuous improvement (or *kaizen,* in Japanese), is a Japanese invention that stands in opposition to the Western concept of technological breakthroughs. As a strategy, it assumes the involvement of all employees, and is based on an optimistic view of human abilities — that they are the keys to ever-rising levels of quality.

New Product "Factory"

The seventh strategy recognizes that continuous improvement must be focused on new products. Customers (whom I liken to "monsters" in Chapter 4) demand increasingly high levels of satisfaction. A company must thus constantly bring new products to market. Through the *new product factory strategy,* a company establishes a "factory" by which excellent new products can be churned out quickly. In a sense, we can describe CWQM as the mechanism that generates a constant flow of innovative and successful products into the marketplace.

Internal Promotion

To ensure that every member of the company is constantly involved with quality and therefore that CWQM is fully operational, management must constantly promote quality within the company. In this respect promoting quality internally is not too different from advertizing one's products or services on the market. Without such constant promotion, the drive toward quality will fall off.

With CWQM, therefore, the role of management acquires the added dimension of quality promotion.

Total Participation

The strategy of involving all employees in process monitoring and improvement represents strong recognition that employees are vital to a company's success. I have not dedicated a chapter to this strategy, both because its meaning is clear and because the concepts underlying it are constantly mentioned and discussed in the text.

To conclude this introduction, let me reiterate that these strategies are at least 25 years old, and some even 30. We, in the West, are forced to call them "new" because it has taken us a long time, and great effort, to understand their importance.

CHAPTER FOUR

The Strategy of Customer Satisfaction: Loving the Monster

Introduction

We have seen that customer satisfaction takes top priority in any company applying CWQM. In this chapter we shall look at the elements of this priority, and its implications for the organization.

Giving highest priority to customer satisfaction accords great respect to the customers themselves. CWQM can be regarded as an approach that attaches great value to human beings in their three most important roles related to business:

- human beings as customers
- human beings as employees
- human beings as suppliers

Respect for customers is the engine that moves excellent companies. It is demonstrated by the attention paid to customer satisfaction. Such attention must come from everyone in the company, or the effort to satisfy the customer will not work.

There are two main reasons for the primacy of customer satisfaction over profit:

- Profit usually affects few people, and implies a knowledge of aspects of the business that are not understood by the great majority of employees.

- Customer satisfaction touches everyone. All employees are also customers, and they know what it means to be satisfied or dissatisfied with a supplier of products or services.

It is, therefore, much easier to sensitize employees to the importance of customer satisfaction.

The Importance of Customer Satisfaction

The importance of customer satisfaction cannot be overemphasized. I will discuss this matter in relation to CWQM, highlighting the most relevant points.

The Customer as Monster

The expression *customer satisfaction* is made up of two words, *customer* and *satisfaction*. To better define the customer, let me introduce the analogy of the customer as monster. I believe that this is the best way to explain customer satisfaction according to CWQM.

In school we learned about mythical monsters such as the Minotaur, the Harpies, the Sphinx, the Cyclops, and dragons. The Minotaur was a man with the head of a bull who each year devoured seven boys and seven girls; the Harpies were birds with women's heads, kidnappers of children; the Sphinx was a winged lion with a woman's head (another man-eater); and dragons were gigantic, scaly creatures who breathed fire.

We might think of the customer as a modern-day monster.

Why link such a frightening image with the human beings we serve? There are, in fact, many elements that link the two. Before going into what they are, however, let me again point out that companies face a "bottomless pit" of customer expectations, which they must try to satisfy as best they can.

Characteristics of the Monster

That said, let us see if we can understand the character of our customer, the monster (see Table 4-1).

Table 4-1. Characteristics of the Monster (Customer)

1. Insatiable hunger
2. Ruthlessness
3. Demanding
4. Slightly shy
5. Vindictive
6. Childish
7. Intrusive
8. Transmutable
9. Self-centered
10. In a word: our boss

Insatiable Hunger

First of all, the monster is insatiably hungry: His hunger is not the result of appetite, it is a deeper, constant hunger for new products. Once he has eaten something, he wants something else, and businesses are there to supply it. Any given product fits the bill for only a limited amount of time, and so companies have the often troublesome task of constantly finding a better replacement.

We are thus faced with a customer who is a "product eater," and one who demands ever-better products to boot.

Ruthless

This monster is also ruthless, caring for no one but himself. If his supplier cannot provide the satisfaction he seeks, he will go elsewhere. A company's own needs for a smooth production flow and healthy budget mean nothing to the monster. Witness the number of people who purchase foreign products in favor of domestic ones, despite the devastating consequences this can have on companies of their own country.

Demanding

The monster demands that we undertake a ceaseless effort to improve what we give him, so as to increase his satisfaction. The monster cannot tolerate any distraction on our part, not even momentary, in our race to provide him with satisfaction. He wants us to be entirely absorbed in him.

Everyone's activity in the company is justifiable as long as it is carried out to the monster's advantage and with his demands in mind. Any distraction caused by internal friction is immediately punishable by withdrawal of the monster's loyalty.

Slightly Shy

The monster is shy, but this has no charm for us. On the contrary, it hurts us, his suppliers, in two ways.

First, it hurts us when we are trying to determine his desires but he does not express them.

Second, it hurts us when we disappoint him by failing to satisfy his needs. In this case, the monster does not inform us of our misstep but simply disappears, never to return.

Vindictive

The monster is not only shy but vindictive. If displeased, he not only turns away from us but poisons others against us. Some studies conducted in the United States show that dissatisfied customers tend to communicate their negative experiences to thirty other potential customers.

Moreover, the monster switches his loyalties to another supplier and forgets all we have done for him except our inability to satisfy him. The Japanese note that it takes between 5 and 10 years for a brand to build solid market foundations, and only one night to lose it all: in other words, it takes a long time to build up trust, and no time at all to lose it.

Childish

The monster's childishness is his weak point, and we must take advantage of it. When the monster discovers something that interests and satisfies him he gets excited, like a child. He must have that thing. We can capitalize on this trait by feeding the monster a steady flow of things that excite and satisfy him.

Intrusive

One of the more insidious traits of the monster is his intrusiveness. He insists on being present in every corner of the company.

The budget manager, for example, would be wrong to believe that he can ignore the customer, for in fact the customer is just behind him, demanding satisfaction, albeit indirectly. We have all seen those American monster movies in which the creatures invade cities, homes, and rooms. Well, our monster behaves in the same way, trying to dominate every small section of the company. His intrusiveness has no limits; he even demands to be with the suppliers and to condition their activities.

Transmutable

In his desire to be everywhere, the monster has a thousand guises. He even takes on the faces of our colleagues.

Self-centered

The monster is also self-centered: he thinks of himself as set apart from the rest and demands that we do the same. He doesn't care about other people's requirements. He wants products and services that are custom-tailored to his needs, and so the challenge for his suppliers is to become artisans for the masses. This egocentricity accounts for the "demassification" process currently underway worldwide.

Our Boss

Many others could certainly be mentioned in addition to the above nine characteristics, but I would like to end with the one that is the most important and strategic from our point of view: Our customer is our boss.

The customer is a boss with life-and-death power over us: not physical death, certainly, but economic death. If we do not serve his or her every need the monster kills us, not by breathing fire, but by taking away our oxygen.

The customer as dominator of the company conditions all aspects of our work. It is not quite true to say that the shareholders own a company: the real owner is the lifeblood of the company, its customer.

A Monster Under a Spell

The monster's story has a happy ending: This monster is under a spell, and, just as in fairy tales in which the monster turns into a prince upon an act of kindness, so does our monster turn into our friend, if we do the right thing.

How do we bring about such a miracle? Just as in fairy tales, there must be love. Though the word may appear excessive, it is the right one. Love for the customer is essential in order to achieve a high level of customer satisfaction.

It may seem difficult to love a creature with so many horrid characteristics, yet it is the only path to excellence, and thus to survival. There is no real substitute for permeating the whole organization with powerful love.

We must understand the joy of being in the service of our customers, and how this improves us as human beings. Each of us is a customer, and thus each of us can understand the value of being loved and served with deep humanity.

It is therefore essential that employees understand that the reward for loving the customer will be the customers' love for the company. They will reward the company with their loyalty and convey their appreciation to others.

What does loving the monster entail? In very simple terms, it entails three activities:

- constantly searching for latent quality
- organizing the customer's invasion of the company
- implementing the customer's invasion into the product

I shall now briefly examine these three activities.

The Constant Search for Latent Quality

What does it mean to constantly search for latent quality? As mentioned in Chapter 1, quality, and thus customer satisfaction, can be viewed from three points of view.

First, there is *required quality,* which addresses those characteristics specifically asked for by the customer. Secondly, there is *expected quality,* that is, those characteristics that satisfy desires the customer has not expressed because he or she takes them for granted. For example, if I stay at a hotel, I expect the sheets to be clean; yet should someone ask me what I seek in a hotel, I would certainly not mention clean sheets.

Required quality and expected quality account for only a small part of true customer satisfaction, however. That is because customers have potential needs, or what we have described as an "insatiable hunger," for things they cannot name and that we as supplier must try to discover. This *latent quality* represents a territory more vast and unexplored than the one the pilgrims faced upon arriving on the American continent.

Latent quality is also called *exciting quality,* because when we experience it we feel great enthusiasm, since we were previously unaware of its existence. Here is a rather simple example, based on personal experience: It is quite normal for the mirrors in a hotel bathroom to cloud up with steam when someone runs a hot shower; the steam that condenses on the mirror makes it hard to use the mirror to shave or comb one's hair. Recently, at a hotel I visited during a trip to Japan, I noticed that a rectangle of the mirror above the sink remained clear and clean even after a very long shower. Something behind the mirror kept it warm, thus preventing it from clouding over. This discovery gave me great pleasure, and, incidentally, the hotel in question is known in Japan for its total quality program, and for the quality of its service. Another famous discovery of latent quality is the Sony Walkman, which hit on a latent need never highlighted before — the desire of young people to listen to music at all times, without having to carry around heavy equipment and without disturbing those around them.

This is where our future lies. Our customer, the monster, wants us to explore this territory, discovering unknown needs and then satisfying them with new products. The better we can do this, the greater will be our rewards.

To discover new ways to satisfy our customers' endless needs, we must have a great deal of love for them, as well as a great deal of patience and the ability to put ourselves into their shoes.

It is worth remembering that latent quality can be discovered not only in a product's hardware, but also in its software, that is, the "human" feature that becomes increasingly important in the "package" we offer our customers.

Organizing the Customer's Invasion of the Company

Let us now examine what we mean by the customer's invasion of the company, and how it can be translated into love for the customer.

We have seen that the client is our boss, and, as such, he or she wants ownership over every part of our company, including offices, departments, warehouses, and subsidiaries.

What do we mean by "invasion"? We mean that every single part of the company must live and breathe love for the customer. Everything we do in every unit of the organization must be defined in terms of the customer. No egocentricity is allowed; egocentricity is the prerogative of the customer alone. Thus one must never "fall in love" with one's system or one's work, forgetting one's function in relation to the customer.

If we look at the company as a whole, such ownership is not so much a difficult concept as a profound one. In a sense we must allow the monster to set the standards of our company, as every boss has the right to do. Terrible consequences might ensue, should we not implement this concept!

The fuller and deeper such an invasion is, the stronger and more competitive the company will be, as everyone will be working for the customer, who in turn will be in the best conditions to be served.

You are probably already familiar with the magical phrase that can, under the right circumstances, create such conditions; it was coined by Professor Ishikawa more than 40 years ago (in 1949): "The process downstream is our customer." The magic of this phrase is set in motion only after the deep love I mentioned has developed.

The sentence clearly points out the ability of our customer to take on different guises within the company. Thus the company becomes a network of customer-supplier relationships, all aligned so that the company can be in the best condition to satisfy its actual customer: the one on the outside.

What is less immediately clear, and yet a product of the same magical phrase, is that, just as hundreds of customers are created, so are hundreds, if not thousands, of products or services that are marketed on the inside of the company.

Let us take as an example the budget office. At first glance, this office might appear to be far removed from the marketplace battlefield. This office too, however, has customers and suppliers. Moreover, it carries out processes that must in turn be organized, like those in a production plant (to use a familiar analogy).

As we can see in Figure 4-1, this "unit" of the company "manufactures products" such as forecasts, goals, and company procedures, and it must satisfy customers such as the executive committee, the board of directors, and the division and functional managers. To do this it must use organizational techniques, including quality control and quality assurance.

I know from working in the field for 10 years that this message is hard to understand, even in the production sectors. Yet, quality control and assurance must be guaranteed for every service and product we produce in our company, from finished goods to internal reports. All this requires a major change in attitude and represents the main difference between ourselves and the Japanese in the matter of customer satisfaction.

Before going to the third and last characteristic, I would like to summarize this second point, as it is a complex one: We must open our doors and lower our drawbridges, and let the customer enter the company so that we can show our love, which constitutes the foundation for customer satisfaction. If we truly wish to achieve excellence, there is no alternative.

How to Carry Out the Customer's Invasion of the Product

Our intrusive customer wants to enter into the product itself, not only the final product but also all those hundreds of products generated within the company.

What does this intrusion mean? Let's consider something seemingly insignificant, such as a bolt within a finished product. Even that bolt contributes to the customer's satisfaction; if it doesn't, we should ask why it is there, since the monster abhors waste.

How does this bolt — or any other company product — get imbued with the notion of customer satisfaction?

The answer lies in a Japanese technique worthy of a Carthusian monk, one that allows the customer's perfect intru-

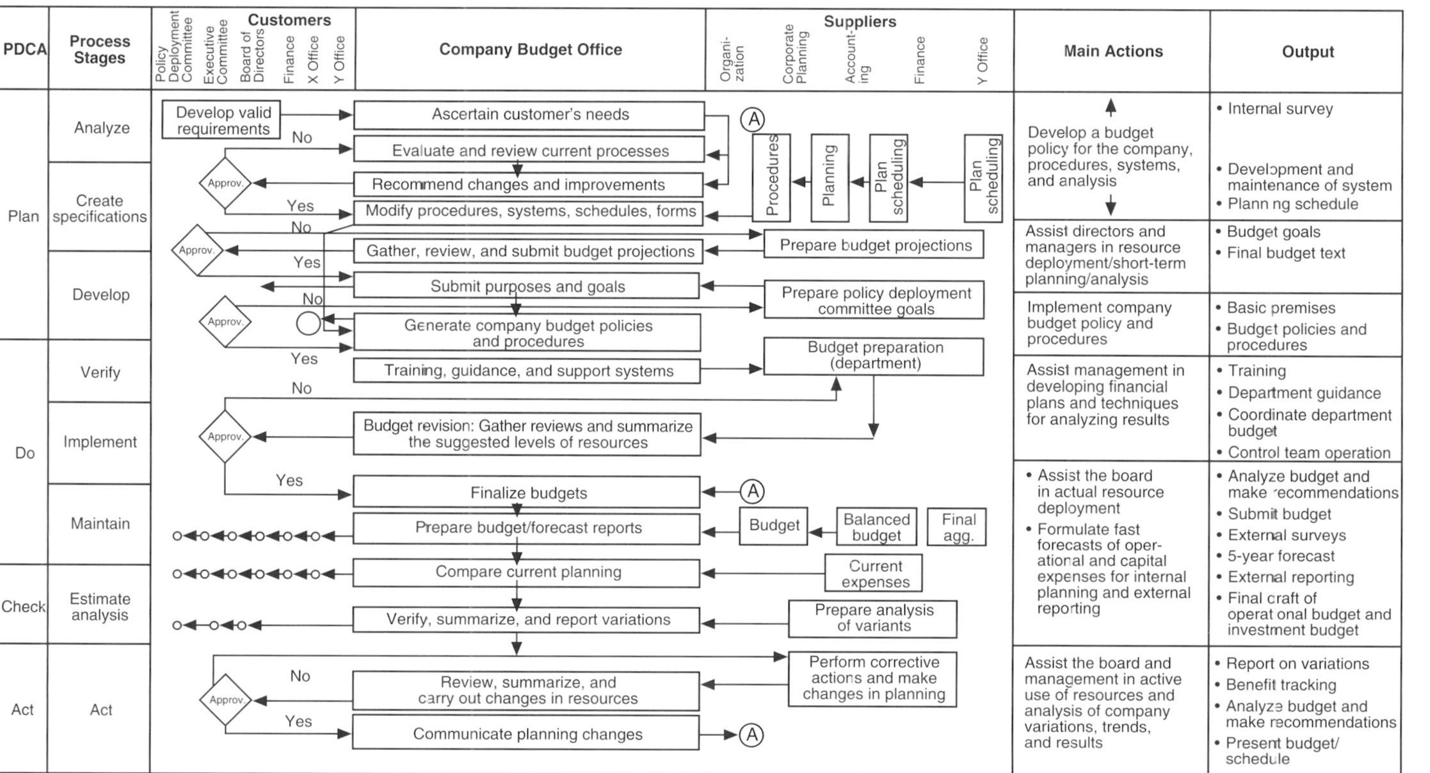

Figure 4-1. Budget Office Processes

sion into every part of the product. This technique is called *quality function deployment,* or *quality deployment* (see Chapter 15).

It has enabled the Japanese to attain superior levels of quality and, what is more important, to perfect successful products in a short time, without the numerous revisions often necessary in Western new product development. It solves the problem of the "weak customer voice" and imbues every part of every company product with the customer's needs. Such is the extent of the passion for the customer exhibited by Japanese companies, and it largely accounts for their success.

Conclusion

To conclude, the customer is our boss, our "monster," and demands to be satisfied. If we want to survive we must make his or her satisfaction our goal; thus, we must love the customer. Only by providing concrete, precise, cohesive, constant proof of this love can a company achieve true excellence. To paraphrase Dante's famous line "the Love that moves the sun and the other stars," we might say that customer satisfaction must become "the love that moves the company and its suppliers."

CHAPTER FIVE

The New Strategy for Human Resources Management

Introduction

One of the greatest Japanese businessmen, Konosuke Matsushita, brilliantly summarized the great strategy for managing human resources in these words:

> "For you, the essence of management lies in extracting ideas from the minds of the executives and putting them into the hands of the workers."
>
> "For us, the essence of management lies precisely in the art of mobilizing the intellectual resources of everyone working for the company."
>
> "Since we have understood the true nature of the economic and technological challenges better than you, we know that the intelligence of a group of executives, impressive as this might be, is no longer enough to guarantee success."

The use of human resources so as to maximize a company's competitiveness is one of CWQM's great secrets. We can call it a secret because this system has been ignored by the Western world. Literature on the subject refers, instead, to lifetime employment, the seniority system, the role of teamwork and of company unions, of the *ringi* decision-making process, and of the informal consultations called *nemawashi*.

These analyses leave out the fundamental aspects of management, however: priority setting in the relationship between manager and staff, and the use of people's highest needs to elicit their highest contribution.

A company's competitiveness is thus based on a new way of managing its human resources. This new system is applicable outside Japan, too, as the results obtained in American and European Toyota, Nissan, Honda, and Matsushita plants demonstrate. What is required is a long-term vision, because according to the Japanese experience the time needed to establish this new human resources management ranges from 5 to 10 years.

The Foundations of Human Resources Management

Human resources management within the CWQM model is vastly different from its Western counterpart. It is based on three important principles concerning human resources. Although they were formulated years ago by scholars and experts such as Abraham Maslow, Rensis Likert, Douglas McGregor, and Frederick Herzberg, they have not been widely accepted or applied, either in America or in Europe.

First principle. The ultimate success of a company depends on how it manages its human resources. No other single factor is more important. New products, sales activities, production quality, and other company output all depend mainly on the capacity and motivation of the company's employees.

Second principle. Human beings have unlimited resources and immense capabilities. The JUSE manual on quality circles states that one of the goals of QC activities is to fully expose human capabilities and their infinite potential. To state the principle another way, men and women can perform miracles if

- they are treated as intelligent human beings
- they are allowed their dignity
- they are treated with respect
- they are involved in the attainment of company goals
- they are well trained
- they are allowed to offer a significant contribution to the work they perform
- they trust that the success they have helped attain affects them positively

Third principle. To develop human resources it is necessary to reinforce people's positive assets. This means that managers must minimize the consequences of employees' negative qualities while helping them to improve. The thrust of a manager's actions should be to help people grow by stressing their positive qualities. The traditional emphasis on negative traits prevents this flowering of human potential.

The Goals of Human Resources Management

In CWQM, the main goals of human resources management are to:

- have employees of all levels react autonomously and coherently to environment
- make optimal use of information flowing from all organization units
- cultivate a strong psychological energy in all members of the organization
- overcome the ambiguities inherent in all human relations

In Chapter 9 we will see that one of the pillars of CWQM, small-step improvement, departs from the traditional focus on profit and results by focusing on process and efforts. Such a difference in approach is also evident in the CWQM model of human resources management. To examine this we will concentrate our analysis on the relationship between manager and staff, which basically represents the "glue" holding together any organization.

The Relationship Between Manager and Staff

The key point in the new management system pertains to the relationship between manager and staff. In the Western business model, this relationship concentrates on *goals* and *results*. Managers establish a relationship with their employees by communicating to them the goals they should achieve. After that, the managers' attention is focused on the results obtained. This might seem like a reasonable approach, given the importance of goals and results. But let's look more carefully at what is going on in such a process.

Let us begin with goals. To achieve a goal, an employee will have to perform certain activities, or, to be more precise, carry out a process. The ways in which such a process is carried out are essential for achieving the goals.

Let us now look at results. It is obvious that, in order to achieve results, an employee will have to make efforts. Just sitting in an armchair is unlikely to produce any results. But we have all met people who make a great effort and yet do not achieve great results. One must know how to transform effort into results. If this know-how were a machine into which we put effort and from which we extract results, it should be a very high-performance device.

The truth is, most people's ability to transform effort into results is limited. The fact that some people can do it owes more to their own personal gifts and determination than to the traditional business system.

Let us now consider the following simple diagram:

Process	Goal
Effort	Results

Let's ask ourselves which side should receive priority attention in the relationship between manager and staff, the left or the right? CWQM focuses on the left, while the Western approach focuses on the right. As we will show, the CWQM approach is the only way for a company to attain its goals.

Priority of Process

What happens when processes take priority? First, managers redirect their energies to the training and preparation of their staff. Since the managerial role is essential in such training, they become deeply involved to ensure that their staff are able to perform effectively. Hence the slogan:

> CWQM begins with training and ends with training.

Priority of Effort

What happens when efforts take priority? Once managers realize that effort precedes results, they begin to reward effort even before they acknowledge results. Parents do the same thing when, for example, they reward their children's first efforts at homework. Though the results may not be the best, the parents praise the children for trying and then offer suggestions on how to improve the work itself. In the same respect, a manager's reward for staff effort is not of a monetary nature, but aims at creating trust and lending support. Employees who are given the full support of their manager will develop the skills to transform effort into ever-better results.

Human Resources Management by Education

Once the relationship between manager and staff is centered on process and effort, the new approach to human resources management can begin. This new model replaces the traditional emphasis on *control* with an emphasis on *education.*

Management by education is largely an indirect way of managing. By developing the ability to manage the process, by cultivating motivation through rewarding effort, and by providing clear guidelines for the staff, managers do away with the need for constant control. Moreover, they exhibit greater trust in people than that shown in the traditional model.

Professor Ishikawa, in his book on CWQM, uses an interesting image when referring to middle managers (whose position is between top management and supervisors). He writes that they should carry out management activities as if they were intelligent traffic cops. Like traffic cops, managers stand at a crossroad in this case, of horizontal and vertical information flows. Their role is to ensure that traffic runs smoothly and that the company's work is carried out safely.

We know that traffic cops can make a situation worse by whistling too often or when it is not appropriate. In extreme cases, they can even cause an accident. In order to regulate traffic, they must not only rely solely on what they see at the crossroad, but they must also be informed about traffic at distant points that might affect the position they are in charge of. They must make estimates and judgments that reflect a perspective broader than the scene in front of their eyes.

Of course, they do not always need to stand at a crossroad. When traffic volume is low, traffic lights are sufficient. Only when traffic is intense is their presence truly needed. If they work hard when they are not needed, they will be tired when their presence is essential.

By the same reasoning, Professor Ishikawa suggests that managers become people whose physical presence isn't always required but who are, nonetheless, essential to their company. For this to happen, the staff must be clear on the company's policies and the manager's interpretations. If these people learn how to work together in a constructive way, then the presence of their superior will be necessary only when special situations require it or when difficulties arise. On such occasions the staff should perceive the manager's contribution as crucial to a solution so that, should another difficult situation arise, the staff themselves will call for the manager's intervention.

The People-Building Process

To implement management by education, companies must activate a *people-building* process, especially at the lower levels of the organization, where it is most needed. To better explain the concept of *people building,* I must go back to what motivates human behavior.

Behavior is motivated by need. Thus, if we wish to motivate the behavior of a company's employees, we must ensure that they feel the need to act. Here we find the support of psychologist Abraham Maslow, who has set basic human needs within a framework of five levels, as shown in Figure 5-1. Although this diagram is well known, it has not been sufficiently analyzed, nor have its implications for personnel development been sufficiently understood.

To understand how each level provides strong motivation, let us imagine the diagram as a fuel tank. This fuel motivates behavior. In most organizations, the two upper tanks — that is, the needs of one's ego and the need for self-realization — are not tapped into. They are mired in a thick sediment and can be

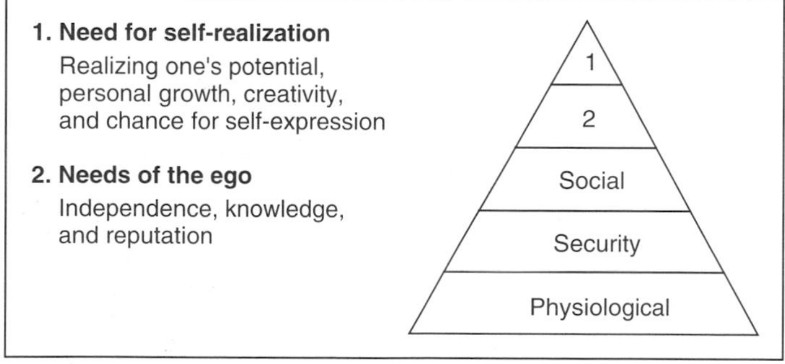

Figure 5-1. The Five Levels of Human Needs According to Maslow

activated only through *people building*. But people building in organizations that have never tackled these higher needs requires a number of years, even in Japan. The process comprises a series of steps, shown in Figure 5-2.

The first stage above the level of individual basic desires is *self-development*. This is activated only when a person feels secure of his or her position within the company, and realizes that there is the potential for both promotion to higher positions and better compensation. During this phase, people realize that

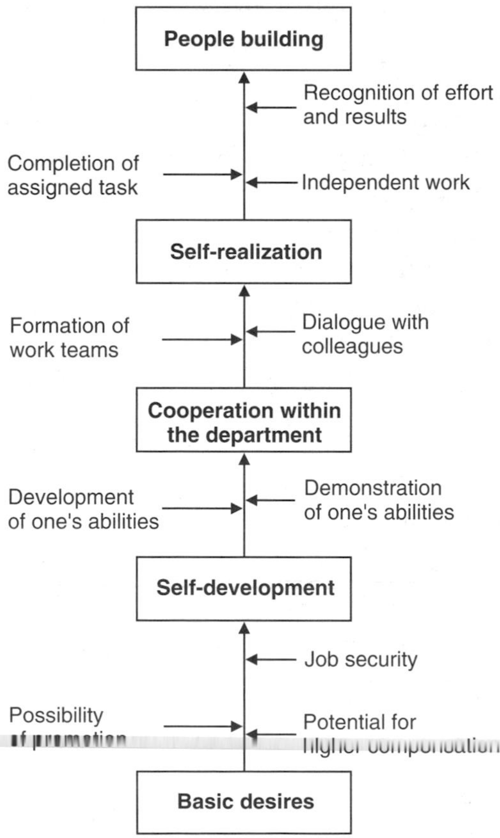

Figure 5-2. The People-building Process

there are new areas to explore and that they can develop their capabilities, thereby greatly strengthening their self-esteem.

Next they move on to *cooperation within the department* (or office). During this stage they further enrich their abilities and develop a new motivation by forming work teams (such as quality circles) that carry out projects. These groups encourage intense interaction among colleagues, which in turn leads to full self-realization and the conclusion of the people-building process. The sense of autonomy derived from carrying out one's work, the satisfaction over a job well done, and the perception that one's efforts and results are being rewarded all "build" a person who is able to:

- react "independently" to his or her environment
- develop spontaneously the psychic energy necessary to offer a greater contribution to the company

Managing One's Superior

Human resources management is not only a top-down process, but also a bottom-up process. It includes not only the actions of managers toward their staff, but also the actions of staff toward managers.

Western business literature gives scant attention to this relationship. Professor Ishikawa stated that employees are truly trained when they can "manage" their superiors. He meant that employees should carry out their work in such a way that their managers will accept their opinions and recommendations. Only then do they become integral parts of the organization.

To do this, employees must be able to "sell" their ideas to supervisors by providing the necessary facts and supporting documentation.

CHAPTER SIX

Partnerships with Suppliers

Introduction

One of the great achievements of CWQM is its acknowledgement of suppliers as one of the company's most important resources. This acknowledgment grew out of the realization that suppliers are fundamental to the development of new products and technology. The principle behind this concept is the following: If appropriately encouraged and assisted, the supplier can provide a unique contribution to design and technological innovation while at the same time actively working toward cost reductions. To get this advantage, however, the customer must have implicit faith in the supplier's ability to play such a role.

The notion of customer-supplier partnerships began taking shape in Japan in the late 1950s. In 1960, at a quality control convention, the first draft of the 10 principles behind customer-supplier relations was defined. These were reviewed, and in 1966 Professor Ishikawa officially presented them at the fourth QC symposium of JUSE.

Japanese industry relies on suppliers to a far greater extent than Western industries. In fact, the Japanese attribute the success of their products in large part to the high quality attained by their suppliers. This vendor-vendee partnership strategy is rare in Western industry, which inclines toward self-sufficiency and mistrust of suppliers. The early Ford Motor Company under Henry Ford offers a classic example, organized for maximum vertical integration.

Foundations for the New Strategy

The customer-supplier partnership is based on three assumptions:

1. The quality of any product depends to a large extent on the quality of its components. In many companies, the procurement costs range from 50 to 70 percent of sales volume.
2. To design and develop new products in shorter times and with higher reliability, a company needs the full cooperation of the supplier, beginning with the initial phases of development.
3. Quality, cost, and delivery are not the only factors to consider when establishing and maintaining a customer-supplier relationship. Technological innovation and constant improvement are also essential.

This collaborative relationship between customers and suppliers differs from the "conflicting" relationship typical of the Western model in a key respect: The Western model focuses on bargaining price. This focus pits suppliers against each other as they vie for low bids, and leads to quick turnover among suppliers, which ultimately increases real purchasing costs. The extra costs are not the fault of purchasing managers, of course, but of the policies handed down by top management.

Characteristics of the New Strategy

In short, the vendor relationship strategy according to CWQM can be described as mutual trust and maximum cooperation within a long-term framework for the purpose of actively ensuring the greatest customer satisfaction. Through this strategy, suppliers become an extension of the customer's company processes and gain awareness that the satisfaction of their final customers largely depends on how such processes are led. Thus, the one-dimensional, transitory nature of the old relationship becomes transformed into something deeper and more enduring (see Figure 6-1). From a simple relationship it becomes a true "link," which requires a management approach focused on long-term results (see Figure 6-2). Let us briefly examine the features of this relationship.

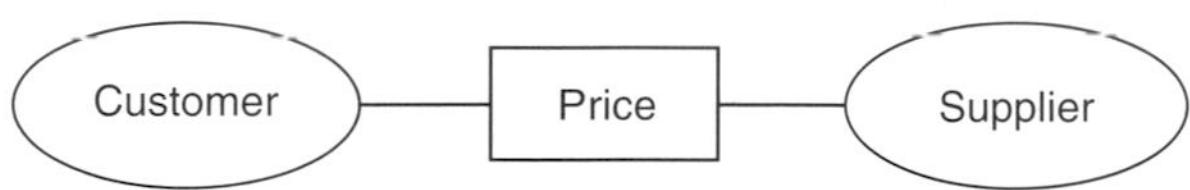

Figure 6-1. Customer-Supplier: Traditional Relationship

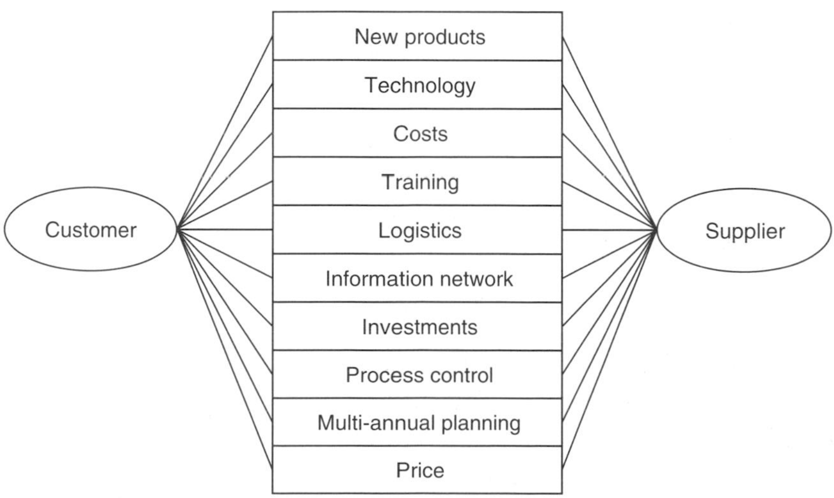

Figure 6-2. Customer-Supplier: Partnership Bond

New Product Development

Suppliers should be involved in the development of new products from the earliest stages, so that they can better understand the customer's requirements at a later stage, provide useful suggestions, adapt processes and technologies, and shorten the development time of the new parts they have to produce.

Technology

There must be a mutual exchange of information concerning the technologies adopted, so that both parties can set the right priorities, avoid bottlenecks, develop synergy, and facilitate product industrialization. Such cooperation can be extended to the research and development stages.

Costs

Customers and suppliers should establish a mutual commitment regarding total cost reduction programs. The deeper the reciprocal knowledge, the better the assessment of the two partners' needs will be; this in turn leads to a more effective focus on the necessary improvement activities.

Training

Suppliers often lack the necessary qualities to become reliable partners. Customers should be ready to offer training, education, and technical assistance in order to increase their suppliers' capabilities.

Logistics

The logistic chain between customer and supplier should be as flexible as possible. The size of lots decreases, while the number of deliveries increases. Wherever possible just-in-time deliveries are carried out, on the basis of open orders. As supplier reliability improves, inventory is reduced by both suppliers and customers.

Information Network

A shared information network should be built for use in operational procedures (deliveries, billing), and management functions (planning, modification management, etc.). Such networks facilitate all flows between partners.

Investments

Given the strength of the bond between customer and supplier, the supplier, in accordance with the customer, is given the authority to make investments that can improve the characteristics of products and services provided. The supplier should no longer be penalized for making such investments; nor should it be afraid of seeing information it provided to the customer used against it.

Process Control

The partnership also embraces the technical aspects of a supplier's process control. The supplier should provide the customer with indicators of *process capability* and *production control* from design through final inspection. A supplier should also invite clients to participate in QC audits held internally.

Long-term Planning

The two partners cooperate in developing long-term plans concerning the main aspects of their bond. They establish common strategies and improvement goals.

Companywide Involvement

The features of the link between vendor and vendee clearly demand involvement by all departments, not just procurement. Communications between the two partners take place daily, and are centered upon the goals to be attained. The people in charge of purchases have the duty to encourage and facilitate such exchanges, and as such they play a key coordinating role.

Number of Suppliers Needed

The partnership strategy leads to a substantial reduction in the number of suppliers needed. Ishikawa mentions the example of a company he worked with to reduce the number of its suppliers. In three years that company reduced the number of suppliers from 400 to 100.

Responsibility in the Customer-Supplier Relationship

A viable partnership strategy between customer and supplier requires clear definition of each party's responsibilities. We can divide these responsibilities into four categories:

1. responsibility for quality control
2. buyer's responsibilities
3. supplier's responsibilities
4. shared responsibilities

The division of these responsibilities should not take precedence over the mutual respect at the foundation of the partnership. Just as the buyer considers the supplier as a valuable resource, so does the supplier view the customer as its top priority.

Responsibility for quality control. Customers and suppliers are both responsible for applying quality control across all systems according to agreed-on precepts. For this purpose the parties must exchange all information necessary to carry out quality control activities.

Buyer's responsibilities. The client is responsible for the accuracy and adequacy of information and specifications given to the supplier.

Supplier's responsibilities. The supplier must guarantee the quality levels of its products and seek to ensure the customer's full satisfaction. It must also provide all necessary data requested by the customer.

Shared responsibilities. Before suppliers and customers enter into a partnership, they should

- adopt a suitable contract concerning quality, quantity, prices, delivery terms, and payment methods
- agree on methods and tools used to evaluate specifications
- agree on the system and procedures to be used in the event of disagreement, so as to permit amicable resolution

In addition, both customer and supplier must ensure control of each phase of their own process, from the issuing of orders to production and scheduling. Throughout the process, each party should keep the interest of the final customer firmly in mind.

Selecting Suppliers

According to the CWQM logic, the customer should consider three criteria in selecting a supplier:

- a good product
- a good quality control system
- good management

In assessing these three items one should bear the following in mind:

- The supplier should understand the customer's company policies and be willing to carry them out. The customer, in turn, must analyze the supplier's company philosophy, assess the knowledge and skills of its management, and gauge the supplier's understanding of the importance of quality.

- The supplier must have a reliable management system and a sound reputation.
- The supplier must maintain high quality standards and be able to adopt technological innovations.
- The supplier's materials or products must fulfill the customer's quality requirements. At the same time, the supplier must constantly strive to improve its ability to fulfill these requirements.
- The supplier must have an adequate quality assurance (QA) program as well as a training program for quality control. The supply cost, moreover, must be fair, and delivery dates should be respected.
- Finally, the supplier must scrupulously carry out its contractual obligations and respect company secrets.

During a seminar he held in Italy Professor Ishikawa illustrated the supplier selection process in these terms:

1. Selection starts with a request for a sample from a large number of companies.
2. An evaluation based on the most important requirements (product quality) reduces the number of potential suppliers to, let us say, 20.
3. Those 20 suppliers then undergo a diagnostic rating regarding their quality control and management system.
4. This further reduces the number of potential suppliers to about 5 or 6.
5. Inspections and checks are carried out, after which 1 or 2 suppliers are chosen.
6. The audit is then repeated for quality control and management. If any results are negative, the supplier is rejected.
7. If results are mediocre for all suppliers selected (even if their products are acceptable), then training begins, both for management and for execu-

tives. After a transition period, the weakest suppliers are eliminated.

Never once did Ishikawa mention price as an element of the selection process.

With proper maintenance of the partnership bond, significant advantages can be gained, especially in terms of quality assurance of the products supplied. In turn, the customer company can maintain a high QA level on the market. From this point of view, the level of supplier-customer relations can make a considerable difference.

As shown in Table 6-1, there are eight levels of customer-supplier relationships. At the lowest level, control is left entirely to the manufacturing departments of the customer company. At the intermediate levels, supplier control increases while the need

Table 6-1. Types of Quality Assurance in Supplier-Purchaser Relations

Level of Relationship	Supplier		Purchaser	
	Production	Out	In	Production
1.	No inspection	No inspection	No inspection	100% inspection
2.	No inspection	No inspection	100% inspection	—
3.	No inspection	100% inspection	100% inspection	—
4.	No inspection	100% inspection	Sample inspection	—
5.	100% inspection	Sample inspection in the presence of purchaser	No inspection; reduced sample inspection	—
6.	Process control and 100% inspection	Sample inspection in the presence of purchaser	No inspection; reduced sample inspection	—
7.	Process control	Reduced sample inspection	No inspection	—
8.	Process control	No inspection	No inspection	—

for inspection by the customer decreases. Thus the quality of supplies increases. At level 8, the supplier-customer relationship is optimal in terms of quality assurance. This is because the supplier is entirely in control of the manufacturing process, making it unnecessary for the customer to inspect products purchased.

Supplier-Customer Partnership at Toyota

The supplier-customer partnership maintained at Toyota, Japan's most successful automobile company, has the following characteristics:

1. *A broadly conceived procurement policy:*
   - Develop stable, long-term relations with suppliers.
   - Stay with the same suppliers.
   - Evaluate suppliers according to total cost, not price.
   - Cooperate with suppliers in order to render their processes less costly and more reliable.
2. *A cooperative relationship with suppliers:*
   - Contracts establish rules for quality control and procedures for managing defective items.
   - The operational relationship falls within the *kanban* system (see Table 6-2), which also embraces suppliers).*
   - The company provides assistance and training to suppliers for the improvement of their management and quality control (see Table 6-3).

---

* *Kanban,* which means card in Japanese, refers to the card based system first developed at Toyota Motor Company for requesting inventory from vendors and previous processes on a just-in-time basis. For more information, see Japan Management Association (David J. Lu, translator), *Kanban Just-in-Time at Toyota: Management Begins at the Workplace* (Cambridge, Mass.: Productivity Press, 1985). — Ed.

Table 6-2. Evolution of the Kanban System

1950	Initial leveling of assembly lines Introduction of kanban within Toyota
1962	Kanban system is adopted with vendors, after being instituted in all Toyota plants
1970	60% of vendors use kanban with Toyota
1982	Kanban is used by 92% of vendors as a system for managing operational relations with Toyota. 50% of them introduced the system into their internal organization (many with the help of Toyota).

Table 6-3. An Example of Supplier Training

Level	Courses
Upper Management	1. Total quality and its management 2. Quality control and reliability
Middle Management	3. Basic course on quality control 4. Basic course on reliability 5. Course on design of experiments
Supervisors	6. Course on managing quality circles 7. Course on 7 QC tools

- The company uses a "comprehensive" selection system to rate suppliers on the basis of global evaluation criteria, which determine the type of relationship to be established.
- The company works closely with suppliers on new product development, technology, and quality control.

3. *Daily information:*
   - Kanban is used for small parts.
   - Sequence (planned deliveries) is used for large parts.
4. *An operational relationship with suppliers:*
   - Toyota tries to limit discrepancies between monthly forecasts and actual daily production to

within 10 percent of plan, and expects supplier to accept this discrepancy.

- Since every automobile model is produced for at least four years, the supplier should not suffer serious damage from such monthly fluctuations, as these fluctuations are generally minimal over a period of many years.
- Toyota guarantees to inform in advance its suppliers when the production of a certain model is about to stop. At that time a compensation system is agreed upon.
- Toyota advises the supplier not to start production until it receives adequate instructions via kanban. Thus, excess production is unlikely.
- To be able to implement an order system based on kanban, the supplier must shorten its production lead time. Toyota teaches how such a reduction can be achieved.

5. *Quality control rewards:*
   - Toyota gives out excellence awards based on an evaluation of control and quality improvement activities in production.
   - Toyota gives out superiority awards based on an evaluation of the entire control management system (including financial and long-term policies). Recognition is granted only if the firm being examined can guarantee systematic improvement with a value exceeding 1 percent of sales volume (variable index).
6. *An association of Toyota suppliers:*
   - The association holds a yearly or semiannual conference on engineering and on quality control.
   - Conferences are given for executives to present and discuss specifications for new products and models.

- Meetings are held to discuss new systems.
- There are regular and frequent exchange of visits between suppliers and Toyota.

7. *Cooperation between Toyota and its suppliers:*
   - Toyota provides training to suppliers. In many cases, in launching a stockless production plan for suppliers, Toyota has invited hundreds of people (managers, department heads, assistants) to its plants to train them in JIT techniques.
   - Toyota provides assistance to suppliers. Toyota experts visit the suppliers' plants in order to assist them in carrying out pilot JIT projects.
8. *Results of cooperation:*
   - Table 6-4 illustrates the results obtained by Toyota's two suppliers, Aisin Seiki and Tokai Rika, and the consequent benefits gained by Toyota. It should be noted that the market share of Tokai Rika has grown for almost every line of product.

Table 6-4. Results of Cooperation Between Toyota and Its Suppliers: Two Examples

Results at Aisin Seiki (1981), suppliers of gears; internal kanban organization in addition to sequence transmitted by Toyota.

1. Lead time between storage of semifinished gears and finished gears is 15 minutes.
2. The sequence is transmitted to Toyota only two hours before the expected delivery time (one hour for production, one hour for transportation).

Results at Tokai Rika (supplier of safety belts, levers for shifts, switches).

Before 1973	Traditional system Push production — monthly lots
1973	Decrease in demand Increase in code numbers Increase in stock on hand (from 24 to 36.2 days) Disorganized shipments Delivery schedules not respected Complaints and recalls by Toyota
1974	Stock reduced to 17 days (better control) Toyota insisted on introduction of kanban system Decision to introduce it with Toyota's assistance, with the following goals: • to cut total inventory in half over a year (from 17.1 to 9.5 days) • to improve productivity and flow of materials
September 1975	Goals not achieved because setup time was reduced and consequently the size of lots remained too large
March 1976	Stock reduced to 6.2 days Plant space recovered 31% decrease in labor costs Improved process control Greater flexibility

June 1982	Raw materials	2.5 days
	WIP	0.75 days
	Finished parts for Toyota	0.3 days
	Finished parts for others	1.3 days
	Total	4.85 days

Results at Toyota

Number of vendors per vehicle	200
Total number of production suppliers	300
Distance of vendors	90% within 300 kms.
Average transportation time	4-5 hours
Frequency of deliveries	Daily
• Most products	15' - 30'
• Motors, transmissions, large-size components	

CHAPTER SEVEN

Process Strategy

Introduction

To fully understand the companywide quality management model and the profound innovations it leads to, one must move beyond consideration of the priorities and decisions made on a companywide basis to those made within each organizational unit of the company. These decisions are illustrated through the second part of Ikiro's story begun in Chapter 2. This reveals the greatest discovery of CWQM at the operational level: the importance of focusing on processes when managing a company and the application of what we will call the process strategy.

Through this story we will enter into more technical concepts, which substantially differ from the traditional organizational culture. In fact the traditional organizational model is basically a functional one, in which analysis prevails over synthesis, the parts over the whole. With CWQM the organizational unit becomes a living part of its environment with sensors that are as important to the company as eyes and ears are to a person.

Traditional corporate culture discovered the importance of focusing on processes only after witnessing the success of

Japanese companies. Thus techniques such as *process management* were created, and often presented as a package. Techniques of this kind, however, are not very successful unless they are set within the framework of the CWQM philosophy.

Organizational Units and the "Process" Priority

Ikiro has not yet finished his mental cogitations in his search for his company's success . He has determined the priorities for the company as a whole, but not for the organizational units (offices, departments, warehouses, laboratories, subsidiaries, etc.) that compose it. To manage these units he must make decisions at the operational level of the units themselves.

The first problem is the difference that exists among the many organizational units: suffice it to think of the difference between an accounting office and a production department. Ikiro is convinced that such differences should not affect the priorities directing the decision-making process for all organizational units.

So Ikiro starts thinking again. The priorities to be set should relate to what is common to all organizational units, whatever their activities and functions are. It is a question of capturing the common "essence" of each organizational unit. Ikiro identifies "processes" as the common characteristic of each unit. Every organizational unit carries out nothing but processes, that is, a series of activities that lead to the transformation of input into output. The output should have some added value in respect to the initial input. This process is the "living" feature of each organizational unit, and it represents its essence. No other outlook so integrates the organizational units; anything else would be too analytical and thus not express the essence of the unit itself.

Ikiro understands that the process, in addition to being the essence of an organizational unit, also constitutes its priority and thus its most important aspect. The focus of management must be on processes.

He feels that such meditations have led him to a great discovery. Focusing on processes as the priority at the unit level is equivalent to choosing quality as the priority at the company level. In these two choices we can say that we have the essence of CWQM. All other decisions descend from those two basic priorities.

Now Ikiro's problem is to determine how to manage a process according to the priorities chosen at the company level: customer satisfaction and quality.

Process: Basic Concepts

With great humility, Ikiro begins from scratch. He needs to learn the basic concepts before he can start examining processes. To do this he turns to concepts laid down by the Western model:

- essential variables
- sources of disturbance
- the regulator

Essential Variables

To explain the role of essential variables, I shall cite the example of a vital process, or essential variable, in the human being: body temperature. If this temperature rises varies much from 98.6 degrees Fahrenheit, the body systems stop functioning.

In an organizational unit, there are two kinds of essential variables:

- those of the process
- those of the output

Just as for body temperature, the values that such essential variables take on are crucial to the process.

Sources of Disturbance

We know that the influenza virus can elevate a person's temperature above normal. To the human organism, the influenza virus is a source of disturbance. One cannot study a process without considering sources of disturbance. In company processes there are innumerable sources of disturbance, each of which causes variations in the essential variables.

The Regulator

The regulator comprises the elements necessary to maintain the process, and thus the essential variables, in the desired conditions, even when sources of disturbance are present. To manage a process, the first thing to do is to design and build a regulator.

Ikiro knows that his study of organizational units is based on a very innovative approach. In the American reference model, the study of an organizational unit focuses on activities, functions, flows, and tasks. The concept of "process" is absent, as is the notion that any organizational unit should require a regulator.

Quality as a Priority Within the Organizational Unit

Now that Ikiro understands the basic concepts of essential variables, sources of disturbance, and the regulator, he can proceed with his meditations. In the organizational unit under scrutiny, processes are carried out, with some inputs and some outputs (see Figure 7-1).

Ikiro knows that every organizational unit operates within the context of a system that gives top priority to quality. What does this mean in terms of essential variables, source of disturbances, and the regulator? Suddenly things seem clear. The process has essential variables that must remain within a certain range in order to produce the required quality level (see Figure 7-2).

Figure 7-1. Diagram of the Unit's Process

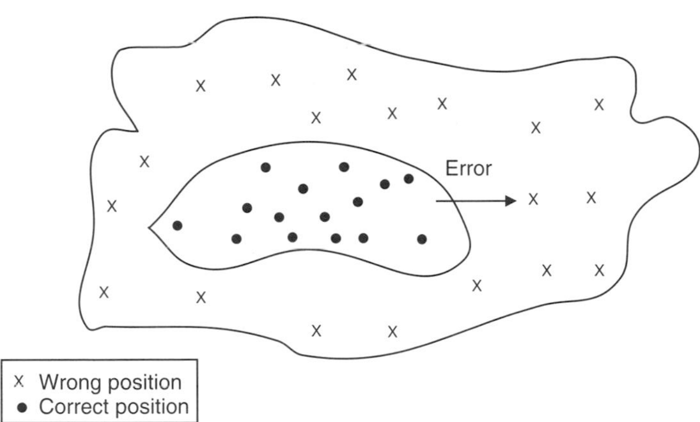

Figure 7-2. Error of the Essential Variable

The source of disturbance tends to lead the essential variables outside of their range, hindering achievement of the quality level. The pursuit of quality is the highest priority, however; thus it is necessary to keep the essential variables within their range. No other factors deserve greater consideration.

So Ikiro discovers a fundamental principle. The real operational priority of each organizational unit is to manage regulators, so that the essential variables will maintain the required level. This type of management action is called *process control.* Therefore, the priorities to be observed are like two sides of a coin:

- process
- process control

Ikiro realizes that by setting these priorities he has abandoned the traditional model, which focuses only on the output of the process. In a production unit, for example, the focus is on production volume, or quantities produced, even though they may remain partially unsold or in need of repair. Ikiro thus knows that he is introducing a true revolution in the management of an organizational unit.

Error-based Control

At this point Ikiro has to find out how to implement process management. We already know that Ikiro has approached the problem by fully accepting and applying the quality control techniques of the American business model (which have since been improved through cybernetics). What does Ikiro learn from such techniques? He learns that there are only two ways to control a process. Actually, there is a third method, one applied by turtles. Turtles defend their vital processes from sources of disturbance by means of a shield. Of course, such a formidable shield is hardly necessary in business organizations, since it would be impenetrable to information as well as to errors, and without information, there is no evolution.

Ikiro meanwhile, understands that the basic method for controlling a process is "error-based control," illustrated in Figure 7-3. This method can be described as follows.

Every operational system, or any organizational unit, has its own essential variables. Sources of disturbance act upon

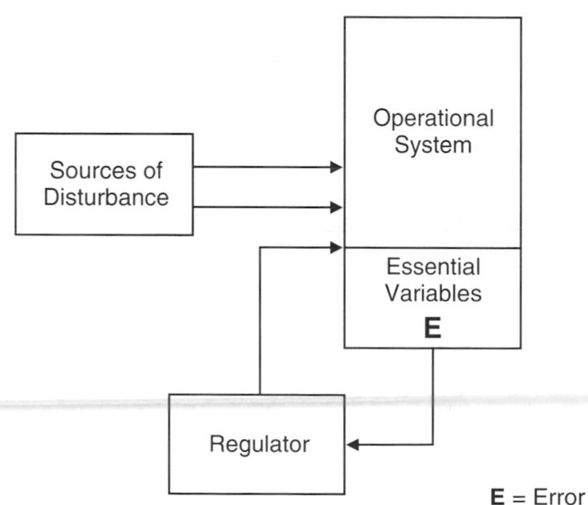

Figure 7-3. Error-based Control System

these variables, leading them out of the range necessary to ensure quality level. Thus an "error" arises. At that point the regulator is activated to identify the error and bring the essential variable back within its expected range. In some cases the regulator is so "intelligent" that it can prevent sources of disturbance from producing errors. Such sophisticated systems are an evolution from the error-based system yet always rely on the former method as a safety valve.

Ikiro knows that to effectively establish the error-based management system he must understand the system's components. As shown in Figure 7-4, several components fall within a feedback loop. They are

- a sensor capable of detecting the error
- a comparator to establish when the essential variable has strayed from its range, causing an error
- a channel to transmit information concerning the error
- a decision maker, who decides what action to take in order to bring the essential variable back within its range

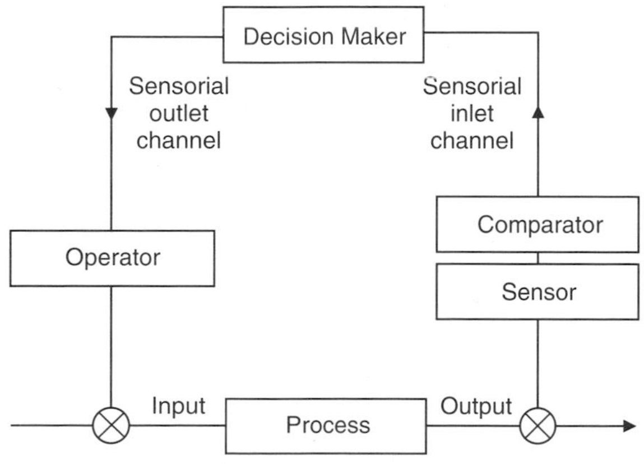

Figure 7-4. Diagram of First-level Feedback Circuit

- a channel to carry the information from the decision maker to someone in charge of acting
- the operator, who actually intervenes in the process to restore it

But this is only the first-level system, as Ikiro discovers. His real goal is to understand the system at its highest, or third, level. In Figure 7-5 there is a second loop, to which a key element has been added: memory. By storing knowledge of the error's history, memory enables the human mind to continuously improve the control system.

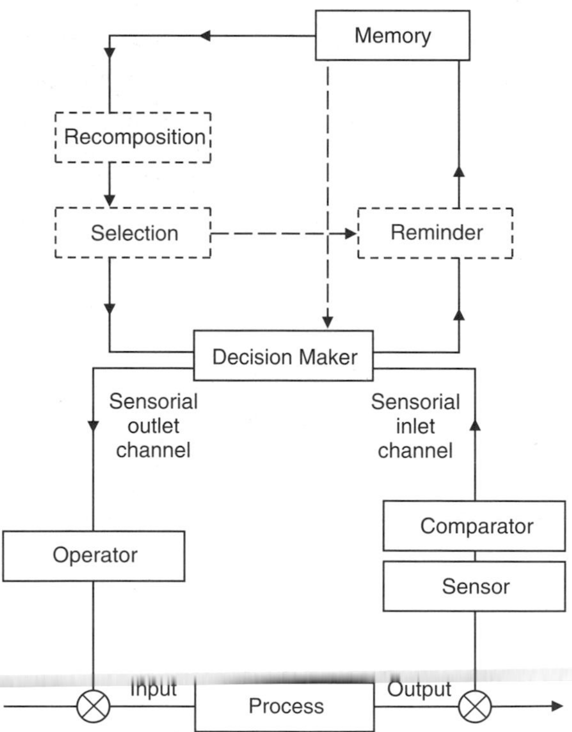

Figure 7-5. Diagram of Third-level Feedback Circuit

Who Establishes the Range of Quality?

We have seen that the essential variables of process control must remain within a certain range. A basic question follows: who can set the parameters of this range, and thus establish when an error has occurred?

In CWQM the answer to this question is brilliant: it is the user of the output of the process, or the customer. Remember Ishikawa's observation that "the process downstream is your customer."

In adopting this rule, one links each part of the company to the market. Hence, the process carried out is not an end in itself, as frequently happens when this connection is missing, but is directed toward customer satisfaction. Organizational units are like many small magnets all oriented toward the same magnetic field, which in our case is the market.

The Design of Feedback Loops

Now Ikiro has all the information necessary to set his priorities. He understands the technical implications of focusing on process and process control. Managing these feedback loops is the true priority of an organizational unit.

This means, first of all, that these loops must be designed. It is not possible to establish process control within an organizational unit without first designing the aforementioned components of that system. That way one can guarantee the quality of the organizational unit at the lowest cost.

Ikiro senses that by establishing process control on the basis of these loops, he will have the most powerful means to ensure maximum productivity in his unit. At the same time he realizes the great competitive advantage he will gain over companies that apply a traditional quality model. In those companies organizational units are designed without consideration for the elements of the feedback loops. Nor do the designers know much about process control techniques. Ikiro now understands why Western companies have such high costs.

With the information he has gathered, Ikiro can now make the right operational decisions to ensure maximum effectiveness in process control.

Priority Choices

Ikiro now makes four decisions, which by themselves largely account for the world leadership achieved in many Japanese industries. He begins by noticing that in the Western model there is very low involvement in the feedback loops. The second CWQM strategy, that of making maximum use of human resources, is completely ignored. As it is 1950, Ikiro concentrates on production. He discovers that in our model such loops are basically supervised by quality control personnel. Line employees are barely aware of these loops, let alone skilled in managing them. So Ikiro makes the following decisions.

The First Decision

Ikiro decides to involve the line supervisors, that is, the people closest to the process, in the management of the feedback loops. His aim is to introduce the ideas of these people into the loops (see Figure 7-6).

At this point, however, he gets anxious, because he knows that taking such a step means that he must instruct all supervisors on process control techniques. Even though Ikiro is still wearing patches on his trousers, he invests whatever is necessary in order to train the supervisors in these techniques.

Once this is done, Ikiro looks at himself in the mirror and tells his image, "This is just the beginning." He knows that control is but a feature of the system, not its true priority.

The Second Decision

Ikiro then makes a second decision: he decides to involve his supervisors in the loop that includes the decision maker. He

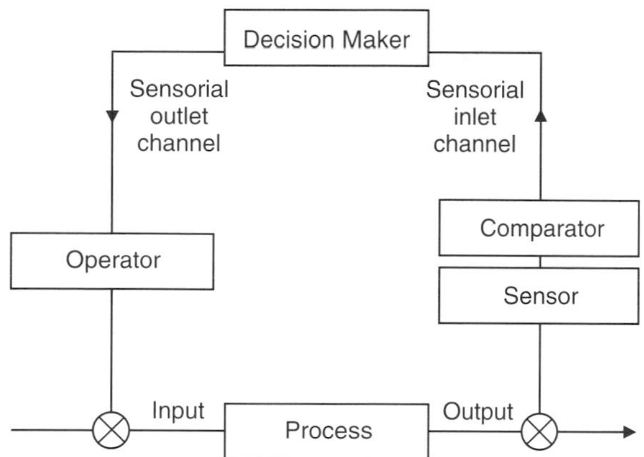

Figure 7-6. Involvement of Supervisors in Process Control

does this to implement the true absolute priority, which is the improvement of processes. Ikiro again gets anxious, as he must train his supervisors in the techniques of process improvement, and thus of quality. Ikiro is consistent, and he proceeds and invests in that direction.

We have now reached the mid-1950s. Ikiro weighs the value of the people he has involved in process control. He recognizes that however many supervisors are involved, it is never enough. Figure 7-7 illustrates the operation of the system.

The Third Decision

Ikiro is aware of the need for maximum use of human resources (the second CWQM strategy) and thus decides to also involve operators in process control, as he had done before with supervisors.

Now he must train all of his operators in the techniques of process control. He realizes how essential it is, however, and makes the necessary investment in training, to allow his operators to manage the feedback loops. He thus implements what we call "self-control."

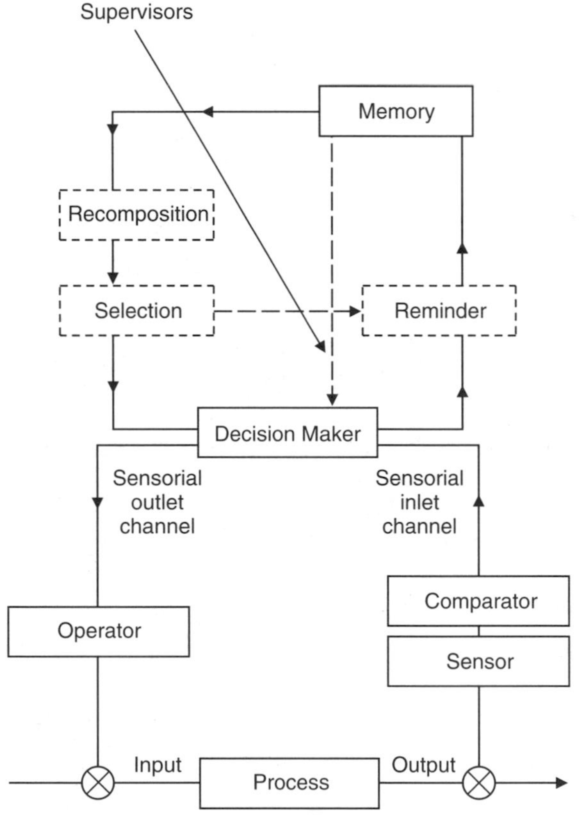

Figure 7-7. Involvement of Supervisors in Improvement

Again Ikiro gazes into the mirror, and again he says "You are not finished yet."

The Fourth Decision

In the summer of 1962, Ikiro makes his fourth decision. He decides to insert operators as thinking minds into the feedback loop that includes the decision maker. Quality circles are born (see Figure 7-8). Now he must train all of his operators in quality improvement techniques. Here too, he stays with his decision and carries out the necessary investments.

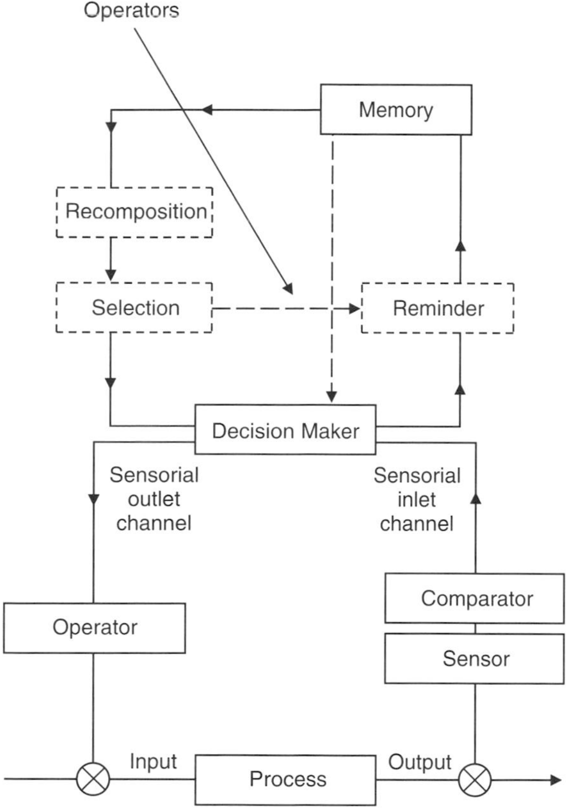

Figure 7-8. Involvement of Operators in Improvement

Summary of the Process Strategy

The process strategy sets the model for all organizational units in the company: the operational level. In the CWQM model, process and process control are the focal points of every operational activity. Only when the process is under control can one begin to improve it, and therefore begin to implement the company's top priority, which is improvement (see Table 7-1).

As we proceed, the matter becomes more technical. In order to control the process we must apply the most appropriate techniques. Here the CWQM model has taken advantage of

Table 7-1. The Role of Process in CWQM

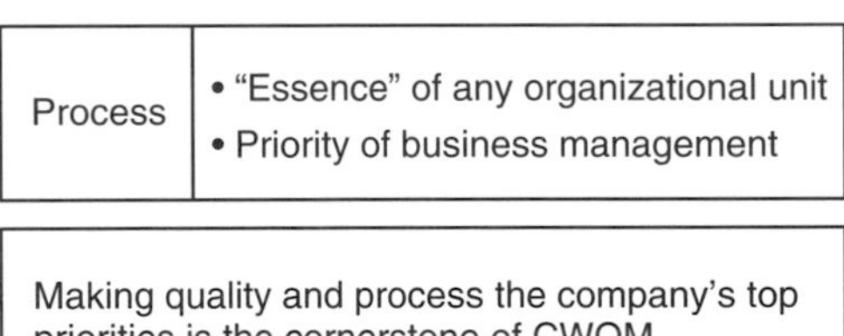

Process	• "Essence" of any organizational unit • Priority of business management

Making quality and process the company's top priorities is the cornerstone of CWQM

techniques perfected in the Western world beginning in the 1920s. The aspects to be considered are new to organization experts: these include sensors, sensorial inlet channels, decision makers, and memories.

The new process strategy leads to the involvement of the entire workforce in the control and improvement of processes. Now quality levels are no longer measured in parts per hundred. In a short time we have reached the point of measuring them in parts per million, even, in recent years, in parts per billion.

The Technologies behind Japan's Success

How is it that the Japanese have outdone Westerners in the field of quality, when the technologies they have applied are all taken from the Western world? In fact, all production processes were designed and developed in the Western world, which possesses, among other things, the most important research facilities and the most advanced universities. So how could the Japanese have surpassed us? We can understand it only by considering three distinct levels of technology:

- process technology
- process control technology
- process improvement technology

Western technology had, with no doubt, the leadership in *process technology,* as it still does in many sectors. But quality isn't built through process technology. It defines processes, their parameters, the conditions for their operation, the machines, and the facilities necessary for such processes, but it does not ensure quality.

Quality is ensured through *process control,* which requires an entirely different technology, and which, more importantly, involves people as a controlling element. Westerners, despite possessing all the necessary knowledge, did not apply this technique seriously, as, the Japanese did.

But neither is the technology of process control sufficient. If we wish to improve our processes, and thus, quality, we must apply a third technology: the technology of *process improvement.* Again, the Japanese have gone way beyond us in this field, a field in which the contribution of people is even more important.

In short, CWQM develops to a very high degree the technology of *process control* as well as the technology of *process improvement.* These, in turn, produce a positive impact on process technologies, as progress achieved in the two technologies will be reflected in the basic technology. This is what we notice constantly when we observe Japanese products.

CHAPTER EIGHT

The Strategy of Quality Control in Management

Introduction

The application of quality control to a company's management activities represents the fundamental strategy of companywide quality management. As the name implies, control and management of quality is extended through the entire company. In this, history repeats itself.

Modern business organization was born with the American efficiency expert Frederick Taylor (1856-1915) and his observations concerning the irrationality of management behavior and the enormous waste within the company for which he worked. Particularly well known and farsighted was his observation about the constant struggle between management and workers concerning the distribution of profits. According to Taylor, the real problem was how to constantly increase the latter, eliminating the great waste of existing resources within a company. Such waste currently varies between 15 and 35 percent of sales volume.

The second Japanese industrial revolution is based on the same premises. The same observations were also made by Professor Kaoru Ishikawa, one of the chief creators of CWQM, who, in his book on the subject, recalls how his experience in wartime industry brought him in direct contact with the enormous waste there. During the early 1950s, his research on quality control persuaded him that, by applying this approach, he could succeed in revitalizing industry and achieving a cultural revolution in management. The contributions of W. Edwards Deming and Joseph Juran added fuel to this purpose.

Ishikawa's ideas were shared by many business and industry leaders in Japan, and thus the foundations of the CWQM movement were laid in that country.

The QC Concept

One must understand the meaning of quality control to be able to apply it extensively to all management activities. Such an understanding is the task and responsibility not of a "quality control department," but rather of all offices, departments, and employees of the company. Moreover, it entails an assimilation of the *QC concept.*

The QC concept includes the following elements:

1. QC is basically prevention.
2. QC is the constant and repeated application of the PDCA cycle.
3. QC is the application of statistical thinking.
4. QC is constant attention to all the factors for customer satisfaction (QCD, or quality, cost, delivery).
5. QC is a revolution in attitude, and a tool to strengthen the company's constitution.

A few comments on each element follow.

QC Is Basically Prevention

The application of this concept represents a basic achievement of CWQM. Usually, this achievement occurs at the fourth stage of the CWQM process, proactive QC (see Table 8-1). Ac-

Table 8-1. The Four Stages of the Quality Control Concept

Evolution of the CWQM Concept	Relations with Customers	QC Approaches	QC Actions	Example of a Solution: A Mosquito Invasion
Stage 1: Primitive QC	Customer activates action	Company reacts to complaints	The problem is not resolved	The mosquitoes are driven away
Stage 2: Slight awareness of QC	Company worries about customer's comfort	Company takes preventive action to avoid complaints	The attempt is made to avoid problems linked to use	The mosquito larvae are killed
Stage 3: A well-assimilated albeit defensive QC	Customer satisfaction is sought	Company eliminates problem	Tests are conducted to forecast problems	Mosquito breeding areas are drained
Stage 4: Proactive QC	Actions are undertaken toward customer expectation	Company foresees problem at the planning stages	Customer complaints are anticipated and prevented	A plan is put in place to maintain areas so they will not become reproduction grounds

cording to the CWQM concept, people's actions must follow this framework:

1. *Recurrent preventive actions:*
   - Isolate problems by analyzing data and facts.
   - Identify real causes and establish corrective actions.
   - Standardize.
   - Monitor and observe the process in an appropriate and permanent way.
2. *Actions to verify process conformity:*
   - Carry out the necessary inspections.

Preventive action is thus carried out by probing ever deeper into *why* a certain event has occurred (asking *why* five times); only thus can one get to the root of a problem. This characteristic of Japanese quality control, all focused on action in relation to causes, is antithetical to the traditional approach to quality control, which is based on action in relation to effects (remedies).

QC Is the Constant and Repeated Application of the PDCA Cycle

The PDCA cycle provides a safe guideline for all QC actions. Each step of this cycle is necessary and must not be neglected. PDCA is essential for examining any activity in need of improvement; with the cycle's rotation attention is focused on the process under scrutiny. The application of PDCA forces us to plan our actions in quantitative terms, that is, through data and facts.

QC Is the Application of Statistical Thinking

With QC one analyzes each fact or situation in statistical terms. This basically means analyzing the variability and the dispersion of phenomena that must be kept under control, in order to reduce dispersion and to keep variability under control.

In a simple yet powerful way, the seven statistical tools help one apply this statistical thinking. Ishikawa's diagram (Figure 8-1) can be very useful in the study of dispersion. A basic concept of the statistical approach is analyzing causes, which are divided into common causes and special causes, as Chapter 13 describes.

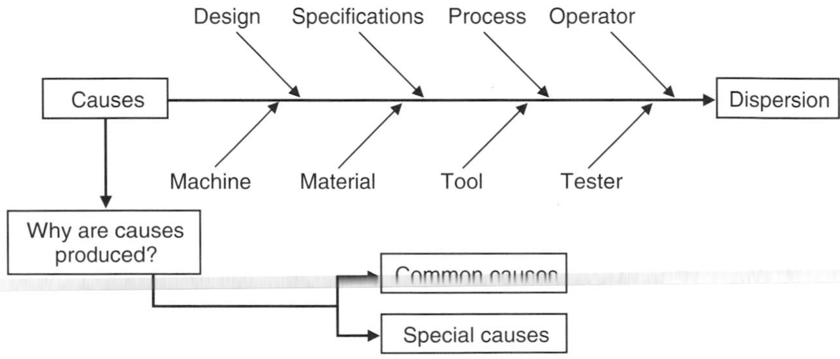

Figure 8-1. Cause/Effect Diagram for Studying Dispersion

QC Is Constant Attention to All Factors for Customer Satisfaction (QCD)

There cannot be real quality if elements for customer satisfaction (quality, cost, and delivery, or QCD) have not been kept in mind. No matter how high the quality, if the price is too high, the customer will reject the product. Thus quality cannot be established without consideration of these other factors.

QC Is a Revolution in Attitude, and a Tool to Strengthen the Company's Constitution

The results obtained by Japanese industry confirm this point in the QC concept, which originated with Ishikawa, who set it as the foundation of CWQM. Specifically:

- QC represents a revolutionary departure in attitude from the traditional one.
- Through application of the QC concept, the company's "constitution" is considerably strengthened, and thus the company is better able to compete in the market. Therefore the QC concept is like gymnastics, which strengthens the human body when it is practiced.

The QA Concept

The QC concept is closely connected to the concepts of *quality assurance* (QA) and *reliability.* In this context, we quote here a statement by Ishikawa at the Seventh QC Symposium of JUSE, held in 1968:

> There are some people, even in Japan, who have the wrong idea that *quality control, quality assurance,* and *reliability* are different concepts. These concepts must be treated as a single one. Reliability is a part of quality assurance, and quality assurance is the basic goal of quality control. Thus, if we consider them together, it is possible to make their relationship a very close one.

The QA concept has 3 main components:

1. QA is an activity carried out for the benefit of the customer.
2. QA is the definition of the quality level demanded by the customer.
3. QA aims to guarantee that the output of company processes satisfies the customer.

The application of the QA concept requires a constant consideration of the customer's need, and great commitment to satisfying that need. Thus the basic imperative of the QA concept is, as Ishikawa says, "quality first."

QA Is the Definition of the Quality Level Demanded by the Customer

Given that every activity must be carried out for the benefit of the customer, one must first of all establish a desired quality level. We often establish this level on the basis of our point of view, rather than the customer's. How many times has the marketing expert as well as the new product designer made this mistake! Establishing this level is one of the most difficult aspects of quality assurance, yet essential to its completion. *Quality function deployment* is one of the main techniques to achieve this goal.

QA Aims to Guarantee That the Output of Company Processes Satisfies the Customer

Every unit or person must carry out quality assurance activities. Let's look at an example to understand this point. Table 8-2 shows the QC and QA activities of a new product development office, as well as the analogous planning activities carried out by the QC office.

Table 8-2. An Example of Definition of QC and QA Activities

Operational activities (new product development office)	Activities of QC	QA
1. Definition of internal organization procedures and planning	X	
2. Definition of standard operating procedures for design	X	
• calculations/drawings/tables	X	
• use of automatic support (CAD, CAM)	X	
• method of issuing drawings, specifications, basic notes	X	
3. Definition of support "formats" (designs and forms)	X	
4. Definition of qualitative requirements for the different stages of the project		X
5. Verification of introduction of qualitative requirements in drawings and documents, and design review		X
6. Tests and experiments		X
Quality office activities pertaining to design	**QC**	**QA**
1. Definition of verification systems	X	
2. Verification of agreement between technical documentation for the design and general documentation (handbook, policies, etc.)		X
3. Participation in design review		X
4. Audit		X

Application of the QC Concept within the Company

With CWQM, the application of the QC concept is truly extensive and complete. We mention here only the QC concept, but it is understood that it includes also the QA concept. This application concerns

- activities directly connected with a product or service
- activities not directly connected with a product or service
- the management of the company as a whole

We briefly consider each item in the following text.

QC in Activities Directly Connected with a Product or Service

The QC concept is applied to all company processes that are directly involved in products or services, from marketing to product development, all the way to after-sale assistance. Through this thorough application it is possible to understand how quality assurance of products and services is obtained by CWQM. Let us examine the various stages in the evolution of quality assurance, using a mountain as our model. The peak represents both the level of satisfaction attained by the customer and the QA level. The path up the mountain represents the effort to reach QA through the QC activities of inspection, establishment of a quality control office, and CWQM.

Inspection Stage

Stage 1 on the path to quality assurance is inspection. In Figure 8-2, the arrow shows how inspection leads to quality assurance, and thus to customer satisfaction.

*Mil-Q-9858A Stage**

At this stage we institute the quality control office, which directly exercises all quality control and quality assurance functions (see Figure 8-3). From here we move on to total participation in QA.

CWQM Stage

At the CWQM stage all company sectors are involved in QA, and to this end each sector carries out the functions of QC and QA (see Figure 8-4). To achieve total participation in QA, a company must make the QA and QC concepts explicit to all employees.

---

* MIL-Q-9858A, *Quality Program Requirements* (Philadelphia: Naval Publications and Forms Center, 1985), is a generic standard developed by the U.S. Department of Defense for development of quality programs in defense industry suppliers. — Ed.

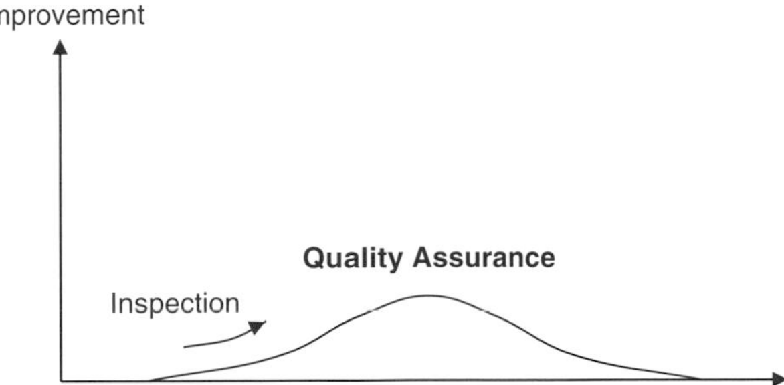

Figure 8-2. Inspection Stage

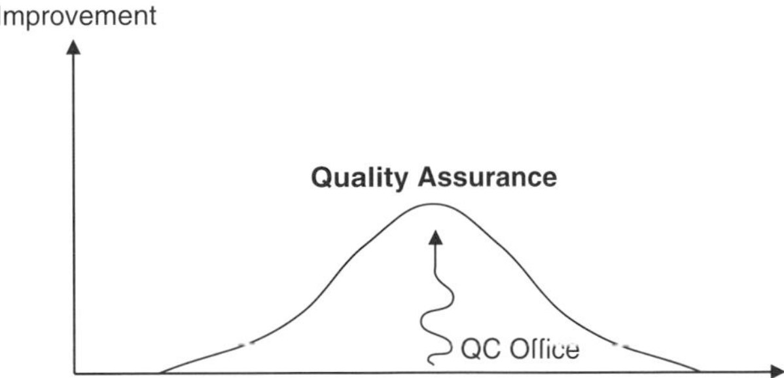

Figure 8-3. Mil-Q-9858A Stage

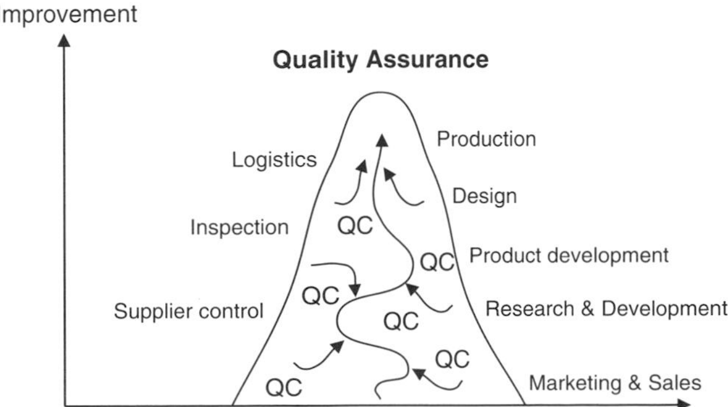

Figure 8-4. CWQM Stage

The QC Concept in Activities Not Directly Connected with a Product or Service

A company must also apply the QC concept in activities not directly connected with products or services, such as budgeting, investment planning, technology development planning, and marketing planning. Each of these activities should begin with the establishment of real and potential problems involved, a study of the causes of such problems and how to eliminate them, and the implementation of solutions. Each supervisor should act in accordance with application of the QC concept.

Management within the CWQM Model

Western companies owe to Henri Fayol the development of the modern concept of management, which he divided into five activities, or functions:

- planning
- organizing
- leading
- coordinating
- controlling

Without abandoning that approach, management within the CWQM approach involves essentially two activities:

- maintenance
- improvement

Maintenance

The first goal of any organizational unit, any process carried out within the company, and every individual is to maintain the performance level achieved. Within CWQM, three fundamental conditions should be fulfilled:

1. maintaining minimal variations within process parameters
2. doing things right the first time

3. minimal time dedicated by management (executives, managers, supervisors) in maintenance activities

The third condition is a prerequisite for carrying out the second management activity. If maintenance takes up too much of management's time, there will be no time to dedicate to improvement activities. Thus, applying the QC concept is essential.

Improvement

Management as improvement is a key characteristic of CWQM and one of Japan's most powerful innovations to management. In CWQM it becomes the measure of a company's success. Improvement activities can be carried out through two different approaches:

- innovation
- small-step improvement

The first approach is the traditional path to improvement in Western companies. The second one, adds a new dimension to improvement, what we might call the "extra gear" that powered Japanese companies to world leadership in industry.

Using the QC concept is also essential for improvement.

The QC Concept in Company Management

The QC concept finds its fullest use in company management. It provides both an approach and a method for the company's managerial process at all levels, beginning with its president.

Every year a company needs to set goals and define guidelines for their achievement. Both directors and managers at different levels must take these goals as reference points for their actions; at the same time, there must be an effective coordination between the various functions.

The definition of goals and guidelines (which, taken together, make up policies), just like every other operational and management activity, must be carried out according to the QC concept, and, therefore, according to a specific process. This process comprises a series of steps, or stages, that are given little consideration in Western companies.

The following is a schematic list of these steps:

- highlighting corporate problems, whether real or potential
- analyzing the causes of these problems
- seeking solutions
- defining company policies on a yearly basis
- extending these policies to all levels and sectors
- developing actions to achieve goals
- periodically revising the results obtained
- examining the causes of any variance
- undertaking adequate countermeasures
- highlighting new problems

The process embracing these phases is carried out through the quality control approach, thus through the QC concept. It requires constant application of PDCA cycles as well as constant study of cause-and-effect relationships. It is only in this way that the essence of company management can take place. This type of management aims at eliminating the causes of nonconformities and at preventing them from recurring.

In CWQM this process is called *hoshin management,* the subject of Chapter 18.

The QC concept is also applied in the essential activities of interfunctional coordination, in order to guarantee the levels demanded by the customer satisfaction factors (QCD). Often those in charge of managing a particular function are not able to solve a problem, as they do not have access to all the necessary information and are thus unable to perceive some cause-and-effect links. In the QC concept, the interfunctional analysis of a problem is centered on concrete data.

Many other approaches and techniques can be applied to company management, but without application of the QC concept, they would lack a supporting framework and thus be useless.

The QC concept can be also applied to control activities within the management process. More detail on control activities can be found in Chapter 18.

CHAPTER NINE

The Strategy of Continuous Improvement: Kaizen

Introduction

This chapter presents the new dimension of quality improvement invented by the Japanese. Here the meaning of quality, as said more than once in this book, is considerably broadened to include costs, delivery, organization, and other factors. In the Japanese language this dimension of improvement is called *kaizen,* while improvement obtained through innovation is called *kairyo.* The main Western languages lack distinct words for the two forms of improvement (although the second type of improvement is particularly tied to Western business culture).

Before companywide quality management can be said to exist, kaizen must have permeated the company culture and have become an everyday activity. According to the Japanese, every morning we should carry out our work a bit better than the day before.

The initial impact of kaizen on a business culture is very hard. It is perceived as "extra work," another burden to bear. But what would our customers think if they knew that we considered efforts to increase their satisfaction as an additional burden?

The revolution in attitude that occurs within CWQM is to a large degree a function of the extent to which kaizen has taken hold. Even in the Japanese business culture, such revolutionary changes in attitude are often needed.

One point that Japanese management experts do not make explicitly is that the kaizen concept is closely connected to that of infinite or unlimited possibility for improvement. This is another great human resource. The main barrier to kaizen is lack of recognition that this unlimited potential exists.

In 1986 Galgano & Associati sponsored the publication in Italy of *Kaizen,* a book by Masaaki Imai explaining the Japanese approach to continuous improvement.

The Diamond Point and the Bulldozer

To explain the meaning of *kaizen,* we will use the analogy of a diamond point, representing kaizen, and crystal, representing the potential for improvement that exists in a company. Let us imagine a crystal mountain of infinite size, into which a diamond point is poised to etch. Of course, a company has more than a single diamond point: it has as many of these tools as there are employees.

Improvement, however, is not achieved by means of the diamond point alone. We in the West have excelled in another approach to improvement. We like to level our mountain with bulldozers. That is, we make innovations through grand gestures such as introducing new machinery, new processes, or new technologies. As mentioned, in Japanese such innovation is called *kairyo.* But we must remember that the "bulldozer" can work only a few days a year. It is not possible to introduce an innovation into the company every day or every month. Kairyo does not allow constant improvement.

Kaizen represents a great revolution to us in the West. We are not used to working intensely in this area, as the Japanese have done. We have not explored the unlimited potential for improvement hidden in a thousand small efforts. Yet its results are no less effective than those obtained through innovation. To quote an AT&T executive speaking to some Italian executives visiting the United States,"We have discovered that the leap in improvement that can be achieved with kaizen is equivalent, during the lifetime of a technology, to the leap attained through technology."

In other words, the diamond point digs into the mountain just as powerfully as the bulldozer.

The Difference Between Kaizen and Kairyo

Understanding the differences between *kairyo* improvement and *kaizen* improvement can better clarify the new features of the continuous improvement approach. Figure 9-1 provides a graphic comparison of small-step and large-step improvement.

There are other differences between the two approaches, the main ones being listed in Table 9-1. Kaizen proceeds slowly, through gradual yet constant changes, whereas kairyo proceeds in spurts, through major but irregular changes. Kairyo involves

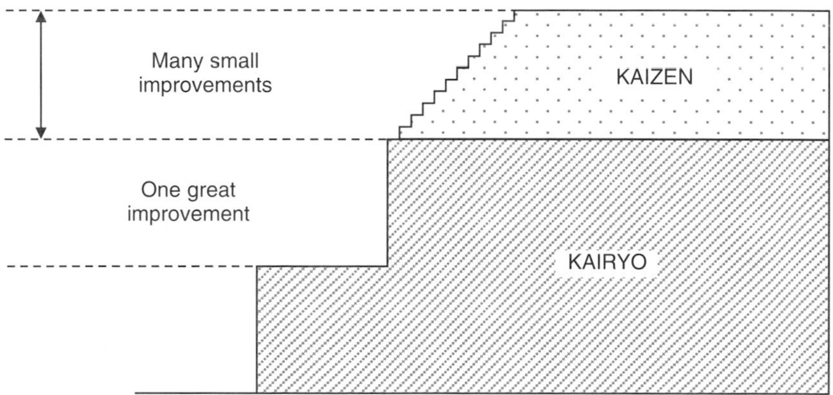

Figure 9-1. Comparison between Kaizen and Kairyo

a select group of people, whereas kaizen involves everyone. Kaizen is a systemic approach based on group effort; kairyo entails a high degree of individualism.

The methods used in kairyo and kaizen also differ substantially. Kairyo dismantles the old and builds the new through investment and new technologies, whereas kaizen improves what is already there. In kairyo the improvement process starts from technological processes and inventions; in kaizen it begins from conventional know-how and the scientific method to problem solving. Kairyo requires less work but large investments, whereas kaizen requires hard work but lower investments.

In the interest of kairyo, Japanese companies were buying technologies from the West only a few years ago; with kaizen, however, they overtook Western companies in many fields.

The kairyo approach is entirely centered on technology, whereas the kaizen approach is employee-oriented. Finally, with kairyo the motivation to improve lies in results and profits, whereas with kaizen such motivation comes from a recognition of processes and efforts.

In this chapter we shall dwell on four essential aspects of kaizen:

- kaizen of processes
- kaizen of time

Table 9-1. Main Differences between Kaizen and Kairyo

Kaizen	Kairyo
Requires little investment but great effort to maintain	Requires large investment but little effort to maintain
Involves everybody in the company	Involves a select few "champions"
Requires recognition of effort before results	Motivated by expected results
Achieved through conventional know-how and PDCA	Obtained by technological or organizational breakthrough

- kaizen of people
- kaizen of technology

Kaizen of Processes

As seen in the previous chapter, a company's activity is nothing more than the sum of many processes. Continuous improvement at the operational level must therefore be carried out in all company processes.

To enable every employee to effect continuous improvement, a simple tool or method is needed that can industrialize small-step improvement. This tool was found in the "Deming wheel," or "PDCA cycle."

Before one can apply this tool, the process that one wishes to improve must be stable. Like a rock climber, one must gain solid footing before taking the next step. Without such a foundation, any improvements obtained through innovation are likely to be lost, as many cases demonstrate.

To achieve this stability, operational conditions within the process must be standardized. Thus, standardization is a prerequisite to application of PDCA, and thus to implementation of kaizen.

The PDCA operational process is based on three cycles:

- maintenance
- corrective action (or recurrent prevention)
- improvement

We define these three cycles as follows.

The Maintenance Cycle

In this cycle, illustrated in Figure 9-2, I am carrying out something previously planned and implemented; thus, my only task is to occasionally check it. If the *check* results are positive, my task is to keep things as they are, and to constantly verify that the process flows in a certain way. I am not always

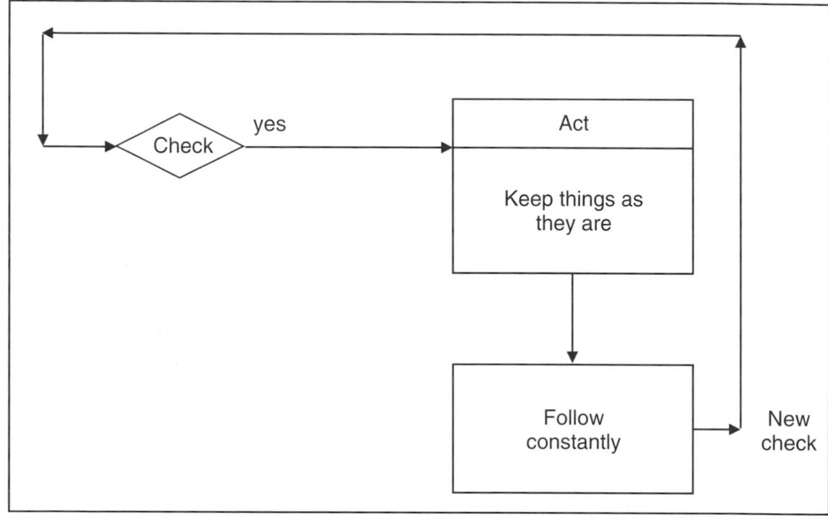

New check = verify whether the plan is always effective

Figure 9-2. PDCA: The Maintenance Cycle

lucky, however. If during the *check* phase I find that something is not right, I must activate the corrective action cycle.

The Corrective Action Cycle

The second cycle (see Figure 9-3) is used when something goes awry in the maintenance cycle. It is easy enough to carry out an immediate remedial action to the problem, but my task is not finished until I work on prevention, that is, eliminate the problem's causes. In other words, remedies act upon results, but true corrective action addresses causes.

The Improvement Cycle

Beyond maintenance and correction is a third cycle, kaizen, or improvement (see Figure 9-4). Like the second cycle, it must be based on the cycles before it or its results will not be stable.

Once I have carried out maintenance activities effectively, I must try to improve processes so that they can be carried out

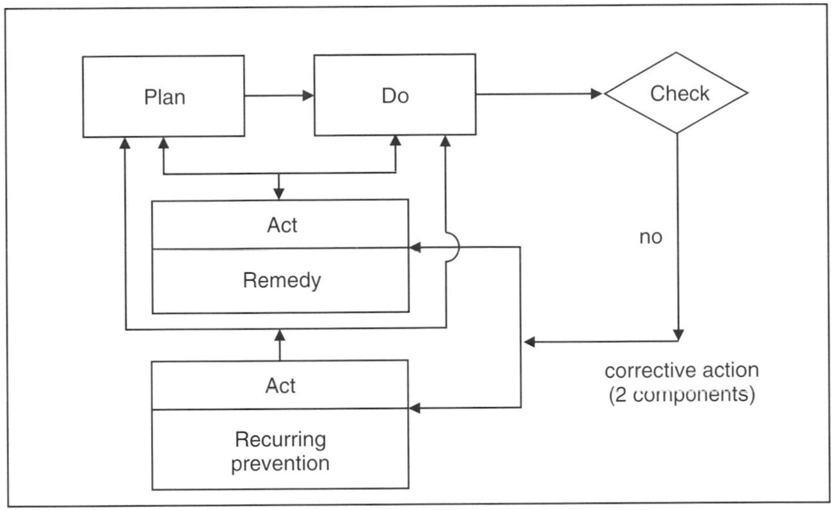

Figure 9-3. PDCA: The Corrective Action Cycle

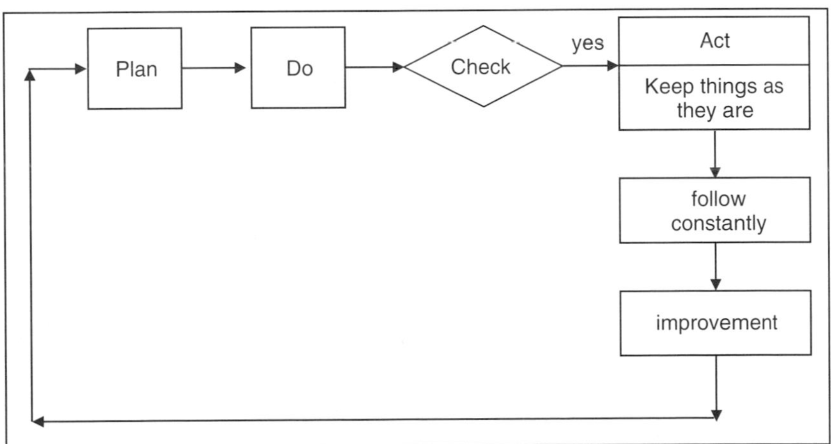

While the maintenance cycle shows positive results, it is necessary to have fresh ideas on how to do better in a simpler, less costly, faster, safer way (that is, ideas for improvement). From these ideas there arises the improvement cycle, beginning with a new plan. If check produces positive results, one returns to the maintenance cycle.

Figure 9-4. PDCA: The Improvement Cycle

in a simpler, faster, less expensive, safer, and more effective way. I will therefore initiate the *plan-do* phases.

The PDCA approach to kaizen is an attitude: anything that is done should be carried out through PDCA. Budget preparation and strategic planning should be carried out through PDCA, as should supervising a machine's workings or a service operation. The three cycles as a whole are shown in Figure 9-5.

This, however, is only one view of PDCA. We know that, in addition to executing the three cycles described above, we must work scientifically. Then PDCA will include identification of the problem, planning, observation and analysis, and identification of the causes (see Figure 9-6). PDCA is therefore an essential work method that must be taught to all employees, so that everyone can achieve improvement.

Each phase of the PDCA cycle (plan, do, and so on) must undergo its own PDCA cycle, as shown in Figure 9-7.

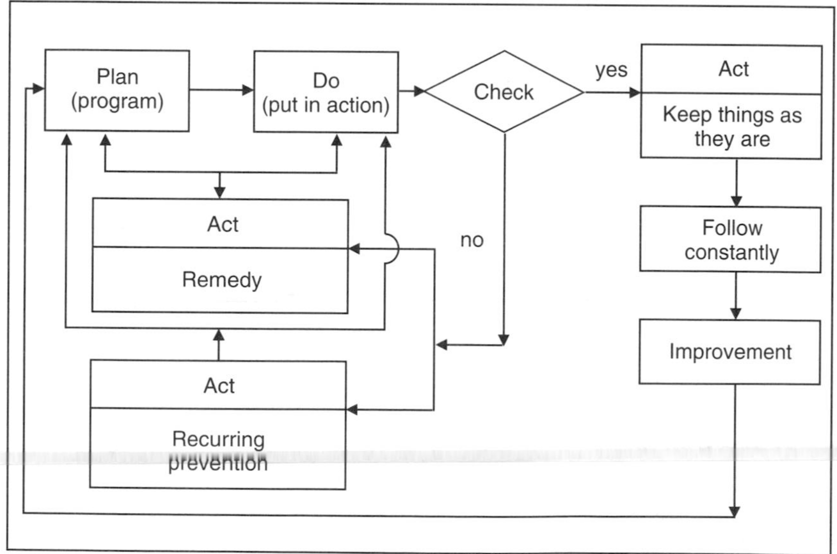

Figure 9-5. The Complete PDCA Cycle

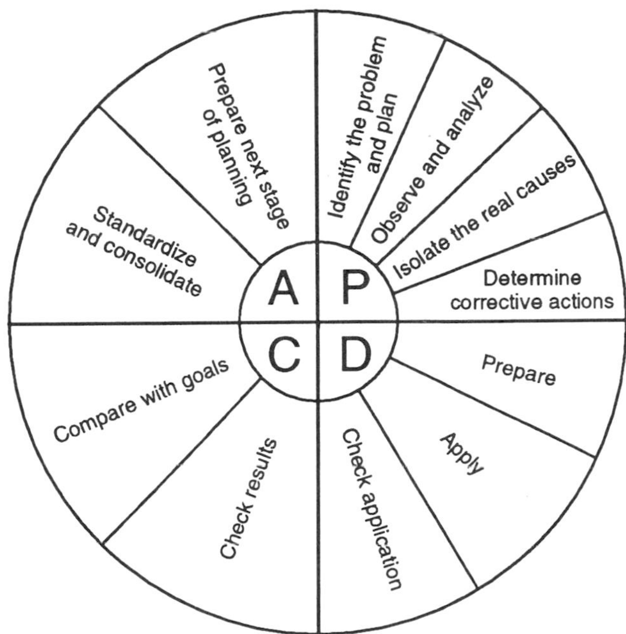

Figure 9-6. The PDCA (Plan-Do-Check-Act) Cycle

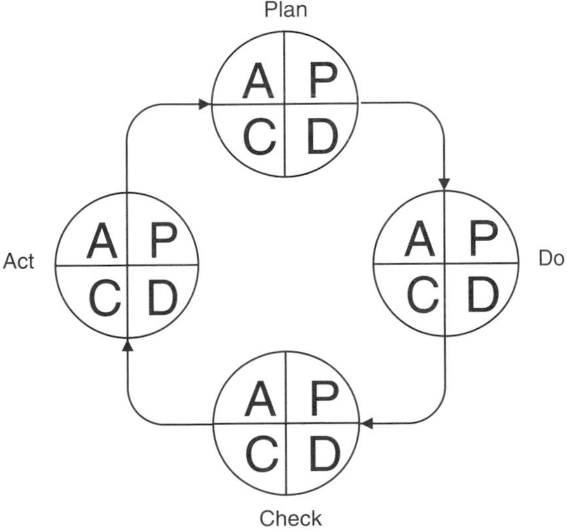

Figure 9-7. Applying PDCA to Its Phases

The entire company must "jump forward" with PDCA, since the improvement process is nothing more than the continuous application of PDCA cycles, by every employee (Figure 9-8).

This is the method. All of kaizen is based on the constant application of this method, in every company process.

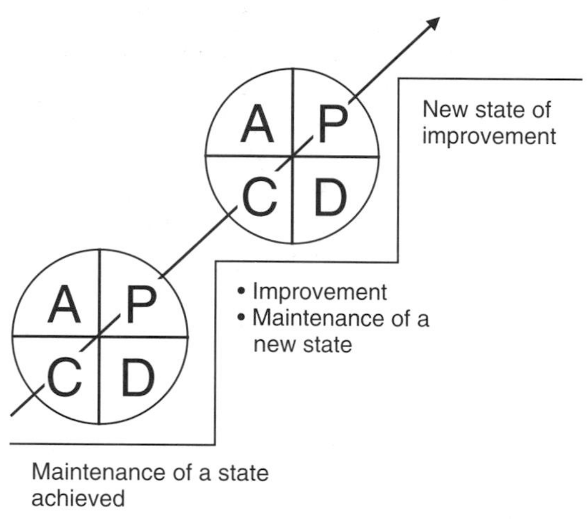

Figure 9-8. The Improvement Process

Kaizen of Time

Time is one of the main factors we have rediscovered today in management. It is something we all share, and something that has equal impact on every company, small and large.

If we apply the diamond point (kaizen) to time, we obtain some revolutionary achievements, as the Japanese experience has shown. But what does this mean? To understand, let us consider another analogy.

Much is said today about the advantages of managing time. Napoleon provided a brilliant example of this. He was extremely successful because he regarded time as a strategic factor: he defeated his enemies because his army moved faster than theirs. In those days, armies were like circuses: They would stop in the evening, set up camp, and then dismantle it the next morning to start marching again. Napoleon's army moved twice as fast by doing something different. When evening came, his soldiers would sleep under the shrubs; they would light a fire to keep warm and do nothing more; in the morning they would simply get up and leave. In this way they reached their destination quickly.

The Japanese have adopted the same concept of time. If we apply kaizen to time in all company processes, we obtain incredible results. For example, Matsushita, a maker of dishwashers, reduced its production cycle from 360 hours to 2 hours. The Just-in-time approach is basically a product of kaizen, as applied to time. For instance, in Japan (although it is becoming more frequent in America and Europe), suppliers have reduced their production cycles dramatically, going, for example form 15 days to 1 day.

Kaizen applied to time makes it possible to increase the variability of products while maintaining the same or lower costs.

Only recently have we become aware that flexible production strategies, rapid response to the market, a great variety of products, and quick innovations are all the result of kaizen, and can be achieved with decreasing costs. In the past we have assumed that such variability brings an increase in costs. Thus kaizen applied to time offers companies a substantial competitive advantage in new product development.

Kaizen of People

Kaizen of people is another concept that offers enormous potential for improvement, since every company is the product of its people.

Although the term *companywide quality management* implies involvement of everyone in the company, it is a mistake to believe that in Japan CWQM does include everybody, as a

Japanese colleague, Ryuji Fukuda, once explained to me. Fukuda conjured up the following image: Four people participate in a regatta. One rows vigorously, two row at a normal pace, and one just floats serenely on the water (see Figure 9-9).

Such are the gradations of involvement, even in Japanese companies. Applying kaizen to people is perhaps the most difficult application of kaizen. This has prevented us from discovering kaizen in the West.

Kaizen of people essentially means creating teams; it is a people-building process based on respect for human beings.

To apply kaizen to people, one must help them to dedicate themselves to higher needs, those for ego-gratification and self-fulfillment. Then they will act of their own accord to improve processes and contribute to kaizen.

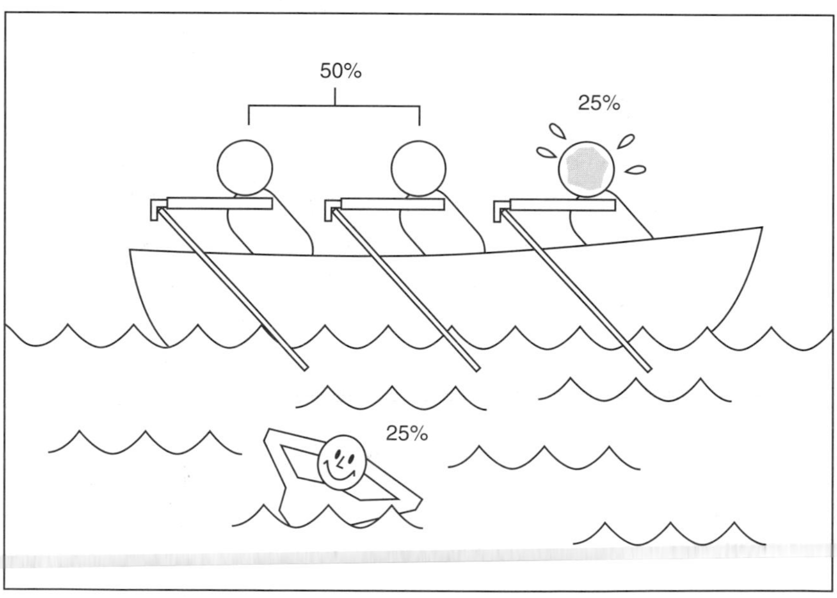

Figure 9-9. Japanese Companies' Commitment to CWQC

Thus kaizen of people is a new way to manage human resources. Western tradition is entirely based on management by control. Through kaizen it is possible to implement a different kind of management, one carried out by education and based on genuine respect for human capabilities.

Kaizen of Technology

Kaizen can also be applied to technology. For example, in consumer electronics and computers, the Japanese have shown incredible ability in developing new ideas and technologies. With kaizen one is not limited to the simple imitation of preexisting products. This is a disciplined method to transform an idea into something new and precious, just as the cutting and polishing of diamonds are industrial processes for the creation of jewelry.

Japanese companies typically adopt four methods for applying kaizen to technology:

- miniaturization
- simplification
- visualization
- transformation

Miniaturization

The Japanese passion for miniaturization is well known, as shown by their compact and extremely light radios, televisions, and automobiles.

The development of portable calculators by Sharp is a good example of this. The cost of a Sharp calculator in 1964 was $4,100, while in 1980 it was only $23. Today solar calculators are sold in any department store for $4 to $9, and they weigh less than 14 grams. By miniaturizing its calculators and continuously reducing production costs, Sharp has remained competitive in this important market.

By forcing producers to reduce the shape and number of parts used in their new products, miniaturization constitutes a strategic tool for moving along the famous "learning curve," based on which costs decrease as production volume increases. Miniaturization is also a technique for developing new product concepts.

Through miniaturization, the Japanese found new ways of reducing costs and opening up new markets. In 1984 Plus and Company introduced Copy-Jack, the first portable photocopier in the world, in the shape of an electric razor, and weighing only 440 grams. Matsushita Electric Company, which took up that idea, introduced a less expensive version and sold 10,000 of them the first day alone.

Simplification

While Americans and Europeans often develop complex solutions to their problems, the Japanese do the opposite, reducing the number of parts, simplifying design, and doing anything else to make products and ideas less complicated.

The "disposable" camera developed by Fuji Photo Film is an example of the Japanese tendency to simplify technology "to the bare bone." By seeking the goal of a new disposable camera that would appeal to teenagers and young adults, produce high quality photographs, and cost less than $12, Fuji Photo was able to penetrate the market with great style, eliminate consumer reservations, and produce a functional and colorful object. Yet from a technological point of view the product was extremely simple. In 1986 alone Fuji Photo sold more than a million of the cameras.

Visualization

Depicting ideas as visual images and improving their appearance are among the visualization techniques favored by the Japanese. Deriving from their sensitivity to imagery and their strong designing capabilities, visualization is also linked to the graphic nature of Oriental languages, which are expressed mainly through ideograms.

This has had a great effect on computer-aided design, or CAD. Daiwa House and Kikusui Homes, for example, developed a design system called Design Your Own Home, which allows the customer to choose the number and size of rooms, the kinds of materials to be used, and other matters related to the design of living quarters.

Visualization techniques are becoming increasingly important in training people in product research and design. NEC is developing four-dimensional workstations, able to simulate three-dimensional objects in the time dimension.

Transformation

Another improvement technique the Japanese apply to technology is transformation, by which parts of one item or system can be changed to develop something entirely different. Probably the best example of this is the traditional Japanese house, whose rooms are used for a variety of purposes.

Because of the high cost of land for construction, Japanese companies have adapted such techniques to shopping centers and office buildings. The Nakagin Capsule Tower Building in the Ginza District in Tokyo, for example, is a modular building that can be changed over time from one shape to another. The idea of "a building that can change" thus replaces the old notion of nonflexible buildings, which are demolished after a few decades of use.

The concept of transformation is rapidly gaining strength in Japanese industry because of its commercial potential. The Transformer toys and the MX-04 car by Mazda, which allows its owner to change its design at will, are two examples of what transformation means in Japan. Given the lack of garage space in Japan, most of the population can only afford one car; transformable cars could thus provide a possible solution to the rapidly changing tastes of consumers.

Conclusions

To describe kaizen in a few words, we might say that it is a diamond point operating in many areas and offering companies an "extra gear" for reaching success. Let me conclude by mentioning the roles that each level of the company should take in kaizen strategy.

- Top management must be committed to introducing kaizen as a company strategy. Specifically, it should support the strategy by allocating resources at least for training activities; it should set policy that promotes kaizen and interfunctional goals; it should achieve kaizen goals through PDCA; and it should build systems, procedures, and structures for kaizen.
- The executives just below top management must formulate and carry out kaizen goals according to guidelines from top management. Specifically, they should use kaizen in their functional activities and in the activities they carry out directly; they must establish, preserve, and improve standards; they must create an awareness of kaizen among employees through intensive training programs; and they must help employees to develop their abilities and the tools to solve problems.
- Supervisors, like everyone else, must use kaizen in their activities. In addition, they must plan for kaizen, and provide guidelines for factory and office workers; they must improve communications with workers and office staff, ensuring that morale is high; they must stimulate small group activities and the individual suggestion system; and they

must ensure discipline (which is essential to carrying out kaizen).

- Workers must be involved in kaizen through the suggestions system and small group activities; practice discipline within the factory; be committed to the development of their abilities so as to be increasingly able to solve problems; and improve their education by co-training (since much can be learned from colleagues).

The Japanese have demonstrated what results can be obtained by applying Western technology to the kaizen "diamond point." It is now up to us to learn that we can add to our "bulldozer" as many diamond points as there are people working in our company.

CHAPTER TEN

The Strategy of the New Products "Factory"

Introduction

The central activity of companywide quality management is the development of new products and services. If it is true that the main operational activity is continuous improvement, then nothing in the company is more important than the development of new products.

As we know, the success of a company is measured by the level of satisfaction it provides its customers, those "monsters" I mentioned earlier. Since the monsters demand new products with ever-increasing frequency, one of the main goals of the new products "factory" strategy is to create a system to produce new products at greater speed, and provide high levels of quality and reliability right from the start.

The Japanese have developed a highly effective strategy for achieving this goal, one that forms the cornerstone of CWQM. One might even describe CWQM as the mechanism by which increasingly new and successful products are quickly brought to market.

Technology is a key element in the development of new products. Once the customer's expectations are defined, quality control plays an essential role both in standardizing and improving technology within the company and in integrating the technological know-how among the different company sectors.

The Premises of the New Products Strategy

New product development within the framework of CWQM is based on the following premises:

1. The success of a company is closely linked with its ability to introduce new products.
2. The new products introduced into the market must provide a high level of satisfaction and guarantee a high degree of reliability right from the start.
3. The time required to develop new products must be continuously reduced: the shorter the period, the higher the competitive advantage.
4. Technology is a key element in the development of new products, and its use as well as its evolution are made easier by the application of quality control.

Through CWQM, management gains full awareness of the importance of these points. A brief explanation of each follows.

1. Broadening competition and the quickening pace of technology development have made a company's success increasingly dependent on its ability to introduce new products that satisfy customer expectations. Therefore, the resources committed to the development of new products and related processes are of a strategic nature.
2. Customer demands for excellent and highly reliable products at an ever-quickening pace are intensifying. At the same time, manufacturing companies are called on to guarantee their prod-

ucts for longer periods. This happens in part for the following reasons:

- Information concerning defective products travels faster and faster.
- Defects are extremely costly to correct and can have a negative effect on the company's success.

3. The time lapse between the decision to study a new product and its availability on the market is one of the main factors for competitiveness. The company that can bring new products to market faster than its competitors obviously acquires a consistent advantage in terms of potential sales volume and turnover, among other things (see Figure 10-1).

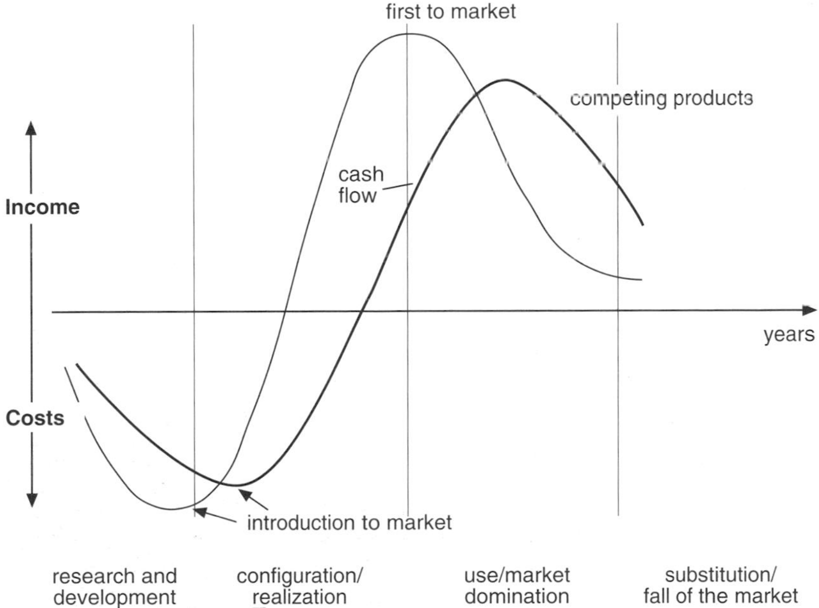

Figure 10-1. Cash Flow in the Development and Introduction of New Products

The Role of Technology and Its Links with Quality Control in the Development of New Products

To understand the vital role of technology in new product development, one must keep in mind four main points:

1. the link between technology and quality control
2. market driven technology development
3. creativity methods in technology development
4. the need for broad training among designers

A few remarks concerning these four points follow.

The Link between Technology and Quality Control

Quality control plays a fundamental role in technology. Specifically,

- it analyzes, organizes, and standardizes the technology used by a company
- it raises the technological level of products and processes

First of all, it is essential to make use of the statistical approach in the application of a particular technology, from concern for the qualitative characteristics of a product to the application of the most advanced reliability techniques. In this way, technology is integrated with the product and with the production process.

Secondly, technological knowledge makes sense only when cause-and-effect relationships can be established and quantified, and when the links between the parts that make up a product and the product system as a whole are also known.

Third, technological knowledge must be disseminated even among nontechnicians, so that it can be used effectively in the development of new products. Sony's Walkman and Honda's four-wheel drive are good examples of success achieved through strong integration between departments involved in the product development.

By integrating technology and quality control, CWQM opens up technology to a wide range of applications and the opportunity for continuous improvement. To achieve such integration, and to strengthen it, researchers and product designers must come out of their shell and extend their knowledge to include the viewpoints of the other departments of the company and also market demands.

Market-driven Technology Development

In order to develop new products it is essential to move technology forward. We now know that with active and intelligent guidance by humans, technology is capable of wondrous things.

In the early 1970s, The Club of Rome published a famous report called *The Limits to Growth.* This report, based on a very pessimistic outlook, caused people working in both the private and public economic sectors to lose confidence in the economy's potential for growth and, indirectly, in the human ability to make continuous progress. Zero growth rate suddenly became an inevitable imperative. Facts proved this idea dead wrong. If one considers the development rate of Japan's gross national product from the first oil crisis to now, it has become about three times as large!

Japanese expert Hajime Karatsu of Tokai University pointed out that the role of humans in progress is that of creating new values by applying technology to natural resources, which would otherwise remain just "stone and soil." According to Professor Karatsu, human capabilities from this point of view are boundless. The use of technology in the development of new products requires a strategy constantly applied within CWQM: simplicity and flexibility. The strategy is the following: to find or create a new and lucrative market, even the most elementary one, that will allow a practical development of the technology (*market-driven* technology). It would not do for an innovative technology to remain at the stage of "idea."

An example of such a strategy can be found in carbon fibers: they are lighter than aluminum yet stronger than steel. Americans have used these fibers in complex applications; the Japanese, on the other hand, used them in golf clubs and fishing rods. In doing this they have been able to perfect production techniques of these fibers that can then be applied to the aeronautics sector. In 1989, 60 percent of the world market for carbon fibers was in the hands of the Japanese.

Creativity Methods in Technology Development

In Japan today the development of technology is widely based on the use of creativity techniques. In no other country are there as many books on creativity. Methods used include the following:

- visionary thought
- global research
- spiral development
- matrix weaving
- technological trees
- technological maps

Let us now consider the second technique, global research. It provides the basis for a global approach to the search for new ideas and technologies. Answers are sought even when the problem itself remains unclear. By investigating new areas and leaving no stone unturned, Japanese companies always succeed in finding new ideas and technologies with practical applications. One of the most outstanding examples of this method is the research for the solar battery calculator developed by Sharp.

Toward the end of the 1970s, Sharp was looking for effective technologies for the application of solar energy to calculators without batteries. After carrying out research at universities and companies that were familiar with ways to generate solar energy, Sharp discovered a small company in Michigan: Energy Conversion Devices (ECD). ECD had developed a new amorphous silicon that enabled liquid crystals to collect solar energy. Its procedures were considered to be unorthodox among major U.S. producers of calculators, but the president of Sharp understood the enormous potential of the company. He took a risk and signed an agreement with ECD for the use of amorphous silicon in calculators. Today, Sharp is the world leader in the solar energy calculator market.

This episode is significant as an indication of the Japanese openness to new ideas, an attitude essential to the concept of global research.

The Need for Broad Training among Design Engineers

To facilitate the development of new products, the technological knowledge of engineers and technicians must be of a "cone-shaped" type rather than a "well-shaped" type. In other words, this knowledge must broaden as it deepens. As Ishikawa suggests, mechanical engineers must have a general understanding of electrical engineering, electronics, metallurgy, chemistry, and statistical methods. If they have a "well-shaped" preparation, they will not be able to move from project C to project D. With a "cone-shaped" preparation, however, they can transfer a positive experience with project A to the development of a new product through project B (see Figure 10-2).

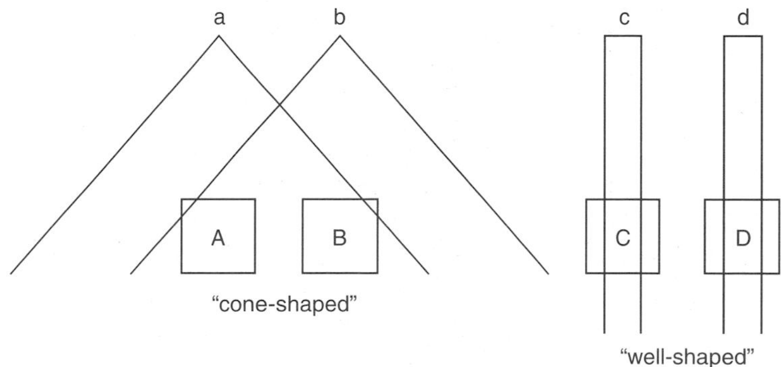

Figure 10-2. Design Engineer Preparation Typologies

The Strategy for New Product Development with CWQM

Having examined the premises underlying new product development, we can now look at the essential aspects of the strategy itself:

1. ensuring the quality of new products already in the development and design stage
2. organizing the planning and development of new products with the most modern techniques of product organization (creation of the new product "factory")
3. studying the market with an interfunctional approach
4. integrating the new product development plan with that of technology

The definition of these four aspects follows.

Ensuring Quality at the Product Development Stage

Ensuring quality by emphasizing the development of new products was one of the achievements of CWQM. Japan's leading companies began applying this approach toward the end of the 1950s with Western industry attempting to catch up only recently, beginning in the early 1980's. Early efforts of Japanese companies to ensure quality focused on two techniques:

- inspection
- process control

Neither approach is sufficient to meet the goal of producing increasingly high quality products, however. The first approach is costly and does not guarantee that defective products do not reach customers. With the second approach it is not possible to correct errors in design; nor is it possible to deal with problems linked with unorthodox use of the product. Lastly, nothing can be done concerning reliability in its broadest sense.

Eventually, it became clear that the quality of a product could not be guaranteed unless quality assurance activities were performed during the various stages of product development itself.

Therefore, if all company activities must center on the new product development process, the critical priority process for the whole company is the quality assurance activities performed during that process. These activities fully involve the following sectors:

- research and development
- sales and marketing
- product planning and development
- design
- purchasing
- technology/industrialization
- production and logistics
- after-sale assistance
- quality

The fundamental problem is twofold:

- Each sector must become aware of its role in quality assurance activities during the new product development stage, and must acquire the necessary technical and methodological competence.
- Each sector must become able to communicate with the other sectors in order to optimize quality assurance activities at the company level.

For this purpose every sector and every individual involved must gain a shared understanding of the goals driving new product development.

This is no easy task. Those Japanese companies that have been awarded the Deming Prize gained sufficient mastery over quality assurance at the product development stage only after four or five years. They did so by rigorously following a multi-year plan like the one described in Table 10-1.

Table 10-1. New Product Development: Improving the System

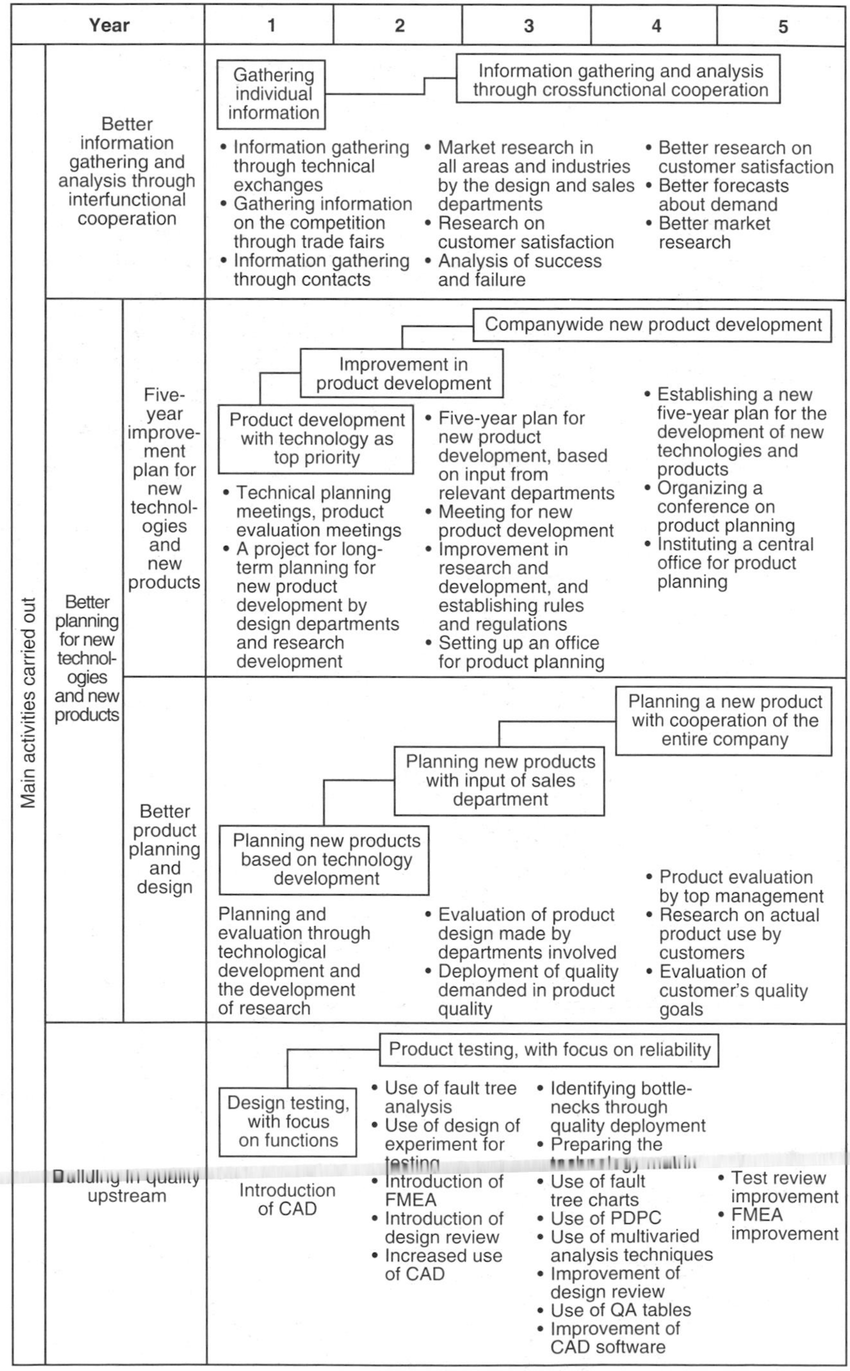

Main activities carried out		Year 1	2	3	4	5
Better information gathering and analysis through interfunctional cooperation		[Gathering individual information] • Information gathering through technical exchanges • Gathering information on the competition through trade fairs • Information gathering through contacts	• Market research in all areas and industries by the design and sales departments • Research on customer satisfaction • Analysis of success and failure	[Information gathering and analysis through crossfunctional cooperation]	• Better research on customer satisfaction • Better forecasts about demand • Better market research	
Better planning for new technologies and new products	Five-year improvement plan for new technologies and new products	[Improvement in product development] [Product development with technology as top priority] • Technical planning meetings, product evaluation meetings • A project for long-term planning for new product development by design departments and research development	• Five-year plan for new product development, based on input from relevant departments • Meeting for new product development • Improvement in research and development, and establishing rules and regulations • Setting up an office for product planning	[Companywide new product development]	• Establishing a new five-year plan for the development of new technologies and products • Organizing a conference on product planning • Instituting a central office for product planning	
	Better product planning and design	[Planning new products based on technology development] Planning and evaluation through technological development and the development of research	[Planning new products with input of sales department] • Evaluation of product design made by departments involved • Deployment of quality demanded in product quality		[Planning a new product with cooperation of the entire company] • Product evaluation by top management • Research on actual product use by customers • Evaluation of customer's quality goals	
Building in quality upstream		[Design testing, with focus on functions] Introduction of CAD	[Product testing, with focus on reliability] • Use of fault tree analysis • Use of design of experiment for testing • Introduction of FMEA • Introduction of design review • Increased use of CAD	• Identifying bottlenecks through quality deployment • Preparing the technology matrix • Use of fault tree charts • Use of PDPC • Use of multivaried analysis techniques • Improvement of design review • Use of QA tables • Improvement of CAD software		• Test review improvement • FMEA improvement

In summary, developing a new product and establishing quality assurance activities regarding the product itself are two sides of a coin. Being closely intermingled, they must progress at the same pace. Only by proceeding in this way can excellent products be obtained. On the operational level, it is necessary to plan and carry out a system of quality assurance during the development and design of new products.

Organizing the New Product "Factory"

Industrial enterprises have developed production processes capable of achieving high levels of quality and productivity. This usually happens as the result of great care and effort on the part of top management.

Through CWQM another production process is highlighted, one that may be even more important than the first: the *new product "production" process.*

Despite its importance, this process has traditionally received little attention in the Western company model. Basically, the production process pertaining to new products must be organized with the same approaches and techniques that are applied to regular production; that is, one must organize the *new product factory.* This work is much harder because, whereas a normal factory is surrounded by four walls and represents one function, the new product factory embraces the entire company and all company functions (see Figure 10-3).

The goals of such a factory are precise: to introduce into the market the greatest number of successful new products at the lowest possible price and in the shortest possible time. To this end, the process of planning and developing new products is divided into a number of stages, each of which is carefully analyzed and organized. There must be coordination among the different stages, and adequate tools for control.

By organizing the development of new products into an "ideal factory," Japanese companies have devised solutions that Western experts have tried to rationalize — self-organized plan-

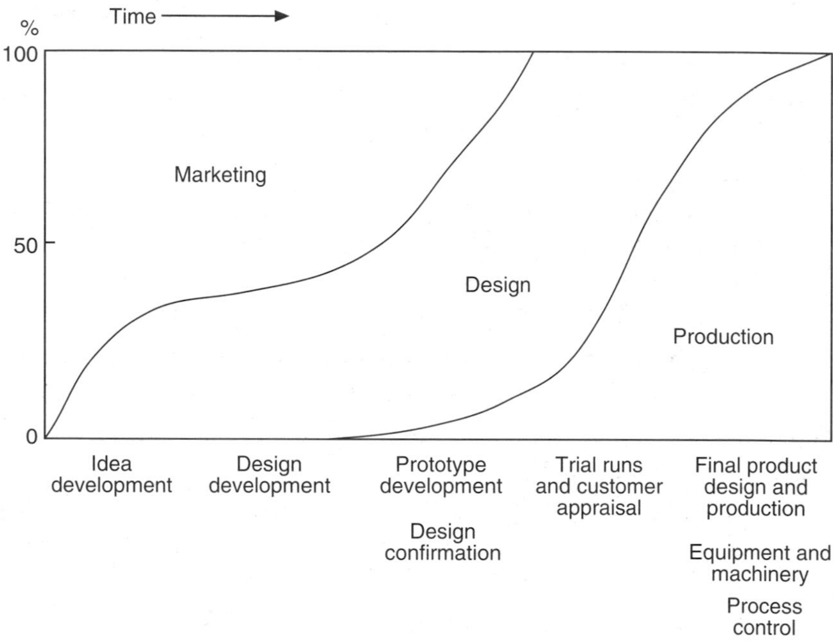

Figure 10-3. Product Development in the Ideal Company

ning groups, overlapping development stages, and multilearning are examples.

The ideal factory would see the use of PERT (program evaluation and review technique) and CPM (critical part method). These techniques reveal the presence of bottlenecks. The main problem is to eliminate all possible causes of delay; QC-PERT tables are useful for this purpose. These are checklists of elements concerning quality and cost, and can be prepared in advance for each stage in the development of new products.

Another feature of QC-PERT tables is the simultaneous evolution of product development and quality (that is, critical characteristics, control characteristics, spare parts characteristics, planning quality guarantees, specifications on available and unavailable technology, planning technology development, and warranty control).

The results obtained by Japanese companies applying the concept of new product manufacturing are clear. Extremely high levels of quality are obtained in very short product development periods. Major automobile manufacturers are able to create a new model in 30 months or less while in the West it takes between 55 and 60 months. Just a few years ago, Western manufacturers of machine tools planned the introduction of a new product line every four years. Today, Japanese companies such as Fanuc and Yamazaki are able to develop a new model from the start in less than two years. Now the consumer electronics industry in Japan measures the time needed to launch a new product in months, not years. Note that the shorter such a period is, the better a product can incorporate the most recent customer demands.

Studying the Market with a Cross-functional Approach

Two points especially pertain to the development of new products:

- Given that products must be renewed with increasing frequency, one must become better skilled at sensing and anticipating customer needs.
- The ability to perceive customer needs is not the task of a narrow group of people, but of the entire company system. This is another argument for cross-functional integration.

To address these needs two important developments within CWQM occurred.

1. The so-called *design approach* sharpens the ability to perceive customer needs by providing criteria through which one can systematically define the strategy toward a certain goal. This approach was standardized with the *seven management tools,* which make it more easily applicable.

2. To extend the task of information gathering beyond the design, planning and development, and marketing departments, a system evolved featuring the following elements:
   - analysis of competition
   - a suggestion list on how to improve new product development
   - the institution of periodic reports
   - reports concerning customer satisfaction
   - information concerning successes and failures
   - the organization of technical memories (past experience in the various sectors)
   - attention to product capability
   - research on product use, and establishment of criteria for best use of such information
   - assessment of compatibility of design and customer needs during the product development stage, through visits to a sample group of customers
   - surveys of current and potential customers for opinions on prototypes

A diagram of the information-gathering process appears in Figure 10-4.

Integration Between New Product Development Plans and Plans for Technology

Given the strategic role of technology in the development of new products, with CWQM the multiyear development plans have been closely integrated with the multiyear plans for new technology (see Figure 10-5 for an example). The two plans must be established and implemented not only in the design and research and development departments, but they must result from an intense exchange among all company departments. There are two critical dimensions:

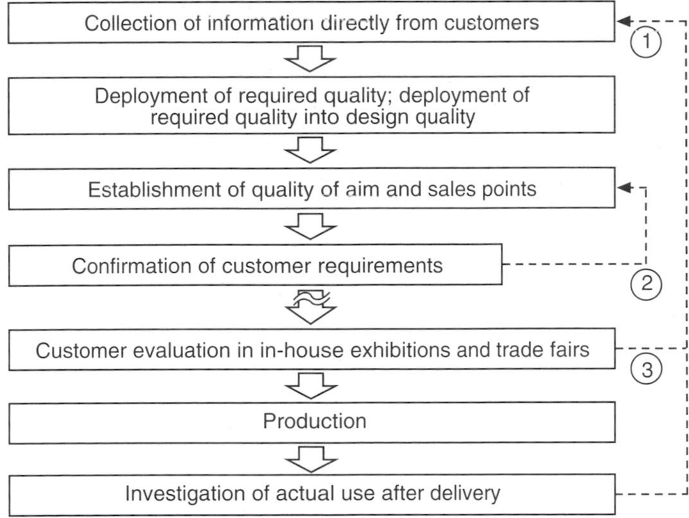

Figure 10-4. The Information-gathering System

- the allocation of resources for product and technology development
- the identification of technological bottlenecks in the development of new products

The period covered by such plans is ordinarily about five years. It must be based on a strategy for the technological development of products and processes.

To discover bottlenecks in advance, and thus save time in developing a new product, one must apply advanced technology, in particular:

- FMEA (failure mode and effect analysis)
- FTA (fault tree analysis)
- design of experiments
- multivaried analysis

To ensure the highest product reliability one must constantly improve reliability testing. Figure 10-5 highlights the integration among plans.

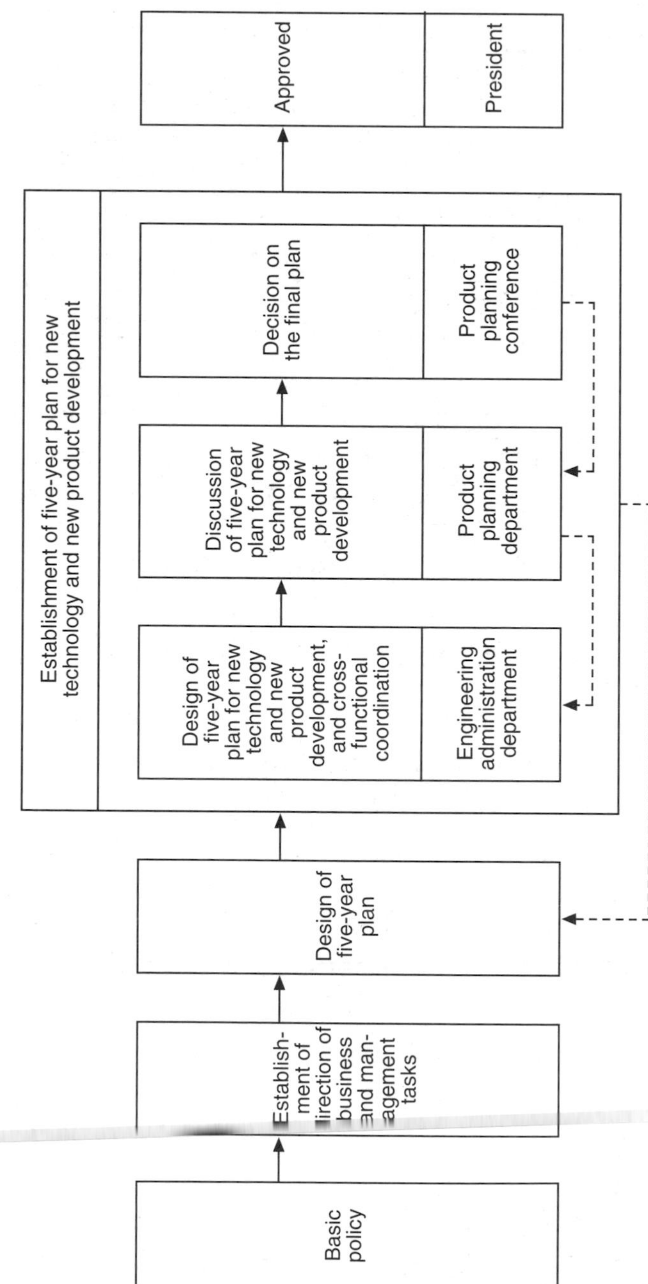

Figure 10-5. A Five-Year Plan for New Technology and New Product Development

CHAPTER ELEVEN

The Strategy of the Internal Promotion of Quality

Introduction

Promoting quality among employees is a fundamental strategy of CWQM , important enough in any country or culture to be supported on a national level. Without such internal promotion, the constant attentiveness to quality that CWQM requires would never develop.

Japan was remarkably forward looking in its concern for quality:

- In 1951 it instituted the Deming Prize to recognize those companies excelling in the area of quality.
- In 1956 it promoted quality through QC courses on the radio.
- In 1960 it instituted the National Campaign for Quality.

Thus for more than forty years the Japanese have been promoting quality. In light of the Japanese culture's traditional inclination toward quality, it might appear absurd to promote that which is already there. It is a little like advertising a brand whose use everyone takes for granted. Why waste the money?

But here we face an apparent contradiction:

- In Japan, where it is said that people have the concept of quality "in their blood," quality is heavily promoted both on a companywide and national scale.
- In Italy, where it is thought that people care little about quality, there is little promotion of quality within companies or the nation as a whole.

The answer, of course, is that it is no contradiction at all, but a case of cause and effect. In Japanese companies with CWQM, the quality culture that has been created is not the cause but rather the effect of massive and ongoing promotion.

The Foundations of the New Strategy

The strategy of internal promotion of quality reflects the following needs:

- to disseminate the values, mission, credo and general policies of the company, so that they become a point of reference for all employees
- to indoctrinate all employees in the CWQM approach, enabling them to undergo the necessary "mental revolution"
- to nurture people's attention to the importance of quality in their work, and to foster constant commitment to the improvement of quality, based on management's annual policies

To satisfy such needs the company must constantly carry out promotional activities involving all employees. They should not be abandoned after the introductory stages of the new approach, but should continue over time without pause. Constant concern for quality and its improvement requires a great deal of effort by everyone, and is possible only with intelligent promotional activity. CWQM requires that a company advertize not just on the outside, to sell its products, but internally, to promote the achievement and maintenance of a high level of excellence. Promotional activity pertaining to quality can be divided into two categories:

- concrete promotional activity at a company level
- promotional activity carried out by individual executives and managers

In this chapter we will discuss the first category, although the second one is no less important. With CWQM, both directors and managers have the important task of constantly promoting quality. As detailed in Chapter 23, the president must also promote quality within the organization. In the case of middle management, and of supervisors, promotion consists largely in supporting quality circle activities, which encourages improvement at the level of office and production operators.

Promotional activities can be divided into five main categories:

1. dissemination of the credo and policies
2. periodic communications
3. focused activities (quality campaigns)
4. suggestion system
5. occasions to meet/compare/verify

Let us examine each of these activities more closely.

The Dissemination of Credo and Policies

To introduce and maintain active CWQM, managers must inform employees of the values to be adopted as guidelines and reference points for all company activities. These values must reflect the company's mission and philosophy. Enlarging shareholder profits is not a sufficient motivator of employees. For this propose, a credo and company *quality policy* are issued.

These are documents issued by the president and distributed to all personnel. Their value is twofold:

- They engender confidence in quality and in top management's commitment to it.
- They provide direction on the path to quality (with the ultimate goal of excellence) from year to year.

The following text gives a few examples of policies set by Japanese companies.

Toyoda Machine Works

The basic policy of Toyoda Machine Works is the following:

> Toyoda Machine Works will contribute to the welfare of society through the development of its business, just as it continues to offer reliable products that fully satisfy customers.
>
> 1. We believe in "quality first."
> 2. We approach the future with a broad outlook and young ideas in order to make our company known for its engineering excellence.
> 3. In our activities we shall use all available human resources, both within and outside the company, supporting the basic values of creativity, participation, and mutual trust.

Mitsubishi

In 1987 the president of Mitsubishi Industries sent the following message to all employees:

> *Policy 1: To increase orders and to fulfill our objective of keeping the business profitable.* We can achieve this mainly by aiming to reduce cost and maintain the attained quality level performance. The primary objective is to reduce costs. Thus we must reduce the cost of raw materials and continuously improve the quality level, while improving product performance and providing the fastest possible delivery

times. Everyone must work together toward this goal on a daily basis if the company is to survive. Our aim over the next two years is to reach, by these means, a turnover of ¥2,500 billion ($15.8 billion at ¥158/$1).

Policy 2: To develop new products and new activities. The development of new products and new activities represents the lifeblood of a company. We guarantee the company's health by revitalizing existing products and developing new products and new activities. In order to do this, we must have everybody's cooperation and effort, along with a shared mental attitude. There is also the need for a determined spirit, to bring a product from concept to reality.

Policy 3: To consolidate the reputation of Mitsubishi Industries as a world-class company. Japanese products are known all over the world. But if Japanese companies were to think only in terms of profits, they would be in trouble in the space of only a few years. We have achieved high product reliability thanks to our technology and to our policy of trying to gain the world's trust. Under that policy, we cooperate with developed countries in developing new products, while cooperating with underdeveloped ones in introducing new technologies. This should be our basic credo, in order to maintain the world's friendship. We must become a worldwide Mitsubishi, a Mitsubishi that has the love and the respect of the entire world. Just as our country cooperates with some 170 other countries politically, socially, and commercially, so should we at Mitsubishi exhibit the same cooperation and respect for others. Let us look ahead to the 21st century, and to continued leadership by Mitsubishi. To conclude, I would like to wish you and your families, who represent the most important part of the company, a year full of serenity, health, and happiness.

Ricoh Company

The Ricoh Company (a manufacturer of photocopiers, telephones, fax machines, data and word processing systems, and cameras), issued a formal commitment to quality to its more than 11,000 employees. This statement, shown in Figure 11-1, rests upon several basic goals and principles:

Building a solid (recession-proof) business:
1. Motivate all employees.
2. Radically change employees' ways of thinking.
3. Develop the abilities of all employees.

Company motto:
1. Love your neighbor.
2. Love your country.
3. Love your work.

Management principles:
1. Improve yourself through your work.
2. Make the company grow through quality.
3. Contribute to society through business.

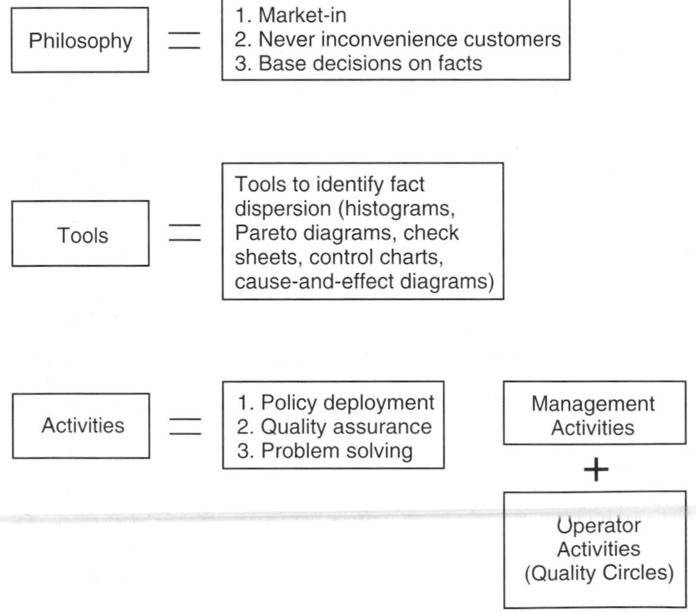

Figure 11-1. Ricoh: Commitment to Quality

Honda

At Honda, too, the personal mottoes of the two founders of the company, Soichiro Honda and Takeo Fujisawa, are constantly mentioned:

- Be original.
- Do not rely on the government.
- Work for your own well-being.

As these examples show, company mottoes tend to embrace the founders' philosophy; they are summarized in five "golden rules":

1. Follow your dreams, and keep a youthful outlook.
2. Respect theory, new ideas, and the times.
3. Love your work and do it with a bright and positive attitude.
4. Ensure a smooth work flow.
5. Make sure that focused research and effort become a daily habit.

Other Examples

The three leading civil construction companies in Japan also adhere to company philosophies:

- Takenaka: Contribute to society through the best possible product.
- Shimizu: Achieve continued prosperity and social responsibility.
- Kajima: Achieve progress and creative development through scientific rationalism and humanism.

Credos can also be expressed at the plant level. The example that follows comes from the plant manager of Texas Instruments Japan:

- Let us strive to be the number-one supplier for quality.

- Quality must become the plant manager's top priority.
- Let us aim for the Deming Prize.

Periodic Communications

Once a company undertakes the CWQM path and starts to involve the entire workforce in quality activities, it becomes essential to give people feedback about their actions and results. Such information allows everyone to monitor their own development and receive new stimuli and new motivation. The most common forms of communication for this purpose are:

- internal newsletters
- videocassettes
- publications on quality, both internal and external

Internal Newsletters

Internal newsletters are a powerful tool for keeping the spirit of improvement alive. Seeing one's results published and being able to compare them to those of others sparks a competitive zeal, lends continuity and stability to the program, and stimulates new ideas.

Also important, newsletters enhance one's knowledge of the company. By printing news on all company functions, the newsletter fosters mutual understanding between departments.

Videocassettes

Videocassettes fulfill many of the same functions of internal publications, but offer more direct and effective visual communication. Because they are more time-consuming and costly to make, however, their use is usually limited to specific subjects.

Publications on Quality

Every company is both distinct from others and integral to its sector, the national economy, and the world economy. It is this integration that makes it important to cultivate in employees the broadest possible outlook onto the outside world. Companies can achieve this by providing (in addition to publications, papers and case histories on internal practices) books and periodicals on the practices of other companies. Making such material available encourages not only personal growth but customer satisfaction. If we wish employees to continuously expand their potential as thinking beings, we must provide them with an adequate source of "nutrition."

Focused Activities (Quality Campaigns)

A company introducing a CWQM program usually launches a series of medium-to long-term activities, embracing quality circles, work teams, task forces, and other small groups. Often the company gives particular emphasis to specific issues, of particular relevance to the company. It does this by means of focused activities, or "quality campaigns." These are initiatives that are limited in time and focused on a specific theme.

Such campaigns (or similar initiatives) are based on voluntary participation and do not affect the normal course of other activities. In this case, promotion has a double effect: On the one hand, it alerts employees to the importance of the problem at hand and motivates them to participate in its resolution. On the other hand, the campaign itself and its results become a tool for quality promotion. During the initial stage promotion occurs when the new initiative is communicated to the entire company during periodic meetings, by means of posted signs and bulletins, or through the distribution of leaflets. Later, the results will be made known in the same way.

Campaigns at Hitachi

Hitachi Denshi, a part of the Hitachi Group, with about 1,600 employees, produces television cameras and broadcasting equipment. Hitachi's campaigns have addressed four areas:

- health improvement
- the creation of pleasant departments
- the discovery of solutions to the problems at hand
- savings and cost reductions

Campaigns carried out in these areas have produced interesting results, as follows:

The campaign for reducing electrical power costs. To prevent lights from being left on unnecessarily within the plant, workers installed cord-operated switches on each light fixture. After this, people participating in the campaign would "patrol" the company at break time and turn off lights that were not needed. Patrols wore an armband that encouraged saving light, and similar reminders were posted around the company. As a result, all employees began paying more attention to this problem, and in some departments the savings reached 30 percent of electrical power.

"One-page messages" campaign. A campaign was launched to encourage people to write concisely to keep letters to one page in length. The aim was to save time for the author as well as for the reader, and to save paper and file space. To this end a manual was drawn up to help employees improve their ability to synthesize. As a result, everyone came to appreciate the importance of writing concisely, and their efforts to do so were significant.

The campaign to reduce office supply orders. After the office supply budget was reduced, a campaign was started to gather unused office supplies and to redistribute them around the company. As a result, more than 3,000 items (such as erasers, pencils, envelopes, paper, and folders) were gathered and redistributed to those in need of them. The effort also created greater order on many desks.

Campaigns at Pentel

The use of posters, photographs, comic strips, and other forms of illustration, make quality campaigns more interesting and amusing. They serve as vivid reminders about a company's, and therefore each employees's, priorities. Rather than indoctrinating, they enrich people's development by familiarizing them with the "culture" of the new approach. The slogans of Pentel, a manufacturer of writing materials, provide a good example of this:

- *Pay special attention to problems.* Problems are not obstacles to be eluded; rather, they should be analyzed, since without problems there can be no improvement.
- *Management means, first, planning and later comparing the results achieved.* Let us turn the PDCA wheel, and operate in a different manner.
- *We are surrounded by mountains of treasure.* Analysis of chronic problems is more useful than analysis of sudden problems in suggesting ideas for improvement.
- *Manage processes by observing results.* Revisions and modifications are a direct consequence of lack of management.
- *Watch out for deviations.* As it is true for chronic problems, analysis of deviations is a richer source of improvement ideas than analysis of average results.
- *Separate before you observe.* Careful classification leads to better knowledge.

- *Improvement begins with one's own sector.* Pay attention to your problems first, then those of others.
- *Eliminate the main cause, and avoid its repetition.* Do not confuse symptoms with causes.
- *Do not forget to standardize.* To maintain good results, use standardization tools.

Campaigns at Canon

In some cases quality campaigns give direction to a company's activities. This was the case in campaigns started by Canon to draw employees' attention to the different types of waste within the company. These campaigns significantly influenced other activities already started in the field of quality (see Table 11-1).

Table 11-1. Canon's Nine Waste Categories

Waste Category	Nature of Waste	Type of Saving
Work-in-process	Items in stock not immediately requested	Improvment in inventory management
Defects	Too many defective products turned out	Fewer rejects
Equipment	Too many machines are idle or break down; setup takes too long	Increase in capacity utilization ratio
Expenses	Overinvesting for required production	Expense reduction
Indirect labor	Excess personnel due to an inefficient indirect labor system	Efficient job assignment
Planning	Products are designed with more functions than are necessary	Cost reduction
Human resources	Skilled employees are used for jobs,that can be mechanized or assigned to less-skilled people	Labor saving or better utilization
Operations	Not working according to work standards	Improvement of work standards
New-product startup	Start in regular production of a new product is slow	Faster shift to full line production

Other Types of Campaigns

Japanese companies often launch another type of campaign, one with a "cultural" purpose. These are aimed at promoting effective problem solving and thus better planned improvement programs. Examples are the *5W and 1H* and *5S* campaigns.

5W and 1H campaigns

The term *5W and 1H* stands for *who, what, where, when, why, and how.* Because answering these questions is a rational, organized, and global approach to analyzing problems and implementing solutions, 5W and 1H can be used in any situation, inside or outside work. It is especially useful for promoting the cultural changes implicit in CWQM through posters and booklets explaining its meaning.

5S Campaigns

The term 5S stands for five Japanese words:

- *Seiri:* Eliminate useless things, and keep only those which are useful.
- *Seiton:* Keep the necessary things in perfect order, so they will be ready to use whenever needed.
- *Seiso:* Keep your workplace clean.
- *Seiketsu:* Share information, so research will not be necessary.
- *Shitsuke:* Follow the procedures thus established.

The value of 5S is similar to that of 5W and 1H. The visual control system that places in view the key aspects of one's work and thus allows for virtually automatic management, is based on the 5S approach. In both cases, considerable documentation pertaining to 5S is distributed within the company.

Suggestion System

The suggestion system enables every employee to submit to management his or her ideas. It is an important tool in a promotional campaign, for two reasons:

- News concerning the suggestions made keeps the focus on quality.
- The number of suggestions is a barometer of employee attentiveness to quality.

The Japanese suggestion system is a highly organic system for harnessing a company's potential for improvement. It encourages the entire staff to constantly think of new ideas, however small, in order to improve all aspects (not just the cost) of their work. Ideas are assessed quickly, and rewards are given on the basis of idea quality.

Thus quantity and quality of suggestions are essential features of the suggestion system, raising the question of which one to emphasize. Generally, during the initial stage, quantity is emphasized. This is because the entire staff cannot suggest major quality improvements until the suggestion system has become a part of their work routine. When the system has reached that level of development (and leaders should be able to recognize it), greater emphasis is given to quality. A classic suggestion system in Japan develops in three stages:

- Stage 1 (from one to three years): Participation and involvement are stressed. The main task of management is encouraging all employees to examine their work and the area of their activities, and to think about how to improve them. During this stage, attention is given to the *quantity* of suggestions.
- Stage 2 (from two to three years): All employees are trained to analyze problems and to seek the best solutions. During this stage, attention is given to the *quality* of suggestions.

- Stage 3 (after five years), management shifts its attention to the *economic impact* of suggestions.

Unlike the American business model, which gives greater and more immediate attention to the economic benefits of suggestions, the Japanese approach focuses on the development of a quality "culture," which does not produce immediate economic benefits. Only later when people have become acculturated to the system, is the economic impact of suggestions stressed.

Two examples follow. Figure 11-2 shows data concerning the suggestion system at Fuji-Xerox. The Aisin-Warner case is reported below.

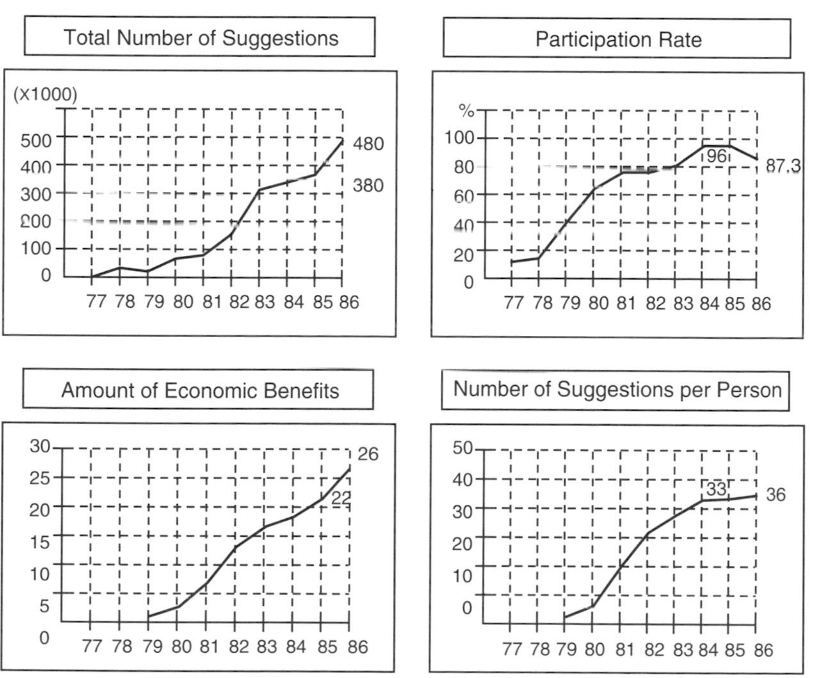

Figure 11-2. Fuji-Xerox Suggestion System

The managing director of Aisin-Warner (automatic transmissions for autos, overdrive, catalytic converters), Haruki Sugihara, notes that employees, when first confronted with a suggestion system, may find it difficult to put their ideas in writing and thus might benefit from a form. In 1982, each worker at the company made at least 127 suggestions a year, and 99 percent of them were implemented. How can a company evaluate so many proposals without taking so much time that the proposers lose interest? Aisin-Warner used a computer to process the proposals, which yielded a significant time savings (by 1987, the time required was estimated at three months). It also used an effective appraisal system, not only for workers, but for department heads, since they were in charge of maintaining the suggestion system.

In 1982, the suggestions made by Aisin-Warner employees fell into the following categories:

- simplifying work processes: 39.0 percent
- improving quality: 10.6 percent
- safety: 10.5 percent
- improvement and maintenance of equipment: 8.4 percent
- environment and hygiene: 7.6 percent
- savings on materials: 3.9 percent
- improvement of office work: 1.7 percent
- other: 18.3 percent

Each suggestion was evaluated according to standard forms that list well-defined merit and scoring factors.

Calls for Meetings/Discussions/Checking

The last aspect to consider for the purposes of promotion includes those special occasions in which conferences and other types of meetings are organized, both within the company and outside it. On such occasions rewards are usually also given out to the most active groups or to the winners of the competitions organized within the company. The most important promotional occasions are the following:

Conferences. On such occasions management groups or quality circles present their projects. Conferences are also held to launch a campaign or to celebrate important company events.

Exhibitions and shows. These can be an occasion to exhibit slogans, QC stories, and defective products. In the last case, products can be labeled with the cause of their problem, its cost for the company, and the solution to the problem. Graphs, diagrams illustrating quality control concepts, and statistical tools can also be shown to help employees visualize and better understand the complete process of quality control.

Meetings/gatherings. Initiatives of this kind keep interest alive, and promote an exchange of information concerning experiences and problems. They are usually held for exchanges of views among quality circles and employees from different plants.

Competitions. Competitions motivate employees to submit excellent improvement ideas and to implement them effectively. Rewards are handed out in both categories. In Japanese plants, worker improvements often extend to equipment and production systems.

Visits abroad. For especially deserving groups, visits to other companies, even overseas, are sometimes organized. Since 1968, JUSE has organized a trip every year for quality circle leaders to study abroad and visit leading companies around the world.

PART THREE

Techniques and Tools of CWQM

Two major priorities of CWQM are to ensure that all company employees are capable of applying an effective approach to problem solving, and to maximize the intellectual capabilities of employees. In this respect, CWQM has gone beyond all other managerial systems. Although it might be obvious to say that a company's competitiveness depends largely on its abilities to define and solve problems and to develop creativity within its staff, in practice, this is not so obvious. The first to recognize it were the Japanese, who developed their industry in real competitive bases only after World War II. The same breakthrough thinking didn't arrive in the Western world until 20 years later.

The great secret of Japanese success in this field has been in the simplicity with which they have approached the problem. The importance of this factor, which they developed through CWQM, cannot be overemphasized. This simplicity is an immediate consequence of the will to have everyone within the company adopt the most effective way of thinking, and the most constructive attitudes, toward their work and their colleagues. In fact, any very generalized phenomenon, if it is to become something real and concrete, must be simple. Alas, in our highly educated culture simplicity is often suspected of implying backwardness.

The Japanese were lucky to have some forward thinking intellects who early on understood the value of simplicity. The greatest, of these may have been Professor Kaoru Ishikawa, who died in 1989.

Part Three is divided into six chapters. Chapters 12 and 13 are devoted to the quantitative and statistical approach to problems.

Chapter 14 treats the qualitative approach to problems, that is, the way to identify a problem before tackling it in a quantitative manner.

Chapter 15 summarizes quality function deployment, a Japanese invention that may be the greatest contribution to business management techniques in the last 30 years.

Chapter 16 describes one of the most brilliant tools perfected in Japan for the visual control system of improvement: the CEDAC chart.

Chapter 17 is devoted to the new attitude that all employees must achieve to implement CWQM.

CHAPTER TWELVE

The Seven Statistical Tools and PDCA

Introduction

What is a company that is made up of scientists instead of ordinary people? It is a world-class Japanese company. To be precise, one should say that the employees within such a company are "little scientists," in the sense that they know and apply the basic tools of science without attaining the level of real scientists. They do, however, have a great advantage over true scientists: they exist in great numbers.

The expression "little scientists" was coined by Galgano & Associati to explain to managers and other employees of Italian companies the great power of the method proposed with the seven statistical tools and PDCA. These tools, which have been "manufactured" by Japanese experts, represent a new use of statistics, which Ishikawa explained during a 1987 seminar organized by Galgano & Associati:

> After the seminars held in Japan by Deming and other American experts during the early 1950s, we Westerners began teaching statistical techniques in our companies. After two or three years we realized that this teaching was not producing any results, and that we were teaching the people a statistical method that was too sophisticated, too

> hard to understand. People started thinking that the statistical method was a very difficult thing and that, therefore, quality control was also something difficult to implement.
>
> To correct this mistake, we taught a statistical method based on two different approaches. Concerning the first, we decided to teach everyone, from top management to line workers, a simpler statistical method, and we therefore developed the seven quality control (QC) tools. By this simple method, 95 percent of a company's problems can be resolved. The remaining 5 percent require a different approach.
>
> We teach the sophisticated statistical methods to engineers and quality control specialists.

This great simplification gave rise to statistical thinking, a basic element of the QC concept and essential for effective and comprehensive resolution of problems.

In Japan, thanks to this simplification, even workers and office staff constantly apply the seven QC tools for the resolution of all types of problems. Deming once stated that in Japan the first language of the people is Japanese; the second is statistics.

Transforming an Ordinary Person into a "Little Scientist"

CWQM enables ordinary people to become "little scientists" over a relatively short time. It teaches them to apply scientific methods to problem solving.

Let us now consider the scientific methods, which in CWQM take the form of the seven statistical (or seven QC) tools and PDCA.

The Data Collection Sheet (Check Sheet)

We know that a scientist relies on data. Without data, there is no science, only approximation and empiricism. We also know that Galileo invented the scientific method when, in order to confirm the correct hypothesis, he measured the time it took for a few marbles to roll along an incline.

We must, therefore, teach an ordinary person who wishes to become a "little scientist" how to collect data. We do this by showing different kinds of check sheet, and explaining the criteria to follow in gathering data.

Figure 12-1 shows one type of check sheet a person might use.

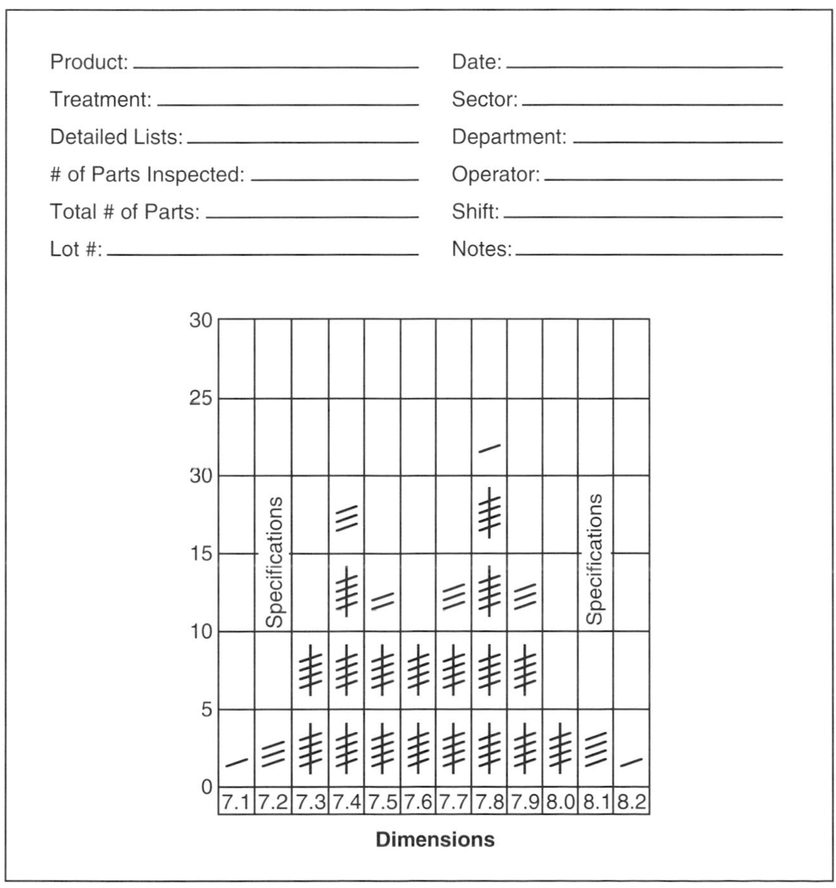

Product: ____________ Date: ____________

Treatment: ____________ Sector: ____________

Detailed Lists: ____________ Department: ____________

# of Parts Inspected: ____________ Operator: ____________

Total # of Parts: ____________ Shift: ____________

Lot #: ____________ Notes: ____________

Figure 12-1. Data Collection Sheet (Check Sheet) for Measurable Quantities

The Histogram

After scientists have collected their data, they face the problem, of reading those data. The problem is, they have only two eyes, while the data gathered are numerous. To solve the problem, they invented the histogram (see Figure 12-2). With this tool, and through the concepts of class, dispersion, and frequency, they can understand the statistical structure of the data gathered, and interpret its meaning.

Thus, we must teach ordinary people who wish to become "little scientists" how to build a histogram. Once we have taught them how to build it, we must explain to them that histograms can be of various kinds: in addition to the regular ones, there are island-shaped histograms, comb-shaped ones, ones with multiple trends, asymmetrical ones, and so on, and we must explain to them the meaning of such irregular forms.

The Cause-and-Effect Diagram

Scientists who have gathered their data and put it into readable form have built solid foundations on which to base

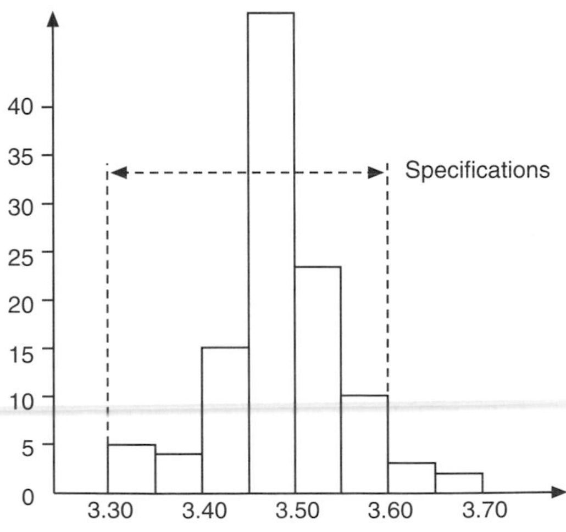

Figure 12-2. An Example of a Histogram

their analysis, their scientific work. So does an ordinary person, at this point, have a solid base on which to proceed to study and resolve the problem.

Next we come to the essence, or pivotal point, of scientific work. This is the study of the relationship between cause and effect, which Galileo invented when he asked himself what might be the effect of a force. By his scientific work, Galileo showed that force did not generate speed, as was believed for 2,000 years on the basis of Aristotle's opinion. Rather, it created an acceleration, that is, a variation in speed.

In teaching the scientific method, therefore, we must teach how to carry out a cause-and-effect study. Within a company, people will pursue improvement goals such as a reduction in rejects or a reduction in through-put time. Well, such goals are always effects. To have an impact on these effects, one must identify their causes. The instrument we teach is the cause-and-effect diagram, also known as the Ishikawa diagram, or fishbone diagram.

Specifically, we teach people to draw a small box, then a horizontal line and some transversal lines. I am here describing a particular cause-and-effect diagram, called the 4M diagram, shown in Figure 12-3. The term *4M* indicates man (employee), machine, material, and method. Employees are told to write down the topic to be studied and then to follow Descartes's advice at the fourth point of his method, that is, to enumerate all the possible causes that they deem connected to the effect under scrutiny. To facilitate such an enumeration of causes, employees may use a technique called *brainstorming,* which is taught for this purpose.

Employees are also told to organize the various causes that come to mind into four categories. Figure 12-4 is an example of a cause-and-effect diagram, with all the potential causes so categorized.

Employees are then encouraged to act like scientists, who are always conscious of their priorities, and to select the causes

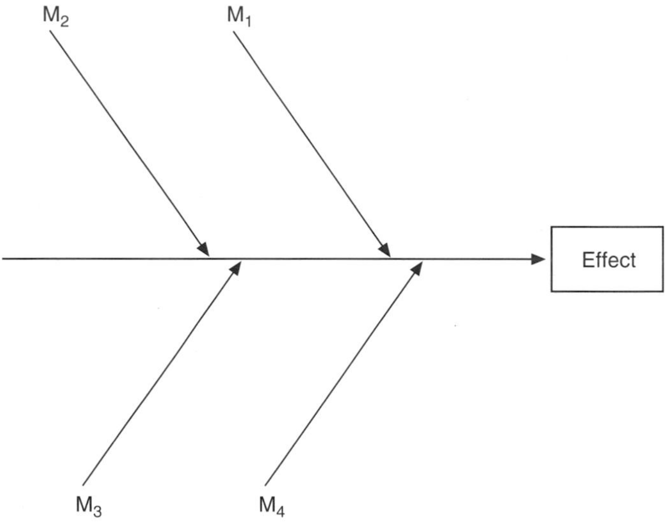

Figure 12-3. Constructing a Cause-and-Effect Diagram (4M)

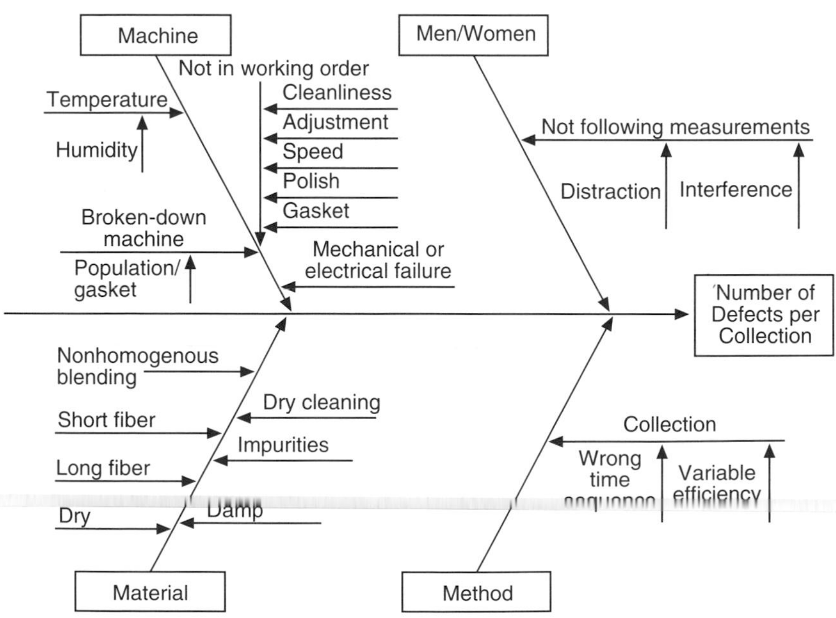

Figure 12-4. Developing a Cause-and-Effect Diagram

they consider most important for the goal being researched. Having established these main causes (normally between two and four), employees are asked to formulate a few hypotheses and countermeasures to eliminate the causes considered. The effectiveness of such countermeasures will then have to be checked against tests.

The cause-and-effect diagram and the Pareto diagram constitute the two pillars of the scientific method.

The Pareto Diagram

The fourth statistical tool is the Pareto diagram. This chart aims at highlighting what I called in Chapter 2 the universal law of priorities.

The diagram was named by Juran in honor of the Italian economist and sociologist Vilfredo Pareto (1848-1923), who, through his studies on wealth distribution, showed that one small part of the population of a country owns most of that country's wealth.

The construction of the diagram is shown in Figure 12-5.

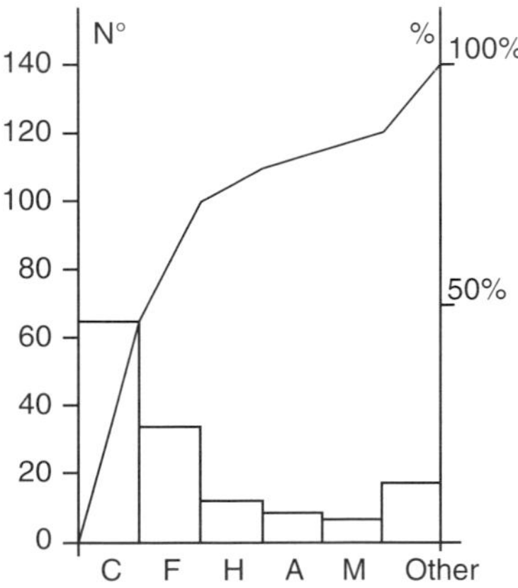

Figure 12-5. The Pareto Diagram

At this point employees are taught to construct the diagram by organizing the data in decreasing order of importance; this exercise helps them to focus on the relevant items.

Stratification Analysis

The fifth statistical tool offers scientists one of the sharpest blades with which to dissect a problem.

Let us imagine a certain department is analyzing a production defect. Data have been gathered and arranged in a histogram. The histogram in Figure 12-6 shows one course data might follow.

In teaching the scientific method we teach employees to ask themselves whether they might obtain useful information by stratifying their data. For example, if a department works in two shifts, they could stratify the same data for the two shifts to see whether there are any differences. In the two histograms shown in Figures 12-7 and 12-8, dispersion in the first shift is higher than in the second. This fact gives us a key to read the situation, for it clues us in to a problem in the first shift. This we can use as a basis for a deeper, albeit more limited, analysis of the first shift.

Scatter Diagram

The sixth statistical tool is among those used most by scientists, who must often determine whether two parameters are correlated with each other.

We tell employees learning the scientific method that when they want to verify whether a correlation exists between two characteristics or two factors, that is, whether one is related to the other, they can use a simple technique. First, they gather data pertaining to the two factors, and then they build a graph charting the pairs of data. Such pairs of data, on a Cartesian plane, are shown as points that may fall into a "cloud" — a pattern with a particular statistical significance (see Figure 12-9).

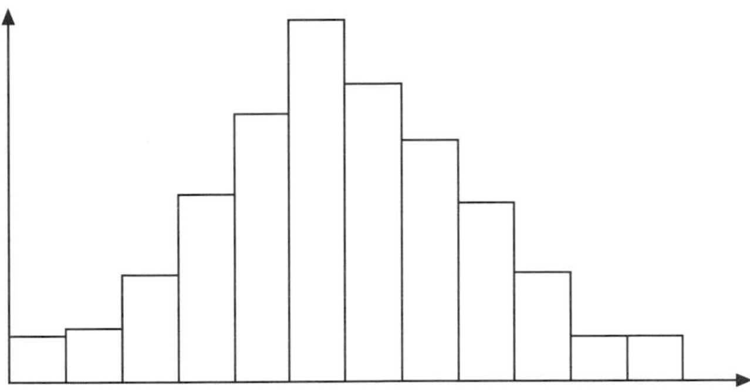

Figure 12-6. Histogram of Department Defects

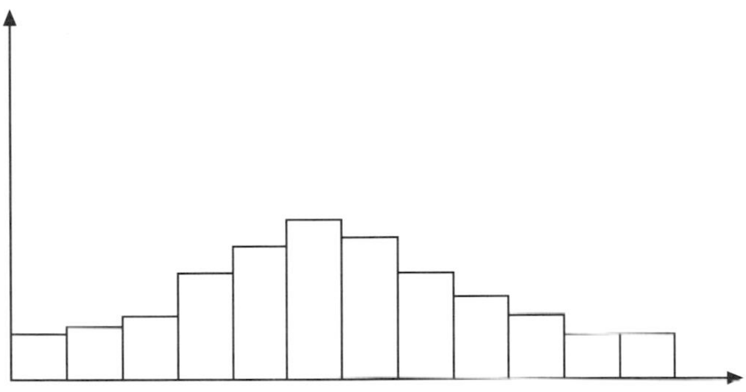

Figure 12-7. Histogram of First-shift Defects

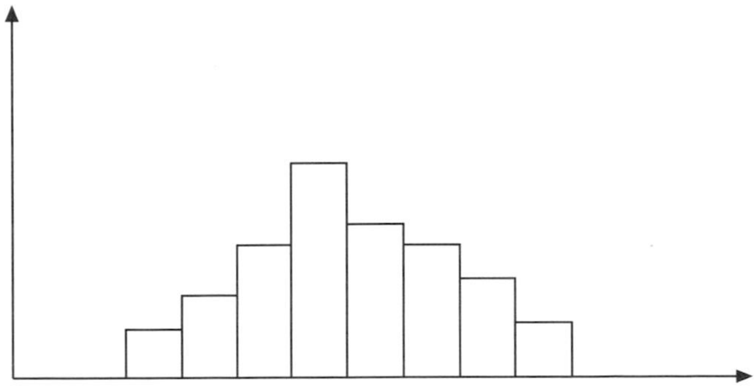

Figure 12-8. Histogram of Second-shift Defects

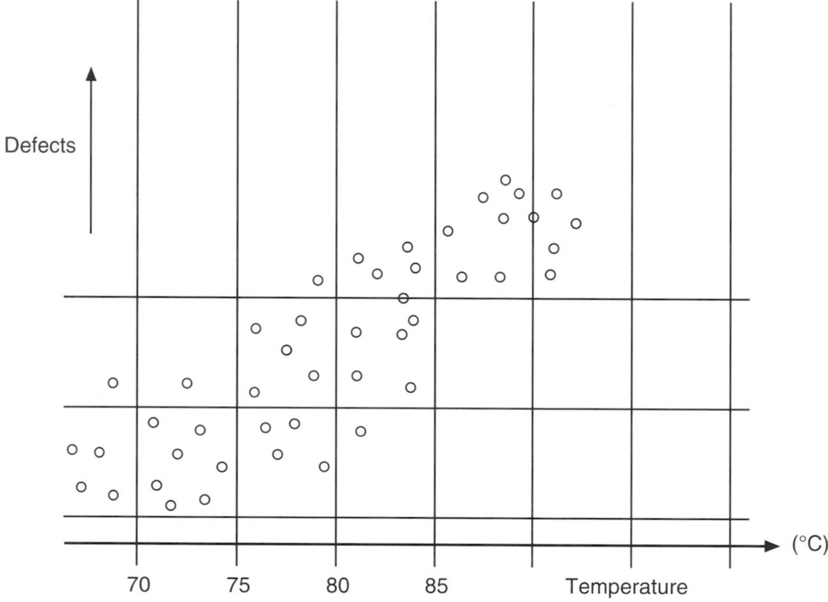

Figure 12-9. Scatter Diagram

Once this cloud has been obtained, it is easy to tell whether there is any correlation.

The Control Chart

The seventh tool is the most difficult one to describe in few words: the control chart.

To teach employees use of this tool, we explain that a process can be under control or out of control. It is very important to understand in which of these two situations they find themselves, since it is impossible to improve a process that is out of control. On the other hand, when it is under control, the process itself is predictable, because its parameters remain within two limits: a lower limit and an upper limit.

One way of seeing whether a process is under control is to draw such limits and check whether at any point the process goes beyond them (see Figure 12-10).

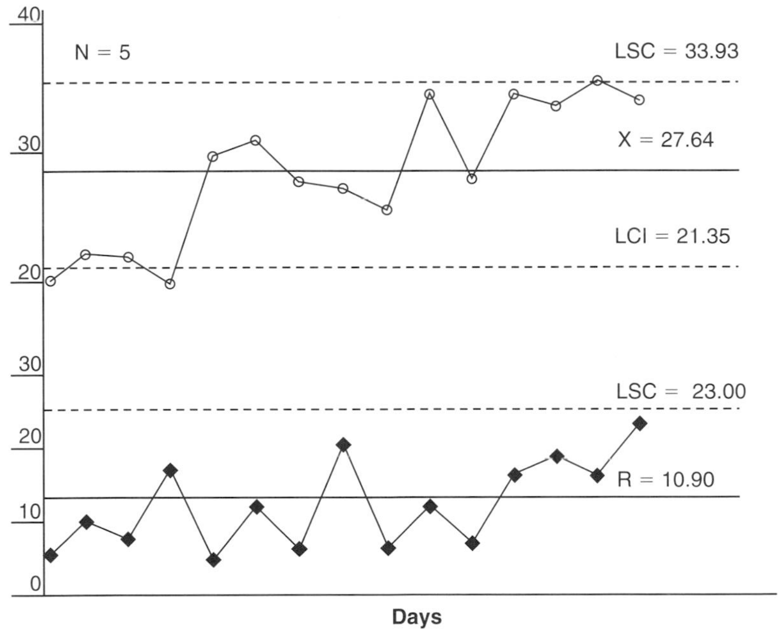

Figure 12-10. The Control Chart

We then teach employees how to calculate these limits (and do other important things that space does not permit me to mention here).

We thus teach employees the scientific method by teaching them how to use the seven statistical (QC) tools. The process takes from 15 to 20 hours.

Only by the repeated use of such tools will employees master them. Leaders, or "facilitators" often assist workers in this task.

These seven tools are extremely powerful. Ishikawa stated that these tools could solve the great majority of problems in companies.

The PDCA Method (or Process)

The tools by themselves, however, are not sufficient to solve a problem. It is also necessary to have a very powerful method of investigation, one a scientist could use and that can be presented in a schematic way with PDCA, or Deming's wheel (see Figure 12-11). I have already explained PDCA from another point of view, in Chapter 3.

To follow the scientific method in solving problems, employees are taught to begin with the *plan* stage. First, they must clearly isolate the problem, that is, gather data in order to understand it better, establish goals, and define its precise dimensions. Second, they must come up with a hypothesis for the solution: they study cause-and-effect relationships, establish the main causes, and then decide which countermeasures to take. Basically, they will have to outline a solution to the problem, but one that is theoretical, not yet confirmed with facts.

At that point they can proceed to the *do* stage, that is, carry out tests to confirm that the plan and hypothesis are correct. To do this they must prepare some tests, indicate how these tests are to be carried out, and explain them to the people who will be carrying them out. Then they can actually carry out the test.

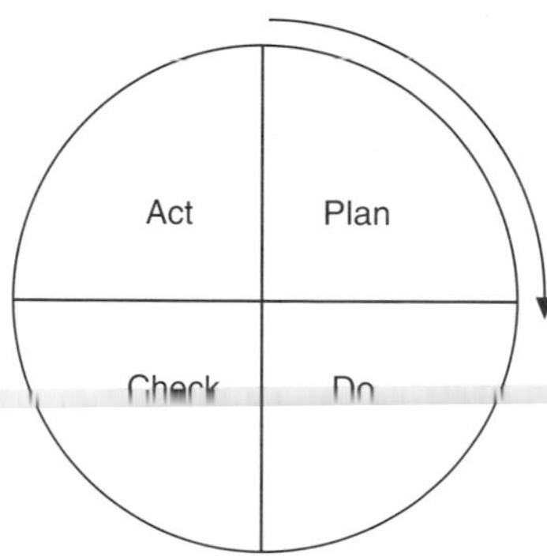

Figure 12-11. The PDCA Cycle, or Deming Wheel

After the *do* stage, employees enter the *check* stage. Here they compare their plan with the results of their tests, doing so with great care, lest the entire effort be lost.

In checking the results obtained by *do,* they might encounter one of two situations. The first occurs when the *check* test confirms the plan. They are then successful, but their work is not over yet, because this success has been obtained at an experimental level. To stabilize the results, they proceed to the *act* stage, which means standardizing the solution and establishing the conditions that allow it to be maintained.

If the solution achieved can be extended to other units, which might include other machines, other products, and other processes, this should be done.

The second possibility is that the test does not confirm the particular hypothesis made. Another cycle must be initiated. The Japanese call this circle Deming's wheel. This involves a new *plan* stage, which will now, however, be more precise, as it takes into account the experience of the first cycle. Various cycles will be carried out until a solution to the problem is found, or, better still, until the goal sought is achieved.

As I said at the beginning, the seven tools, in addition to PDCA, are the means by which an ordinary person can be transformed into a little scientist. Over the course of their work lives people face a great number of problems. CWQM gives them the tools to solve these problems and improves their solid contribution to their company.

The QC Story

Use of the PDCA process as a problem-solving tool follows a procedure that can be likened to the unfolding of a story or of a play. In Japan, this way of proceeding is called the *QC story,* and it evolves through seven stages:

1. Identify the problem (*problem*).
2. Understand the characteristics of the problem (*observation*).

3. Search for its causes (*analysis*).
4. Eliminate the causes (*action*).
5. Validate the effectiveness of the action (*checking*).
6. Make elimination of causes permanent (*standardization*).
7. Review activities and plan for future work (*conclusions*).

If applied in the order just described, the QC story is a fast and safe method to obtain significant results in improvement activities. Here we will briefly describe the principles behind each point.

Problem. Choosing which problem to deal with is related to the priorities one has established. Given this awareness, it is then necessary to tackle the problem by seeking to understand it in the fullest possible way. For this, one must follow its evolution through time by quantifying the negative results it generates, and the potential for improvement. The latter must be expressed through clearly defined goals. During this stage, therefore, the importance of the problem must be clearly established, in order to increase the awareness and the commitment of the people who will be attempting to find a solution.

Observation. The problem itself usually provides the elements needed to solve it, but in order to recognize the elements, one must know how to look at the problem. The goal of observation is to discover what causes the problem, by observing it from various points of view.

The most frequently followed approach is to look at the problem from four angles: time, place, type, and symptoms. This enables one to see how the problem varies in relation to these items (for example, in a furnace one must examine the variation in the percentage of defects in relation to the position of the products within the furnace itself). The results of observation are very useful for the next stage.

Analysis. Analysis enables one to discover the main causes of a problem, and thus concentrate on them. Analysis comprises two stages: the first, that of formulating hypotheses, is directed at choosing the most likely causes; the second, that of controlling hypotheses, aims at choosing the main causes among those put forward in the first stage. The reason for such a procedure is the need to obtain scientifically established causes.

Practically, one identifies the main causes on the basis of a cause-and-effect diagram that carries out all the elements connected to the problem. Once the observation stage has revealed the irrelevant causes, these are eliminated and the remaining causes then analyzed in greater depth, so that priorities can be set.

Action. Countermeasures can aim either at correcting an existing phenomenon or preventing its causes. Ideally, one applies solutions aimed at eliminating causes, keeping in mind any possible side effect that might derive from a particular action.

Checking. Checking tells one whether the measures adopted have been effective in preventing recurrence of a problem. To verify the effectiveness of an action, one must compare the situation before and after the application of the countermeasures, making use of the same evaluation parameters. It is also important to evaluate economically the results obtained.

Standardization. To prevent recurrence of a problem, one must standardize corrective actions, and ensure that all the people involved consider such standards integral to their actions and habits. To this end, one makes use of the 5W and 1H approach, to properly analyze all aspects worthy of consideration.

Conclusions. Conclusions summarize the problems that are still unsolved, thus paving the way for a future QC story. As a final step in the QC story, one performs self-analysis, examining the procedure just completed for help in implementing future actions.

The power of PDCA, and of its version as a QC story, is considerable. All employees, from the top executives to front-line worker, should follow this process when tackling a problem.

During presentations, too, it is important to follow the PDCA diagram and the QC story, since use of such an outline strengthens the ability to analyze a problem.

CHAPTER THIRTEEN

The Statistical Approach to More Complex Problems

Introduction

After Japanese companies had introduced the scientific method, via the seven tools and PDCA, to all levels of employees, the need to strengthen diagnostic abilities for problem solving emerged. They solved this problem by integrating more powerful statistical tools.

Some complex problems cannot be analyzed through the use of the seven tools alone, but require the use of more sophisticated statistical techniques. So statistical education was added to a field already deeply impregnated with scientific methodology.

In Japan, statistical methods are taught primarily through practical application, contrary to what happens in the West.

An understanding of the theoretical algorithms linked to statistical tools is seen as secondary to an understanding of the use of such tools in practice, as well as to an understanding of the goals linked to application of each tool. In other words

---

This chapter was edited by Maurizio Montagna, a consultant with Galgano & Associati.

(thanks also to information technology), the method was to apply first and understand second. The results of such an approach are evident: statistics are normally, and correctly, applied by department heads, so that they can manage and improve processes.

Solving Complex Problems

For problems that cannot be solved through the use of the seven statistical tools alone, more powerful statistical tools are available, whose use can be understood through examination of a three-staged approach:

- analyzing the effect
- analyzing the causes and the definition of the most important factors
- optimizing the most important factors

This approach is, in fact, a funnel-shaped process, in which, through a sequence of steps, the factors that most affect results are highlighted.

In applying this method, we place specific tools, particularly effective in problem solving, within each of the three stages. Such tools are described in Table 13-1.

Before we examine the three stages, however, let's consider the four principles to be followed in studying a problem, especially a complex one.

Table 13-1. Advanced Statistical Tools for Problem-solving

Effect Analysis	Process capability studies Analysis of variance (ANOVA) Series analysis Concentration analysis Principal component analysis (PCA)
Cause Analysis	Multiregression analysis Principal components analysis (PCA)
Optimization of Principal Factors	Design of experiments (DOE)

Four Principles of Tackling Problems

The effectiveness derived from application of statistics is greatly increased when the statistical method is integrated with a few fundamental principles, and with a rigorously logical analysis.

In tackling improvement-related problems, we face omnipresent reality: phenomena are variable in their appearance. Improvement consists in reducing and controlling such a variability.

In pursuing this process it is very important to save effort, that is, to obtain a maximum amount of useful information from the least amount of data and elaboration. To achieve this goal, we apply four principles, which can be described as follows.

First Principle

The first principle is the universal law of priorities, which states that in every situation there are few truly important factors, while all the others scarcely matter. In our case, we can state that few factors account for most of the variability.

Obviously, process performance will be optimized if those few factors are controlled. The identification of the most important factors leads to two concrete results:

- strong economy of resources dedicated to the problem
- shorter time to resolve the problem

Second Principle

The second principle states that any phenomenon is multivaried: for example, a steel product has a particular cohesiveness, a particular hardness, a yield load, a breaking load, and so on. In other words, since a product is defined through many characteristics, the goal of an improvement study is their optimization related to customer satisfaction.

If all characteristics were independent from each other, there would be no particular problem in optimizing all characteristics: each aspect could be optimized quite apart from all the others. Reality is different: a product's characteristics are linked with each other, and thus, optimization of one characteristic cannot exist without an awareness of such existing links.

Third Principle

The third principle is that processes are to be considered as systems. It is possible to isolate different hierarchical levels within such systems: causal factors can be classified at various levels according to the influence they exercise on output variability. In particular, variability can be divided into two macrocomponents, one spatial, and the other temporal, and each of these, in turn, into subcomponents related to identified hierarchical levels.

The spatial analysis, as well as the temporal one, is often essential for the resolution of a problem.

Fourth Principle

The fourth principle is that variability is due to two large families of causes: common causes and special causes.

Common causes are intrinsic to the process, and are linked to design and construction of equipment, use of raw materials, operational procedures, the skill and education levels of employees, and other factors. *Special causes* are maladjustments, errors in managing equipment, faulty raw materials, and other disturbances.

In terms of the influence on variability, that total variability is the sum of two components:

- basic distribution due to common causes
- disturbance patterns that are superimposed on and thus broaden the basic distribution

Careful application of such principles through use of statistics leads to an interpretation of variability and to isolation of the most important factors. It is often easy to identify priority factors, and simple statistical tools are sufficient to highlight them; for more complex problems, it is necessary to use more powerful magnifying lenses, more sophisticated statistical tools, to penetrate deeply into the problem.

Effect Analysis

Analyzing an effect usually involves studying output variability in all aspects necessary to fully understand it. One of the goals of this stage, for example, could be establishing natural distribution (that due only to common causes) of a particular product characteristic, and establishing which variability component has greater weight.

Process Capability Studies

The tool used to define natural variability is the study of *process capability*. Use of this tool enables one to identify what response a process is capable of providing. In other words, it enables one to determine process performance when it is affected only by common causes.

Knowing process capability makes it possible to compare intrinsic dispersion with specifications. When faced with an intrinsic dispersion wider than required specifications, one is confronted with processes that are not intrinsically adequate. By contrast, capabilities that are within required specifications indicate a more favorable response.

Analysis of Variance (ANOVA)

An even more effective tool for a deeper analysis of dispersion is *analysis of variance* (ANOVA).

Studying process capability may have shown whether the system is able to fulfill specifications or not. Especially in the latter situation, it is important to understand the "structure of the variability" so that one can act effectively on the more important components.

As we have seen, global variability can be divided into a temporal macrocomponent and a spatial macrocomponent. That is, it is possible to have a phenomenon that is modified over time but at the same time to have different results at different points of the process.

A few examples will clarify the concepts of variability structure and variability components.

Example: Production of Mechanical Tappets

Let us consider the production of mechanical tappets on a numerically controlled lathe equipped with six chucks, where the product characteristic in need of study is the diameter of the tappets.

Through the data gathered concerning these characteristics, it is possible to verify variability both in time and in space — that is, the variability that occurs at the same moment on different chucks. By analysis of variance, one can divide overall variability into these two components, isolating the weight of each.

In practice, it is often necessary to further divide both the temporal and spatial variability into subcomponents, as a function of the different hierarchical levels that the process involves. This identifies which component or subcomponent accounts for the greatest variability. This step is essential if one is to narrow the range of causes that might influence the process in a decisive way.

Example: Packaging Frozen Vegetables

In a company that packages frozen vegetables there exists an excessive variability concerning the weight of each package.

The machinery for filling the packages consists of a feed hopper, loaded with spinach every half hour; four prehensile mechanisms for removing the spinach from the feed hopper; and four loading positions where the packages are filled. There are also systems for the automatic transportation of the packages.

One can divide the overall weight variability into two components:

- temporal variability, that is, the variability that exists between packages filled by the same prehensile mechanism at different times
- spatial variability, that is, the variability that exists between packages filled at the same moment by different prehensile mechanisms

After a careful examination of the process — in particular, of the temporal logic behind the system's operation — it was possible to isolate three levels of temporal hierarchy:

- a short-term level, pertaining to weight variations detectable between consecutive takes of one prehensile mechanism
- a medium-term level, pertaining to weight variations detectable over a time of half an hour, equal to the emptying time of the hopper
- a long-term level, pertaining to weight variations detectable between packages from different hopper loads

Through consideration of the data gathered, the variability structure of the phenomenon, and analysis of the variance of data, the company identified the greatest cause of variance as occurring at the medium-term level (that is, during emptying of the hopper). From the study it appeared that this component explained 75 percent of the variability, and that a decreasing trend in the weight of the packages occurred between the time the hopper was full and the time it was empty. This information narrowed the range of possible causes to attack. A solution was found in a short time, reducing the overall variability of the phenomenon by 70 percent.

It was therefore demonstrated that the causes that generally affect spatial variability differ from those which affect temporal variability.

In a high percentage of problems, analysis of the variability structure of a phenomenon is sufficient to precisely define the number of causes that might affect the phenomenon itself. In this case, one proceeds to the subsequent stage: the study of cause-and-effect links between process parameters and product characteristics. Other times, the effect cannot be entirely determined and thus, the problem will require further investigation.

Fourier's Analysis and Analysis of Historical Series

Should temporal variability prevail, Fourier's analysis and the analysis of historical series can provide effective tools. Let us briefly present the goals of such tools.

Fourier's analysis is a temporal analysis of the consecutive values of a variable. One uses it to determine whether the data show one or more frequencies in the cyclical swings inherent in the system. It shows its effectiveness particularly in the case of constant causes, such as games, eccentricities, systematic behavior of a mechanical nature, and response inertia.

Example: A Cookie Manufacturer

In a cookie manufacturing company, the weight dispersion of individual items when they were removed from the oven at the end of the cooking cycle was too high, and this resulted in problems maintaining the weight stated on the package. Furthermore, it had been learned through previous studies that the dispersion of raw product was equal to 25 percent of the dispersion of cooked product. It was obvious that the cooking phase induced too high a product variability.

At this point the company decided to analyze the weight of hundreds of products in succession. From the data gathered and analyzed through Fourier's analysis, it was shown that the weight dispersion could be graphed as a sine curve, with a period of six minutes. This fact was in itself very serious, since the packaging was done with 30 consecutive cookies and some packages came out with only light cookies, while some came out with only heavy cookies. Thus, the difference in weight between packages was considerable. The study, however, was essential to the search for causes; the decisive factor was the cycle time of the phenomenon, lasting six minutes. This data coincided with the period between the switching on and off of the oven's thermostat. A careful analysis of the internal temperature of the oven revealed a direct correlation between this cycle and the variation in weight. An intervention was carried out on the reaction of temperature control, thus reducing the variability of the cookies by 70 percent and bringing all packages back to specification.

Another tool used in analyzing temporal data sequence is the *analysis of historical series*. This technique is even more powerful than the previous one, insofar as it is able to identify any law pertaining to the dependence between values, not only cyclical phenomena. In practice, very often the law by which a sequence of values for the same product is shown is not of a sinusoidal shape, but very different. The analysis of historical series makes it possible to identify any type of law in which there is not a perfectly causal variability.

At this point of the investigation, when the effect has been clearly defined, one can begin research into the most important causal factors. To this end one uses powerful statistical tools, which enable an analysis of the dependency among many factors and isolate the characteristics to be improved.

Cause Analysis

The goal of any improvement activity is to control the most important causes or factors. This implies identifying links between the causes themselves and the characteristics to be improved. By understanding these links, one can narrow the range of variability of phenomena.

Analyzing such links is especially demanding. Once the effect has been clearly established, an effort is made to establish the possible factors affecting the results. To such end, one can rationalize the search for possible factors by using the cause-and-effect diagram. This diagram can be applied in three stages:

Stage 1 (creation): classification of all possible causes in the diagram

Stage 2 (analysis): isolation, on the basis of experience, historical data, and elements derived from analyzing the effect, of probable causes

Stage 3 (verification): determination of the few most important causes

For complex problems during the verification stage, it becomes necessary to apply advanced statistical techniques, such as multiregression analysis.

Multiregression Analysis

Multiregression analysis is without a doubt one of the most effective techniques for tackling problems related to processes, since it points out the most important factors and expresses the link between these factors and the result.

The application of such a tool requires the use of both historical data and data gathered ad hoc once the problem is identified. This method of data collection is undoubtedly preferable to the first one, since it promotes greater care in the data collection.

The number of variables to consider is not a binding aspect, since it is possible to manage hundreds of process variables with use of a calculator.

Example: Polymers for Molding

At a chemical manufacturer's, one of the main problems was to supply polymers for molding that complied with specifications pertaining to humidity content. Excessive humidity within the polymer led to quality problems for customers at the molding stage, while insufficient humidity caused too many rejects in the production phase. Polymer production is characterized by numerous parameters, such as the die-plate temperature (Xl), the cooling water temperature (X2), the period spent in the water (X3), and the diameter of the drawn polymer (X4). A study was undertaken to analyze the dependency between such parameters and product humidity, with the aim of isolating the most influential parameters, and the laws of dependency. To such end, data from 30 samples were collected, showing for each sample the value of the process parameters Xm, as well as the humidity value for the corresponding product Y. Figure 13-1 shows the table used to gather data.

Through a series of computer calculations, the most influential parameters were isolated:

- the time spent by the polymer in the cooling water
- the temperature of the drying air

These accounted for 75 percent of the total humidity variability. The law of dependency between the two main parameters and the polymer's humidity was also determined. This led to the establishment of new process specifications concerning

Sample	X1	X2	X3	X4	....	Xm	Y
1							
2							
3							
....							
....							
n							

Figure 13-1. Check Sheet for Multiple Regression Analysis

the time spent in the water by the polymer, as well as the temperature of the drying air, which led, in turn, to a humidity of the polymer in line with specifications.

In collecting data to study multiregression, one should also point out the values of other product characteristics, in order to show any link between product characteristics or between process variables and product characteristics. The goal of this further investigation is to avoid optimizing one characteristic of a product to the detriment of another. This approach derives from the fact that any phenomenon is, in fact, multifaceted, as noted at the beginning of this chapter. In any case, optimizing one characteristic at the expense of another would compromise product quality.

Principal Component Analysis

The full understanding of a statistical problem leads to the so-called optimization of response surfaces of all product characteristics. *Principal component analysis* is a particularly effective technique for this purpose. This tool has many applications; particularly, it can be used to analyze links between product characteristics or between process variables.

The first application is definitely the more interesting one. A product is defined by many characteristics; if they were all independent from each other, there would be no particular problem in optimizing all characteristics. In reality, however, product characteristics are all linked with each other; thus, it is not possible to optimize one characteristic without understanding its links with the others. Through statistics it is possible, however, to take advantage of these links, with the resulting economies both in research and in control.

Example: The Production of Yarns

In a textile company, routine controls called for measuring five characteristics, such as spinning count, regularity, strength, stretching, and resistance to traction. Routine controls were very demanding, so the company performed principal component analysis to check whether there might be precise links between some characteristics, and whether it might be possible to measure only a few items (with the others being determined through their links).

It turned out that the five parameters were strongly linked, with particularly strong links between stretching and strength, and between regularity and resistance to traction. In other words, by knowing the degree of stretching, one could determine strength with a considerable amount of precision, while by measuring regularity one could determine resistance.

Upon concluding the study, the company decided to carry out controls on three characteristics, instead of five.

Optimization of Principal Factors

When tools such as multiregression are applied, the factors that most affect the results and the law expressing the links between them become clear. Sometimes the law discovered is used to determine optimal conditions. Often, in order to establish the highest point in the response curve, a company performs a series of planned experiments.

Design of Experiments

In designing an experiment, one plans a series of tests in which realistic values are established according to a previously determined plan. These tests are carried out repeatedly, until the highest response is obtained.

Statistics offers various models for the application of experiment design; the most frequently used are the following:

- full factorial design
- fraction factorial design
- Latin square design

In terms of information, the most effective model is the full factorial one, as it allows one to determine the existence of any interaction, and to quantify it.

Once two, three, or four of the most likely causes affecting results are specified, tests are designed for the purpose of isolating the must influential factor or factors, and the best operational conditions. The most widely used method for designing experiments is the so-called *2n* method, where *n* indicates the number of factors to be tested with the experiment and *2* indicates the levels chosen for each factor. One usually determines the levels for each factor by considering the highest possible realistic value (shown conventionally by plus sign or 1), and a lowest realistic value (indicated conventionally by minus sign or 0). For example, the highest and the lowest could coincide with the standard parameter variation limits.

Sometimes one tests more than two levels for each factor, to obtain a range of the most significant tests. The full factorial method allows verification of the effects produced on the results of tested factors, and of any interaction among the factors themselves. It is important to evaluate the impact of interactions on results, as they are often the controlling factor. (We are faced with an interaction when the combined effect of various causes is different from the sum of the effects of the individual causes.)

One example can better clarify the concept of interaction: Four braking tests were carried out at 100 kilometers per hour, according to the conditions shown in Figure 13-2. In each the space required for stopping was recorded.

We consider as factors A and B, respectively, "road conditions" and "tire conditions." If we consider also two levels, for factor A we will have "dry" and "wet," while for factor B, we will have "new" and "worn." Note that the first test shown in the chart can be seen as a reference condition, for it represents the best conditions: as can be seen, all tests provide braking space higher than the results of the first test. For the fourth test,

Test	Road Conditions	Tire Conditions	Braking Space
1	Dry	New	50 meters
2	Dry	Worn	70 meters + 20
3	Wet	New	70 meters + 20
4	Wet	Worn	200 meters + 150

		A- Tungsten	A+ Aluminum
1 L/minute	B- = 15,5	44 42	48 49
	B+ = 30.5	30 31	37 36
1.5 L/minute	B- = 15, 5	37 35	54 52
	B+ = 30.5	26 24	43 46

Figure 13-2. Braking Distance and Lathe Production

the braking space is not 90 meters (50+20+20), but 200 meters, that is, a much higher value. Thus, the simultaneous presence of a wet road and worn tires drastically reduces the braking ability of the vehicle.

In practice, in order to facilitate the designing of experiments, researchers prepare matrixes, whose margins contain the value of the factors tested. Following are the diagrams for:

- the two factors A and B, with two levels for each factor:

	A-	A+
B-		
B+		

- three factors, A, B, and C, with two levels for each factor.

		A-	A+
C-	B-		
	B+		
C+	B-		
	B+		

The results obtained in the practical experimentation are reported in the boxes shown and then analyzed.

Example: Mechanical Precision Company

Figure 13-2 shows the project diagram used to study the effects of various factors on the number of parts produced per hour on a lathe. These factors included:

- the type of tool (A)
- the work angle (B)
- the quantity of coolant (C)

The boxes further contain the results of

- a randomized sequence of tests
- repetitions for each box (that is, a repetition of testing for each set of operational conditions).

With this data, one can evaluate the contribution of each parameter to the results, and thereby isolate the set with the best conditions.

CHAPTER FOURTEEN

The Seven Management Tools: The Qualitative Approach to Problems

Introduction

Chapters 12 and 13 described the quantitative tools used in companywide quality management. With these tools one fights the battle for quality improvement by correctly isolating, quantifying, and communicating elements pertaining to existing problems of any kind: process defects, excessive time, useless procedures, and so on. These tools enable companies to obtain significant improvements.

Yet the work carried out with the aforementioned tools is of a reactive nature; that is, it is performed in reaction to unfavorable situations, especially to customer dissatisfaction (including internal customers). If a customer complains because of a delay or product defect, it is imperative to address the problem immediately and as high upstream as possible. We have seen that to resolve problems in a definitive manner, one must eliminate their causes, rather than simply carry out a superficial corrective action. In the long run, however, improvement by

---

This chapter was edited by Francesco Zucchelli, a consultant with Galgano & Associati.

elimination of causes will not suffice. There are many reasons for this:

- As we have already seen, complaints represent the tip of the iceberg in terms of customer dissatisfaction.
- Eliminating causes is paying attention to only one aspect of quality, *negative quality. Negative quality* refers to the gap (thus, something negative) between the actual situation and an ideal reference situation. Excessive downtime for a machine, too high a rate of defective products, overly complicated procedures, and excessively long delivery times are examples of negative quality. Improvement is basically a matter of identifying the gap to be reduced, and then eliminating its cause. Thus one is reacting to a negative situation. Companies are now beginning to realize that negative quality is no longer going to guarantee them supremacy over the competition.
- Although expressing company processes and other activities in terms of numbers is necessary for an initial assessment of problems and areas for intervention, it does not provide all the necessary elements for a correct and deep analysis of them. This applies, for example, to processes that are less closely linked to production, such as finance and control, human resources management, marketing, and product development processes. In these areas there are important factors that don't translate to numbers but cannot be ignored, such as impressions, comments, judgments, and personalities.

For these reasons, companies have adopted a second approach to improvement, while staying within the total quality strategy. This approach is more demanding, but also more stimulating. More active in nature, it is called *positive quality,* and it involves a new set of tools. Between 1972 and 1977, a committee of JUSE developed what are known as the *seven management tools,* or *seven new QC tools.* These tools, too, clearly fit into the general logic and methodology of CWQM.

Characteristics of the Seven Management (New) Tools

With the seven management tools, the approach to problem analysis and definition is simple and based on standard criteria. There follow some observations on the tools:

- They allow the elaboration not only of numerical information, but also of verbal information.
- The term *management* indicates that these tools are addressed essentially to a company's management, in opposition to the seven statistical tools, which are aimed at all employees. This is because their use is intended mainly for the resolution of more complex or less-defined problems.
- As is the case for the seven statistical tools, the seven management tools were not invented out of thin air but derive from methods used in other fields.
- The seven statistical tools and the seven management tools do not together make up the totality of problem-solving tools. For particularly complex or specialized problems, there also exist tools that are not part of either of these groups. These tools, in addition to being based on mathematics and statistics, are also based on semantics, that is, on the study of language and verbal expression.

In any case, the use of the seven management tools must occur simultaneously with, not as an alternative to, the seven statistical tools, which maintain their full usefulness for the processing of numerical data (see Figure 14-1).

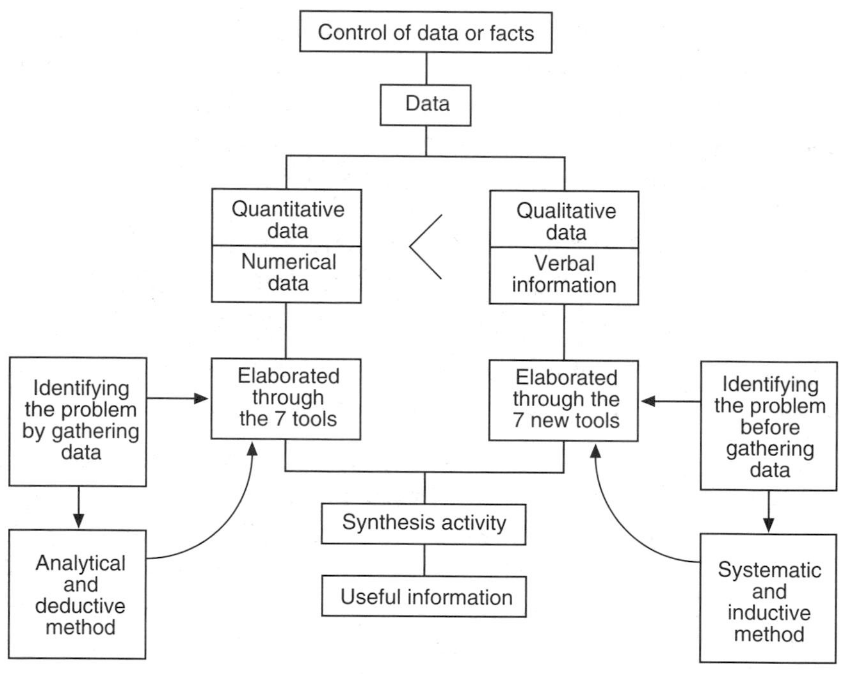

Figure 14-1. Integration of the Seven Statistical Tools with the Seven Management Tools

The Seven Management Tools

The seven management tools are the following:

- *Affinity (KJ) diagram:* For synthesizing, classifying, organizing indefinite ideas
- *Relationship diagram:* For isolating cause-and-effect relationships
- *Tree-shaped diagram:* For deploying general concepts into details
- *Matrix diagram:* For correlating in a logical form, in order to evaluate, select, decide
- *Decision tree (PDPC):* For identifying alternatives

- *Arrow diagram (PERT):* For planning
- *Matrix data-analysis:* For quantifying relationships

A description of each tool follows.

Affinity Diagram

One uses an affinity diagram to collect a great number of verbal expressions (ideas, opinions, observations, etc.) and organize them in groups according to natural relationships between individual items. With this tool a creative process, rather than a logical one, is used. An example is shown in Figure 14-2.

The affinity diagram (or KJ diagram, after its inventor Jiro Kawakita) is perhaps the most innovative of the seven management tools. This is because, in its extreme conceptual and logical simplicity it allows a clear view of the largest and most complex problems. Basically, it is a way to structure and classify unclear or vague ideas. It is therefore very useful when one wants to rationalize and focus on complex and multifaceted problems.

Specifically, the tool organizes information into homogeneous classes ordered according to importance, on the basis of their affinities. It is used when one wants to

- determine logical priorities, especially in cases where it is not possible, or where it would be restrictive, to think only in terms of numerical priorities
- extract the greatest amount of useful information from few or scattered data, or from unrelated ideas
- understand and organize problems that are not clear
- create new concepts

Other benefits of using this tool are

- making use of verbal information even in confused situations, and identifying problems by synthesizing the available data

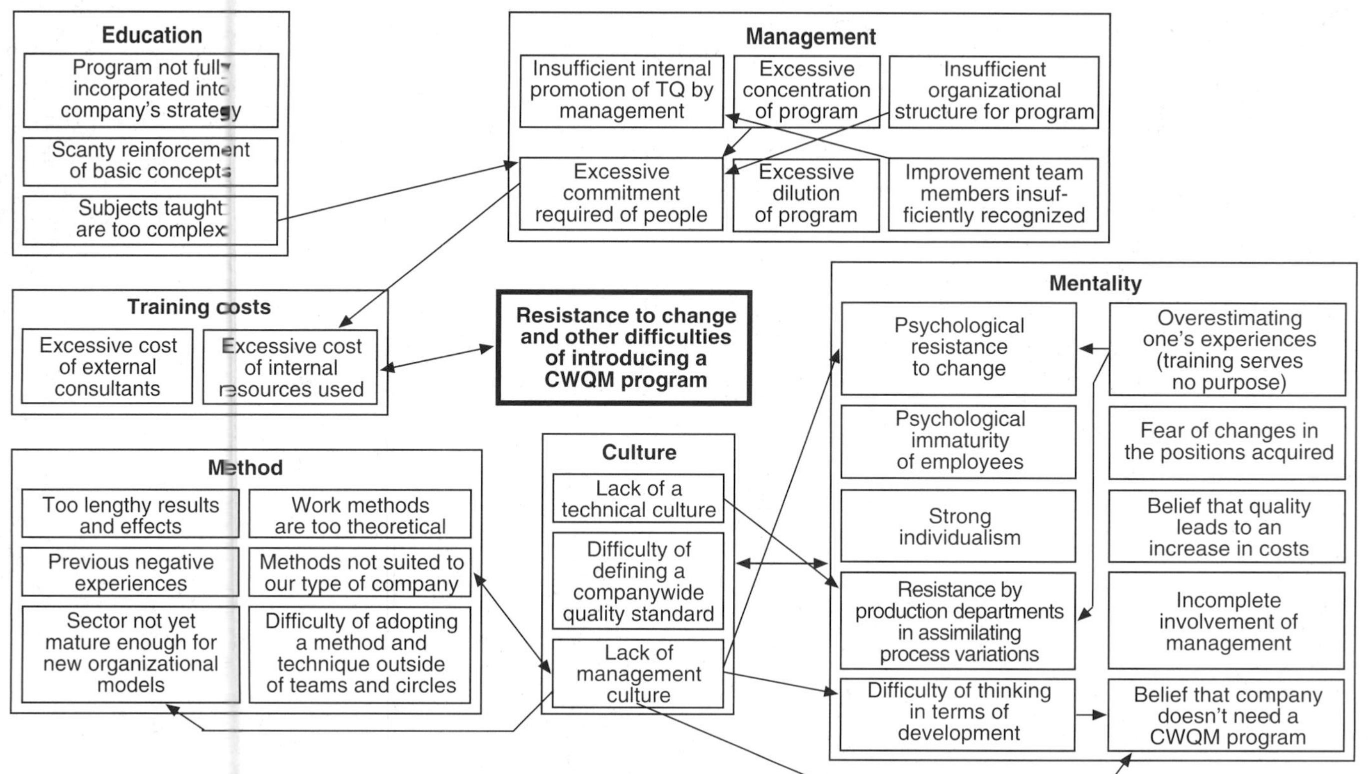

Figure 14-2. Affinity (KJ) Diagram

- developing new ideas through innovative thinking
- identifying the essential issues of a problem, and getting everyone to understand priorities
- transforming ideas into actions, and increasing motivation
- integrating various points of view
- identifying the relationship among different aspects of a problem, by organizing them in order of importance

Again, because it involves several people for hours at a time, it should be used only for truly important matters.

Relationship Diagram

A relationship diagram is used when one wants to build a map of the logical consequential links among items that are interconnected and related to a central idea, problem, or issue. It facilitates the solution of problems where causes interact by dividing a problem into its basic components and isolating the relationships between causes and effects. The basic logic behind this tool is, therefore, the same as those of the cause-and-effect diagram. (See Figure 14-3.)

This tool offers the following advantages:

- It allows one to examine causes that interact among themselves and reveals the relationships that exist among all causes.
- It facilitates consensus among participants on the relationships among the various causes.
- It encourages creativity in identifying new relationships.
- It helps one to isolate vital problems and relationships, thus promoting a shared understanding of the problem.

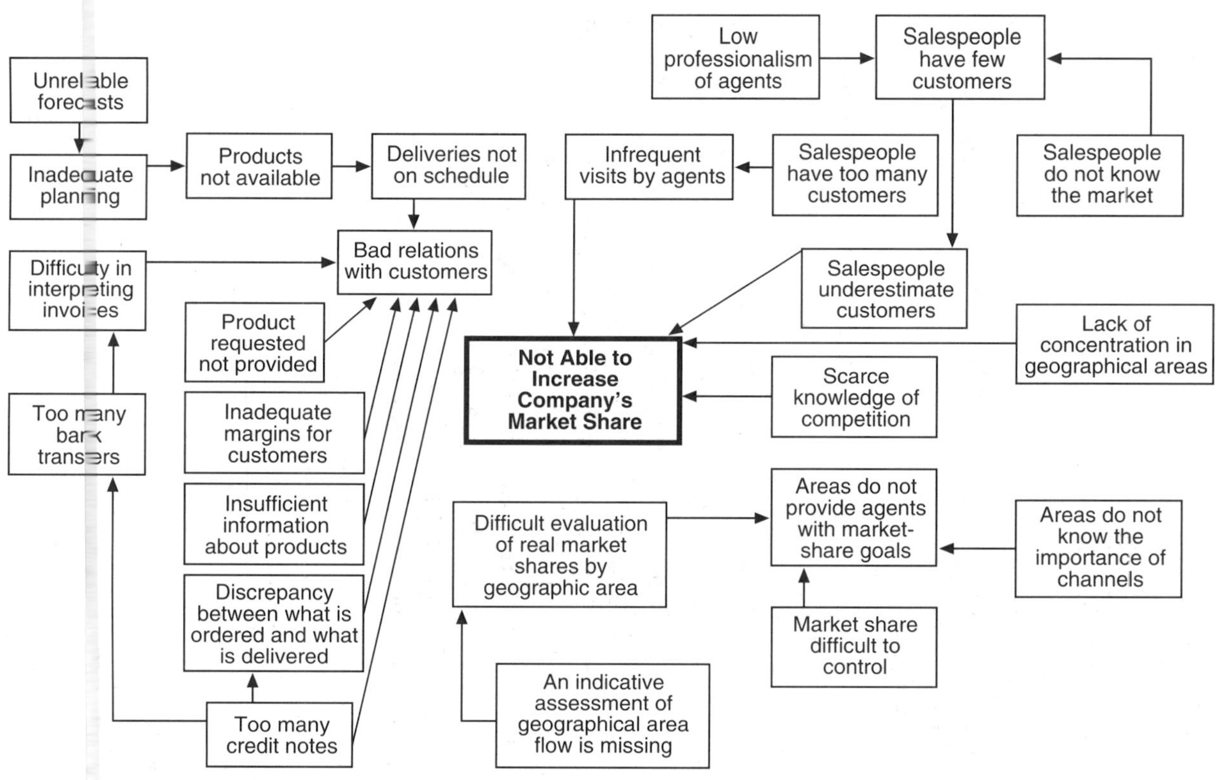

Figure 4-3. Relationship Diagram

Tree-shaped Diagram

The tree-shaped diagram systematically outlines the complete spectrum of paths and tasks that must be carried out if one is to achieve a primary goal and its subgoals. Use of this tool takes one from generalities to details. By isolating all intermediate conditions that must be satisfied, it leads to identification of the most appropriate procedures and methods by which to achieve the established goals in order to solve a problem.

It possesses vast application possibilities: It can be used, for example, to represent and organize company policy, to detail activities within each company function, to determine actions that guarantee and improve quality, and to analyze customer wishes pertaining to new products.

In practice, it underlies all deployment activities; taking one toward a goal by helping one define actions with increasing precision and fullness. With this tool, the process can be carried out systematically, without errors or omissions. (See Figure 14-4.)

Matrix Diagram

The matrix diagram organizes a large group of characteristics, functions, and tasks so that elements that are logically connected are presented in graphic form. It also shows the importance of each connecting point in relation to each correlation. One uses it to establish and effectively present the relations that exist among a number of variables expressed in verbal form. A typical example is correlating the needs of customers with product and service characteristics within the context of quality deployment, or verifying the consistency of the various steps in hoshin management (see Figure 14-5).

Decision Tree (PDPC)

The decision tree, or process decision program chart (PDPC), outlines every conceivable occurrence as one progresses from def-

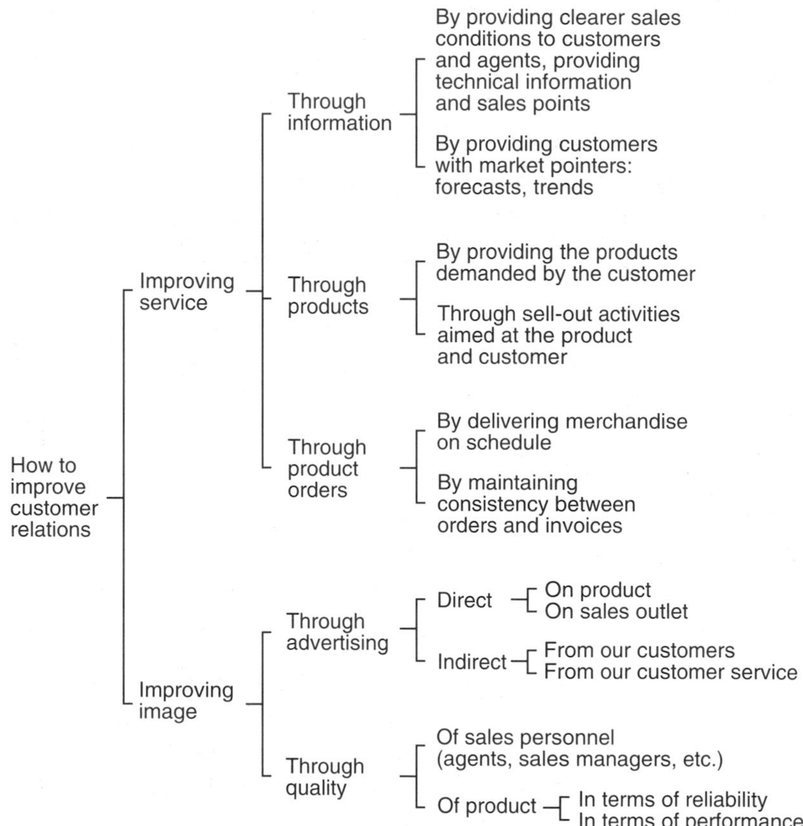

Figure 14-4. Tree-shaped Diagram

inition of a problem to possible solutions. It is useful when one wants to plan all possible chains of events that might occur during a project; it is useful, therefore, when one is not familiar with the problem or goal.

The PDPC diagram is a support tool to establish which procedures and actions are most appropriate to a project. It is used during the planning stage to forecast all circumstances that may be encountered during the course of a project, and to indicate the means for preventing them or counteracting them, weighing various alternatives.

<table>
<tr><td>Cutter footboard</td><td></td><td></td><td></td><td></td><td>●</td><td>●</td></tr>
<tr><td>Mixers</td><td></td><td></td><td></td><td>●</td><td></td><td>●</td></tr>
<tr><td>Batch preparation</td><td></td><td></td><td>●</td><td></td><td></td><td>●</td></tr>
<tr><td>Warehouse (raw materials)</td><td>●</td><td>●</td><td></td><td></td><td></td><td>●</td></tr>
<tr><td>Effect
Causes
Solutions</td><td>Emptying mill boxes</td><td>Inadequate palletization</td><td>Batch preparation on a few footboards</td><td>Overflowing loads</td><td>Difficulty in cleaning cutters</td><td>Lack of equipment for gathering waste</td></tr>
<tr><td>Intake vent</td><td>●</td><td></td><td></td><td></td><td></td><td></td></tr>
<tr><td>Hamper alteration</td><td>●</td><td></td><td></td><td></td><td></td><td></td></tr>
<tr><td>Metal containers</td><td></td><td>●</td><td></td><td></td><td></td><td></td></tr>
<tr><td>Increased number of footboards</td><td></td><td></td><td>●</td><td></td><td></td><td></td></tr>
<tr><td>Planning loads with lower weight</td><td></td><td></td><td></td><td>●</td><td></td><td></td></tr>
<tr><td>Substitution of the cutting-screening system</td><td></td><td></td><td></td><td></td><td>●</td><td></td></tr>
<tr><td>Planned gathering of appropriate bins</td><td></td><td></td><td></td><td></td><td></td><td>●</td></tr>
</table>

Figure 14-5. Matrix Diagram: A Plan to Reduce Waste of Plastic Materials

PDPC is widely used in decision making when sufficient information is lacking, or when a particularly unstable environment exists, in order to identify useful methods or procedures to solve difficult problems. It is typically used in new product development, building and equipment, and data processing programs. It can also be useful for representing operational procedures in a production cycle or a system cycle, or for procedures to study and repair damaged machinery. (See Figures 14-6 and 14-7.)

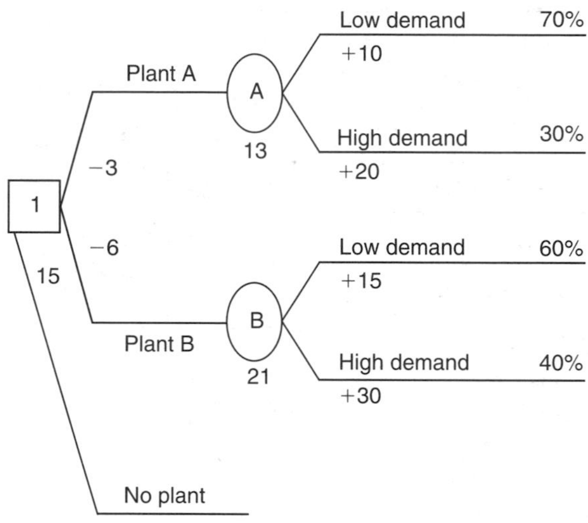

Figure 14-6. Decision Tree

Arrow Diagram (PERT)

The arrow diagram is useful for defining the most appropriate schedule for any task, and for ensuring that the task or actions proceed in the most effective way.

The PERT approach (*program evaluation and review technique*) is based on this diagram. One uses it, therefore, to represent a work program through a network of activities and events whose interdependence is fully displayed. It allows the establishment of a critical path, that is, the sequence of operations that conditions the total length of execution. It can also be used to effectively control work progress and optimize work schedules and procedures.

The arrow diagram is indispensable for long-term projects, such as the construction of a plant or the development of new products. (See Figure 14-8.)

Matrix Data-Analysis Diagram

The matrix data-analysis diagram is applied when one wants to analyze the data shown in a matrix diagram, so that each vari-

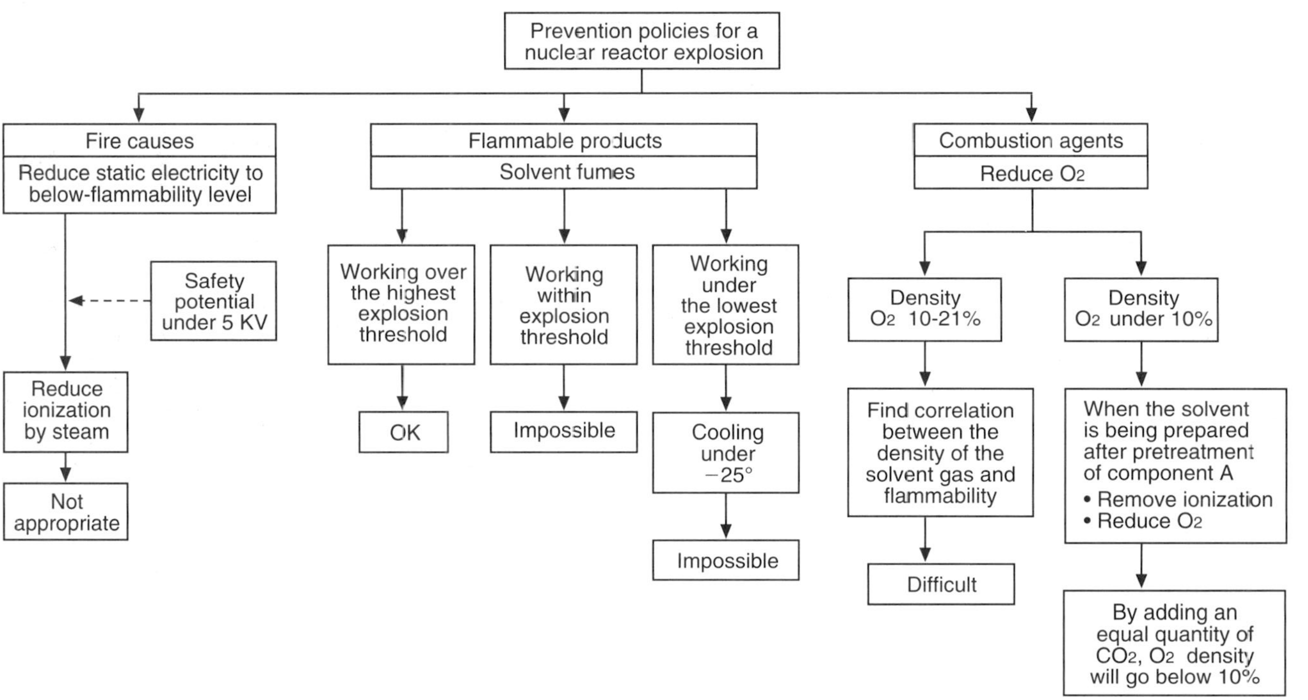

Figure 14-7. Decision Tree

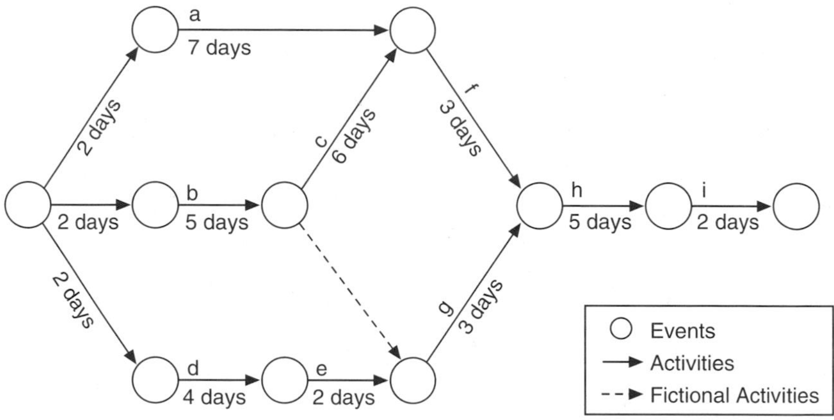

Figure 14-8. Arrow Diagram (PERT)

able can be easily examined, and the real strength of relationships between variables revealed. It is the only one of the seven management tools to be based on complex processing of numerical data, requiring the use of a computer. It allows a clear interpretation of great amounts of numerical data, isolating the principal variables; that is, it seeks the principal components (*principal component analysis*) with multivaried analysis techniques.

There are many applications of this tool. In fact, any time the phenomena being studied are a function of a high number of interacting variables, this diagram greatly facilitates the analysis and isolation of priority factors. Its use, therefore, appears advantageous in studying the parameters of production processes, in analyzing market information, in finding links between numerical and non-numerical variables, and so on. A simple example of these tools was shown in the previous chapter.

Analyzing and Defining Problems

Before we examine the characteristics and purposes of the seven management tools, let us consider a few concepts pertaining to the logical and mental processes involved in analysis and definition of problems. Stimuli from the outside world are received and memorized, forming a "mental picture" of the outside world that tends to organize itself in a hierarchical "tree-shaped" structure, of the kind shown in Figure 14-9.

The ideal structure to represent the outside world (for example, a problem) does not always appear evident from the start, since data appear a little at a time and in random order. As available information increases, it may become necessary to reorganize the tree, to take into account the new elements.

This process, in itself slow and random, can be made faster and more predictable through the adoption of systematic work procedures. For this purpose it is useful to carry out the analysis by gradually shifting attention toward levels of greater detail (top-down), or lesser detail (bottom-up). Top-down or bottom-up analysis must take place gradually, that is, without excessive jolts. Gradual analysis offers the following advantages:

- greater ease in understanding the problem
- greater clarity in the logical connection among elements of a problem
- better means to a more complete analysis

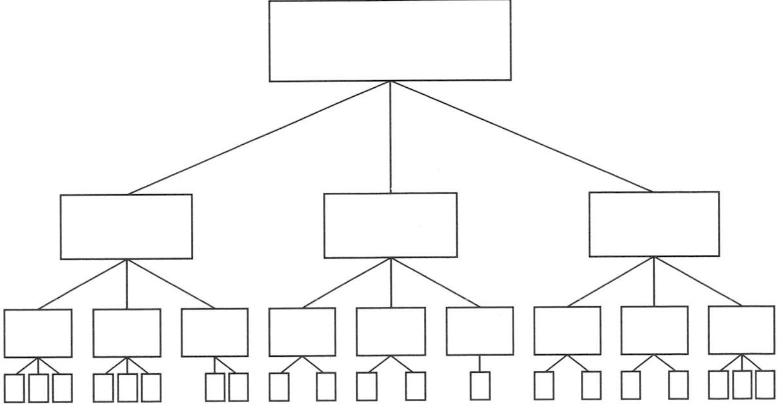

Figure 14-9. Hierarchical Tree Structure

Applications and Contributions of the Seven Management Tools

The seven management tools can be seen as:

- semantic tools, as they aid in understanding the meaning of available verbal information
- creative tools, because they help to reorganize available verbal information (reorganizing information is the mechanism at the base of the creative process)
- tools for problem solving, since they are used specifically to define and solve problems

Contributions of the seven management tools are listed in Figures 14-10 and Table 14-1. Such contribution is particularly essential in the following areas:

- improvement activities in the area of clerical work
- analyzing information from outside the company
- new product development processes
- areas in which one must operate and reason in terms of extremely low rates of defects (parts per million)

More generally, these tools can be put to good use wherever there is a need to pay attention to all details, and to analyze and set verbal data into a framework that gives them a clear and univocal meaning and thus leads to rational decisions.

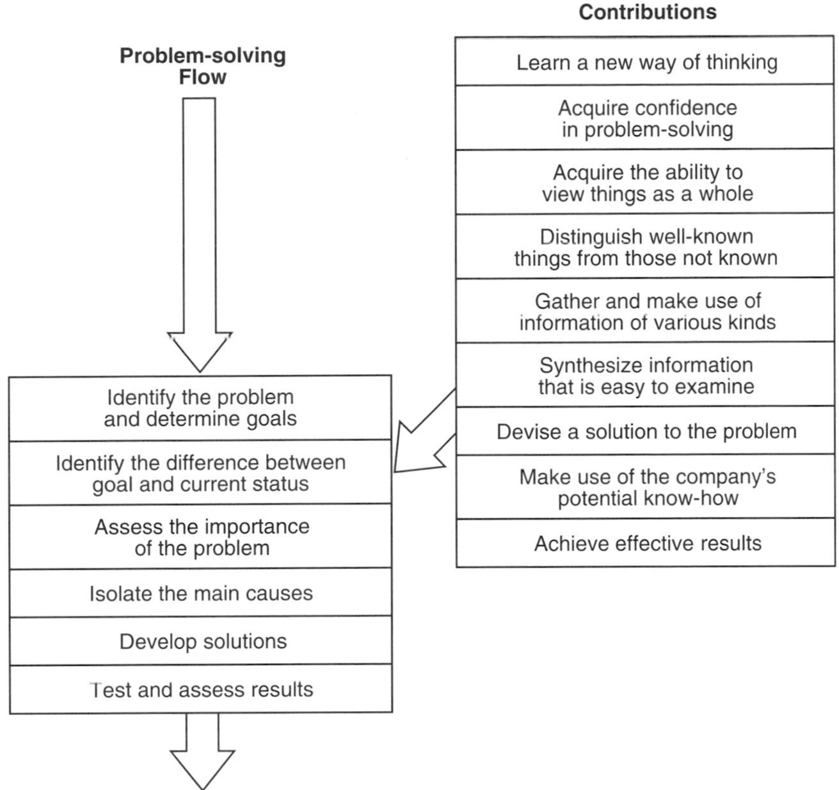

Figure 14-10. Contributions of the Seven Management Tools

Table 14-1. Applications of the Seven Management Tools

Area	Applications	Relationship Diagram	Affinity Diagram	Tree-shaped Diagram	Matrix Diagram	Matrix Data-Analysis	Decision Diagram	Arrow Diagram
Design and quality assurance	Understanding needs and translating them into product characteristics		●	●	●	●		
	Connection between product characteristics and process parameters			●	●			
	Clearly establish facts that increase product reliability	●	●	●	●	●	●	
	Clearly establish relationship between function and cost			●	●			
	Assess research and development departments		●					
Production	Clearly establish reasons for shipping delays			●	●			●
	Reduce defects at receiving stage			●	●			
	Analyze reasons for nonconformity	●		●	●	●		
	Management of complaints and quality improvement	●		●	●	●		
	Productivity improvement	●			●		●	
	Checking and reducing inventory	●			●			
	Cost controls and reduction by value analysis	●		●				
	Plant control and improvement through planned investments						●	●
	Safety control and improvement against accidents and mishaps	●	●			●	●	

Area	Applications	Relationship Diagram	Affinity Diagram	Tree-shaped Diagram	Matrix Diagram	Matrix Data-Analysis	Decision Diagram	Arrow Diagram
Management	Policy deployment	●	●	●	●			
	Defining responsibilities				●			
	Development of a realistic plan						●	●
Personnel	Establishing priorities for education and training activities in relation to goals	●	●	●	●			
	Clearly establish areas of responsibility in relation to tasks			●	●			
	Strengthen the activities of circles	●	●	●				
Marketing and Sales	Classify needs and correlate with new or current products	●	●	●	●	●		
	Analyze competition			●	●	●		
	Demand forecast			●		●		
	Stratify by product, channel, area					●		
	Develop activities and sales promotion	●						●
	Rationalize information and market feedback			●	●			

CHAPTER FIFTEEN

Quality Function Deployment

Introduction

Quality function deployment (QFD) is a method to ensure quality of new products starting from the planning and development stages. It enables a company to determine upstream the quality of design needed to satisfy a customer and, subsequently, to extract the key points linked with quality assurance (QA).

QFD evolved from QA: In Japan during the 1960s, when it was understood that the winning strategy lay in the constant development of new products, it became increasingly obvious that QA activities aimed primarily at production processes were no longer sufficient. It was necessary to ensure quality from the upstream stages of production, "building in" quality at the planning stages. This need led to QFD, which is a technique to guarantee QA at the initial stages of a product's life cycle. QFD can therefore be viewed as a part of QA, as shown in Figure 15-1.

Historically, the beginnings of QFD can be placed around 1966, the year in which Kiyotaka Narumi, from Bridgestone Tires, submitted a list of quality assurance items (the customer's real demands), juxtaposed to those features which the

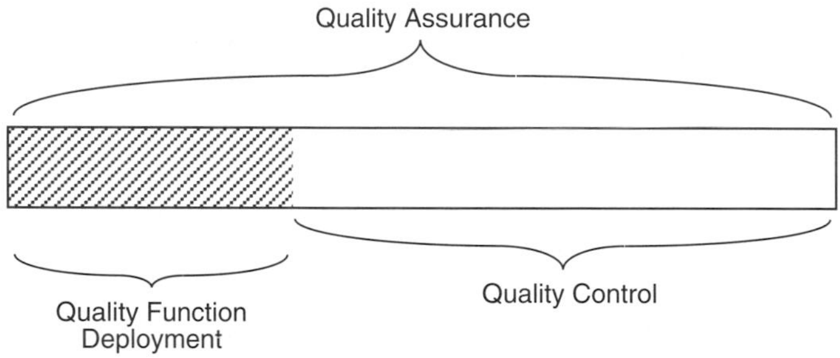

Figure 15-1. Relationship between QFD and Quality Assurance

product should possess in order to satisfy the customer (substitutive features).

In 1967, a perfected version of the list developed by Narumi was applied to the components division of Matsushita Electric Industries (now Matsushita Electric Parts). However, until that time, applications of the basic techniques of QFD did not yet permit the establishment of an overall plan for quality, since too much importance was given to deployment.

This obstacle was overcome in 1972, by Professor Akao, who, in cooperation with Professors Mizuno and Furukawa, submitted a quality chart to a department of Mitsubushi Heavy Industries, operating in the shipyard business.

In the following years, applications within Japanese industry gradually increased. This is confirmed by the number of publications devoted to the subject, which increased from 5 in 1971 to 45 in 1986.

The Principles Inspiring QFD

A few thoughts about the principles characterizing QFD follow.

Customer Demand

A customer of any product or service hopes to have the fewest possible problems deriving from its use — ideally, none.

In fact, however, such a perfect product is hard to find. One might legitimately ask, why does a product not always present the features required by the customer? or why do new products create problems for the customer?

To answer these questions, one must examine the company process that leads to creation of a new product.

The Traditional Process for New Product Development

The process generally followed by a company starts from customer demands, which are usually expressed in vague terms, through qualitative criteria such as "pleasant appearance," "easy to use," "works well," "safe," "comfortable," "long-lasting," or "luxurious." While these criteria are important for the customer, they are vague and difficult to fully understand for the company. Developing a new product typically requires the following stages:

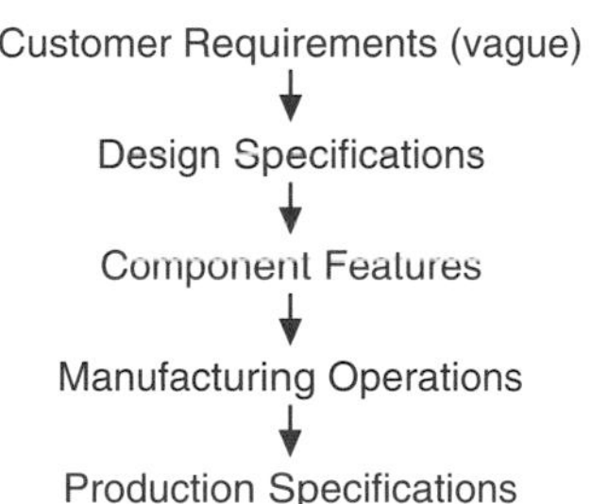

This process is intended to promote customer satisfaction, and it would, were it not for one detail: in most cases the customer's needs are studied far less carefully than the product's subsystems and components. This is precisely because of the vague terms in which those needs are expressed. Not enough attention and resources are paid during the initial stages of product research, and this causes problems and dissatisfaction (and, consequently, costs) after a product is launched. This void is filled by QFD.

Figure 15-2 compares the distribution of resources within Japanese companies with that of American ones at the various development stages of a product. As is evident, these distributions constitute two mirror-image curves. This shows how the Japanese make a greater effort at the development stage of a product, focusing on strict planning and on problem prevention, thus reducing problem-solving activities when the product is on the market. The key is to carefully design a product at the initial stages, devoting much effort to understanding in detail a customer's needs, and dividing them into basic elements that can be precisely correlated with the product's features or components. This requires a great initial effort, as in-depth research must be carried out not only on the technical characteristics of a product, and its implications for production, but also on the needs, both explicit and implicit, of the customer. On the other hand, this preventive approach is more effective than the reactive one that occurs at a more advanced stage.

The Definition of Quality Function Deployment

QFD constitutes a framework of procedures and techniques to determine the quality of product design, through a

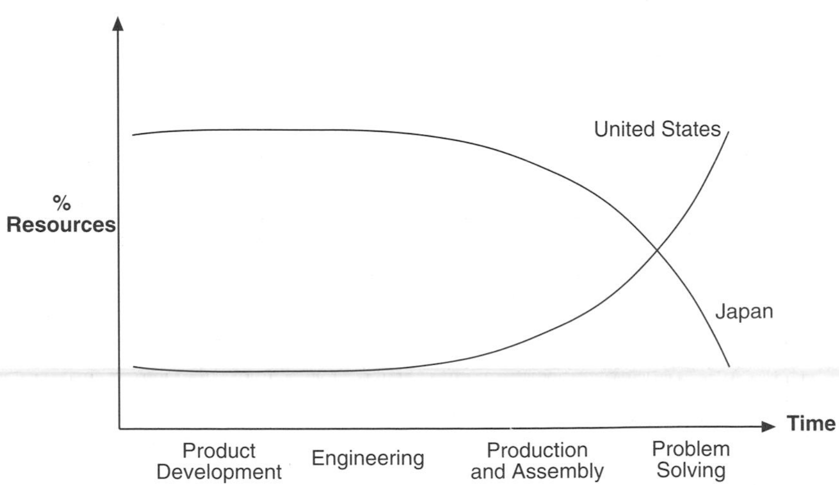

Figure 15-2. Resource Allocation for New Product Development

process that transforms a user's needs into the corresponding features (quality features) that a product must possess. This process systematically develops existing relations

- between product features and each functional component of the product
- among all activities and resources that directly affect the quality to be developed, by defining goals and means at each stage of the process

The last part of this definition requires a brief explanation. To transform customer needs into product features one must abandon the traditional new product development process, summarized in Figure 15-3, in favor of a new one, shown in Figure 15-4.

The new process is no longer a strictly functional job, with a constant deferment of activity, but a highly integrated activity at all stages of product development. It can thus prevent interpretation errors or misunderstandings caused by subjective thinking. It also overcomes communication problems: In the traditional process, marketing executives sometimes have problems understanding technical language, while technicians may consider customer needs to be intrusions on their work. This creates distance between the customer's request and the company's response, and makes the response inadequate.

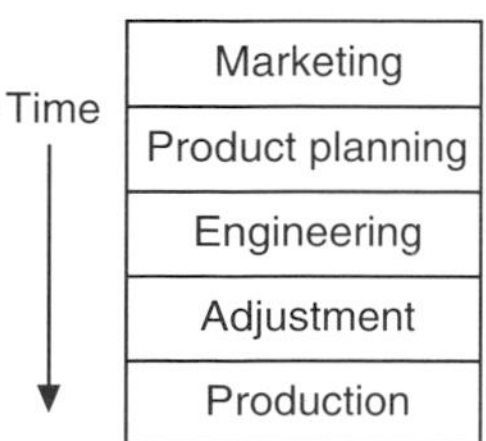

Figure 15-3. Traditional Product Development

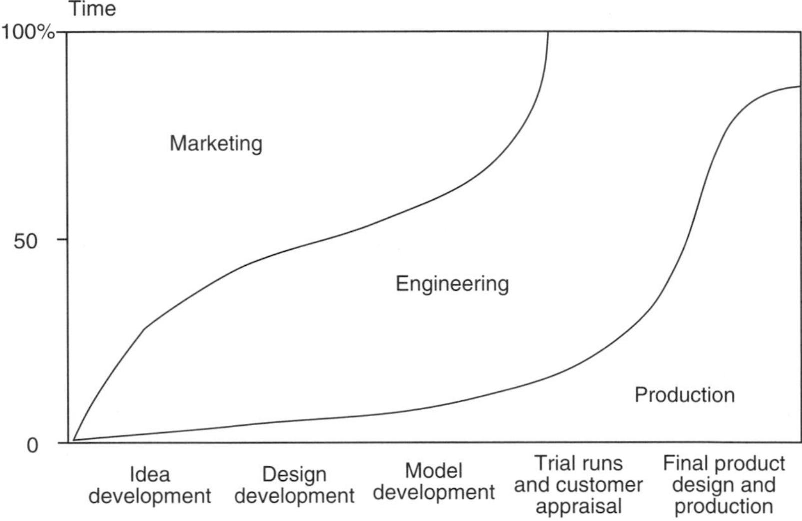

Figure 15-4. Ideal Product Development

With QFD, on the other hand, one can give quality concepts a concrete form from the beginning. The technique ensures that quality is already "built-in" to the product from its planning and development stages, and it promotes consistency among the various stages. In essence, QFD prevents companies from creating products that correspond perfectly to specifications, but that nobody wants.

QFD consists of basic activities and techniques that each company "personalizes" according to special needs.

"Upstream" Quality Construction

Besides allowing a better focus on customers needs, QFD virtually eliminates the number of design modifications needed. In Figure 15-5 Japanese and American automobile companies are compared with regard to product modifications before and after introduction on the market. An American company increases the number of changes it makes over time, with problems shown and resolved through testing of the product. After pro-

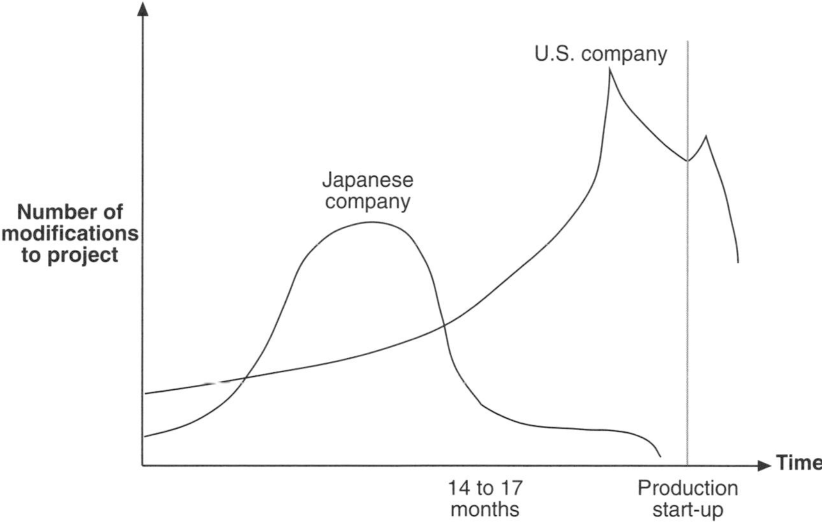

Figure 15-5. Number of Modifications to New Projects (Car Industry)

duction has begun, new problems are discovered, and these lead to further modifications. A Japanese company, on the other hand, carries out fewer but more significant modifications during the initial stages, and does 90 percent of these more than a year before production begins. The crucial aspect of this method is that modifications are less expensive because they are made on paper, and they anticipate problems, rather than pursuing them. This leads to considerable savings in the time needed to develop a new product, which is one-third to one-half of the normal period.

The Simplified Process of Quality Function Deployment

The flow of QFD, according to a simplified process, takes place in four stages:

- planning
- design

- preproduction
- initial production

The logical process that underlies new product development with QFD can be enclosed within a chart; to describe it in brief, one can make reference to the quality chart (one of the basic QFD charts), a graphic meeting point of customer needs, production capabilities, and all comparisons and parameters needed to determine the necessary quality. The quality chart is illustrated in Figure 15-6; the text following presents a few clarifications of the six areas described therein.

Area 1: quality needs deployment. In this area, the customer's primary requirements are detailed according to a branch struc-

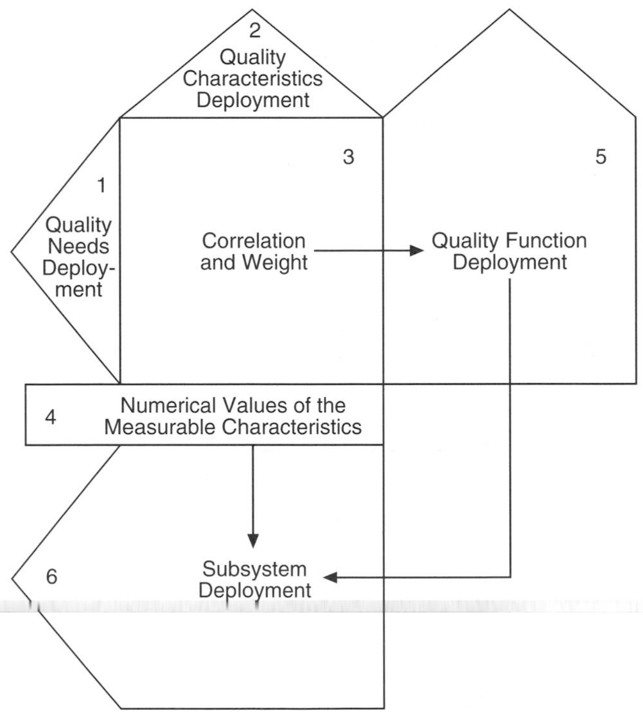

Figure 15-6. Quality Table

ture, from the general to the particular (see example in Figure 15-7). In essence, the procedures necessary for achievement of the primary purpose are established. Such procedures, in turn, constitute the secondary level of goals, which call for the identification of their own procedures, and so on, until the fourth or fifth level of details pertaining to aims and needs is reached.

Preparation of area 1 is completed with the identification of priority needs among all elementary needs listed, through, for example, surveys among potential product users.

Also, in relation to all elementary needs, one compares the position of a company with that of its competition to determine items of superiority and items of inferiority.

Area 2: quality characteristics deployment. In this area, all technical requirements necessary to make the final product correspond to the original needs and desires are displayed. In essence, one translates the required features into measurable quality features, which can be represented with precision. Starting with lower-level quality requirements, one isolates the corresponding quality features and then groups them together according to a tree-shaped structure analogous to that of quality needs (see Figure 15-8).

Customer's Quality Requirements		Quality Detail	Quality Characteristics	Measurement Unit
Clear and precise vision potential	Sufficient visibility of distant objects	Sufficient luminosity	Electric power	W
		Sufficient width of light band	Depth of band	MT
			Penetration ratio	
			Reflexivity	K

Figure 15-8. Quality Characteristics Deployment

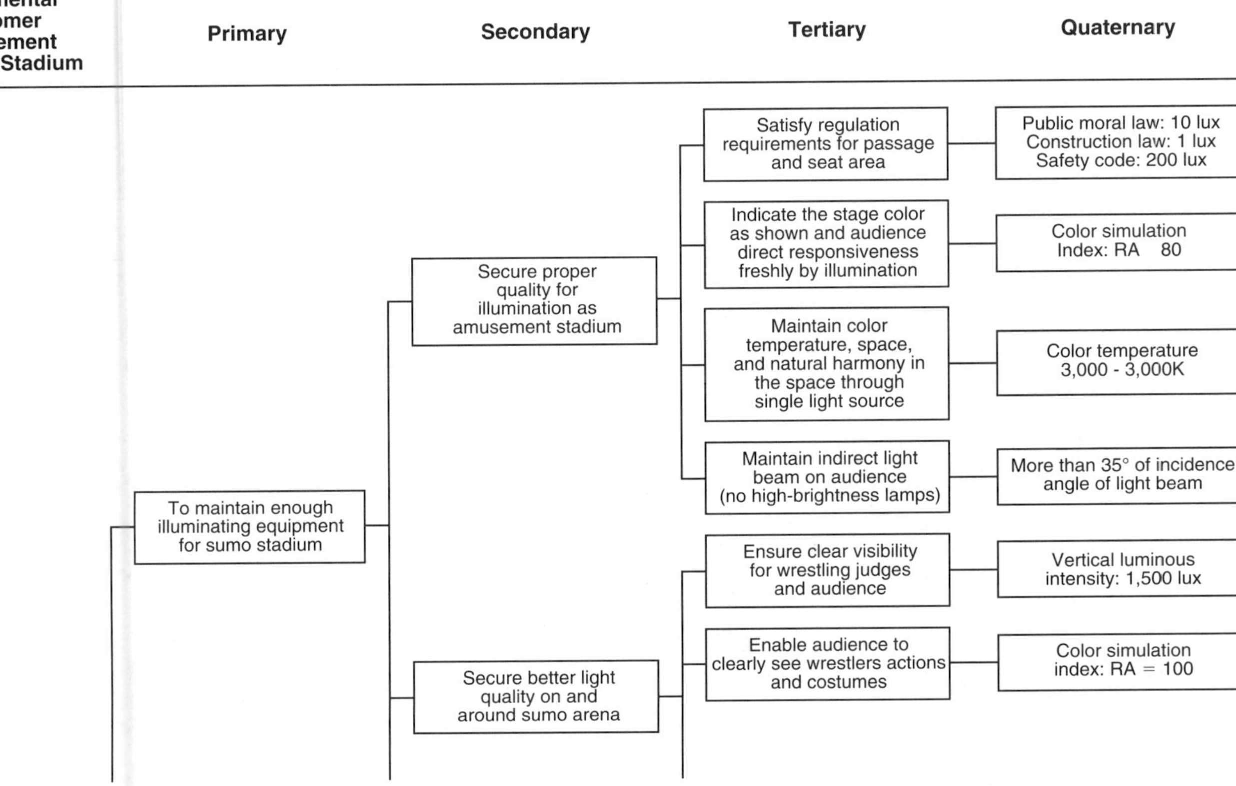
Fundamental Customer Requirement for Sumo Stadium
Primary
Secondary
Tertiary
Quaternary
To maintain enough illuminating equipment for sumo stadium
Secure proper quality for illumination as amusement stadium
Secure better light quality on and around sumo arena
Satisfy regulation requirements for passage and seat area
Indicate the stage color as shown and audience direct responsiveness freshly by illumination
Maintain color temperature, space, and natural harmony in the space through single light source
Maintain indirect light beam on audience (no high-brightness lamps)
Ensure clear visibility for wrestling judges and audience
Enable audience to clearly see wrestlers actions and costumes
Public moral law: 10 lux
Construction law: 1 lux
Safety code: 200 lux
Color simulation Index: RA 80
Color temperature 3,000 - 3,000K
More than 35° of incidence angle of light beam
Vertical luminous intensity: 1,500 lux
Color simulation index: RA = 100

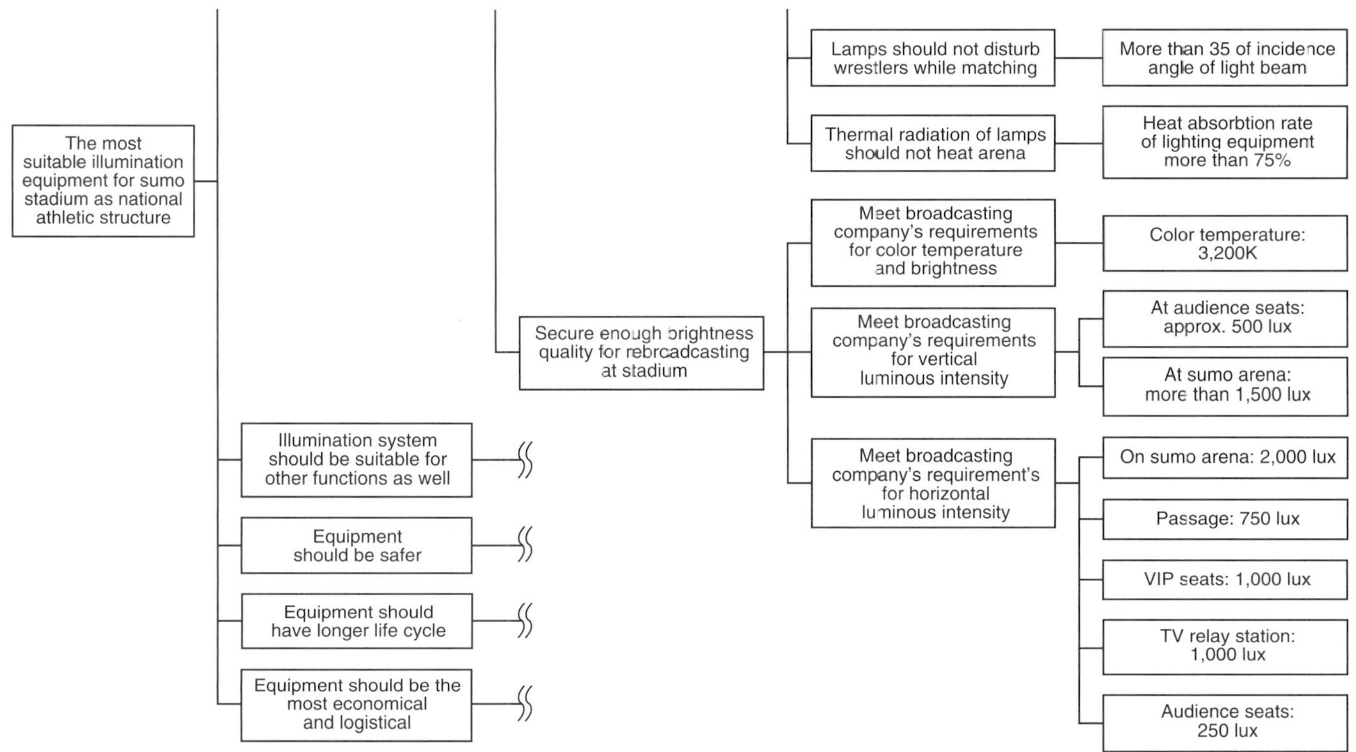

Figure 15-7. Quality Table of Illumination in Stadium (Deployment of Requirements)

Area 3: correlation and weight. After completing areas 1 and 2, as described above, one must determine relationships between the quality requested and quality features established later. In essence, it is necessary to establish whether there exists a relationship between every elementary need and every quality feature identified, establishing also the "intensity" of this relationship (strong, normal, uncertain). One does this by compiling the matrix in area 3, which results from the meeting of needs (area l) and features (area 2). An example pertaining to a car's headlights is shown in Figure 15-10 (pages 242-243).

The joint processing of information concerning elementary priority needs, as well as the most essential qualities and the intensity of relationships between areas 1 and 2, all point out the priority development criteria for the new product.

Area 4: numerical values of the measurable characteristics. In this area the numerical values to be assigned to each quality feature are shown. These values should guarantee the fulfillment of all the needs for which a relationship has been established with the feature under scrutiny. The value to assign to each feature also derives from a comparison with products previously created, as well as with those of competitors (Figure 15-9).

Area 5: quality function deployment. Once customer needs and related quality have been identified and explained, the next step consists in identifying which technologies are needed in order to transfer and integrate into the product the designed features. This area consists mainly in connecting individual needs to product function, by analyzing the use of the product itself.

Area 6: subsystem deployment. The purpose of this area is to facilitate the integrated design of quality specifications for individual components, in order to prevent problems related to connection or integration.

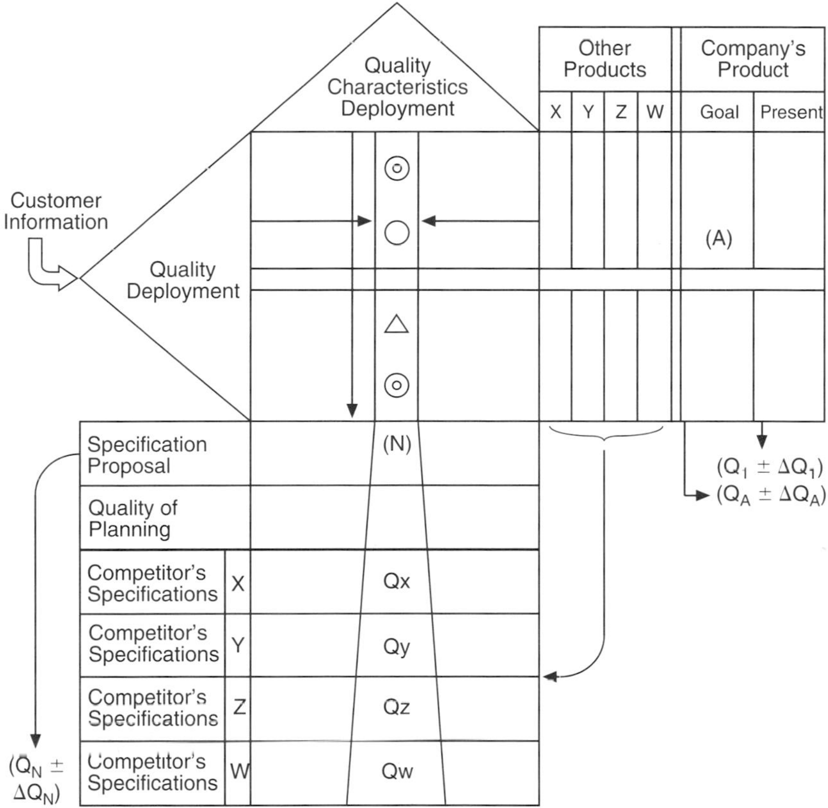

Figure 15-9. Quality Characteristics: Assigning Numerical Values

Once a product's functioning has been determined and described, one must ensure that the development of individual components, subsystems, and systems takes place in a coordinated and well-integrated fashion. Compiling this area involves detailing for each subsystem and component all that we indicated in previous steps. After such an area has been compiled, one can draw up a table for each component, showing quality features, and the corresponding values, as well as an index of their importance. With this the planning stages and design input are completed.

Quality Deployment: Primary	Secondary	Tertiary	Quaternary	Light Distribution: Light distribution angle: Beam-lens light distribution angle	Beam-lens size	Filament-changing angle	Beam-changing angle	Light Distribution: Light beam: Light intensity	Transmission factor	Reflectivity	Color temperature	Electric power	Voltage	Longevity: Efficiency: Airtightness	Filament strength	Sealed gas property	Bulb size (volume)	Consumed electricity	Safety: Redundancy	Recovery angle
Provides unobstructed visibility to front	Driver's visibility is clear	Distant objects visible	Lamp bright enough	○	○	△	△	○	◎	◎	○	◎	○					◎		
			Light beam spread enough	◎	○	△		△	△	△		△						△		
			Light beam straight enough			△	◎													
			Light beam focused on the object	◎																
		Close objects visible	Low beams bright enough	○	○	◎	△	△	△	◎	◎	○	◎	○				◎		
			Light beam spread enough	◎	○	△		△	△	△		△						△		
			Light beam straight enough			△	◎													
			Light beam focused on the object	◎																
		Enough visibility in any circumstances	Enough visibility in all weather conditions	○		△														
			Enough visibility when steering to both sides																	
			Enough visibility in bumpy conditions																	
			Stable visibility in any loading conditions																	
		No glare to driver	No glare to driver	◎	△	○	○	△												
		Enough brightness to read road signs	Beam to upper directions	◎																
		Enough brightness to identify colors	Beam bright enough to show colors					○			◎	○						○		
			Beam bright enough for color-blind drivers								○	○						○		

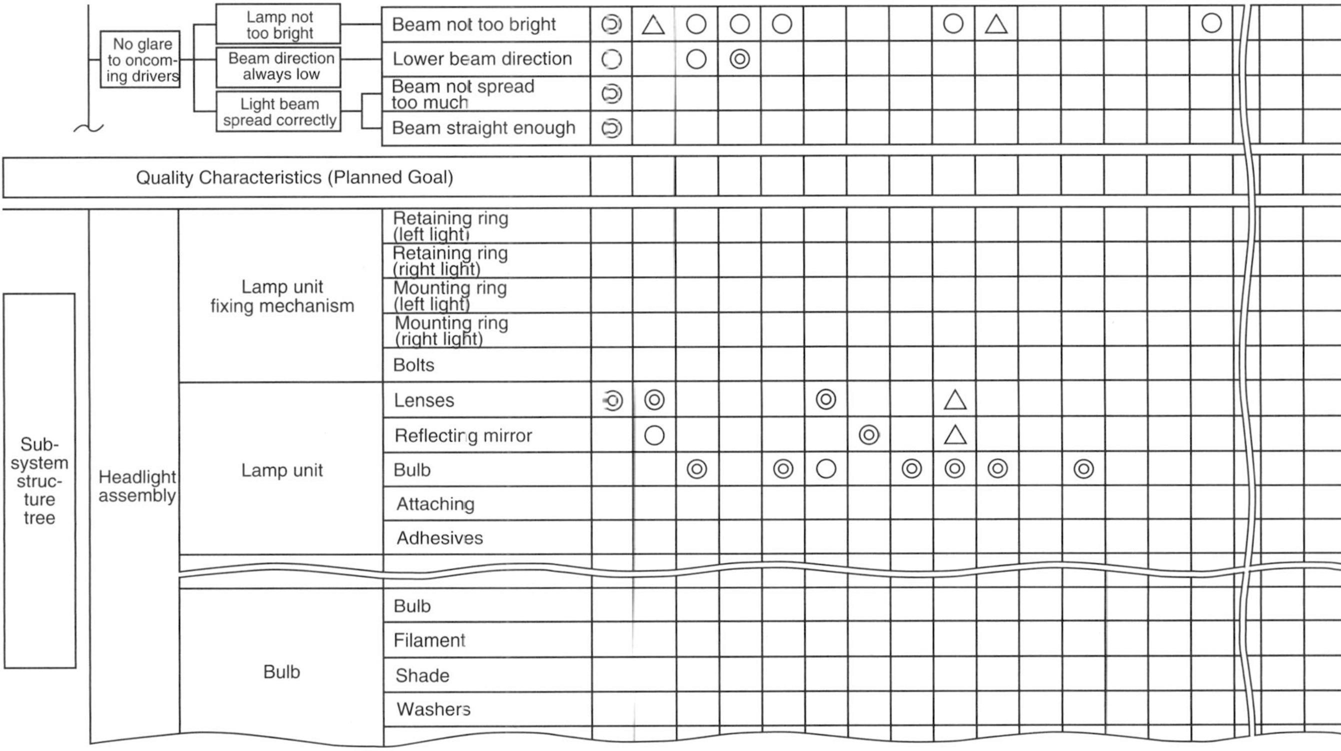

Figure 15-10. Quality Table for Car Headlights

Once the components have been determined and correlations between them and previously identified features established, one can construct QFD tables for each component:

- development of component detail design
- identification of the aspects linked to the production process
- definition of quality control broad procedures

QFD, therefore, enables all these activities to be consistent with each other, and to reflect the initial quality tables, thus allowing customer wishes to guide all stages of product development, design, and production.

The Complete QFD Process

Beginning in the 1980s, the structure and activities of QFD were further refined to make new product development increasingly effective. This happened, on the one hand, through a growing integration among the various activities involved, and on the other, through an increasingly organic use of other methods and tools (*fault tree analysis,* etc.). In this context, further *deployments* have been developed, such as: *cost deployment, technology deployment,* and *reliability deployment.*

The introduction of this advanced plan within a company implies the completion of experimentation according to a basic plan ("simplified process"). To give an idea of how it is articulated, we have shown, in Figure 15-11, a comparison between the simplified process (sketched) and the complete process.

Results Obtainable with QFD

QFD is a relatively simple yet very detailed system. It may appear too detailed and weighty, yet the results obtained by Japanese companies speak clearly. First of all, it should be reiterated that QFD's main strength lies in its promotion of product development through *prevention* rather than *reaction,* with a positive impact on the number of modifications requested of the product, as already shown in Figure 15-5. This causes a direct reduction in the costs linked to launching a new product.

The example shown in Figure 15-12 refers to Toyota. It shows the impact of QFD after seven years of application, during which four new van models were launched. The sketched area represents the costs encountered after production was launched. At Toyota such costs are considered losses, which must tend toward zero. The light area represents preparation costs, especially operator training. We see that in seven years there was a 61 percent reduction in start-up costs.

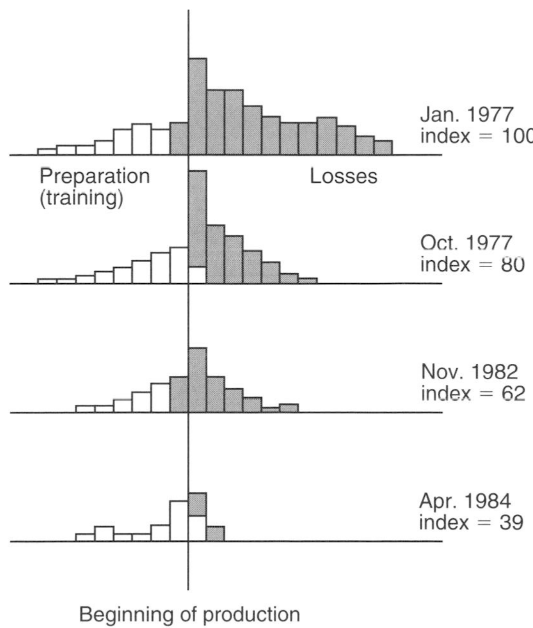

Figure 15-12. Toyota: Costs Associated with Production Start-up

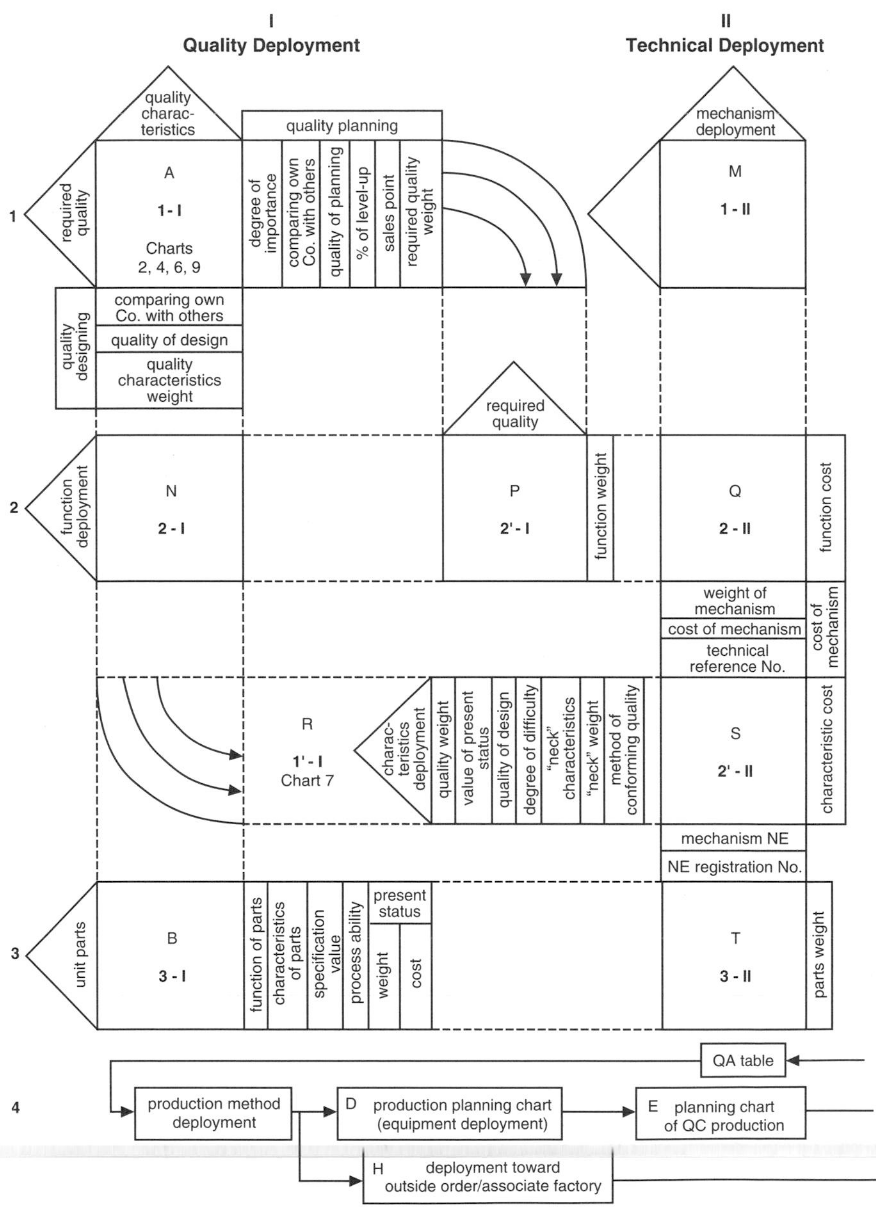

Source: Futaba Electronics Industries example in Yoji Akao, ed., *Quality Function Deployment: Integrating Customer Requirements into Product Design* (Cambridge, Mass.: Productivity Press, 1990).

Figure 15-11. Quality Deployment (Including Technical, Cost, and Reliability Deployment)

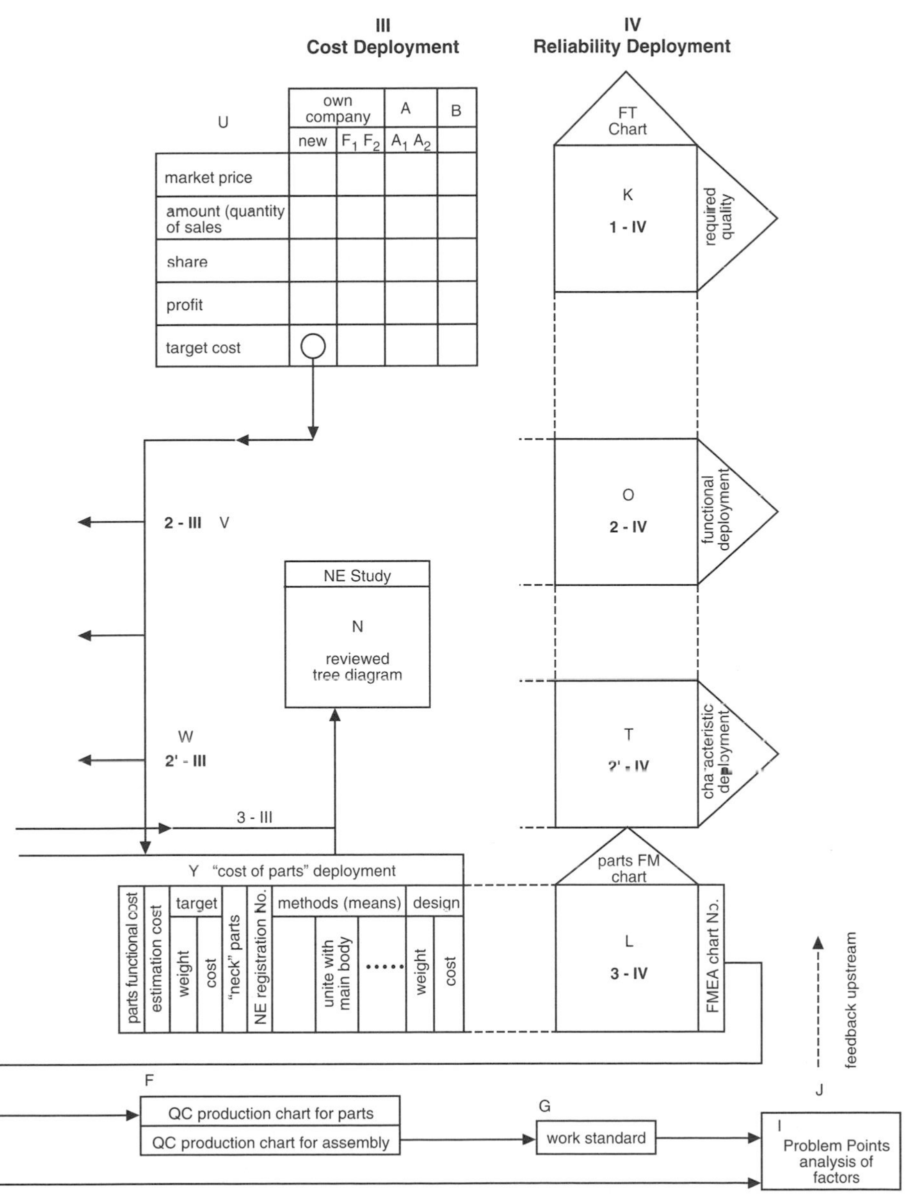
III
Cost Deployment
IV
Reliability Deployment
U
own company
A
B
new
F1 F2
A1 A2
market price
amount (quantity of sales
share
profit
target cost
FT Chart
K
1 - IV
required quality
O
2 - IV
functional deployment
2 - III
V
NE Study
N
reviewed tree diagram
T
2' - IV
characteristic deployment
W
2' - III
3 - III
parts FM chart
Y "cost of parts" deployment
parts functional cost
estimation cost
target
weight
cost
"neck" parts
NE registration No.
methods (means)
unite with main body
design
weight
cost
L
3 - IV
FMEA chart No.
feedback upstream
J
F
QC production chart for parts
QC production chart for assembly
G
work standard
I
Problem Points analysis of factors

Beyond this example, it is possible to summarize the benefits of QFD in three categories linked to three key moments in the life of a product:

Benefits Linked to the Stages Preceding the Market Launch

1. Full understanding of customer needs: By asking what is important to customers and what their expectations are, one is less likely to start off on the wrong foot. With QFD, it is impossible to miss the messages sent by the customer along the path of product or service development.
2. Lead time reduction: By increasing investment, particularly in (human resources development) design, there is a later savings in product development time.
3. Development time reduction: Use of QFD leads to rationalizing of resources, which has a positive influence on development costs.
4. Increase in action speed: QFD makes things move faster, because planning takes place at the initial stages and mistakes in setting priorities and goals are minimized.

Benefits Linked to the Start-up Phase

1. Minimizing start-up mistakes: Products that are correctly planned and designed require fewer modifications when they go into production.
2. Start-up cost reduction: Improvements in planning and testing carried out during the first stages of the development process result in lower costs. This is because modifications carried out 12 months before a product is launched are less expensive than those carried out, for example, 9 months later.
3. Improvement in product quality: Well-designed products are usually better in quality.

4. Increased productivity: Products that are carefully designed develop fewer problems during the production and assembly stages. This leads to increased productivity, a better use of installations and tools, and lower costs.
5. Improved communications: Designing with QFD keeps all those responsible for the various stages of the process informed about relations between output features at each stage, as well as about the features of the final product.

Benefits Linked to the Stage Following Start-up

1. Reduction in breakdowns and warranty interventions: A product that works well from the beginning performs better and generates fewer costs linked to warranty repairs.
2. Improved customer satisfaction: To give what the customer demands, and something more, at a lower cost (exciting quality) is a very important plus.
3. Know-how continuity: QFD paves a "path" that can be followed at later stages. It also becomes a valid model for new people entering the company, and prevents the loss of know-how when people leave the company.

CHAPTER SIXTEEN

The CEDAC System

Introduction

The CEDAC system is a method for simply and effectively defining, managing, and carrying out improvements.* It has been implemented successfully in many companies in Italy and in a number of other countries, including Japan and the United States.

CEDAC means causc-and-cffcct diagram with the addition of cards. The CEDAC system is based on three basic assumptions for carrying out improvement activities in the most effective way:

- Always concentrate on the precise feature of a problem.
- Always have within sight both problems and actions to overcome them.
- Carry out the improvement on site, that is, where the waste is generated.

* CEDAC is the registered trademark of Productivity, Inc. for its training events and related materials.

The CEDAC system is extremely flexible, and is useful in the management of various aspects of improvement. The principal aspects are

- setting out and defining improvement activities (*policy deployment*)
- continuous improvement and monitoring of company performance indicators
- improvement projects
- standardization of improvement solutions

The CEDAC system was developed by Ryuji Fukuda, professor at the University of Kobe and a consultant to many international corporations. In 1978, the Deming Prize Committee awarded Fukuda the prestigious Nikkei Prize for his article "The Application of the CEDAC for Standardization and Quality Control." He is the author of several books about CEDAC and related improvement systems.*

The CEDAC System

The purpose of the CEDAC system is to deal with and eliminate any kind of waste within the company (product defects, inventory, delays, etc.), that is, any element that does not add "value" to the company's product or service. The system is based on three techniques:

1. window analysis
2. window development
3. CEDAC diagram

This chapter will be devoted to analyzing the CEDAC diagram. However, a brief explanation of the other two techniques will help to clarify the system.

---

* See *Managerial Engineering: Techniques for Improving Quality and Productivity in the Workplace* (Cambridge, Mass.: Productivity Press, 1986), and *CEDAC: A Tool for Continuous Systematic Improvement* (Cambridge, Mass.: Productivity Press, 1990). — Ed.

The goal of *window analysis* is to "code" the types of waste found, so that one can effectively determine what actions are necessary to eliminate them. It is based on a double-entry matrix, on which two units involved in a problem confront each other on how to prevent waste (see Figure 16-1). The meeting point between the two knowledge levels that characterize the units determines the identification on the matrix of one of the possible nine boxes, which are grouped according to four possible situations:

- *Situation A:* The method is established, known, and applied in its entirety by all parties involved. This constitutes the ideal situation, and does not require further analysis.
- *Situation B:* The correct method is established and known by all interested parties, but not implemented correctly, in its entirety, or at all by some. This category includes human error, intentional negligence, lack of time, and distraction.
- *Situation C:* The correct method is established, but some individuals involved are not fully aware of it. This happens because of information or communication.
- *Situation D:* The correct method is not established and not known by anyone.

Window analysis, therefore, provides a quantitative view of the division of defects in various situations (areas B, C, and D).

Window development (situations B and C) is useful for further analysis of those situations in which a correct method has been determined but not altogether known or implemented. It is developed through specific techniques, such as

- on-error training (OET)
- human error analysis (HEA)
- skill analysis

			Method for Preventing the Problem		
	Unit X / Unit Y		Known		Unknown
			Practiced	Not Practiced	
Method for Preventing the Problem	Known	Practiced	A		
		Not Practiced		B	
	Unknown			C	D

Figure 16-1. Window Analysis

- visual control system
- day-to-day management

For area D, in which the correct method has not been determined, (and thus there is great improvement potential), the CEDAC diagram is applied (see Figure 16-2).

The CEDAC Diagram

The CEDAC diagram is both a tool and an organizational form to manage important improvement plans. With CEDAC one applies cause-and-effect logic, by focusing the analysis and participants' contributions more sharply.

Upon initial analysis, CEDAC appears like a simple cause-and-effect diagram (see Figure 16-3). As a matter of fact, this diagram operates on a scale higher than that of the traditional cause-and-effect diagram. CEDAC gathers in one place both the "description" and the "proposal" (how to intervene on the causes that generate an effect).

It looks like a poster, placed where a problem is to be dealt with (department, office, etc.). It must be highly visible, and everyone must have access to it. It is represented graphically, as

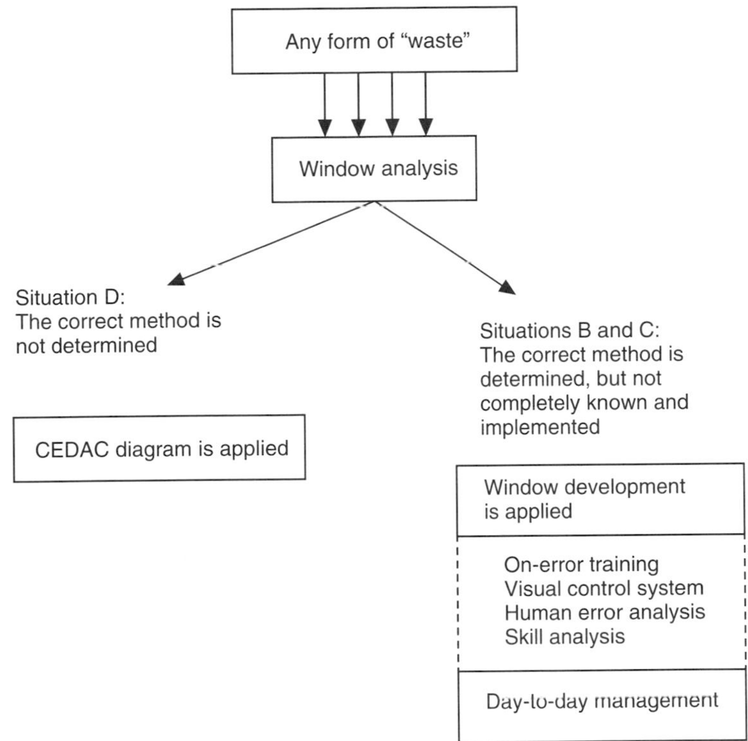

Figure 16-2. Use of the CEDAC System

said, by a cause-and-effect diagram. What increases its power is the fact that, on the effects side, there are some indicators (graphs, tables, histograms, etc.) that are continuously updated on the progress of the problem under scrutiny (number of defective products per day, accidents per month on a particular machine, number of warranty repairs, etc.). This allows all the people interested in the problem to "see" at all times the evolution of the problem itself.

Across from the effect side, the cause side is open to anyone, at any time. Once the main branches have been identified, anyone can signal the problems encountered or regarded as relevant through a special card, which has to be signed in case any

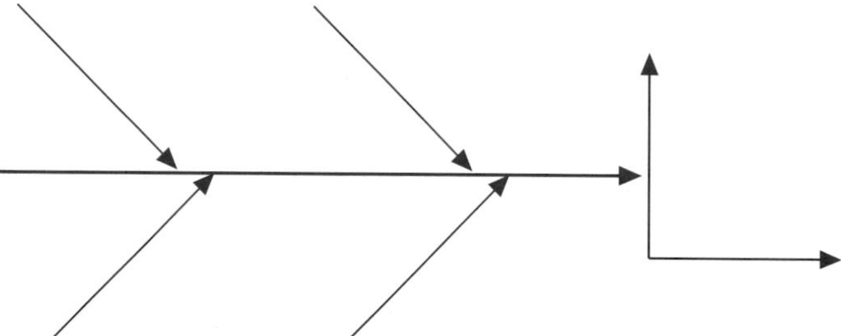

Figure 16-3. Basic CEDAC Diagram

further clarification is needed. At the same time, with a different color card, anyone can suggest a remedy to a particular problem.

Since on one side there are problems and suggestions to solve the problem, and on the other side there are indicators, one can easily verify how these indicators move as countermeasures are tested one after the other.

The problem chosen must be of considerable importance in terms of quality, so that those participating do not see their efforts produce insignificant and unmotivating results.

With CEDAC there is no need to hold meetings so that people can contribute, since they can do so on the spot as the idea strikes them. This eliminates the problem of ideas that are forgotten and makes the contribution more immediate. The CEDAC diagram constitutes a tool for

- collecting and depicting the ideas of many people, without having to organize special meetings
- keeping attention focused a problem that the company regards as important to overcome
- keeping people informed in real time about new process standards

Participants in Use of the CEDAC Diagram

These are two key players in the use and management of a CEDAC diagram: the leader and the team. The problem to be solved is entrusted to the CEDAC leader, who sets up and manages the CEDAC diagram while coordinating all activities created by it. To enlist support in these activities, the leader may decide to form a team of people (the CEDAC team). Individual skills may be useful in relation to organizational, technical, operational, or other aspects of the problem, and the leader may assign particular tasks to members of the team. The CEDAC leader organizes brief but frequent meetings with the team as needed during the project. Team members must actively participate in the CEDAC diagram with their cards.

Building and Managing the CEDAC Diagram

The CEDAC diagram can be divided into two parts (see Figure 16-4):

- the effects side (usually the right side of the diagram), where all graphs monitoring the progress of the project are contained
- the causes side, where all cards from all participants in the CEDAC diagram are placed

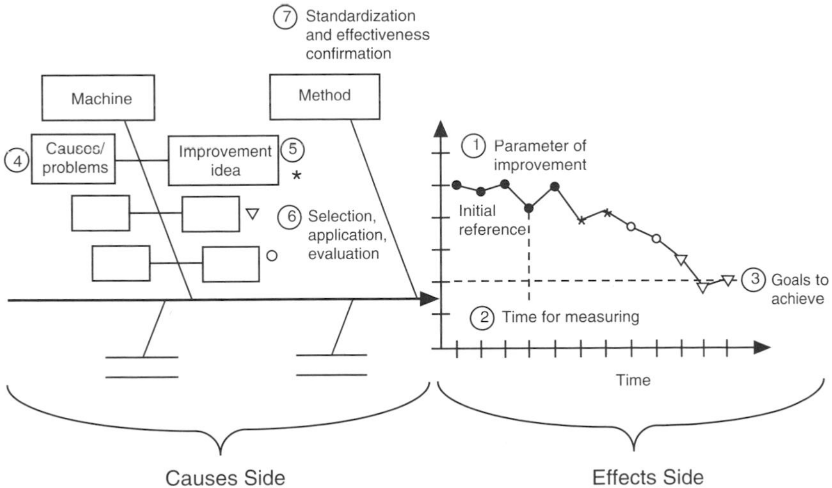

Figure 16-4. Building a CEDAC Diagram

The construction and management of a CEDAC diagram takes place in seven basic stages, some concerning the effects side, others concerning the causes side:

1. Identify parameters (*performance indicators*) to measure the results of improvement actions.
2. Determine how often performance indicators are to be updated.
3. Define the goals of performance indicators.
4. Collect cause cards.
5. Collect cards with improvement ideas.
6. Select and test improvement ideas.
7. Define and apply new standards.

Identify Parameters (Performance Indicators) *to Measure the Results of Improvement Actions*

It is essential to establish the parameters, or performance indicators, that best represent the various aspects of the problem to be solved. These allow one to monitor the progress of the improvement action. The parameter should always be represented by graphs that show progress in the clearest possible way (examples would be point diagrams, bar diagrams, Pareto diagrams, control cards, and layering). The parameters, and their graphic representation, should provide useful information to determine causes and countermeasures.

Determine How Often to Update Performance Indicators

To guarantee the effectiveness of the CEDAC diagram, one must keep the time interval for the updating of the graphs regarding performance indicators as short as possible.

Define Goals of Performance Indicators

Every performance indicator on the CEDAC diagram must have a goal, which should be clearly shown on the graph. If necessary, this goal can be quantified in economic terms, to point out the economic advantages of some of the suggested actions. The quantitative goal, which can change during the course of the project, must also be expressed in terms of the time allotted for resolution of the problem, which does not usually exceed four to five months.

At the end of stage 3, the CEDAC diagram is ready to be implemented through the following steps:

1. Prepare the poster, noting
   - project title
   - leader's name
   - initial date
   - all performance indicator graphs
2. Display the CEDAC diagram in the appropriate location, explaining to all those involved how to read it, what its goals are, and so on.
3. Systematically update graphs, according to a preset frequency.

At this stage the CEDAC displayed will be as shown in Figure 16-5.

Collect Cause Cards

The CEDAC leader encourages all the people involved in a problem to fill out cause cards (notes on the obstacles that interfere with goal achievement). Anyone can fill out such cards — executives, managers, technicians, and line workers alike. Participation by a large number of people in this phase is essential, as the aim is to analyze causes noted in various company cultures.

The CEDAC leader must not simply wait for the cards to arrive, but must directly encourage their compilation, especially by those closely involved in the problem.

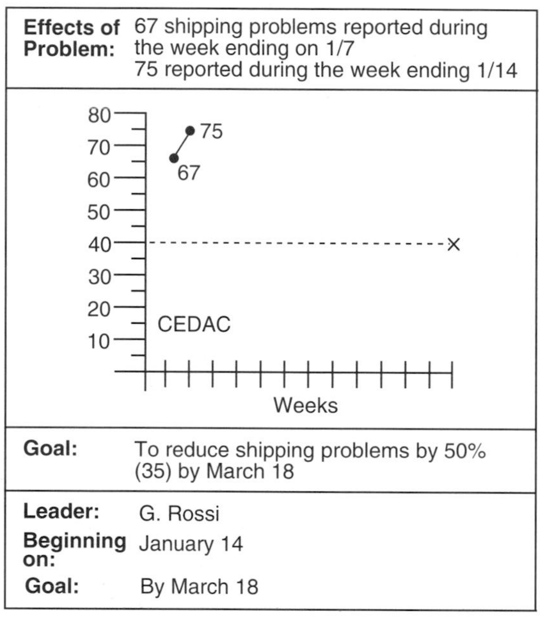

Figure 16-5. Building a CEDAC Diagram: Effects Side

Collect Improvement Idea Cards

The people involved in the problem are invited to think about how to overcome or eliminate the obstacles shown on the cause cards. They are to suggest countermeasures on improvement idea cards, which are of a different color from the previous ones and are to be placed on the diagram to the right of the pertinent obstacle cards (see Figure 16-6).

Select and Test Improvement Ideas

The next step is to analyze and evaluate each improvement idea card. For this purpose a meeting is held, involving everyone who might have something to offer to the task. The person who has filled out the card is either present at the meeting or informed in detail about the evaluation, which is also shown on the poster by means of visual symbols.

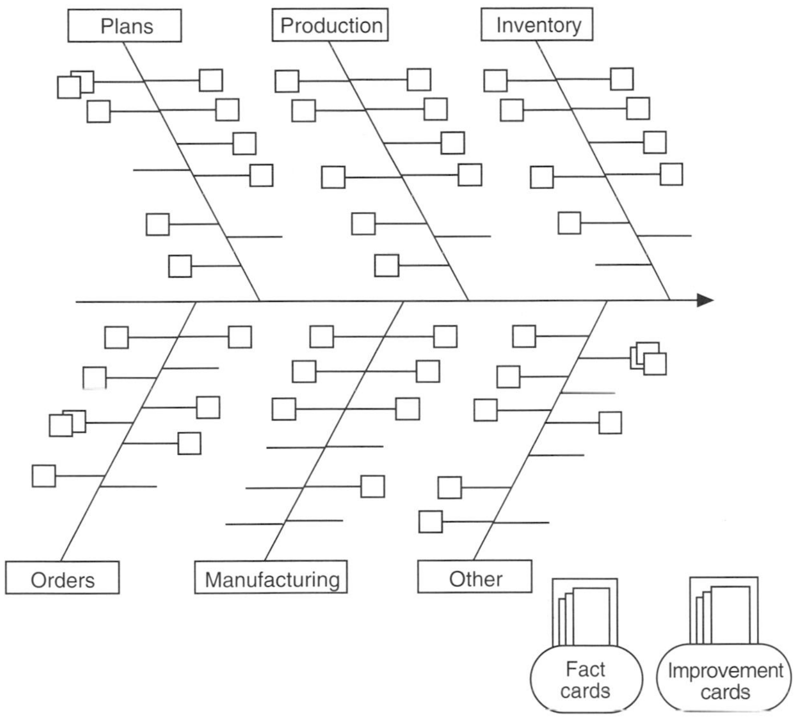

Figure 16-6. Building a CEDAC Diagram: Cause Side

Define and Apply New Standards

Once an improvement idea is tested, it is possible to evaluate objectively whether it has a positive or a negative impact on the performance indicators. If its results are effective, an improvement idea is highlighted and made the new standard. The CEDAC diagram is especially useful in the definition of standards. First, it eliminates the risk that ideas will be selected on the basis of influence by higher authority rather than on the basis of their merit. By this principle everyone is given the same opportunity to establish standards. Second, it ensures that improvement ideas reflect the experience, work knowledge, technology, and management techniques of the area involved.

Above all, the CEDAC diagram is not a system for "hanging up cards"; it is an improvement tool that workers can use.

Strengths of the CEDAC Diagram

The strengths of the CEDAC diagram can be divided into three groups:

1. Strengths pertaining to the high number of people involved: The CEDAC diagram focuses attention on and motivates involvement in problems that are important to everyone. By stimulating and serving as a vessel for ideas across a wide spectrum of the company, it encourages an integrated approach to problem solving. Moreover, it is visible to all, giving everyone access to standards.
2. Strengths pertaining to methodology: Because the CEDAC diagram takes cause-and-effect relationships as its focal point, it constantly strengthens the culture and practice related to them. It provides immediate feedback to everyone concerning the results obtained, creating a sense of solidity and achievement. All interested employees know the process by which standards are developed, and how standards affect process parameters. Also, it helps to spread the new standardization.
3. Strengths pertaining to the development of the improvement culture: Because it promotes the concept of continuous improvement on a daily basis, the CEDAC diagram encourages integration between improvement and operations.

CHAPTER SEVENTEEN

The New CWQM Mentality

Introduction

The application of companywide quality management requires a revolution in a company's way of thinking. "Way of thinking" means the way in which problems and people are dealt with, the criteria with which priorities are established, the perception of one's main role and duties — in short, all the things that determine behavior within a company. With this new mentality, people acquire the desire and the will for self-improvement.

This change must be propelled from the top, through a series of messages and concrete actions to indicate and confirm the line adopted for the development of this mentality. One of the originators of this revolution was Ishikawa. We can make two observations regarding the change in mentality.

- Quality is not intrinsic to the culture of Japanese companies. In his book on CWQM, Ishikawa claimed

---

This chapter was edited by Cristina Galgano, a consultant with Galgano & Associati.

that Japanese industry functioned irrationally, and that a managerial revolution was necessary.
- the first one to call for a mental revolution by both managers and staff members was Frederick W. Taylor, the father of the scientific analysis of work. His teachings paved the way for CWQM.

Japanese experts maintain that three to five years are needed to create the new mentality underlying CWQM. This can be achieved only if management is actively committed to translating the system's basic principles into concrete action.

Aspects of the New Mentality

If CWQM is to be truly operational, a company's workers need to absorb its basic concepts. The following are the most important:

- Respect employees as human beings.
- Put quality first.
- Focus on the market (*market-in*).
- The downstream process is your customer.
- Analyze facts and speak through data.
- Concentrate on a few important things.
- Control within the process (*in-process control*).
- Control the upstream (*up-stream control*).
- Do not attribute fault to others.

A description of each concept follows.

Respect Employees as Human Beings

A company employs human beings, who should be able to achieve their full potential in terms of ability, creativity, and motivation while working. For management, this means delegating as much power as possible to people on all levels. As human beings, people must be allowed

- to react independently to stimuli that originate from the working environment
- to develop spontaneously their psychic energies, in order to contribute to the achievement of company goals

In short, people have minds, and they want to use them. It is management's task to create conditions in which this potential is realized — through focused and effective actions for the improvement of activities.

Such a system might be called "management by humanity," because it encourages the full development of boundless human potential. This system assumes that employees

- work in positions where their dignity is unimpaired
- are always treated with respect
- must be involved in achieving company goals
- must be well trained for their job
- must be allowed to offer a significant contribution to the work being carried out

The responsibility for implementing this system falls largely to management.

Quality First

Quality first means incorporating attention to quality into one's daily activities, which is basic operational strategy referred to in Chapter 3. Each person must know that no compromise is allowed concerning quality: it is top priority in every situation. All employees must understand that by applying the concept of *quality first* to all activities, they earn the customers' trust and make the company highly competitive in the long run.

Focus on the Market (Market-in)

Market-in refers to the orientation of a company toward the market and customer needs, as opposed to an orientation toward internal efficiency. This expression is meant to strengthen employees' awareness of the fact that the market and the customer are the true owners of the company.

A market orientation by itself is not sufficient to guarantee customer satisfaction. The customer must enter the company and guide every activity and function. Everything must be seen from the customer's point of view, the customer being the internal customer, as well as the external one.

Each sector of a company, however distant from the market, must be able to distinguish direct and indirect links between its function and the market. This promotes greater effectiveness in defining actions that enhance a company's competitiveness.

The Downstream Process Is Your Customer

Each organizational unit and each individual has one or more internal customers.

The notion of the *internal customer* was defined by Ishikawa in 1949, and represents a basic concept for the application of CWQM. Ishikawa remembers a conversation he had with a department supervisor in 1949, while working as a consultant in a steel mill. The two were looking at a problem, and in the course of their discussion, Ishikawa suggested that they go together to consult the head of a department downstream to the supervisor's. On hearing this, the supervisor said, "Professor, you want me to go and consult my worst enemy." This remark made it clear to Ishikawa that in any company where antagonism exists among people who are closely linked to each other, quality cannot be achieved. Hence the creation of a new rule of behavior: orientation toward the internal customer.

This orientation provides guidelines for each organizational unit, as well as each person, on how to perfect their output. In carrying out daily work, everyone strives to meet the expectations, requirements, and needs of those who use the output. This is the *market-in* concept.

Analyze Facts and Speak Through Data

By nature, people approach problems subjectively, on the basis of personal impressions and experiences. Thus any solution undertaken tend to be hypothetical and ungrounded in facts. With CWQM we replace this subjective approach with a new approach, expressed by the statement "Analyze fact and speak through data." Essentially, all employees are asked to acquire a scientific mentality. This means that

- Employees must understand the importance of facts, and must learn to observe them;
- Employees must learn to express facts with accurate data.

Data come at us from all sources. The trick is to separate correct from incorrect data.

Concentrate on a Few Important Things

Employees must apply the universal law of priorities (described in Chapter 2), and be aware that in every situation there are only a few truly important factors. When employees grasp this, the effectiveness of their actions increases considerably, to the company's advantage. To facilitate the application of this concept, one usually uses a Pareto diagram.

Control within the Process (In-process Control)

In-process control is nothing more than the extension to all employees of the management guideline "focus on processes." control is to be exercised not on results, but on the various process phases. With such a system, the action will be focused on prevention of recurring defects, thus gradually reducing the variability of the processes themselves.

Control the Upstream (Upstream Control)

Being aware of what happens within a process is not sufficient if one wants to exercise effective control over it. It is necessary to go back upstream in order to discover the factors that affect process, so as to keep them under control.

The late Taiichi Ohno, former vice president of Toyota, used to give an example about determining the true cause of a machine's breakdown:

> When confronted with a problem, have you ever stopped and asked *why* five times? It is difficult to do even though it sounds easy. For example, suppose a machine stopped functioning:
>
> 1. *Why* did the machine stop?
>   There was an overload and the fuse blew.
> 2. *Why* was there an overload?
>   The bearing was not sufficiently lubricated.
> 3. *Why* was it not lubricated sufficiently?
>   The lubrication pump was not pumping sufficiently.
> 4. *Why* was it not pumping sufficiently?
>   The shaft of the pump was worn and rattling.
> 5. *Why* was the shaft worn out?
>   There was no strainer attached and metal scrap got in.
>
> Repeating *why* five times, like this, can help uncover the root problem and correct it. If this procedure were not carried through, one might simply replace the fuse or the pump shaft. In that case, the problem would recur within a few months.*

Do Not Attribute Fault to Others

The tendency to blame other units or people for problems creates a strong obstacle to improvement. People tend to find justifications for their own mistakes, thus losing their grip on what needs to be done. With CWQM, everyone focuses only on his or her own area, seeking continued improvement from within its confines

---

* Taiichi Ohno, *Toyota Production System: Beyond Large-Scale Production* (Cambridge, Mass.: Productivity Press, 1988), p.17.

The New Company Constitution

Once employees understand and apply the basic CWQM concepts, the company system, or "constitution," becomes substantially modified. The company acquires new strengths, new abilities to react to its environment, and greater flexibility. At that point the company can begin adopting specific practices that are simpler, safer, more integrated, more effective, and more economical than earlier ones. It will then be easier to change current management systems and approaches according to their effectiveness and appropriateness for the task. This means that all employees must commit themselves to defining critical areas of the new culture. These are:

- development of new processes and products
- mechanisms for participating and involving all employees
- improvement of problem awareness
- awareness of the need for quality improvement, based on an annual schedule
- freely flowing communications among management, staff, office workers, and line workers
- management style and policies that are human-oriented

PART FOUR

CWQM Processes and Executive Leadership

By examining CWQM processes, we enter into the operational aspects of the new management system. The figure opposite is a graphic representation of how the six CWQM processes become a part of the company structure. Each one of them constitutes a great innovation and a piece of the puzzle in this new way of managing a company. *Hoshin management* is management of main improvements handed down yearly by top management, whereas *daily routine work* is maintenance of performance level and continuous achievement of small improvements. Hoshin management is also cross-functional.

The *president's diagnosis* keeps both processes under control, and management guidelines direct all company activities.

Through *quality circles,* operators are allowed to participate in improvement activities, while at the same time succeeding in the operator's basic people-building process, both in the office and in the production departments.

The process of *intensive education* provides oxygen for the company as an organism, and is based on the conviction that employee performance can constantly improve.

The last process, that of *product or service management,* will not be analyzed in this book. This process begins with market research for the development of new products, and, after a whole series of stages, ends with after-sale service. Upstream, it concerns relationships with suppliers, and downstream, with the various links of the distribution chain.

Basic CWQM Processes

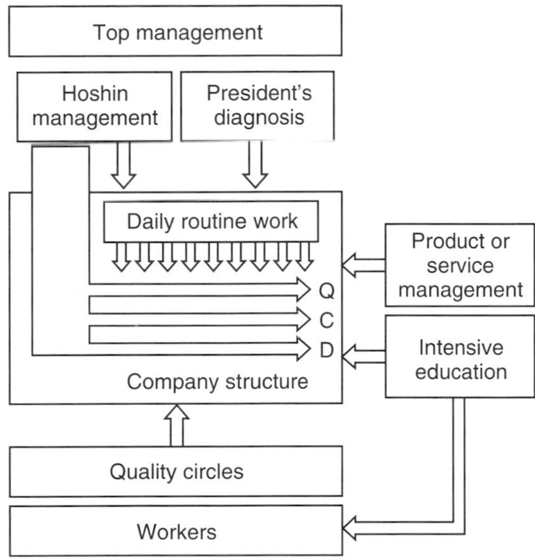

CHAPTER EIGHTEEN

Hoshin Management

Introduction

Companywide quality management amounts to a new "constitution" for a company, so great are the innovations it brings to management. The key process by which CWQM is implemented is *hoshin management,* which represents the highest evolution of the new approach to quality.

Hoshin management is carried out in annual cycles and provides a guideline for pursuit of major improvements (whereas small improvements are effected through *daily routine work*). Hoshin management is the Japanese version of the American *management by objective* approach.

Hoshin management grew out of the application of quality control to companywide improvement. During the first years of CWQM development companies did not separate improvement activities from maintenance activities. The central activity was "process control," by the application of PDCA. Eventually the companies realized that such an approach was inadequate. They understood that the most important improvement activities needed to be incorporated into corporate management by means of "policies" issued by top management. In fact, policies were the first area to be considered in the Deming Prize checklist. The first company to separate maintenance and improvement was Komatsu (1962), with its *flag system,* and in 1965 Bridgestone officially defined the annual cycle, through *deployment* and other stages that now characterize hoshin management.

Basic Points of Hoshin Management

Hoshin management (HM) is a management process by which company strategy is converted into operational guidelines. Specifically,

- Annual operational policies are established, on the basis of the medium- and long-term ones.
- Such policies are carried out by concrete actions involving the company's entire organizational structure.

From a different perspective, HM can be seen as a series of activities through which the company each year brings about important improvements in clearly defined areas. Its significance can be best understood through an examination of its aspects:

- definition of policy
- foundations of annual policy
- basic features of the process

Definition of Policy

The entire CWQM management system is based on the concept that a company needs a guideline, or policy, for the main improvement activities to be carried out during the course of a year. A policy includes three elements:

1. an area of action, which acts as a theme or direction (for example, cost reduction)
2. a quantitative target to be reached in the chosen area (say, a 10 percent cost reduction)

3. a direction concerning a course of action, that is, the means for reaching the target (following the example above, by improving the logistic system).

Foundations of Annual Policy

An annual policy must derive from a broader vision, one related to a company's basic values and goals. The diagram in Figure 18-1 shows such a derivation.

Basic Features of HM

Four features of HM stand out because of their importance:

1. All employees focus on a small number of priorities, normally two to three but up to five. Thus the

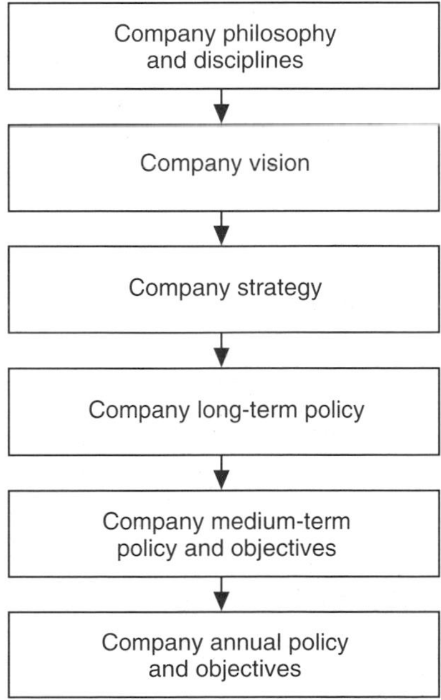

Figure 18-1. Foundations of Annual Policy

company applies the universal law of priorities by concentrating all efforts on a few goals. The purpose is to obtain *breakthroughs,* that is, innovative improvements in areas that are most important for the success of the company, within the framework of a long-term vision. It is impossible to explain the success of Japanese companies other than as the sum of many breakthroughs, obtained each year by this concentration of effort.

2. The entire process tends to polarize attention on the cause-and-effect links pertaining to goals, so that any difference between established targets and results actually achieved is reduced to a minimum. This basic CWQM process is like a large gym in which to exercise the employee abilities that are essential to company success.
3. Through *policy deployment* the targets and guidelines of upper management are communicated to lower levels. Specifically, executive policy is translated into a new set of policies that can be understood and developed by the staff. This happens at all levels. In this communication process an integration between top-down and bottom-up flows takes place. Without such integration, there can be no true employee participation.
4. The PDCA process (plan-do-check-act) is extensively applied at all stages and in all procedures. PDCA is the operational essence of hoshin management. In this way, greatest emphasis is placed on the evaluation of operational processes, whose management is based on the continuous use of facts.

The Six Stages of Hoshin Management

The implementation of HM takes place in six stages (see Figure 18-2). The process is circular, in the sense that the last stage constitutes a reference point for the beginning of a new cycle the following year. From a conceptual point of view, it is correct application of the PDCA cycle during all activities for communicating policies and goals throughout the company. The seven management tools are used to implement the various stages.

The six stages are:

1. preparation for the definition of the annual policy
2. president's definition of the annual policy
3. policy deployment
4. policy execution
5. periodic verification of implementation (*check*)
6. president's diagnosis

Preparation for Definition of the Annual Policy

The first stage can be divided into three substages:

- A critical analysis is made of the previous year's results, in which information on errors or failure to achieve targets is highlighted, since it indicates any possibility for improvement. Thus, the emphasis is on cause-effect relationships, not on seeking guilty parties.
- The external environment is analyzed, with consideration for any important changes in the national or international economy; the company's particular market, as well as others that have a bearing on the company; technology; and other pertinent factors.
- Medium- and long-term policies and plans are verified.

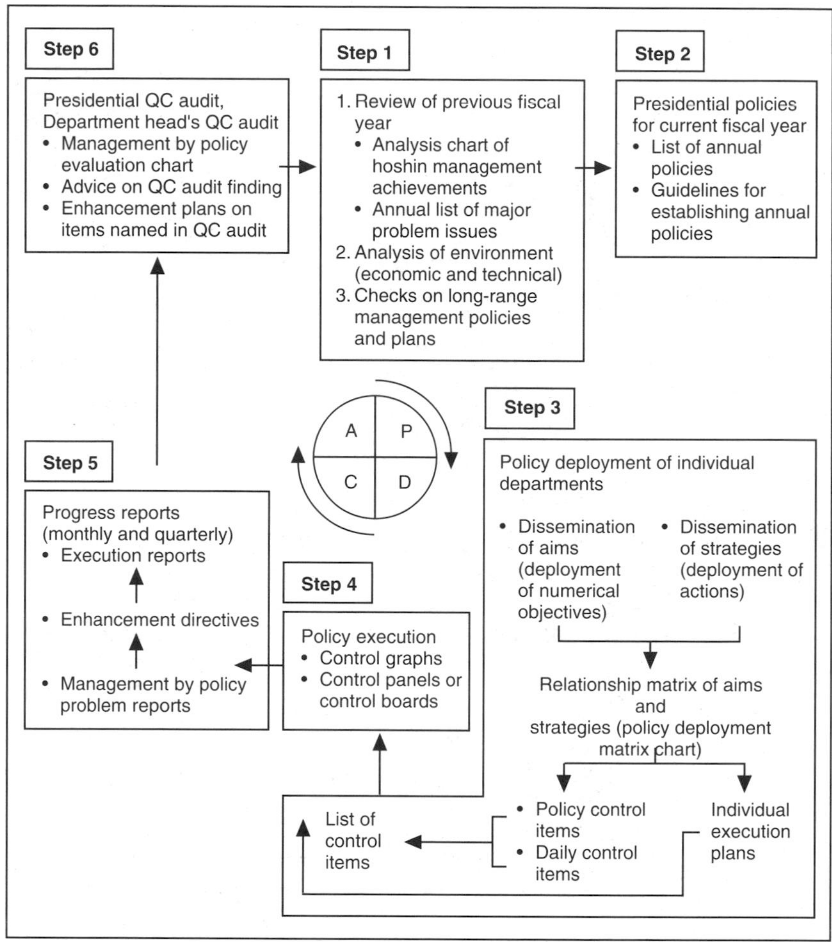

Figure 18-2. Diagram of Hoshin Management Stages

These activities take place through a bottom-up process, which permeates the entire structure. Checks and audits carried out in each unit throughout the year facilitate this process. Through a series of summaries the data gathered reaches top management for a final report.

The management tools used during this stage include the affinity diagram (for structuring any problems in need of a solution) and the relationships diagram (for establishing causes).

President's Establishment of Annual Policy

Establishment of the annual policy is generally done jointly by the president and top executives. The task is carried out along with preparation of the budget and investment plans, and it results in the written formulation of a few priority items.

Turnover and profit targets are expressed in numerical terms, while priority activities are expressed numerically only if they are truly critical.

The president's policy (except for turnover and profits) is distributed among all employees at the beginning of the year, so that all workers can feel involved in the achievement of goals and can transfer this awareness into their work.

Policy Deployment

The president's policy is "exploded" through an increasingly detailed tree-shaped diagram, which outlines all steps down to establishment of a plan for concrete actions to be carried out in daily work. This involves a correct definition of modalities and schedules for implementing the responsibilities of people and departments. At the same time, it is necessary to establish modalities and schedules for control, an indispensable element in the evaluation of the progress of policies during their implementation phase.

Deployment activities must take place gradually, so that they are neither too specific at a high level nor too general at the lower levels. The main difficulty lies in correctly evaluating how gradual the process should be. It is also necessary to make sure that there is consistency between policies at different levels, and among targets and actions at the same level.

Three categories of actions are established:

- actions to be carried out directly by those undertaking deployment
- actions to be carried out by staff
- nonpriority actions

Support management tools, in addition to the tree-shaped diagram for deployment activities, include the matrix diagram (to check for consistency), PDPC (to choose the best alternatives), and the arrow diagram (to plan execution and checking).

Execution of Policy

This stage involves execution of policy, as described in the items above, by each person or unit to which responsibility has been assigned. Each person carries out the plan according to the HM execution plan; this requires individual discretion and self-control. Control boards and control panels are used for daily control of the results. Execution is followed by a daily check, which is carried out with the aid of management tools such as arrow and Gantt diagrams.

Periodic Implementation Verification (Checks)

The checking activities mentioned at the previous stage are accompanied by periodic checks, set up to verify policy implementation status.

The periods vary (monthly, quarterly), depending on the extent to which numerical targets have been achieved, executive plans have been implemented, activities are consistent with targets, and problems have been resolved.

The checks are carried out by the same people responsible for carrying out the policy, and are discussed during regular meetings. This bottom-up process applies PDCA to all anomalies discovered.

It should be pointed out that data and information pertaining to the periodic checks of each policy are examined and stored for use in a critical analysis of the year just ended. The management tools associated with this stage are the arrow diagram (to show progress), the relationships diagram (to show the reasons for any discrepancy with expected results), and the PDPC diagram (to point out the best corrective actions).

The President's Diagnosis

The *audit* stage, or president's diagnosis, is specific to HM, and it consists of the periodic check (annual or semestral) of CWQM development within the company. The diagnosis is a direct and official contact between the highest executive and a particular company department, allowing the president to personally verify the consistency and progress of the application of CWQM. As this diagnosis is particularly significant, it is treated separately in Chapter 22.

The six stages described can be represented with another diagram that shows all parties involved, from the president to the managing staff (Figure 18-3).

On the extreme right of the diagram the procedures and documents that support the various implementation stages are reported. Whereas the earlier six-stage diagram emphasized the circular process based on PDCA, this diagram gives a clearer picture of the flow, which comprises a meeting or discussion stage as well as an action stage, always with a clear view of the necessary feedback.

Figure 18-4 shows a typical example of how HM is incorporated into the management process of a Japanese company. Note that its introduction takes five years.

Policy Deployment

Within HM, policy deployment represents the process of spreading the president's policies throughout every company department. As shown in Figure 18-5, this is a waterfall-shaped process, through which top-level policies are successively translated into increasingly explicit and concrete terms for the level

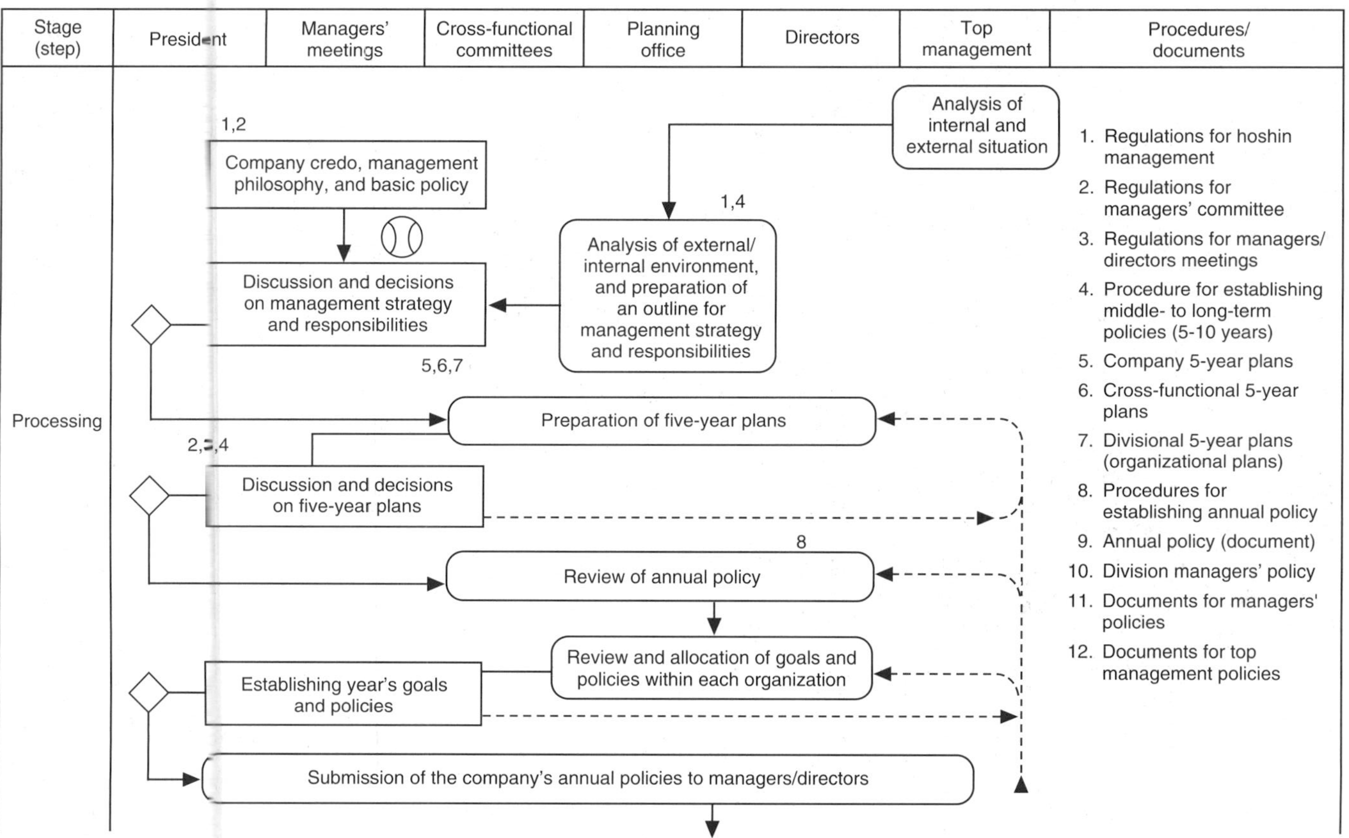
Stage (step)
President
Managers' meetings
Cross-functional committees
Planning office
Directors
Top management
Procedures/ documents
Processing
Analysis of internal and external situation
1,2
Company credo, management philosophy, and basic policy
1,4
Analysis of external/ internal environment, and preparation of an outline for management strategy and responsibilities
Discussion and decisions on management strategy and responsibilities
5,6,7
Preparation of five-year plans
2,3,4
Discussion and decisions on five-year plans
8
Review of annual policy
Review and allocation of goals and policies within each organization
Establishing year's goals and policies
Submission of the company's annual policies to managers/directors
1. Regulations for hoshin management
2. Regulations for managers' committee
3. Regulations for managers/ directors meetings
4. Procedure for establishing middle- to long-term policies (5-10 years)
5. Company 5-year plans
6. Cross-functional 5-year plans
7. Divisional 5-year plans (organizational plans)
8. Procedures for establishing annual policy
9. Annual policy (document)
10. Division managers' policy
11. Documents for managers' policies
12. Documents for top management policies

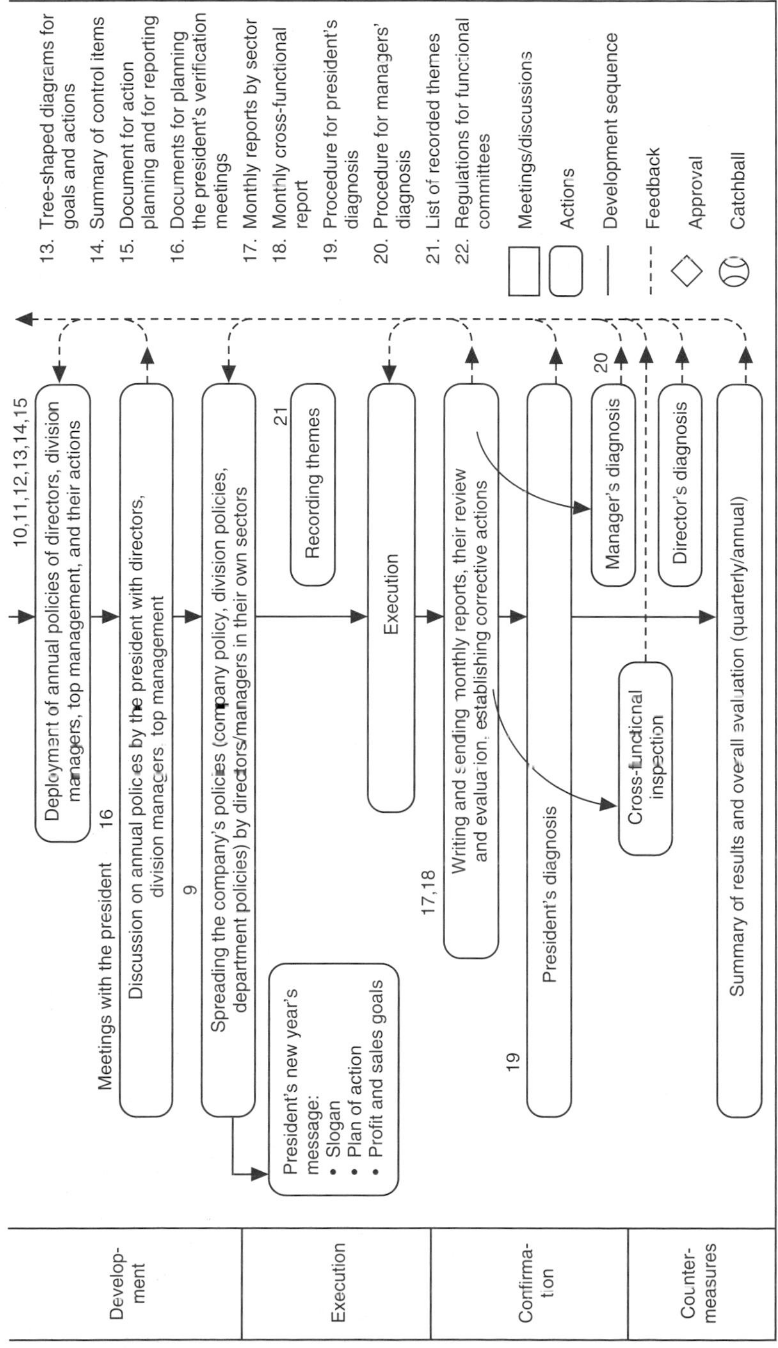

Figure 18-3. Hoshin Management Flowchart

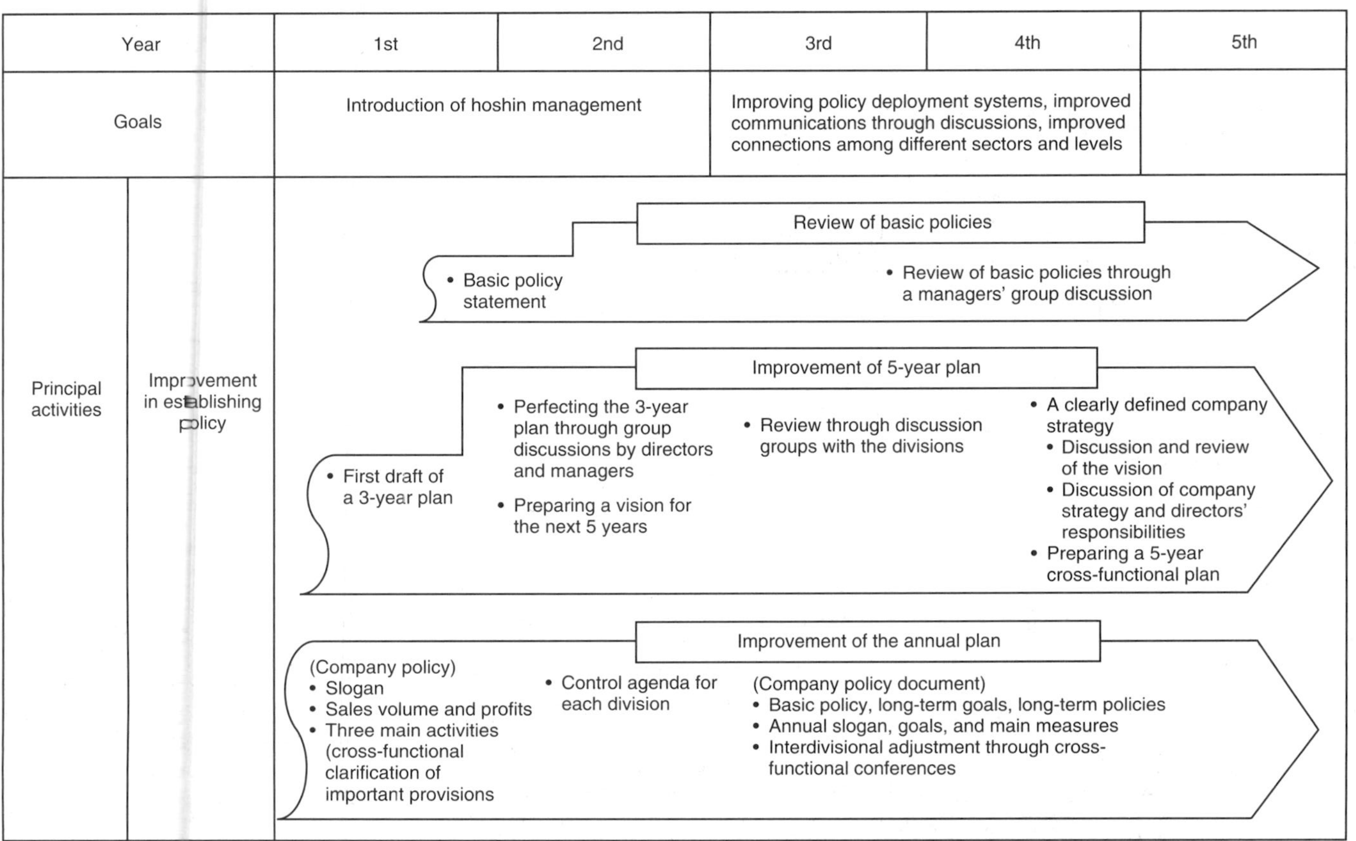
Year
1st
2nd
3rd
4th
5th
Goals
Introduction of hoshin management
Improving policy deployment systems, improved communications through discussions, improved connections among different sectors and levels
Principal activities
Improvement in establishing policy
Review of basic policies
• Basic policy statement
• Review of basic policies through a managers' group discussion
Improvement of 5-year plan
• First draft of a 3-year plan
• Perfecting the 3-year plan through group discussions by directors and managers
• Preparing a vision for the next 5 years
• Review through discussion groups with the divisions
• A clearly defined company strategy
• Discussion and review of the vision
• Discussion of company strategy and directors' responsibilities
• Preparing a 5-year cross-functional plan
Improvement of the annual plan
(Company policy)
• Slogan
• Sales volume and profits
• Three main activities (cross-functional clarification of important provisions
• Control agenda for each division
(Company policy document)
• Basic policy, long-term goals, long-term policies
• Annual slogan, goals, and main measures
• Interdivisional adjustment through cross-functional conferences

Principal activities	Deployment between numerical goals and measures	• Adjustment and deployment of the policies of sector managers		• Introduction of project recording • Improvement in coordinating goals and measurements by improving documentation	• Review of documents	
		• Confirmation of policy by sector at the beginning of each period		Improvement verification meetings with the president • Implementation by sector • Cross-functional and cross-sector coordination		
	Improvement in implementing follow-up	• Follow-up on goals during management meetings	• President's diagnosis (research problems of each sector)	• Evaluation by the vice president of the annual plan • Manager's diagnosis • Evaluation of results in policy deployment	• President's diagnosis (development of policies by sector, verifying progress and actions)	
Effects		The development of the policy has been gradually understood and a systematic approach has begun	The 5-year plan was established for the first time through group discussions	Developing a system for coordinating policy among the different levels	Good hopes for carrying out the annual plan through policy deployment	
Problems		The policy deployment system is not yet adequate	Coordination and discussions still insufficient, data surveyed not sufficiently specific	Action deployment still insufficient with cooperation between various sectors and levels	Policy deployment still in need of strengthening	

Figure 18-4. Schedule for the Application of Hoshin Management in a Japanese Company

below. Thus, policies are detailed to the extent that they become a precise reference for improvement activities of the current year. Of course, how the sales manager translates the president's policies will differ from how the production manager does it. Normally, in Japanese companies, deployment stops at the level above supervisor.

The entire deployment process is particularly delicate. Just as blood circulation enables a body's parts to function, so does policy deployment enable all parts of a company to contribute to its success. And just as an embolism can paralyze a human limb, so can an obstruction in the deployment process prevent the downstream process from functioning.

An important development of policy deployment was the introduction of the target/means matrix. This matrix allows one to examine the correlation of the targets that flow from the policies, with the necessary measures to achieve such goals. This is an important link. Figure 18-6 represents the flow of the two deployments at a large Japanese company.

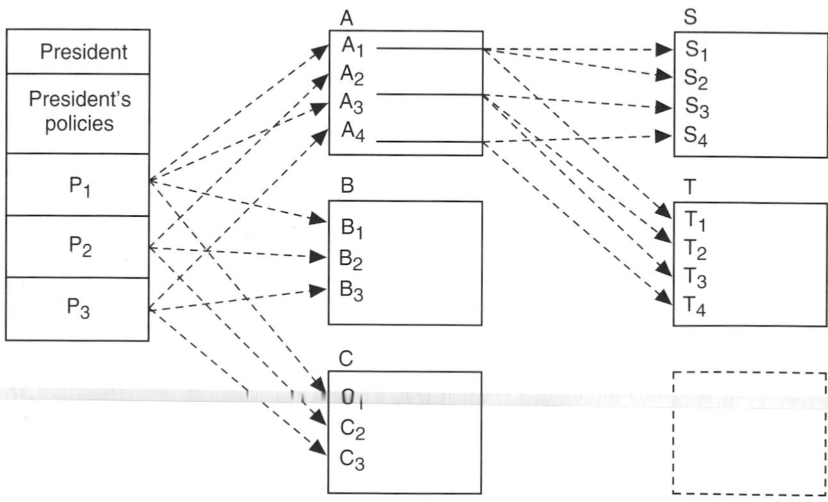

Figure 18-5. Policy Deployment Process Diagram

The target/means matrix allows an in-depth examination of the cause-and-effect relationship between goals and actions, and an evaluation of their consistency. Figure 18-7 shows an example of the target/means matrix.

An Example of Plant Manager Policy Deployment

Let us consider an example of policy deployment within a plant. The example concerns a Japanese industrial company, and it shows how the plant manager's policies become those of the production managers, who translate them into actions for their lower-level staff, highlighting also the checkpoints, goals, and reference period. The policies of the plant manager are the following:

- more flexible manufacturing system and establishment of quality, cost, and competitive strength on new product through smoother start-up implementation
- promotion of administrative efficiency
- more vital workplaces, and nurturing of employees' talent

Table 18-1 shows the deployment of such policies.

Control Items and Check Items

The application of HM requires constant verification of the status of implementation and achievement of target goals. One does this by establishing a large number of "control items," which become an integral part of the process structure, as they control criteria, targets, and results achieved. This activity is very important, since when work is proceeding well, people tend to fall back into reliance on subjective evaluations.

HM's control items thus make it possible to follow activities in a thorough way, and to react appropriately and effec-

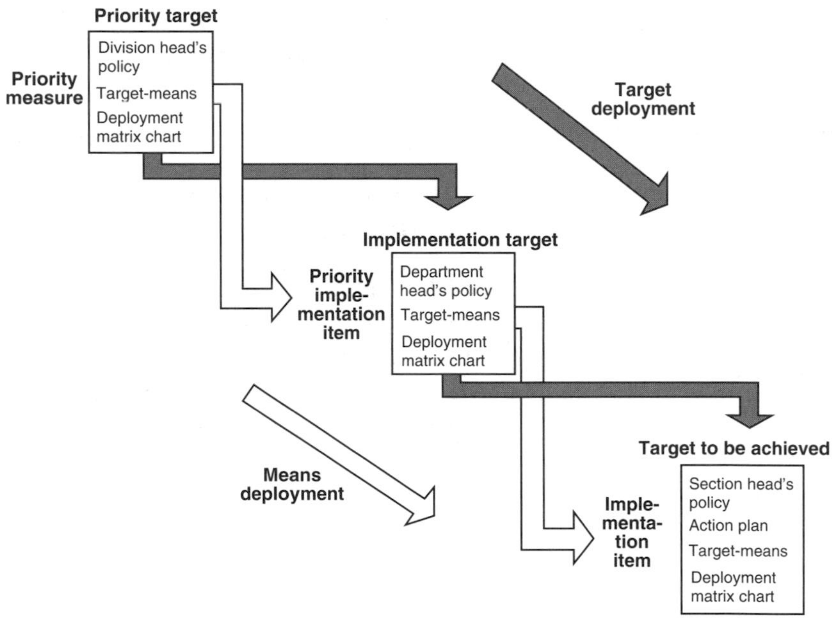

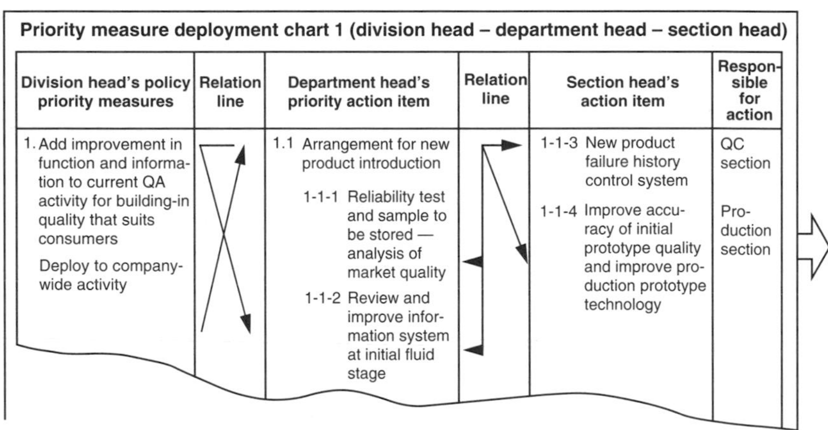

Priority measure deployment chart 1 (division head – department head – section head)

Division head's policy priority measures	Relation line	Department head's priority action item	Relation line	Section head's action item	Respon-sible for action
1. Add improvement in function and informa-tion to current QA activity for building-in quality that suits consumers Deploy to company-wide activity		1.1 Arrangement for new product introduction 1-1-1 Reliability test and sample to be stored — analysis of market quality 1-1-2 Review and improve infor-mation system at initial fluid stage		1-1-3 New product failure history control system 1-1-4 Improve accu-racy of initial prototype quality and improve pro-duction prototype technology	QC section Pro-duction section

Note: Adapted from Yoji Akao, ed. *Hoshin Kanri: Policy Deployment for TQM* (Cambridge, Mass.: Productivity Press, 1991).

Figure 18-6. Target and Means Deployment

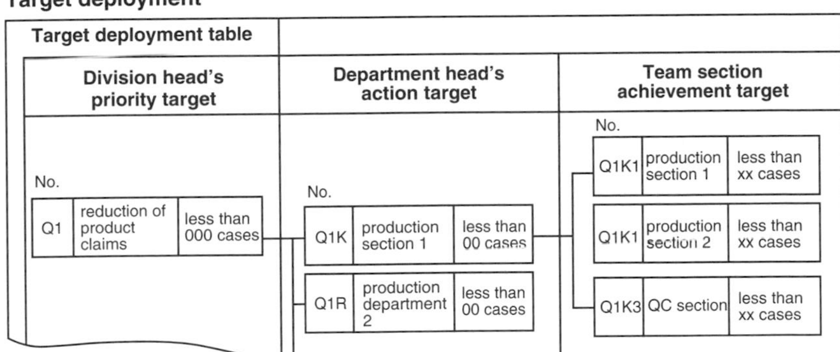

Figure 18-6. (cont'd)

				Department Goals								
				1			2					
				Cost			QA					
			Num. Val.									
		Plant Manager Actions	Department Manager Actions	De-scrip-tion	De-scrip-tion	De-scrip-tion	De-scrip-tion	De-scrip-tion	De-scrip-tion	Code	Param.	Control Sheets
Actions	Cost	I.1.	I.1.1									
			I.1.2									
			I.1.3									
			I.1.4									
	QA	II.1	II.1.1									
			II.1.2									
		II.2	II.2.1									
			Code									
			Parameter									
			Control Sheets									

Figure 18-7. Matrix of Goals/Actions Relationship

Table 18-1. Manufacturing Department Manager's Policy

Policy	Priority Items (Activity Plan)	Control Point	Goal	Period
1. To strengthen cost competitiveness through promotion of a single workpiece flow between each process, and to accumulate manufacturing technologies toward FMS (flexible manufacturing system)	1. Improve machining method • activity expansion for cutting conditions improvement • machine tool operation improvement	Work-hour reduction	7.5%	By June
	2. Improve workpiece flow • utilization of waste-cutting techniques for carrier system improvement • work preparation improvement on the assembly line	Turnover for work-in-process	25%	By December
	3. Improve cutting tool change	Changing time	7%	By June
	4. Improve energy efficiency	Electricity Fuel Resource	7.5% 10% 6%	By June
2. To stabilize the startup operation for new models through the use of the best knowledge at the workshop	1. Shorten the lead time for prototype product manufacturing	Lead time and cost	10%	By December
	2. Fully implement manufacturing process plan	Process capability assurance and cost	100% 100%	At the startup
	3. Advance establishment of all required technology • prevent crankshaft bending	Assembly defects	0.2 item per set	At third month

3. To promote and expand mistake-proof activity	1. Leak stop activity 2. Careless mistake stop activity			
4. To educate employees so that they may improve their creative, managerial, and technical capabilities	1. Adapt computer technology to FMS trend 2. Install office automation equipment	Numerical control operator rank A B C	 10% 30% 60%	By December
5. To make the workplace safe, active, and cheerful	1. Promote workplace cleanliness through "5S" activity 2. Eliminate accidents by preventing causes	Staff study Number of accidents	 Zero	 Throughout the year

tively to the data obtained at preestablished control points. Control items are actually two kinds of items:

- *Control items* verify whether results agree with established goals. They particularly enable higher levels to evaluate their results and targets, by assigning responsibility for implementing corrective action in the case of any discrepancy between results planned and results obtained. Control items also serve as a reference for the following year's policies and goals.
- *Check items* enable one to measure and evaluate the causes that contribute to determining the outcome of any particular activity. They are established by the upper echelons for their staff, in connection with control items, in a "waterfall" process in which the *check items* of an upper level become the control items of a lower level (see Figure 18-8). Check items thus enable one to evaluate the status and adequacy of action to achieve targets and to maintain appropriate procedures each successive corrective action.

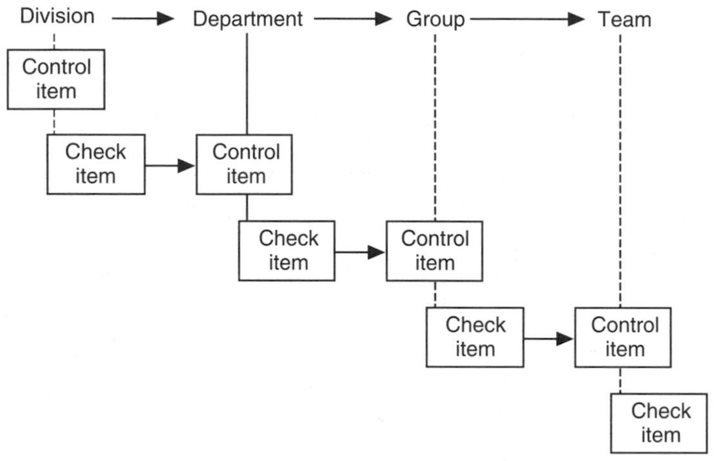

Figure 18-8. "Waterfall" Process for Defining Control Items and Check Items

The link between control items and check items, in terms of goals and actions to achieve them, is shown in Figure 18-9. In Table 18-2 some typical control items and check items are shown in diagram form.

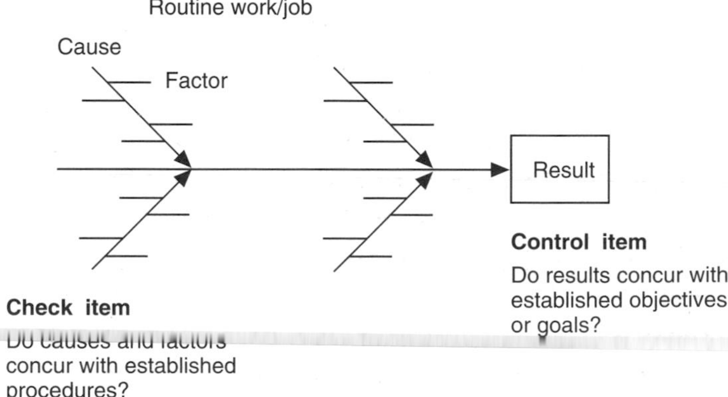

Figure 18-9. Cause-and-Effect Link Between Check Point and Control Point

Table 18-2. Control Items and Check Items

Control Items

Tangible	Intangible
Profit	Company's image improvement
Sales turnover	User's degree of satisfaction
Production output	Community relations
Productivity	Employee morale
Financial characteristics	Status of suggestion system
Yield ratio	In-house communication
Claim ratio	Management/staff relations
Complaints report	
Quality failure rate, etc.	

Check Items

Tangible	Intangible
Conformance of operation sequence	Improvement of standard operating procedures
Conformance of operation actions	Improvement of equipment or facility
Expenses consumed	Status of training program
Time consumed	
Availability of equipment	
Operator efficiency	
Absenteeism	

Cross-Functional Management

The application of hoshin management is not complete without strong integration among the company's department and functions. CWQM's great innovation was to organize this integration around the three factors in customer satisfaction: quality, cost, and delivery. As a matter of fact, improvement activities activated in each company department on an annual basis with HM must be coordinated. The final goal of each department or function is to contribute to the constant improvement of the three factors just mentioned.

Of course, there are other basic activities within the company that must be coordinated cross-functionally, such as new product development, technology development, and human resources management. To enact this coordination, *cross-functional management* was created.

Professor Ishikawa, who first developed this management process at Toyota in 1960, describes it as the weft that is woven into the warp to make the cloth. Without it the warp (here represented by departments or functions) would be disconnected, and would not have any texture of its own. Figure 18-10 shows the weave that must be created by cross-functional management.

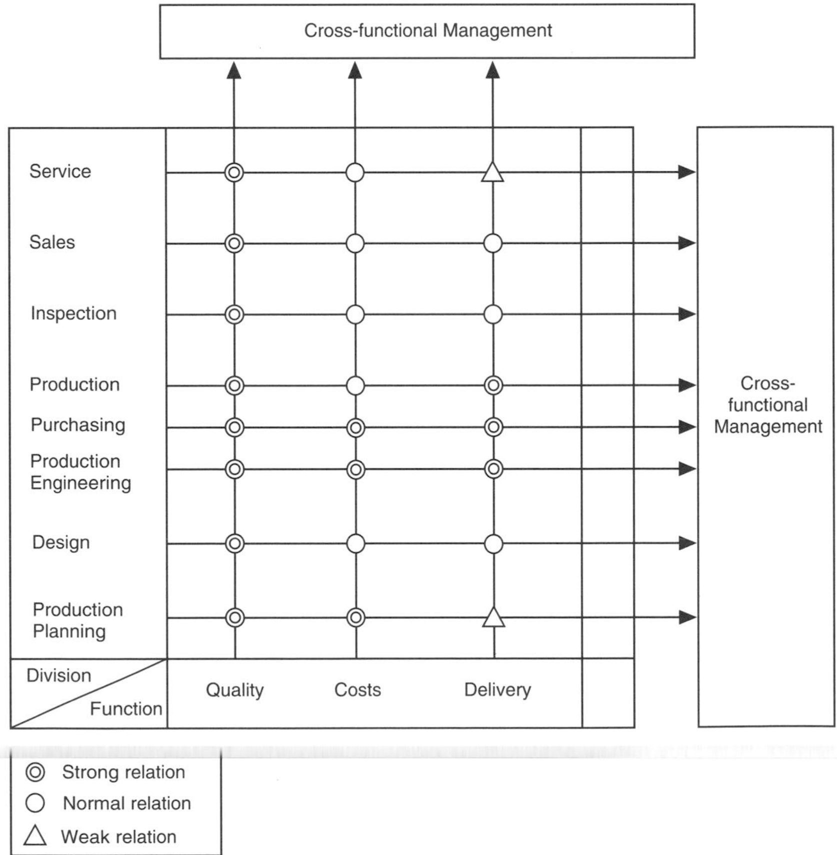

Figure 18-10. Cross-functional Management Diagram

In CWQM, cross-functional management is carried out by various high-level committees, which coordinate each of the basic factors. For example, the head of the cross-functional committee for quality will be one of the senior executives, with members being managers from departments directly or tangentially involved with quality. The number of members is generally between 5 and 10. These committees meet once a month. Each committee should choose a secretary belonging to the department associated with the factor in need of coordination. The committee may assign particular problems to project groups. The proper functioning of these committees may require a few years. Ishikawa notes that for a large company such as Toyota, it may take 10 years.

Comparison between Hoshin Management and Management by Objective

To conclude this chapter on HM, we show a comparison between this management process and management by objective (Table 18-3). Such a comparison is the result of efforts by a committee of the Japan Society of Quality Control and of research by Kozo Koura.

Table 18-3. Comparison between Hoshin Management and Management by Objectives

	Hoshin Management	Management by Objectives
Background Concept	Start with the concept of the control cycle, which is born in the development process of CWQM	Start with a score system, and add the concept of behavioral sciences and management system
Type	Organization-oriented Group-oriented Function-oriented	Personnel-oriented
System	• A system of fusing the process of companywide participation with the bottom-up and top-down processes • Use of PDCA cycle and a trouble-shooting system	• A system for having all the related people work together • Use of troubleshooting and decision by objectives
Priorities	• Quality first • Total object of quality (Q), cost (C), and delivery (D)	• Profits and cost
Introduction Promotion Implementation	• Education and flexibility • Promotion based upon the principle of companywide participation	• Political pressure emphasized not only in education, but also in implementation • Selective use of top-down process and participation management
Method of evaluation	• Emphasis on process as well as results • QC audit by president, QC audit by department manager • Organizational self-analysis of difference between goals and results • No direct link with personnel management	• Centered on results • Linked to personal management (1) selection of workers by objectives (2) job evaluation system (3) score system (4) salary control system
Method	• Control item • QC techniques • Policy deployment	• Index • QC, IE, and OR are subsystems

CHAPTER NINETEEN

Daily Routine Work

Introduction

Together with hoshin management, *daily routine work* (DRW) represents the other pillar of the CWQM managerial system. Aims and fields of its application become evident when set within a framework that links them with the two key activities of CWQM, maintenance and improvement, and that highlights their differences from hoshin management.

Hoshin management is the principal tool for improvement; it presents a few peculiarities, such as

- application on a global level throughout the company
- concentration on a few priorities linked to the company's business factors
- consistent improvement goals, aimed at a *breakthrough*
- a top-down approach for its implementation, with priorities chosen by top management, and deployment and implementation of policies carried out by lower-level managers.

This chapter was edited by Giancarlo Pagliughi, a partner with Galgano & Associati.

It goes without saying that the effectiveness of hoshin management depends on whether it fits into a generalized context in which each unit has a proven maintenance system, that is, control and continuous improvement of its own processes. The essence of DRW is to carry out this maintenance and improvement system, which, therefore, is characterized by

- its local application within each organizational unit of the company (it can reach the individual level)
- local autonomy, with responsibility delegated to each company unit
- maintenance (control of one's processes) and continuous improvement (constant improvement of unit's performance level)

The features of DRW are, therefore, centered on the autonomy given to each unit, on control and maintenance of processes, and on the constant improvement of performance.

The term *daily routine work* may sound vague and demeaning, but it describes the process aptly.

Names provide a way for classifying or identifying content; the important thing to do is to define the essence and the methods applied. Of course, as for all components of CWQM, daily routine work has its own application method, comprising various steps and supported by various tools and methodologies.

Definition and Features of Daily Routine Work

Daily routine work can be defined as follows:

- It is a management process (*what*).
- It is carried out by all units of the company (*who*).
- It pursues the goal of full customer satisfaction (*why*).
- It is based on systematic control and continuous improvement (*how*).

- It is applied to each activity and process (*where*).
- It is performed on a daily and permanent basis (*when*).

Following is a description of a few basic features of this CWQM process.

The Downstream Customer(s) as a Priority Reference

The DRW process is geared to the satisfaction of customer needs, that is, to the requirements of the unit downstream. This customer could be someone other than the "final customer," and, in such a case it will be defined as an "internal customer."

The idea, in DRW, is to arrange all activities carried out by individual units in logical "customer-supplier" chains. The DRW process involves the unit under consideration mainly as a "supplier" (see Figure 19-1).

DRW is a management element of CWQM, in which the concept of internal customer, as well as the view of a company as a group of customer-supplier chains, is stressed and applied.

Local Autonomy in Taking the Initiative

Each unit promotes and develops DRW independently, with methods varying according to the unit activities that are most critical to the customer. This means that in a company that has assimilated the CWQM culture, each part of the company (as well as each person in it) develops the DRW process in-

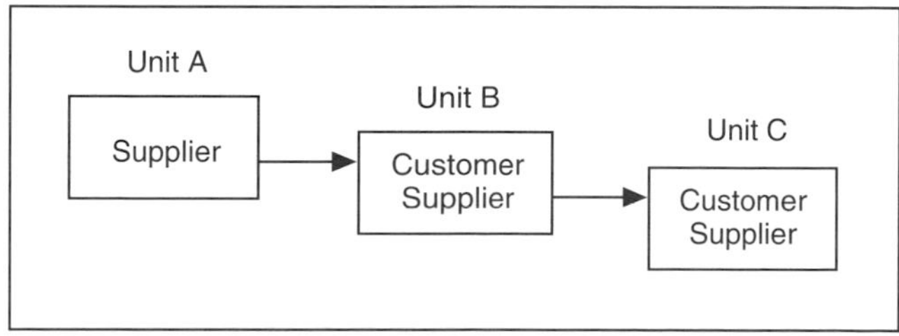

Figure 19-1. The Customer-Supplier Chain

dependently and permanently. At the same time, through other mechanisms typical of CWQM, this process is rendered consistent and in tune with relevant priorities.

Maintenance through Systematic Control

To satisfy downstream customers through output and products, one must develop the ability to control one's processes, through the maintenance process. The first basic aim of DRW is, thus, process control. This requires a "technology" specific to process control activities, one based on standardization both of the way processes are carried out and of the control system. The systematic control is gradually extended to all "important" processes or activities of the company on a continuous and daily basis.

Continuous Improvements

Although the ability to control processes is essential, it does not guarantee customer satisfaction in a dynamic context of constant evolution of needs.

DRW adds to the capacity for maintenance that of constant improvement of local activities. This part of the DRW process becomes central once the control process has reached a high level of effectiveness. Improvement activities involve a constant commitment and are concentrated on the priority processes and results of the moment.

Applicability and Implementation

Because of its orientation to customer satisfaction, DRW is theoretically applicable to all company activities. In fact, as a continuous process, it is particularly effective in activities of a repetitive nature (both high and low frequency). Concerning their implementation, DRW activities take place "in" and "during" a unit's operational processes; it is thus expressed by day-to-day management, both of maintenance and of improvement activities.

Methods for Applying DRW

In order to translate its goals into concrete facts and results, the DRW process takes an approach based on a precise method.

- DRW is characterized by *four basic approaches:*
  1. process approach
  2. customer approach
  3. process control approach
  4. improvement approach
- DRW is structured in *10 operational phases* for its implementation:
  1. Identify the priority process.
  2. Define its goals.
  3. Identify customers and their needs or expectations.
  4. Identify the quality indicators.
  5. Establish control goals and limits.
  6. Define a control system.
  7. Implement the control system.
  8. Verify the results.
  9. Implement countermeasures through PDCA.
  10. Standardize.

Each of these stages is aided by techniques and tools that facilitate application. In Figure 19-2, the 10 stages of the PDCA process are divided among four main "blocks," which correspond to those that have been defined as DRW's basic orientations.

The Four Basic Orientations

The following text briefly describes the four basic orientations.

Process Orientation

Process orientation involves the unit "vision" in terms of activities or processes that produce "products" (parts, documents, drawings, information, etc.), more generally called "output."

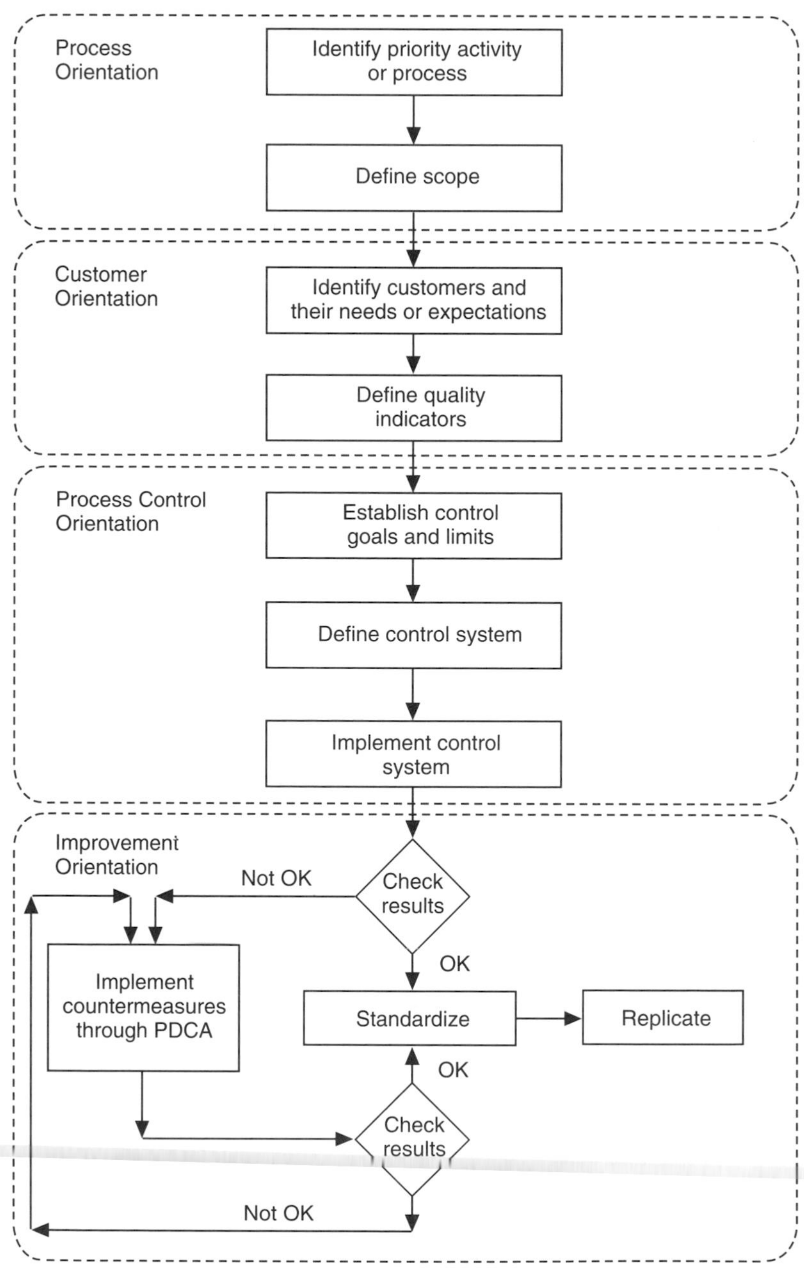

Figure 19-2. The DRW Process

Customer Orientation

Customer orientation involves identifying one's customers (those who use the process output) and understanding their needs or expectations.

Process Control Orientation

Process control orientation involves defining and implementing a control system for one's activities or processes, in order to maintain the required performance.

Improvement Orientation

Improvement orientation involves identifying, pursuing, and maintaining the improvements necessary to satisfy customers, through the involvement of all individuals within the unit.

Purposes of the 10 Implementation Stages

Each implementation stage has a specific purpose, as follows:

1. *Identify the priority process* to identify the process on which to concentrate.
2. *Define its goals* to fully understand what needs to be ensured with regard to the company organization and processes.
3. *Identify customers and their needs or expectations* so that the unit's efforts can be effectively aimed toward the real needs of the customers (those who use the unit's output).
4. *Define quality indicators* in order to have concrete and consistent indicators though which to check the unit's performance from the point of view of the customer.
5. *Establish control goals and limits* in order to have quantitative means for determining when performance is unsatisfactory and requires countermeasures.

6. *Define a control system* for the unit's process or activity in order to assure correct running of the process.
7. *Implement the control system* in order to put into practice and make the established control activities "come alive."
8. *Check results* in order to verify the degree of customer satisfaction, the need for countermeasures, and the latter's effectiveness.
9. *Carry out corrective actions through PDCA cycles* in order to determine effective countermeasures in the case of insufficient performance.
10. *Standardize* so that, when the results are satisfactory to the customer, the process becomes "standard operating procedure" for the unit.

DRW as a PDCA Cycle

The DRW process is, in fact, on application of the PDCA (plan-do-check-act) cycle (see Figure 19-3).

- The *plan* stage (planning, preparation) encompasses the first six stages, during which the control system for the chosen process is established.
- The *do* stage (execution) consists in implementing the control system (stage 7).
- The *check* stage (verification) consists in identifying the needs for improvement (stage 8).
- The *act* stage (countermeasures and standardization) calls for establishing effective countermeasures, checking them, implementing them, and standardizing them (stages 9 and 10), in order to carry out improvement actions.

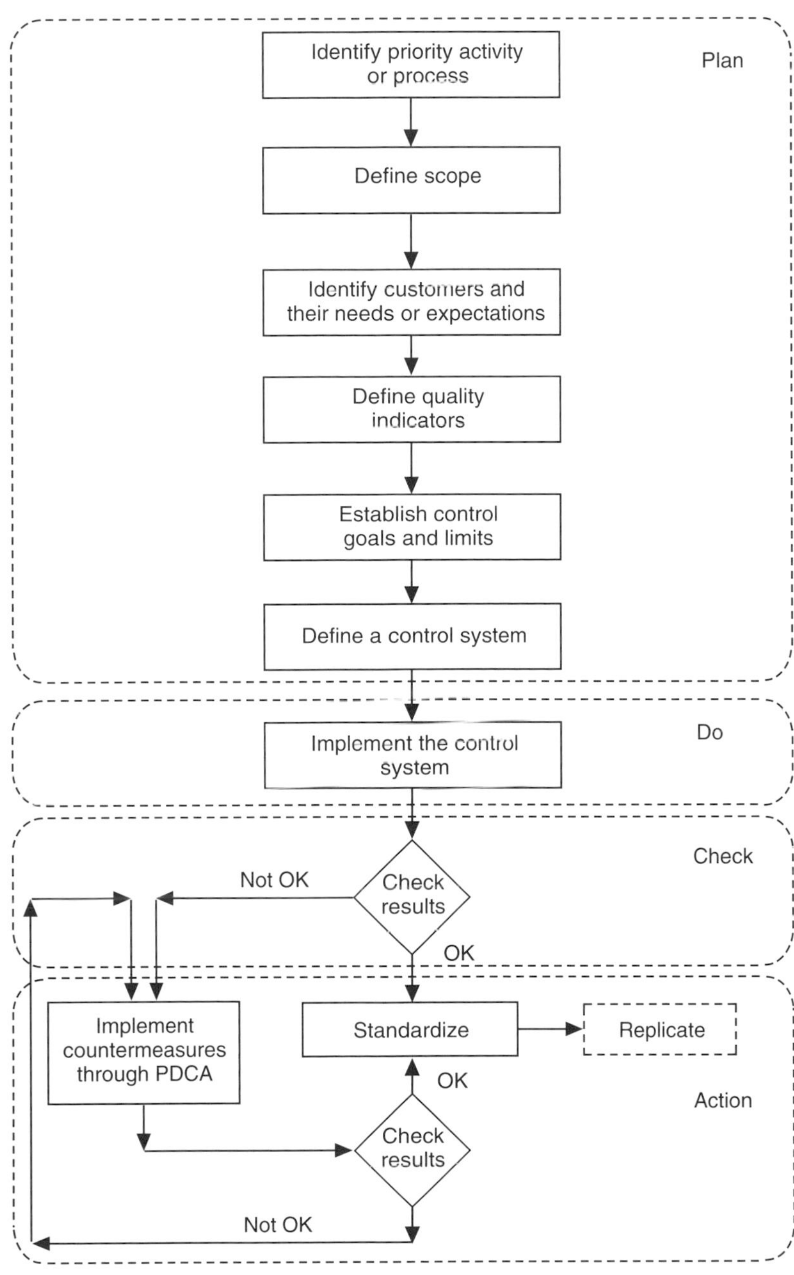

Figure 19-3. The DRW Process as PDCA

The 10 Operational Stages of DRW

The following sections explore the implementation of the 10 operational stages in carrying out daily routine work.

The application of DRW within a company usually requires a written internal manual so that all units and their employees share a common reference. Here we propose not to present a manual of that kind, but to show the capillary nature of the method.

First Stage: Identify the Priority Process

The scope of this step is to correctly identify the unit's priority processes and outputs; the recipients of these activities and outputs (the customers) will have already been identified.

This stage is useful because, in practice, it is not possible to apply DRW to all processes at the same time. DRW therefore begins with one or more of these priority activities or processes, and is later extended to the remaining ones. The useful operational stages are summarized in the tree-shaped diagram shown in Figure 19-4.

Second Stage: Define the Process

Once the unit's top priority process has been identified, it is necessary to understand how the company makes use of its output. Especially drawn-up checklists can be helpful in defining the scope of a process. The outcome of this stage results in a brief sentence describing the process scope.

Third Stage: Identify Customers and Their Needs or Expectations

At this stage, customers have already been identified. The focus here is to determine their needs, so that one's performance can be evaluated on that basis. It is a good idea to first determine all relevant needs or expectations, then to establish which have priority. The basic tasks are to perform a complete

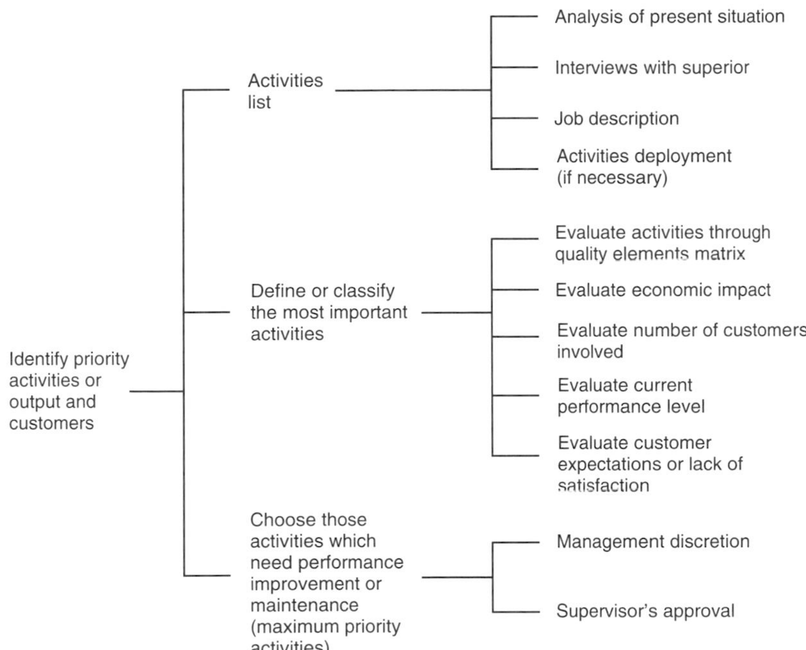

Figure 19-4. Tree Diagram for Determining Priority Process

analysis and make an objective and speedy determination of priority needs.

To facilitate this step, checklists of the type shown in Figure 19-5 can be useful.

Customer needs and expectations are generally shown in a tree-shaped diagram. At the next stage, needs and expectations will be "translated" into parameters that are more directly linked with the unit's process.

Fourth Stage: Define Quality Indicators

Customers and their expectations are satisfied through output, that is, through "product" provided to them by the unit. Quality indicators are meant to provide the unit with a tool to measure its effectiveness in achieving the customer's

Activity ____

Output ____

Customer ____

— Am I providing my customer with what he really needs?	
— Does what I provide help him achieve his goals?	
— Is it in the form he needs?	
— Do I really understand what he needs?	
— Do I know his activity well?	
— Do I know he uses what I provide for him?	
— Do I know why he carries out such an activity?	
— Do I know what problems I could cause him with a mistake?	
— Do I know why he is sometimes not satisfied with what I provide?	
— Have I discussed it directly with him?	
— When did I speak with him last?	
— When is the last time I went to visit him?	
— Would he like something I have not yet been able to offer?	

Figure 19-5. A Checklist for Determining Customer Needs

needs and reasonable expectations. As such, they must have two features:

- They must be directly linked with the unit's process and output.
- They must be directly linked to the customer's needs and expectations.

To correctly identify quality indicators, it is useful to follow the logical sequence shown in Figure 19-6. The goal of this stage is, therefore, to translate such needs into measurable indicators that are clear to unit members.

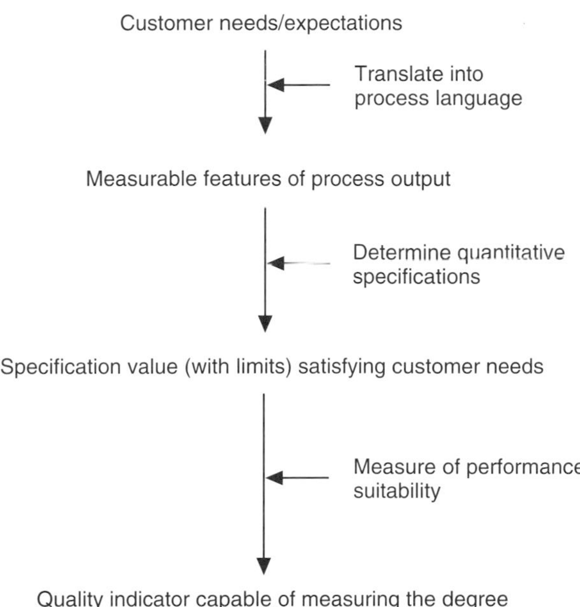

Figure 19-6. How to Develop Quality Indicators

Fifth Stage: Establish Control Goals and Limits

After developing a set of quality indicators, one must establish control goals and limits through appropriate diagrams. This gives one the ability to check performance progress. The objective is to find the desirable or necessary level of the quality indicator in order to satisfy the customer. One establishes it with the downstream customer after analyzing historical data, and sometimes by establishing temporary intermediate goals.

The limits, on the other hand, express in a quantitative form the acceptable variation of a quality indicator, that is, those variations that do not call for any corrective action. (This is the concept of statistical control limits).

Finally, once quality indicators and their goals and limits have been defined, they are graphically displayed through charts or control cards. This allows one to access current process performance quickly, in relation to the established goals and limits.

This stage, therefore, is based on the "visual control system" for the constant monitoring of quality indicators.

Sixth Stage: Define a Control System

With this stage, DRW moves its focus into the internal processes of a unit. The result is the definition of an effective process control system. It is a complex stage, rich in detail but essential to the satisfaction of the customer downstream.

The former stages, focused on customer needs and definition of quality indicators, are essential but only preparatory to this stage. Achievement of customer satisfaction in practice requires definition and implementation of an effective process control system. The output then becomes simply the consequence of how the process is carried out and controlled. As such, this stage as well as the later ones aimed at continuous improvement are crucial to DRW.

In determining a control system, the DRW approach makes use of a logic that is fundamental to total quality: standardization. Determining the control system through standardization involves four aspects, that should be dealt with in sequence:

1. *Determining how the activity or process is to be carried out.* This is a preliminary condition, aimed at ensuring a continuous and uniform unfolding of the process over time (successive cycles). It constitutes a "standardization" of the *modus operandi,* which allows for more effective development of the control system and the following stages of DRW.

   It would be difficult to control and continuously improve a process through use of haphazard operating methods. One of the main outputs of this step is the establishment of standard operating procedures (SOP).

2. *Identification of control points.* This step involves analyzing the process to define activities, intermediate output, or process conditions that must be constantly observed in order to control the process (monitoring). At this stage it might be useful to draw cause-and-effect diagrams to determine those causes which have greatest influence on the quality indicators. The final result is a list of "critical" causes for the different steps of the process.
3. *Definition of process quality indicators.* Once the control points have been established, it is necessary to determine what needs to be measured and by what criteria is control judged to be necessary (process limits and specifications). The establishment of control points and process quality indicators often requires a "statistical approach" as well as appropriate statistical techniques, so that one can isolate the basic cause-and-effect relationship and determine process control limits.
4. *Definition of organizational framework.* Once the more technical aspects have been taken care of during the previous stages, it is necessary to establish organizational methods for the implementation of the control system, in particular, aspects such as
   - the method and frequency for data collection
   - the method of data representation (charts, control cards, etc.)
   - who is responsible for collection of data
   - who is responsible for checking activities and intervention

The use of a specific synopsis table allows one to synthetically summarize and display the designed control system.

Seventh Stage: Implement the Control System

We have already shown how the 10 operational stages of DRW represent the application of the PDCA cycle in the activity or process under scrutiny. Once the control system is defined, the *plan* stage is completed. The next stage involves implementation. This seventh stage, therefore, constitutes the *do* stage of the cycle (see Figure 19-7).

During implementation it inevitably becomes clear that what was planned is not always appropriate, effective, or simple to apply. Therefore, one makes changes and applies them for the scope of improvement. There are two aspects of this stage that are particularly important:

Employee Involvement and Education Training

The implementation of a control system represents a change, and thus may incur resistance. One of the most effective methods to reduce resistance consists in providing all necessary information and instructions to the employees and, wherever possible, actively involving them in establishing change. This might require explaining the following:

- customer needs and expectations

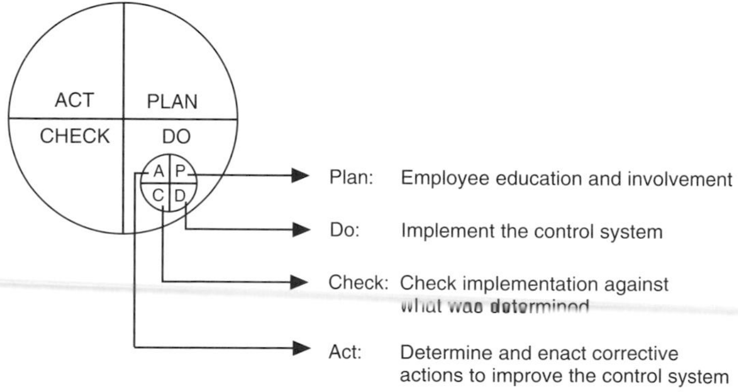

Figure 19-7. PDCA in Implementing a Control System

- which features of the unit's output affect these requirements and what the customer's specifications are
- why particular control points were chosen
- why specific control methods were established and process indicators defined
- what activities and implementation methods are required of individuals within the control system

When people understand the aims to be attained, what is expected of them, and how they are to act, they are more likely to welcome change.

Checking the Essential Aspects with Method

There are many aspects that influence the process; thus it is important to make sure that the established system is applicable, that it works as planned, and that it is adequate for the process scope. One should proceed with the method and check essential factors: (people's behavior, work methods, tools, materials, machines, etc.) as described in the tree-shaped diagram in Figure 19-8.

Eighth Stage: Check Results

Through the control system it is now possible to check process and output results by comparing them with the preestablished limits, as well as with goals. If the results fall within the preestablished limits, the next step is to standardize. Should this not be the case, it will be necessary to take the appropriate countermeasures and then check the results again (that is, activate an improvement cycle).

This stage calls for a constant check action toward the defined control system in order to "select" and direct the downstream activity. Specifically, it highlights

- what needs further standardization
- what needs improvement

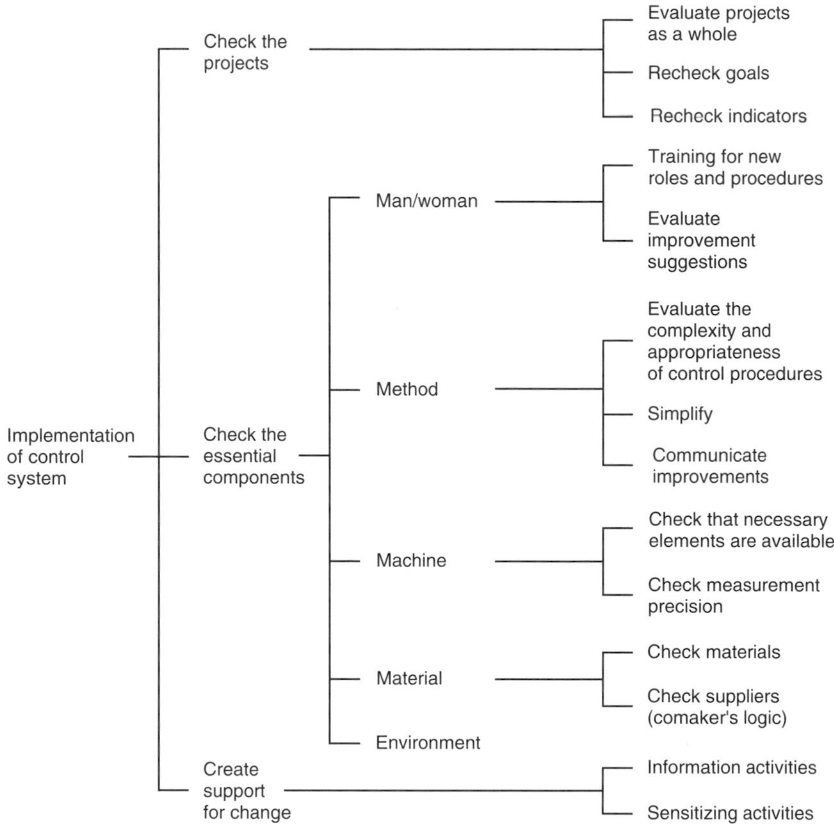

Figure 19-8. Checking the Essential Aspects of the Control System

Ninth Stage: Implement Countermeasures through PDCA Cycles

If, through a check of results, discrepancies arise between unit performance and customer expectations (negative quality), or when it is considered appropriate to supply the downstream customer with a new performance standard (positive quality), improvement actions are developed. This stage, therefore, perhaps the most important one of DRW, interprets the principle of continuous improvement on a permanent basis.

The action can be extemporaneous, triggered by a particular circumstance, or identified and planned over a longer period of time as a result of critical reflection on one's performance. The important point is that such an initiative is propelled by the organization, or rather, by the people working in it. These people work under the pressure of responsibility toward the downstream customer, and are aided by the system they have set up to fully satisfy the customer.

In developing improvement activities, DRW enacts the two main aspects of industrializing improvement in accordance with total quality:

1. *Plan-do-check-act:* following the PDCA cycle to guarantee the development of effective solutions. Even though problem solving, as we have said, requires action on causes, in certain cases it may be necessary to establish remedies or actions that limit or eliminate the consequences of a problem in the short run. For example, poor service delivered to the final customer calls for operating procedures that provide for the application of specific remedies. The important thing is for such remedial action to be followed by countermeasures based on prevention.
2. *Effective involvement and organization of human resources:* Identifying the most appropriate organizational form to adopt in relation to the nature of the problem. A reference point can be identified among the various and flexible activities typical of total quality:
   - individual activities
   - project teams (functional and cross-functional)
   - open teams with visual control system (CEDAC teams)
   - quality circles and other small groups

Of course, most resources will be drawn from the unit itself, but when necessary, employees in external units (suppliers or customers) can be involved.

Tenth Stage: Standardize

At this stage, standardizing means, above all, consolidating the positive results of improvement actions. This is necessary, given that

- the eighth stage has highlighted the need to adopt countermeasures
- the ninth stage has developed one or more PDCA cycles, in order to identify effective countermeasures (improvement action)
- new operative procedures have been established within the process so that the unit can better respond to customers' needs and expectations (new standard)
- at this point such new standards must be applied systematically (completing standardization)

This stage is developed through the following operations:

- reviewing documentation
- identifying the persons involved in applying countermeasures
- training and preparing employees
- determining whether the new standards are being applied correctly
- determining whether the new standards continue to be effective

Utilization of the Results in Other Processes

The DRW process flowchart contains a further box, signifying the transfer of results to another unit. This step maximizes the advantages of the results obtained. In this context, "transfer" means to duplicate a particular countermeasure in other sectors, plants, or departments, that have an affinity to the unit under scrutiny. The underlying concept is that of "repeating the best wherever it is reasonable and possible."

Links Between Hoshin Management and DRW

Taking place within the same company, hoshin management and DRW, two fundamental processes of CWQM, are closely linked. As shown in Figure 19-9, the two processes converge in the standardization of company operations, insofar as improvements, both the major ones and the minor ones deriving from DRW, lead to modifying standards. Another connection concerns the chronic problems that are revealed by DRW. These problems are considered and given the appropriate weight at the time of policy formulation.

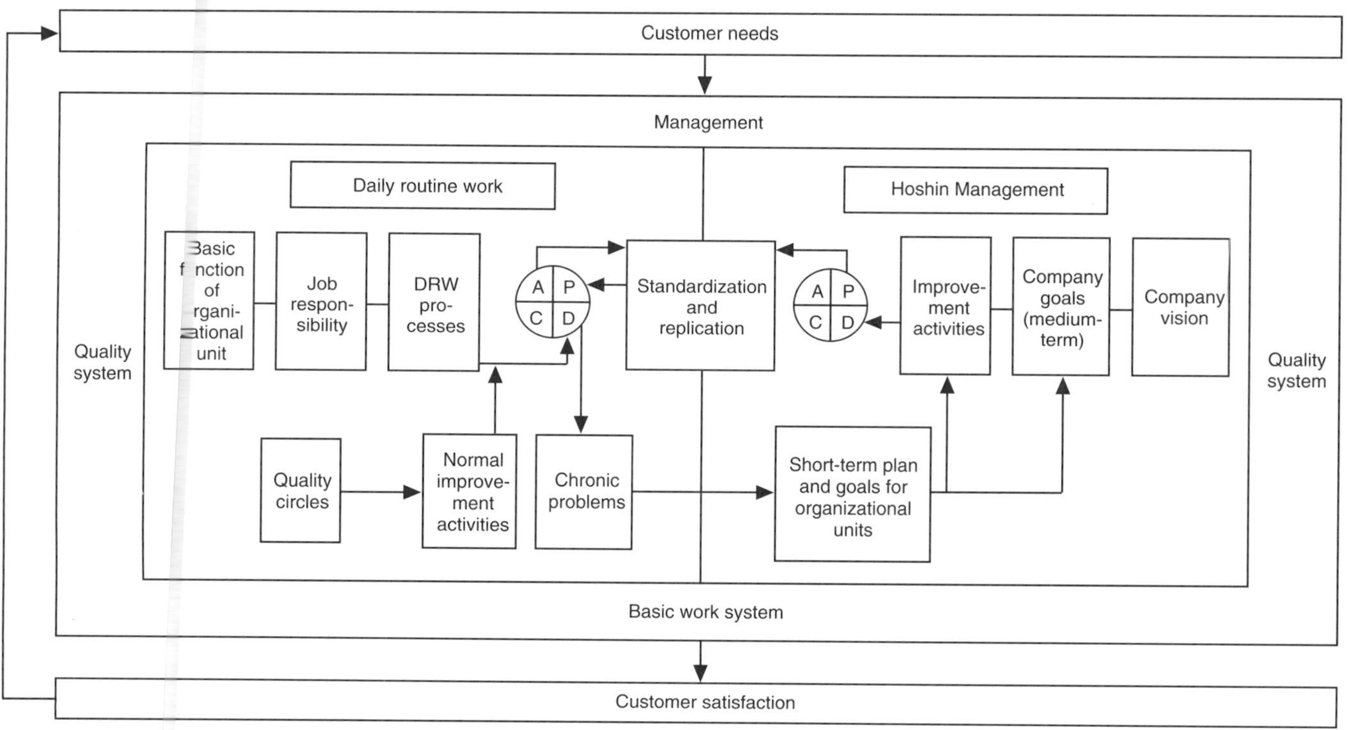

Figure 19-9. Links Between Hoshin Management and Daily Routine Work

CHAPTER TWENTY

Quality Circles

Introduction

The quality circles process is the most innovative aspect of CWQM, precisely because it represents a major breakthrough and is a great forerunner to the most delicate area of company management, that of human resources.

As is well known, the first circles were introduced in Japan during the summer of 1962. To understand how farsighted Japanese company management was, one must go back to the reigning Western model of the early 1960s.

For a number of years (1980-85), quality circles were the best-known aspect of Japanese companies; later, the *just-in-time* system and the "company without inventory" displaced quality circles as elements of renown. During the period mentioned above, to speak of Japan and of quality meant talking about quality circles.

The considerable number of articles and books in English on this subject is out of proportion to their actual limited success in Western companies. In the great majority of companies that adopted quality circles, the number of employees involved in active circles is quite small. Often the circles are only a gimmick, soon forgotten. This is because the companies adopt the circle system without understanding their real importance and without shedding the lack of trust in human resources that characterizes the management of so many companies.

In introducing circles, the company undergoes deep changes. Unfortunately, many people still do not understand the role of circles in the success of a company.

The Quality Circles Process

The quality circles process engages employees in quality improvement activities.

In Japan, as we have said, quality circles have been active since 1962, and to date they have been introduced in many companies in over 50 countries. The simplest definition of quality circles is the following: *A quality circle is a small group that voluntarily carries out quality control activities within an organizational unit.*

Based on a philosophy of total participation, such groups promote self-development and mutual support as a part of CWQM, as well as improvement of every kind within the organizational unit, through effective use of quality control techniques.

In 1962, when the first quality circles were organized in Japan, the following guidelines were set up for their activity:

1. Improve the leadership and management capabilities of supervisors by encouraging improvement through self-development.
2. Raise morale among employees while creating an environment in which each person is more aware of quality, of existing problems, and of the need for improvement.
3. Operate as a CWQM nucleus at the department level. The circles support assimilation and implementation within their organizational units of the policies issued by the president and depart-

ment manager, as well as the achievement of quality assurance.

Within the framework of these guidelines, the promotion of quality circles within Japanese companies aimed at achieving the following three goals:

- contributing to the improvement and the development of the company
- respecting human beings, and creating a serene environment where it makes sense to work
- letting human capabilities emerge, and developing the innumerable opportunities they are offered

Other important concepts underlying the operation of quality circles are the following:

- The workplace is not only a place to carry out operational activities, but is also a place to apply creativity.
- Quality circle activities should not be limited to the workplace; QC members should also participate in meetings for exchanging experiences, both inside and outside the company, as well as in internal and external conventions and presentations. The idea is to widen the mental horizon, and to strengthen personal determination regarding improvement activities.
- The group provides a meeting point to cultivate and to train individuals in their effort to establish relations with others.
- Participating in circles helps to develop one's personality.
- Circles can grow only if a company's management is truly committed to providing guidance, training, support, and to maintaining a deep respect for people.

Quality Circles and the "Quality Circle" Company

The difficulties encountered by companies in developing and maintaining the quality circles program are mainly due to the program's deceptively easy beginning. In fact, it seems easy to start out with a small number of circles, an impression confirmed by employees' interest in the program. On the other hand, managing such a program in order to maintain and develop the number of circles within the company is one of the most complex activities. This complexity is made evident by the fact that the circles program is characterized by its ability to create a "company" within a company: the quality circle company.

The company created by the circles program has as its main activity the "production" of projects at the level of line workers and office staff. In a sense, then, it can be viewed as a consulting company. This is an original view that aims at better defining the process of starting up and managing a quality circles program. Although the new company does not in fact exist, it is important that employees see it as real.

In Figure 20-1, we show the structure of the two companies. The structure of the first is represented by its organizational chart. The second has a very different structure: there are circles, facilitators, and the quality office. If the company has more than one plant, there will be an office in each of them.

In the "quality circles company," many activities are carried out beyond that of implementing a great number of improvement projects. For example, circles might do the following:

1. Create an awareness and work at promotion in order to fuel quality circles activities. This activity must never stop if the number and commitment of these circles is to increase, or in the worst case, not decrease.
2. Hold training activities for facilitators, supervisors, leaders, and circle members. This activity is central

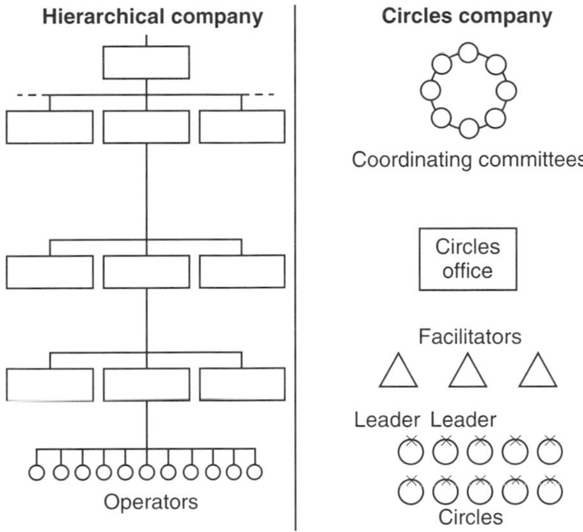

Figure 20-1. The Quality Circles Company

to the circles program: it requires possessing a specific know- how, very different from that which exists in the training departments of most Western companies.

3. Hold regular meetings of facilitators and leaders. These meetings are essential for strengthening the circles program and for improving the performance of facilitators and leaders.
4. Perform support activities for projects being carried out. These include:
   - the facilitators' activities
   - the intervention of other internal managers for the purpose of assisting individual circles in their activities of information gathering, diagnosis, and establishment of countermeasures
   - the intervention of the circle's executive committee

5. Perform logistical support activities. They include:
   - providing material needed for carrying out projects (forms, computers, audiovisual equipment, etc.)
   - making available a conference room for meetings
   - providing material for presentations
6. Present of project results. Such presentations are made at various levels:
   - to colleagues in other departments
   - to department managers
   - to top management
   - at conventions held outside the company
7. Evaluate project results. These results must be evaluated without delay, and a series of procedures implemented to ensure this goal.
8. Apply the proposals formulated in the projects. This application is the final activity of the quality circles for the project under study. This activity, too, must be carefully organized.
9. Give recognition of circle activities. This entails managing the vast array of rewards that is needed to keep the program alive.
10. Exchange experiences with other companies. This is very important, both for motivating employees and for its cross-fertilization effects.
11. Regularly audit circle activities. The audit must take into account the effectiveness of the different organizations and activities:
    - oordinating committees
    - administrative offices
    - training for the program
    - case presentation
    - presentation of facilitators
    - support given to supervisors
    - overall activities

12. Manage costs. Carrying out the aforementioned activities often involves some cost, which must be accounted for if the economic picture of the quality circles company is to become clear. Each of these activities requires resources, and activities must themselves be standardized. Standardization is particularly necessary if the company is large.

Accentuating the complexity of circles management are the problems found in all companies:

- changes or shifts in personnel
- changes in machinery, work systems, and products
- high-pressure work times
- work reduction periods
- negotiations with trade unions

Only with an adequate structure and continuous leadership can quality circles endure in a company.

The Circles Office

Following is a comprehensive description of the quality circles office duties. In Japan, the functions of a circles office are carried out by the CWQM office, which usually reports directly to the president.

Promotion of Quality Circles

Promotion is carried out through two activities:

- establishing the concept of quality circle, based on the policies of top management, and spreading it among all employees
- organizing the promotion section of the CWQM office, and assigning the appropriate personnel to manage quality circles

Management of the Training Program

Managing the training program entails the following:

- establishing a long-term and a training schedule plan divided into annual periods
- preparing material for training and for the instructors
- carrying out training according to schedule

Supporting Circle Activities

To support circle activities means

- providing the facilitators with the necessary suggestions and assistance concerning the themes to pursue, the way to manage meetings, analysis techniques, and so on
- following the circles' activities and introducing corrective actions in order to eliminate weak points
- establishing the forms for quality circles' end-of-project reports, for project evaluation, and for overall evaluation of circle activities

Management Activities

Management activities include

- managing the following systems:
  1. circles records
  2. project evaluation
  3. prizes and recognitions
- preparing the schedule for internal meetings for the presentation of projects (by division, plant, and at a company level)
- organizing a committee for evaluating projects for internal conventions
- preparing the quality circles activities budget

- setting up newsletters or other publications for quality circles
- organizing regular meetings of the management committee

The Facilitator

The role of the facilitator is essential to quality circles success. Here we list the tasks assigned to this role.

Planning Activities

Planning activities consist in

- establishing criteria for elaborating a plan of action for the circles
- participating in the planning committee for circles activities
- supporting the leaders in preparing an annual plan, in choosing themes, in defining and solving problems and in editing the *QC story*
- promoting meetings with high-level executives so that goals and guidelines can be confirmed to circle members

Assistance to Circles

Providing assistance to circles means

- making contact with leaders and circle members on an individual basis, supporting their work and acting as advisor
- carrying out assistance in a planned fashion, in order to support the circles entrusted to one
- promoting circle activities to nurture both the creativity and development of their members' capabilities.

Training

The task of training involves

- preparing educational materials for circle members' training programs
- developing training sessions and training reinforcement for leaders and, where necessary, for members

Promotion of Circles

Promoting circles means

- publishing of newsletters on circle activities, in which the articles have been contributed from various departments, and promoting their distribution
- spreading the circles concept in the different departments, so as to promote a real understanding of them and to create an environment conducive to such activities
- spreading the concept of *people building* throughout the entire organization, as part of the guidelines handed down by top management
- promoting meetings between circles and their management, as well as with front-line workers, for the purpose of facilitating their common tasks and their degree of cooperation

Presentation of Projects

After a project has been completed, the facilitator sees to it that its results are presented. This means

- promoting sessions for the presentation of results at the level of department, divisions, plants, and so on
- promoting presentation of the more active circles to others, so that their experience can be shared
- preparing diplomas and prizes to confer upon the most deserving circles

Evaluating Activities

Evaluating activities comprises the following tasks:

- evaluating the projects presented with a critical analysis undertaken jointly with managers of the department involved
- evaluating performance and results obtained by the circles
- submitting the results of the evaluation to the central circles office

Meetings of Leaders and Facilitators

Leaders and facilitators meet regularly to exchange impressions and opinions with other facilitators, to learn new techniques, and to improve their own capabilities.

Exchanges with Other Companies

These exchanges take two forms:

- visiting other companies and participating in conferences where circles efforts are being presented, to see the level of realization and the development stage
- developing a program of visits to other companies for the training and advancement of circle leaders, as well as of individual members

Activities Budget

The facilitator prepares a budget for implementing activities; specifying the responsibility for expenses.

The Real Significance of Quality Circles

Earlier we showed a few elements that explain the meaning of the quality circles process. In this paragraph we wish to go further in attempting to clarify the great bearing of this process within the context of CWQM. To this end, we must take into consideration the following factors:

- the need for a new role for front-line employees
- the profound human demands of these workers
- quality circles and the supervisor
- the role of circles in the care for details
- the people-building process

The Need for a New Role for Front-Line Employees

The management structure (executives, middle managers, specialized technical employees) and front-line employees (production and administrative workers) went for years in different directions, and never tried to cooperate in any real way. The role given by management to front-line employees was very limited, and could be summarized as "managers think, operators work."

Today, more than ever, companies must struggle to survive. Technological innovations, the speed of change, and intense competition make a breakthrough necessary in these relations. In the past the management structure faced these challenges alone, but today they overcome the actual capabilities of this structure. Front-line employees, too, must actively participate in resisting these challenges.

Consequently, the relations between managers and employees should be based on new foundations; the employees also must bear part of the burden arising from the competitive challenges facing the company. Quality circles create such new foundations, providing workers with an opportunity to actively contribute to the company's improvement goals. Employee participation is voluntary, but it is up to management to promote among its ranks the need for the company to make the best use of all available resources.

The Profound Human Demands of Front-Line Employees

Everyone who works seeks human dignity on the job; this is especially true of front-line employees. Unfortunately, the Tayloristic organization did not take this need into account.

The leap that is required is a matter of seeing employees as creative, thinking human beings rather than merely arms and legs to do physical work. This change is accomplished by using the famous Deming Cycle, more technically known as the PDCA cycle. The widespread use of the PDCA cycle on the part of all employees underlies the mental revolution specific to CWQM.

If the profound human demands of employees are to be satisfied, it is necessary to move from the first to the second PDCA, as shown in the diagram in Figure 20-2. The jump from one cycle to the other is reflected in, among other things, the higher cultural level of the individuals, and their richer social life.

Quality circles make full use of the operators' mental faculties. Among other things, they call upon operators to use the scientific method, which is based on use of the seven statistical tools, as described earlier.

Quality Circles and Supervisors

The role of supervisor is enlarged in companies aiming for excellence (supervisors are people who directly supervise and coordinate front-line employees, both in departments and in offices). All operational problems are brought to these individuals; workers and office staff turn to them for guidance on behavior and resolution of any problems that arise.

In fact, supervisors are involved in a great number of small problems, yet at the same time must reach the goals for productivity and quality. To achieve this, they must, first, maintain and stabilize standards, and, second, strive to improve them. Because executives and top managers are generally removed from operational activities, they are unable to attend to their details. Thus the responsibility of supervisors is almost total.

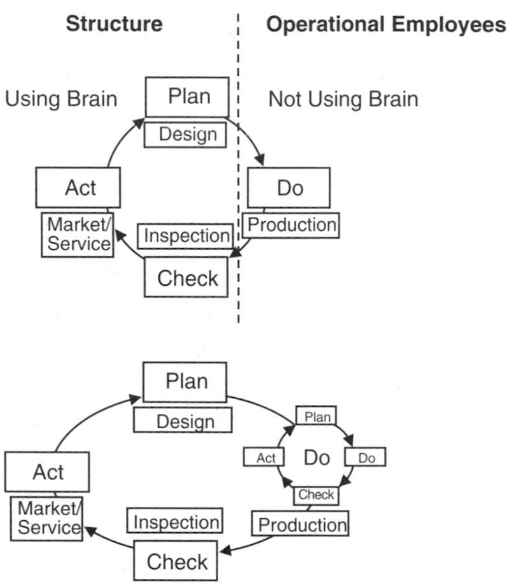

Figure 20-2. Role of Operational Employees

They represent, therefore, the real "link" between operative work and managerial work. From this point of view, their role as link with front-line workers becomes increasingly important, as it strengthens the employees' identification with their company. This role as a link has been well understood by the most dynamic Japanese companies.

In practice, supervisors must

- assist their superiors in their managerial tasks and in the decision-making process and, at the same time, assist the technical staff in carrying out improvement activities
- help their front-line employees by providing precise control of the processes they are entrusted with and constantly seeking small improvements.

In Japanese industry, quality circles have been the main tool used to achieve the twin goals of control and continuous improvement. To properly understand the meaning of the circles, one must understand that, in a sense, the circles' real goal is that of enhancing the supervisor's. Enhancement is essential if the company is to continue in its pursuit of excellence. Quality circles are structured to be a mirror of the entire company (executives, middle managers, and operational staff). Because the circles are self-reflective, this structure can evolve in a positive manner in the constant search for increasingly better results, respecting the balance between authority and internal democracy.

With quality circles supervisors must become trainers. In this way, a process of self-improvement by members is initiated under their leadership, which in turn nurtures the professional growth of the supervisors. They can then better assist their superiors in their managerial responsibilities. Without such mutual growth, the circles have no future. In companies that have understood the deep meaning of the circles program, (currently they are almost exclusively Japanese) the program itself has progressed to the point that management considers the circles a vital part of the development of the managerial capabilities, not as an isolated activity related to operational levels.

The Role of Circles in the Attentiveness to Details

The best-selling book in the history of modern management is the work by Tom Peters and Robert Waterman titled *In Search of Excellence* (1982), which sold about five million copies. It was followed by another book by Tom Peters, with Nancy Austin, called *A Passion for Excellence.* The two books are the result of research aimed at discovering the principal factors leading a company to success. The authors' interpretation of the way to obtain excellence, and thus to beat the competition, can be summarized this way:

- Management and directors must give the company a sense of leadership; to do this they must provide

values, vision, and a show of integrity. Without values and without vision, a company's employees cannot give their best.
- Excellence is pursued through obsessive attention to detail. It must emanate from highest management and be evident in all employees' work, including that of front- line employees.

The two characteristic features of an excellent company are profoundly different, yet they must coexist: this is the paradox of excellence. Circles play an essential role in fostering attentiveness to details, and thus they help to overcome this paradox. Front-line employees, the people most qualified to follow the detailed aspects of processes and procedures, are put in a position to be able to offer a solid contribution to improvement. It is important to remember this slogan, "Within the company, the highest experts in operational work are the workers themselves".

The People-Building Process

When the management structure understands that front-line employees are a company's greatest resource it will become actively involved in people building. Quality circles play a decisive role in the people-building process, and in a system of management based on education, as detailed in Chapter 5.

Table 20-1. A Few Parameters for Operating Circles

Parameters	Stage of Circle	
	Initial Period	Operational
Frequency of group meetings (# of times per month)	1 to 2	3 to 4
Percentage attending meetings	65	85 to 95
Percentage of speakers at meeting	80 to 90	100
Type of projects	Easy	Difficult
No. of projects carried out per year	1	3 to 4
No. of tools used per year	3 to 5	4 to 7
Number of presentations per year within department/office	1	1 to 2
Three-year activities plan	No	Yes

CHAPTER TWENTY-ONE

Intensive Education

Introduction

In CWQM the function of education is to position all employees so that they can make the best use of their intellectual capabilities. In a sense, CWQM represents the "discovery" of the brain, and of its boundless abilities.

Simple development of personal abilities is considered important, yet limited in and of itself. Training is believed to lead to a certain plateau in the execution of a specific task, beyond which it is impossible to proceed. If, however, people are taught to use their brains, there exist no limitations or final plateaus.

Once it becomes understood that the human brain has unlimited potential, education becomes of necessity intensive. That is because such realization prompts another: that education is the only factor that can distinguish one company form another, since technologies, machinery, and products, tend to be similar in all companies operating in the same field.

Elsewhere we said that the main purpose of education is to change people's mentality, and that one of the principal aspects of the new mentality is the desire and will for self-improvement. The role attributed to education by CWQM is based on trust: in people and in their ability to use their intelligence for the benefit of the company. Education programs are therefore developed on the principle that every person, with few exceptions, has sufficient potential to constantly learn and grow. A Japanese company with CWQM carries out three or four times more educational activities than an ordinary Western company does.

The Use of the Brain in Intensive Training

We all know what long and demanding preparation the Olympics require. The Japanese, by applying CWQM, understood before anyone else that the competition faced by companies is like a never-ending Olympic game, and that employee education represents a decisive factor. Hence two famous slogans:

> "CWQM begins with education and ends with education."
> (Kaoru Ishikawa)
>
> "Before manufacturing products, we must produce men."
> (Konosuke Matsushita)

These slogans summarize the process we have called "intensive education." In the West, the need for intensive training is fully highlighted by companies that are more advanced in their application of total quality.

The management of Hewlett-Packard Corporation made the following statement to a group of Italian executives who were visiting their company, "For years we thought we had done a lot of education, but when total quality was introduced, we realized we hadn't done enough."

Intensive education involves every person's brain, which one can view as black box (see Figure 21-1). In the central part of this diagram is a black box (the brain), which, like all black boxes, can be analyzed only through its input and output. At the operational level, when the black box is not used, and one input directly becomes an output, the work cannot be considered really as value adding; nor can we really speak of productivity. The same analogy applies to conceptual work, which without use of the black box becomes more intuitive than conceptual — obviously a dangerous way to operate.

CWQM attempts to ensure that all actions make use of the black box, relying on the boundless capabilities of the brain. To maximize this brain potential, a company must invest heavily in education; even more important, however, it must seek favorable conditions for such a process to be carried out.

The Essential Features of Training

The process of intensive education within CWQM has four main features:

1. It emphasizes human relations.
2. It assumes a company commitment.

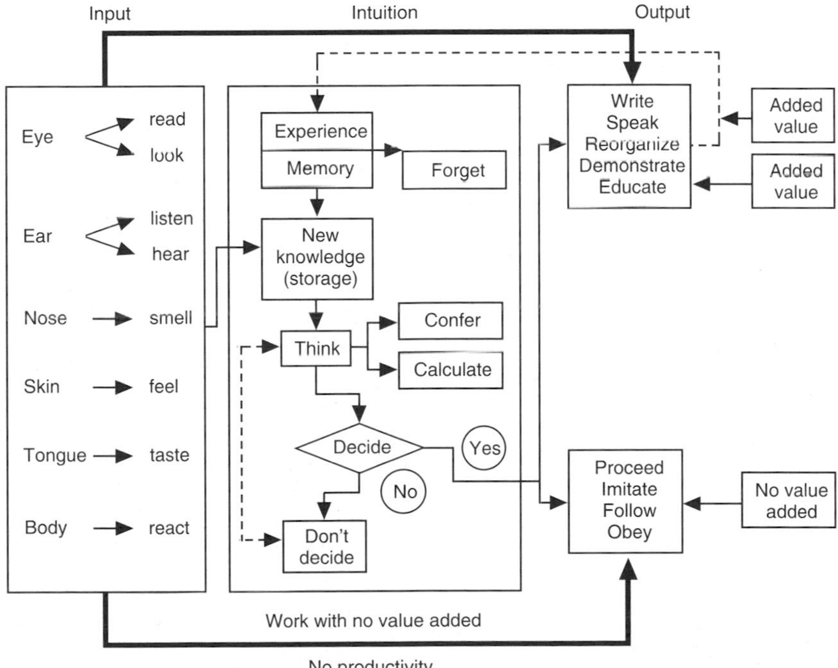

Figure 21-1. The Brain as a Black Box

3. It is continuous and flexible.
4. It has multiple goals.

A few comments on these features follow.

1. The education process is based on people rather than on techniques. People make a significant contribution to their company only if they are integrated within the system; professional training alone is not of much use. In Japanese companies, the process of transferring technical knowledge takes place in a very effective manner, through direct exchange from one person to another, as can be done among colleagues while they carry out their work.
2. Education constitutes a basic responsibility of the company, as it does in a family. Great emphasis is placed on the development of its members, as borne out by ceaseless investment of time and energy into such development.

   Cooperation among fully trained people and people who are in training enhances education, especially within a framework of long-term employment (given the educational value of communication flows).
3. In a marketplace where sudden changes are routine, it benefits neither the company nor its employees to restrict workers to a specific task that could soon become obsolete. With CWQM, companies promote various training and education cycles so as to "build" versatile employees. In this sense, education is continuous. With special reference to human relations, it is often set up in an informal way. This is one of the reasons why the monetary cost of training is normally quite low.

Intensive education strengthens the identification of employees with their company, and facilitates transition from one task to another. It also helps "future" managers to gather more technical and human relations experience within the various production units.

4. Education has multiple aims, related both to multiple demands and to the constant changes within the company: product quality and productivity, good personal relations on the job and technological innovations. In companies with solid experience in CWQM and in problem solving, the emphasis is on training in *problem finding,* which is essential for the development of positive quality.

Methods and Procedures in Intensive Education

There are many methods and procedures to implement intensive education. Figure 21-2 shows the most commonly used ones for employees in any area within the company. Note that quality control training is common to every area.

Great emphasis is placed on *on-the-job-training* (OJT), even though this type of training is not sufficient by itself. It should not be forgotten that the basic assumptions for the development of an individual's capabilities is personal will and commitment to learning.

Methods and procedures must be introduced into the flow of training activities. Figure 21-3 represents such a flow, outlined in terms of PDCA.

Different Education Areas

Intensive education concerns five different areas, as shown in the chart in Figure 21-4.Each area is important for education, and none of them should be neglected. The last step to be developed is *people building,* which mainly concerns operational

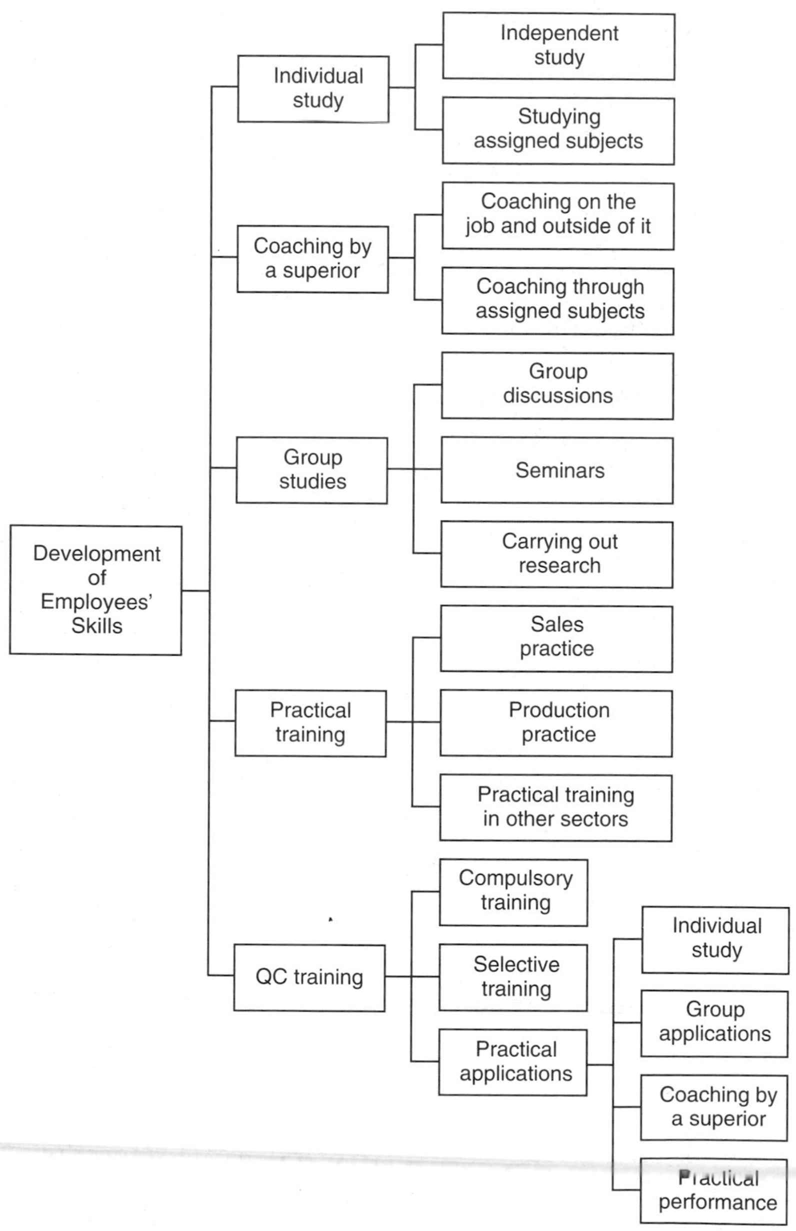

Figure 21-2. Development of Employees' Skills

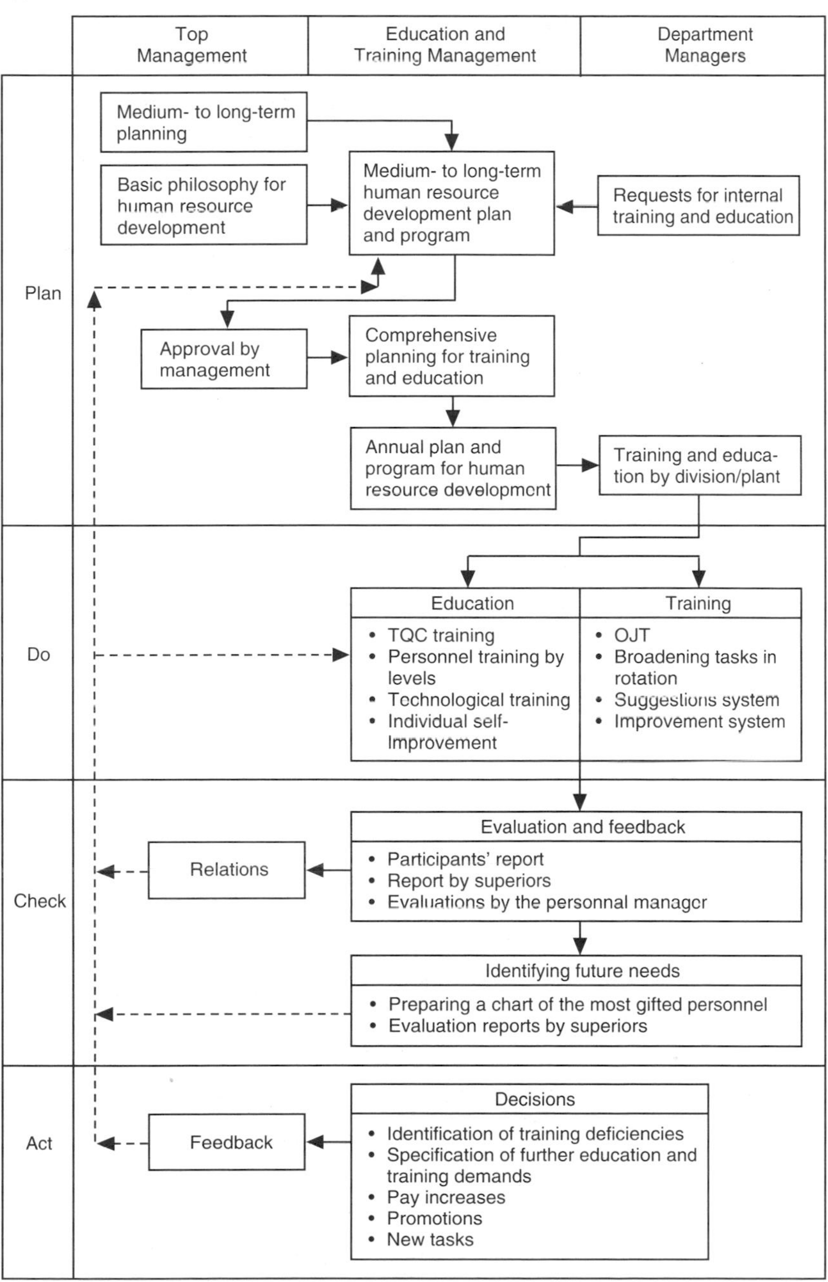

Figure 21-3. Flowchart of Human Resource Education and Training

employees. The internal operational training process relies on another basic process of CWQM, quality circles, as well as on the suggestions system. Both serve the purpose of developing "thinking" persons, that is, people who make maximum use of the above-mentioned "black box." The importance of education is immediately clear if one considers the extent to which it allows companies to develop the communications capabilities, participation, and creativity of employees. Figure 21-5 shows a chart of such development.

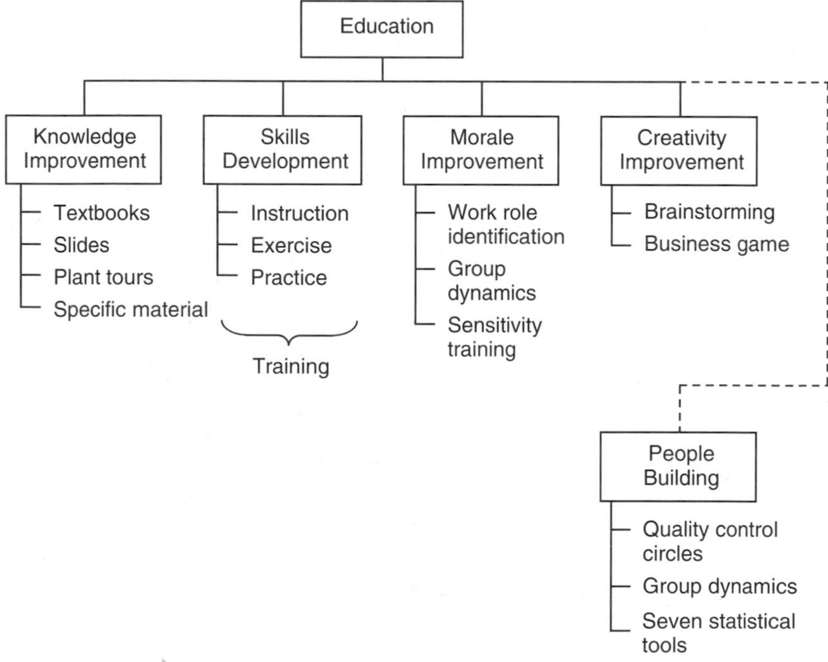

Figure 21-4. Areas of Education

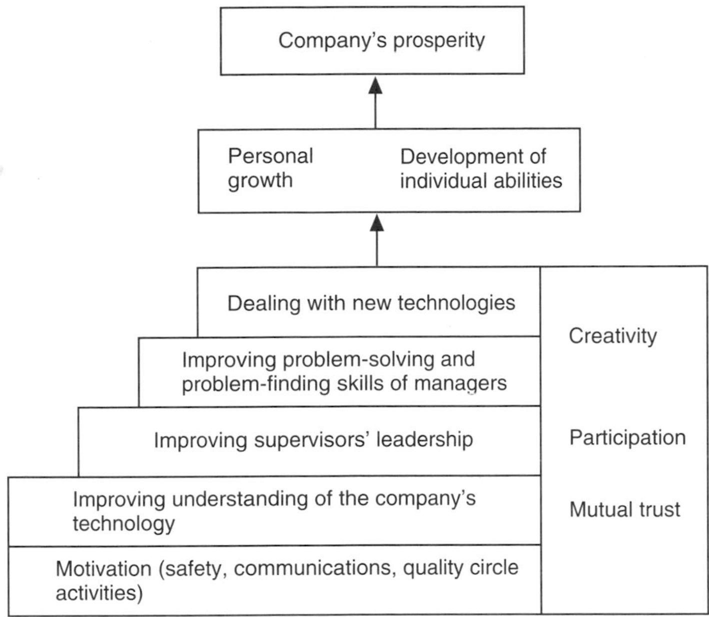

Figure 21-5. Human Resources Development Process

The Use of Communication Processes for Education

The intensive education process involves more than implementation through various methods; it must also be continuous and ever-active (hence the term *intensive education*). This continuous process is developed through use of communication flows as training tools. Consider that each person within a company "receives" information flows and at the same time "broadcasts" other flows. Such an information flow contains an educational value in the sense that it can be used to improve capabilities, broaden the view of jobs in relation to the company's needs, improve creativity, and increase motivation. For this value to be the highest possible, information flows must be as rich as possible. This requires that "broadcasters" be clear on the importance of communicating the greatest possible amount of information to their staff or colleagues. The most important communication flows are

- between managers and staff
- between colleagues in the same office or department
- between different offices or departments
- between the company and outside organizations

The education value of information flows will not be maximized unless a company creates conditions necessary for its development. Such conditions address two factors:

1. Mental attitudes of both receivers and broadcasters
   - *Receivers* must be eager to absorb all the information they receive
   - *Broadcasters* must be willing to transfer all the information in their possession and experience. Managers, for example, must be willing to communicate to staff information on company policy, work programs, and the reasons for doing certain things and not doing others.
2. Company culture
   - It should offer opportunities to intensify the flow of communication.
   - It should outline career paths with changes of position.
   - It should assign tailored tasks.

In summary, a CWQM company is a university in which employees are given constant opportunities to learn.

The quality control culture strengthens the orientation to education. The continuous study of problems and situations leads to an increasingly high level of awareness of the work carried out, and, thus, people's ability to control and improve processes continues to increase. The process of intensive education becomes a part of everyday activities.

The Key Function of the Career Plan

The *career development plan* is the basic support for education activities in the framework of CWQM. Without such a plan, the reference point necessary to determine education activities for every manager would be missing.

Figure 21-6 illustrates a typical example of career development, that of a sales person in Japanese company. This plan covers a 10-year period and calls for a shift in level, a rotation of the various company units, positions to be held, and the development plan. As the figure shows, career development broadens the role traditionally played by office workers, and thus promotes professional and personal growth among employees.

To establish a career plan, the company must draw up tables containing the qualifications required of people at different levels. Career progression is determined on the basis of an evaluation of employees' professional features. Such an evaluation takes place automatically, through an interview or test, depending on the career level sought. Table 21-1 shows an example relating to marketing personnel.

The Role of the Education Office

The education office plays an important role in intensive training within a CWQM framework. It must, first of all, be able to integrate the human resources development policy of the company with the actual organizational needs of the areas involved. Moreover, it should provide advisory support in the implementation of education policies. Such a task is carried out both through direct consultations with division and function managers and through implementation of the education program, with external support and by encouraging employee self-improvement.

Name	Position	Organizational Chart	Current Level
	Salesperson	Sales Department	6th

Year	1	2	3	4	5	6	7	8	9	10
Age	23	24	25	26	27	28	29	30	31	32

	Age 23–25	Age 25–27	Age 27–31	Age 31–32
Development Plan by Level	6	5	4	3
Department	Sales Department	XXX Plant	Commercial department General planning department	Marketing office
Function	Sales of essential goods	Production control	Sales control (27–29); Sales planning (28–31)	New product planning
Self-improvement Planning	Tests for sales personnel; Lessons in English conversation	Production control tests (25–28); Test on the handling of dangerous materials	Marketing test (28–31); Understanding procurement activities (28–31)	Lessons in English conversation

Figure 21-6. An Example of a (Ten-Year) Development Plan

Table 21-1. Qualifications Table (Marketing)

	Category			
	6	5	4	3
General Notions				
Language	X	X	X	X
Product knowledge	X	X	X	X
Understanding regulations	X	X	X	X
Total quality control	X	X	X	X
Composition trends		X	X	X
Applicable laws			X	X
Basic SQC	X	X	X	X
Basic economy			X	X
Basic technology			X	X
Job Knowledge				
Cost surveys				X
Commercial decrees				X
Work rationalization			X	X
Marketing theories				X
Marketing systems			X	X
Marketing control			X	X
Sales control		X	X	X
Commercial regulations				X
Production planning			X	X
Production control			X	X
Process lines				X
Product knowledge		X	X	X
Guarantee level	X	X	X	X
Product quality		X	X	X
Treatment of complaints	X	X	X	X
Treatment of accidents	X	X	X	X
Management policy			X	X
Management planning			X	X
Establishing goals		X	X	X
Marketing trends:				
• national		X		
• international			X	X
• competition				X
Individual Features				
Intuition			X	X
Ability to plan and schedule			X	X
Leadership abilities		X	X	X
Daring	X	X	X	X
Ability to establish relations	X	X	X	X
Ability to organize work	X	X	X	X
Ability to . . . (specifying for different roles)				

To summarize, the role of the education office can be represented as follows:

1. *Establishment and control of companywide human resources development system:*
   - understanding of top management policies for human resources development
   - preparation of human resources development system (program and plan)
   - identification of management and supervisor responsibilities regarding their subordinates' development
   - organizing the education system
   - establishment of education system regulation and standards
   - estimation and allocation of educational budget
   - establishment of long- and medium-range career development plan
   - evaluation of job-site education plans established by each organization, and follow-up
2. *Identification of education needs for human resources:*
   - identification of education needs or weakness based on top management policy, each organizational status and weakness, and technical and technological trends analysis
   - prioritizing of above findings on the basis of criticality, and inter-organizational analysis
   - decision on physical implementation program
     - participant selection
     - instructors selection
     - duration
     - budget
     - goals

3. *Support and counseling of site management and supervisors:*
   - furnishing of OJT procedures, tools, and methods to each responsible manager and supervisor
   - consultation on OJT implementation to improve their effectiveness
   - furnishing of OJT site education material
4. *Establishment and implementation of education program:*
   - establishment of in-house classroom-type education program organized by level of skill and technology
   - establishment of participation program organized by outside facility
   - establishment of long- and medium-range programs for above
5. *Support of self-development concept:*
   - promoting the need for self-development in every employee (people building)
   - encouraging employees to participate in the people-building program
   - persuading employees to recognize the importance of the people-building program by showing them the positive results that can be achieved

CHAPTER TWENTY-TWO

The President's Diagnosis

Introduction

What in Japan is known as the *president's audit,* or *president's diagnosis,* is certainly one of the most original approaches from a managerial point of view (by "president," we mean here the chief executive officer). This process represents the clearest evidence of the great revolution brought about by company-wide quality management. Several principles inform the president's diagnosis:

- At certain times of the year the president personally tackles processes, not just results.
- The president assesses basic problems of the company and takes on the responsibility of providing suggestions to the staff concerning such problems.
- The president applies quality control, in the search for the cause of problems.
- The president provides an example for the entire organization how to correctly apply the quality control (QC) concept.

Companies that have adopted CWQM have institutionalized the president's diagnosis and perform it at least once a year. Early in the process of introducing CWQM, companies often perform the diagnosis twice a year. The first application of the president's diagnosis occurred in the early 1950s at a Japanese company, Shin-Etsu Chemical Industry, which won the Deming Prize in 1953.

In this chapter we describe the managerial audits, or diagnoses. These should not be confused with the technical ones, such as the product quality audit and the quality system audit.

Goals of the Diagnosis

The main goals of the president's diagnosis are the following:

- checking the consistency of each unit's daily activities with company policy
- checking for proper application of the president's policies
- identifying important internal problems as well as ones related to emerging situations
- identifying the main organizational problems involving the entire company
- promoting the application of CWQM through the president's interaction with staff

The president's diagnosis assures the company of a greater capacity, over the long term, to achieve goals set by policy. An indirect goal of the diagnosis is that of educating the president to the correct application of quality control, and to obtain more precise information in order to define the company's policies for the following year.

This diagnosis is not intended to criticize the results obtained by executives and managers but rather to highlight the processes that led to such results. People are taught to recognize possible gaps while being provided with all necessary support to improve the situation. For this reason, and to eliminate any association of the term with control, the term *diagnosis* is preferred to *audit*.

The diagnosis also provides a useful opportunity and incentive to improve the flow of vital communications for the promotion of CWQM. Interaction rather than one-way communication, should take place to promote closer relations between the president and staff.

How the President's Diagnosis Is Carried Out

The president's visit to the department in question is announced a few weeks in advance. Before the visit, the president receives from the department manager a short report on the status of the department itself. On the visit, which usually lasts a whole day, the president is accompanied by the vice president or other top-level executive.

The diagnosis evolves over a number of stages. A typical example is the following:

- *Stage 1:* The action of the previous diagnosis is examined and compared with all actions developed in the meantime, which were detailed in the department manager's report.
- *Stage 2:* The unit undergoing the diagnosis illustrates its priority activities, and indicates new internal and external needs that could evolve into priority activities.
- *Stage 3:* A debate is held, with questions and answers based on examination of a series of control items. Typical control items might involve policy deployment, DRW, employee involvement, training, or financial resource problems. A checklist guides the questions, and the quality of the answers is carefully evaluated on the basis of the documentation and data provided. The questions could include:

1. What problems have been encountered in pursuing the president's policies at the department manager's level?
2. What procedures were followed to achieve these results?
3. What problems can be foreseen in the near future?
4. What suggestions does the unit wish to give the president and his staff?

- The department manager must be prepared to exhibit whatever data is necessary to strengthen the arguments. During the day, the president can make short visits to some offices or sectors of the departments under scrutiny.
- *Stage 4:* In this stage, the information that has emerged is reviewed, positive results are stressed, improvement areas are identified, and further research is delegated. The object is not to blame individuals for problems, but to find the causes of any shortcomings.
- *Stage 5:* The list of actions taken during the day is checked, summarized, and reported. In carrying out a diagnosis, the following aspects deserve special attention:
  - Don't just check results, but evaluate the process through which the results were obtained.
  - During the diagnosis, discrepancies among different data may appear. In such cases, concentrate on the problem and seek its causes. Avoid looking for a culprit to blame.
  - Use visual information and other documents showing the activities carried out. Diagrams, control charts, and similar materials are helpful for confirming information.

- Allow sufficient time for the debate so that the information can be communicated effectively.
- Finally, be sure to provide the department involved with all suggestions and recommendations it needs in order to assimilate the CWQM concepts.

Positive results that can be obtained with the president's diagnosis include the following:

1. First, this activity is useful for the president, who is forced to study CWQM concepts in depth. In analyzing the operations that take place in the various units, he or she has the chance to broaden his or her own understanding of the company.
2. The president can assess the true health of the company. The president normally receives information that has been filtered through the hierarchical ladder, which inevitably tends to highlight positive aspects. The president should encourage the presentation of reports focused on problems within the company, as this is precisely the aim of the diagnosis.
3. Human relations between top management and staff, which are often poor or nonexistent, have a chance to improve. To this end it may be useful to plan an informal meeting, such as a reception or dinner, after the diagnostic stage.
4. It is an important occasion to stimulate all those involved in CWQM activities.

Diagnosis at the Lower Management Levels

The diagnosis must also be conducted at managerial levels below that of the president. Two or three levels may be involved, depending on the size of the company. The goals are similar to those of the president's diagnosis, but related to the dimensions of the smaller unit under scrutiny.

The executives who report directly to the president evaluate activity planning, the analyses carried out in order to set goals and develop countermeasures, the status of business plan implementation, and the results achieved within the organizational unit. The managers who report to these executives, should in turn, evaluate staff who report directly to them. The audit carried out at the lower levels resembles the president's audit, with the five stages previously mentioned. Sample questions follow for policy deployment and for education and training.

Policy Deployment

- How were company's policies translated into concrete terms?
- Have adequate indicators and goals been set for each priority activity?
- Are countermeasures evaluated appropriately?
  - has the budget been considered?
  - has a cost-benefit analysis been carried out?
  - have the tools been used correctly and effectively?
- Is there a detailed schedule for the implementation plans?
  - has the required cross-functional cooperation been considered?
  - what contingency plans have been worked out for critical activities?
- Have the countermeasures been checked correctly?
- Have any actions been undertaken to address shortcomings?
- Has standardization been updated, based on improvement activities?

Education and Training

- How was the education program developed (what analyses were carried out)?
- What training program do you have (what is it, who, and how many people will be involved)?
- Is training used in daily activities (any examples)?
- Have any training programs been developed to support policy deployment activities?
- How is the effectiveness of training measured?
- Is there a need for further training?
- If there are deficiencies (in the above), what countermeasures are taken?

Managers' diagnoses usually take place every six months. Managers in charge of these diagnoses are required to prepare and submit to their immediate superior a report about the most relevant issues identified.

The President's Diagnosis at Komatsu

Komatsu, a Japanese company founded in 1921, is one of the world's largest manufacturers of machinery for the building industry (bulldozers, etc.). Diagnostic activities are structured on three levels: The first concerns the company as a whole, the second the individual divisions or plants, and the third affiliated companies. Whereas the second-level diagnosis is carried out by the executive in charge, the president works directly on the evaluation concerning affiliated companies and, of course, the company itself. The latter is the so-called president's diagnosis. In this activity, the president is assisted by the general managers and, in some cases, by one or more external consultants.

The diagnosis is carried out on an annual basis, and each year is focused on three or four priority issues, selected in relation to quality, cost, and delivery. One week before the diagnosis, the auditors receive a progress report on CWQM activities;

this document, called *jissetsu*, contains the answers to the following questions:

- Has the cooperation between the various departments been productive?
- Have goals been attained?
- If goals have not been obtained, what are the causes of failure?
- To what extent have customer expectations been satisfied?

During the audit, the people responsible of the various departments illustrate the data submitted and furnish any other explanation needed.

Jissetsu must be short and concrete, following a rule requiring that each hour of evaluation produce a document not longer than two pages: thus for a six-hour audit, there will be a 12-page *jissetsu*. This rule was introduced because, earlier, each manager participating in the evaluation would submit a 30-to 40-page report, in eagerness to show all he or she had accomplished. The effectiveness of the meeting was thus considerably compromised, because of the time needed to provide all the necessary explanations.

Those involved in the diagnosis must be able to present upon request full documentation pertaining to the activities reported in the *jissetsu*. This custom implies that the document itself will contain only that has in fact been done, and prevents the diagnosis from becoming simply a formality to be carried out.

The diagnosis then becomes the basis for subsequent activities: the unit that has undergone the diagnosis then develops a plan of action for each weak area identified. These plans are submitted to the quality committee and become a part of the unit's policies for the following year.

CHAPTER TWENTY-THREE

The Chief Executive Leadership Role for CWQM

Introduction

In Part 1 we presented an overall view of the company-wide quality management. One of the system's four building blocks is the chief executive officer's leadership, which we described as the real engine behind CWQM. In fact, the successful introduction of CWQM *totally* depends on the commitment and the enthusiasm devoted by the company's chief executive in the area of quality. Commitment and leadership must be translated into constant leadership action, necessary to guide the entire organization toward the fundamental changes involved in CWQM.

The crux of such leadership action is the CEO's recognition of quality (and therefore customer satisfaction) as a priority equal to that of profits and results. Surely one cannot expect a company's employees to become positively involved in quality if the CEO does not provide an example.

In Japanese companies, before the development of CWQM, the CEO was barely informed on quality-related problems and on the operating of the quality systems; therefore, he or she devoted very little time to quality. With the introduction of CWQM, this void was filled. The company's top management must be the first to practice quality control, and to create an approach to work that respects quality. In Japan, the commitment of top executives to quality control was the key factor in that country's success.

Mistaken Attitudes of Top Management Toward Quality

In his book *Total Quality Control,* Ishikawa maintains that in Japan many top executives do not understand the importance of this new approach. They have scarce and erroneous knowledge of CWQM concepts, as evidenced by certain common attitudes. Whereas many exhibit a strong interest in result indicators (such as profits, turnover, and technological investments), the interest in quality appears to be weak. Considering quality to be a problem pertaining to the production area, top executives pay little attention to process factors and parameters, which are decisive for quality. Often the CEO does not have a detailed picture of how the quality level of the company's products and services compares to that of the competition's products and services.

The shortsighted preconception that attention to improvement of quality leads to cost increases comes from the mistaken conviction that quality management means control and inspection. A few typical statements show a mistaken approach to quality: "We do not need CWQM. Our sales continue to grow. Why should we need CWQM? We have our quality specialists; I am sure they are doing their best." Such statements reflect the CEO's lack of direct involvement in quality problems. Some point to their employees' participation in seminars as evidence of their great commitment to training. Yet training is not sufficient if people are not allowed to put into practice the knowledge acquired.

Another typical attitude is, "Let us cut costs, and not worry too much about quality." Many top managers are convinced that cutting costs is their main mission. It is, of course, an important aspect of managing a company, and CWQM can be a great help in achieving this goal. However, operating with this aim alone, and thus taking a short-term view, harms quality and ultimately costs a company the trust of its customers. There is also a lack of awareness of how quality needs change over time: that which was sufficient one or two years ago might be inadequate today.

Even the belief that one's standards are the highest in the national market signals a narrow outlook: competition lurks around every corner, waiting for a chance to enter our markets and thus make our lives more difficult.

The Most Dangerous Managers for CWQM

Professor Mizuno divides managers who hinder CWQM into four categories:

1. those who know nothing about CWQM
2. those who know about CWQM but are not interested in it
3. those who oppose CWQM, since they believe it is not necessary
4. those who believe that CWQM is already being applied in their company, when in fact, it is not.

According to Mizuno, the managers belonging to the fourth category are the most resistant to the introduction of CWQM. In particular:

- They are held back by their prejudices concerning the meaning of CWQM, and usually have a fuzzy view of their company's real performance.
- They tend to distort CWQM into a spiritual movement or reduce it to a flow of reports and paperwork.

- They are too busy to take the time to carefully examine the real meaning of CWQM, and to realize all the details necessary to its application
- They do not have a feeling for operational activities, and find it difficult to understand their details.
- They do not understand that CWQM involves radical change in company priorities and employee attitudes.

Responsibilities of the Chief Executive

The CEO must take the lead in guiding the organization toward the deep changes associated with CWQM. This leadership cannot take shape if the CEO does not demand extremely high goals of top and middle managers. On this point there must be no doubt: if a company wishes to, it can achieve goals that are unimaginable within a traditional framework.

Many Japanese companies have achieved great results; an example is Yokogawa Hewlett-Packard, which won the Deming Prize in 1982. In that company, assembly nonconformities were reduced from 4,000 to 400 parts per million (ppm), and the wave solder defect rate went from 4,000 to 4 ppm — using machinery considered obsolete by the company's American counterpart. Figure 23-1 shows other significant data on the subject.

Given the need to provide very challenging goals, the CEO has 10 responsibilities in applying CWQM.

1. The CEO must carefully examine quality control and companywide quality management concepts, and fully understand the problems related to their application.
2. The CEO must be personally committed to all processes preliminary to the application of CWQM.
3. The CEO must formulate directly the principal policies regarding quality, within the framework of hoshin management, after analyzing the state of quality and of the internal product quality system.

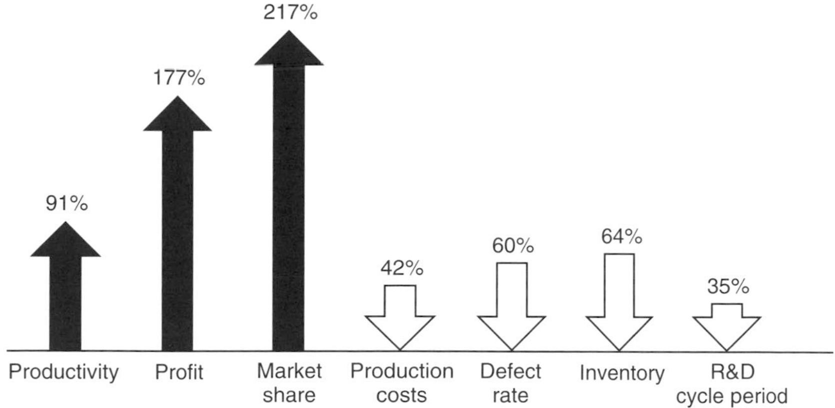

Figure 23-1. Yokogawa Hewlett-Packard: The Results of Five Years of CWQM

4. The CEO must become actively involved in implementing the "quality first" strategy, by specifying the quality levels necessary for long-term goals related to the international market situation.
5. The CEO must take a leadership role in implementing CWQM concepts, promoting them personally.
6. The CEO must ensure the training activities necessary to the implementation of the program, on the basis of medium- and long-term plans.
7. The CEO must personally verify the state of application of policies and programs related to quality, and take any corrective action necessary, through the president's diagnosis.
8. The CEO must specify his or her own responsibilities concerning quality assurance, and endorse the company's quality assurance system.
9. The CEO must endorse the control system to be assigned to each organizational unit.
10. The CEO must spread concepts such as "the downstream department is your customer."

Top management cannot exercise a leadership role in the area of quality if it does not possess information that motivates actions undertaken in the various departments. Essential knowledge concerns the following subjects:

- management responsibilities in the area of quality
- PDCA
- quality data for management
- an information system regarding quality and customer satisfaction
- hoshin management
- daily routine work
- In-process control
- quality assurance
- the president's diagnosis
- the career development plan
- quality control circles
- relations with suppliers

Since 1962 JUSE has sponsored a course for top executives of Japanese companies. The 33-hour program covers the following subjects:

1. management and quality control: quality control for new product development (3 hours a week)
2. quality assurance (4 hours)
3. how to use statistical methods (3.5 hours)
4. quality control in manufacturing processes: small group activities (3.5 hours)
5. quality control in procurement and sales departments (3.5 hours)
6. quality control administration (3.5 hours): organization, promotion, education, and training
7. status and trend of quality control in Japan and in the world (3.5 hours)

8. case study on the initiation and promotion of quality control (3.5 hours)
9. group discussion and conclusion (5 hours)

The Chief Executive's Commitment to CWQM

The chief executive's duties are numerous and diverse. According to Ishikawa, in a medium-large company, the estimated time devoted to these activities should be between 15 and 20 days a year. Such activities can be listed as follows:

1. Initial period:
   - acquiring the basic concepts of CWQM, and acquiring the methodologies and tools for its correct application and for resolution of problems
   - visiting a few companies in the forefront of CWQM application
2. Later period:
   - chairing the CWQM executive committee (bimonthly meetings)
   - participating in the periodic presentations of management plans, and discussing them (at least twice a year)
   - participating (at least twice a year) in the official presentations of the quality circles, and making comments
   - providing guidelines and approving the monthly messages concerning quality to be communicated to all personnel
   - defining the policies to be used as a point of departure for the annual cycle of hoshin management
   - carrying out the president's diagnosis every year (twice a year, during the first years)

- applying PDCA to cases concerning one's work, in the framework of improving one's output (personal quality)
- visiting the distribution network and customers, in order to better understand problems related to quality
- participating in specific initiatives for the promotion of quality within the company

Taking a leadership role in the CWQM program requires a considerable commitment on the part of management. It is not sufficient to issue policies; rather, top managers must act as guides and as driving elements.

It is important to be aware that substantial change in the organization will not be evident for a few years after CWQM introduction. In Japan this period lasts at least five years, while in Western companies the period is certainly longer.

Even when it might seem natural to feel gratified by the results obtained, and to be content with the levels attained, continued effort on the part of the company's top management should be maintained. The entire organization should constantly be reminded that, with rapid market changes and the increasingly pronounced competition, successes are only temporary, and thus the company's drive toward continued improvement should never be slackened.

The Chief Executive's Responsibilities in Quality Assurance

One of the CEO's tasks is to define his or her responsibilities in quality assurance and to endorse the company's system pertaining to it. This duty is important because with CWQM, the customer becomes the company's top priority. Given this priority, it is necessary to constantly improve the level of "satisfaction" that products or services ensure for the customer, while at the same time striving to eliminate problems. Who, if not the chief executive, can guarantee this goal? Nothing can replace the direct responsibility of the CEO: this person is the only one who can fully protect the client's interests within the company. Hence the CEO must have complete responsibility concerning quality assurance. In particular, the CEO is responsible for

1. establishing and spreading the policy of quality
   - at all levels
   - for each product
2. setting quality goals and procedures to achieve them, taking as a reference
   - the development of basic products and production capability
   - basic products and decisions pertaining to their quality
   - maintenance and assistance at the clients' premises
   - safety
   - improvements in the level of design and development of new products
   - improvements in the quality of procedures
   - reductions in manufacturing and assembly defects
   - reductions in customer complaints
3. establishing a quality system
   - analysis and research concerning the quality demanded by the market (customer needs)
   - production planning
   - design and engineering
   - production engineering (industrialization)
   - purchasing
   - production
   - inspection and testing
   - storage
   - packing and transportation

- customer service
- complaints and regeneration (or recycling)

4. organizing quality assurance
   - organizational structure and functions
   - assigned personnel
   - responsibilities and level of authority
   - delegation
   - evaluation criteria
5. planning quality: in the development of new products, establishing a "quality plan" in order to determine
   - quality goals to achieve
   - the systems responsible for quality at the various stages
   - the need to implement new technologies, materials, equipment, and methodologies
   - the personnel needed (human resources)
   - inspections, tests, measuring systems, and tools needed
   - other tools for quality evaluation and demonstration
6. carrying out a quality diagnosis of pertinent activities, by
   - defining the group in charge
   - defining the audit program containing system audit procedures, process audit procedures; and product audit procedures
7. reexamining the quality system
   - following the results of the audits
   - for the introduction of new technologies
   - for new market strategies
   - for market changes due to social or international factors, or to changes in the competition's attitudes

PART FIVE

Introducing Companywide Quality Management into a Company

The introduction of companywide quality management into a company is critical to the system's effectiveness. It is not enough to understand the concepts underlying this new management system; one must also be able to apply it specifically to one's company. The problem is even more complex because of the time needed for such an introduction, which varies between 4 and 6 years in Japan, and 6 to 10 years in the Western world. In the West, only a small number of companies have 7 to 8 years of experience in the application of CWQM, while the great majority have no more than 4 to 5 years.

If one considers that managers need at least 2 or 3 years to learn the meaning of this new approach, and that an effective application of CWQM can be initiated only after such a level has been reached, one can understand why most companies in the United States and Europe are still in the early stages of introducing CWQM. Further complicating the process are the barriers of the Japanese language and of Western prejudice toward Japanese culture.

The first chapter in Part Five is devoted to a description of the ways in which Japanese companies introduce CWQM. A section of this chapter was written by Professor Ryuichi Kobayashi, the 1987 Deming Prize winner.

In the second chapter we describe the entry point for the application of CWQM, which Galgano & Associati has applied extensively in Italy and in some European companies through the launch of quality improvement program. It was through this program, applied in over 250 companies, that Galgano & Associati developed and enriched its know-how in this field.

In the third chapter we illustrate the CWQM application plan. We believe that this "second-generation" plan will be the model for effective introduction of the new approach, both in industrial and in service companies, during the next few years. This plan has already been tested in important Italian companies, and it addresses global introduction of CWQM. Being developed by the company's management itself, it is, thus tailored to the specific reality of that company.

CHAPTER TWENTY-FOUR

The Introduction of CWQM in Japan

Introduction

The introduction of companywide quality management into a company assumes full awareness of the two major changes to be made:

- a "mental revolution" among all employees
- a new "constitution" for the company

Such changes require years of careful CWQM implementation. Generally, five years is the shortest period needed for the full implementation of the CWQM plan in a medium-large Japanese company. Thus, the steps needed to fully implement a CWQM plan must be followed precisely.

Roughly half of all major companies in Japan have introduced CWQM, while the rate among mid-size or small companies is of two out of five. The most advanced industrial sectors, from this point of view, are transportation companies, paper manufacturers, electronics companies, and ferrous and nonferrous metal industries.

Introducing CWQM into a Company

According to the experience of the best Japanese companies, the introduction of CWQM occurs in two phases:

1. the preparatory phase
2. the implementation phase

Of course, the length and intensity of each phase, as well as the transition from one to the other, depend upon the company's culture, size, and features, as well as on its management's decisions. The model described in this Chapter is a general guideline only.

Even before embarking on the preparatory phase, a company must carry out sensitizing activities. The most important of these are the following:

- establishment of a long-range plan and an implementation program
- establishment of organizational guidelines for CWQM
- assignment of employees for management
- establishment of implementation procedures
- establishment of medium-term policy, based on long-term policy and objective
- training of managers for dissemination of the policy and objectives
- adaptation of managers to concept of hoshin management

The Preparatory Stage of CWQM

The preparatory stage is perhaps the most delicate phase in CWQM introduction, because successful implementation depends on it. The main points of this phase are the following:

- establishment of fundamental policies (quality, quality control, and quality assurance)
- training of management in the concepts of CWQM

- top-level support for the development of CWQM
- support of the "critical problem solution" program
- promotion of standardization and daily routine work
- trial run of hoshin management in a limited area

This model, and that given for implementation, is for reference only. Moreover, it applies only to medium-large and large companies. In fact, a company's reality does not lend itself to schematic representations, and over a period of about five years, events within the company force many changes.

There follows a detailed description of the activities concerning each item.

- Establishment of fundamental policies (quality, quality control, and quality assurance)
  1. commitment to the essentials of management policy
  2. definition of *quality*
  3. definition of *quality assurance* and its execution policy
  4. definition of *quality control* and its execution policy
  5. commitment to necessity of CWQM implementation and formulation of its definition

- Training of management in the concepts of CWQM (basic concepts, quality control system, quality assurance system, statistical methods, companywide participation).
  1. determination of policy for CWQM implementation by organizational levels
  2. establishment of training program
  3. preparation of education material for all levels
  4. determination of training procedures
  5. training of upper and middle managers

- Top-level support for development of CWQM
  1. establishment of support program for CWQM management in each office on a consultant basis
  2. assignment of instructors
  3. preparation of training material by organizational level
- Support of the "critical problem solution" program (for executives, upper, and middle managers)
  1. request for identification of "critical problem areas" within their assignment job
  2. explanation of PDCA conception (plan-do-check-act) concept
  3. explanation of CWQM approach and its effectiveness
  4. explanation of use of scientific method to identify and correct problems
- Promotion of standardization and daily routine work (DRW)
  1. establishment of standardization program (company standards, management standards, and technological standards)
  2. establishment of standardization committee
  3. determination of standardization system policy
  4. appointment of standardization facilitators in each organization
  5. establishment of standards
  6. campaign for dissemination and enforcement
  7. preparation of DRW handout
- Trial run of hoshin management in a limited area
  1. dissemination of top management policies to department managers
  2. setting of lower-level policy and goals
  3. determination of control item and control point

4. preliminary run, the length of which is to be defined
5. implementation of PDCA cycle activity
6. explanation of statistical method utilization

The Implementation Phase of CWQM

The most important activities in the implementation phase of CWQM are the following:

- regular use of hoshin management by all executives and managers
- full training in quality control for all employees
- assistance to departments starting improvement activities
- introduction of the daily routine work concept
- development of the quality function deployment concept, in addition to that of hoshin management
- full application of the quality assurance concept in every department over the lifecycle of the product
- extension of standardization activities to nonproduction
- establishment of a system to gather, analyze, and evaluate information pertaining to quality
- extensive application of quality audits

There follows a description of activities pertaining to each item.

- Regular use of hoshin management by all executives and managers
    1. developing with top management the policies for each department
    2. identifying basic goals and establishing a priority index
    3. establishing control points and actions

- Full training in quality control for all employees
  1. creating awareness of the quality control concept
  2. instruction on developing quality circles
  3. presentations by executives, managers and circle leaders

- Assistance to departments starting improvement actions
  1. to improve product quality
  2. to improve reliability
  3. to prevent product defects
  4. to reduce costs

- Introduction of the daily routine work process
  1. promotion of the concept of internal customer
  2. identification of internal customer needs in each department
  3. definition of processes to be controlled
  4. development of performance indicators

- Development of quality function deployment and hoshin management concepts
  1. establishment of quality function deployment roles and responsibilities
  2. establishment of procedures to deal with complaints and to define appropriate corrective actions
  3. implementation of procedures in every organizational area
  4. report and evaluation from each area
  5. report on the deficiencies of each area
  6. partial revision of each area's goals

- Full application of quality assurance concept in every department and over the lifecycle of the product.

1. definition of quality assurance policies and their implementation schedule
2. establishment of a new product development policy
3. establishment of a policy for dealing with complaints and of appropriate corrective actions
4. establishment of a quality improvement program for all types of products
5. coordination of department's plans according to quality function deployment concept
6. collection and analysis of data concerning quality
7. assurance of safety and reliability

- Extension of standardization activities to nonproduction units
  1. establishment of programs and schedules for the marketing organization
  2. establishment of programs and schedules for other management offices
  3. establishment of standardization systems for nonproduction activities

- Establishment of a system to gather, analyze, and evaluate information pertaining to quality
  1. establishment of an information-gathering system
  2. establishment of a system for synthesizing and evaluating information
  3. creation of a feedback and follow-up system
  4. analysis and evaluation of internal information
  5. analysis and evaluation of external information

- Extensive application of the quality audit
  1. setting of goals, policies, and management structures for the diagnosis

2. establishment of audit program
3. establishment of systems and procedures for the audit
4. preparation of control sheets
5. implementation of top-management program and that of the other offices (CWQM office, etc.)
6. delegation of responsibility for the audit
7. evaluation of audit's effectiveness

Development of a CWQM Plan Within a Small to Medium-Size Company

Even in Japan, difficulties sometimes arise in the application of CWQM in small and medium-sized companies, particularly in the application of hoshin management. The reason is that the management culture of these companies is not well developed. The model shown in the preceding paragraphs is not easily applicable in companies of this size.

Experience has taught that it is easier to implement CWQM concepts if the following steps are taken:

1. Start from a departmental level (depending on the size of the company). Hold brainstorming sessions to identify the following within the organization:
   - the best processes, procedures, products
   - the worst processes, procedures, and products (sometimes called "problems")
   - customer complaints for which the various units are responsible
   - the highest rates of unsuccessful processes and products and their costs
2. Identify, according to perceived priorities, areas that require corrective actions.
3. Define goals to pursue for every area.
4. On the basis of the improvement projects established and through the plan-do-check-act cycle,

define corrective actions that need to be carried out with the participation of all management.

5. After successful completion of the first project, start a second one, following the same sequence of steps.
6. Once everyone has become familiar with the PDCA cycle, and every problem has been eliminated through cooperation, implement hoshin management in every area, according to the policies set by top management.
7. If difficulties are found in carrying out hoshin management, initiate further training, getting the assistance of external consultants

The Development of CWQM in a Japanese Company

Figure 24-1 shows the process by which a medium-large Japanese company (more than 3,000 people) introduced CWQM. Note that this example does not precisely correspond to the model just described. Rather, it displays the vital actions that were carried out from the first to the fifth year.

The more general model takes into account all the most innovative CWQM processes, which are set up and begun during the first year and then carried out gradually over subsequent years, in accordance with the following criteria:

- Clearly define the goals pursued during the five development phases of the plan. These phases must correspond to specific actions aimed at reaching full implementation.
- Support the introduction of CWQM through creation of appropriate organizational structures (CWQM office, QC management committee, division or plant QC committee, quality assurance committees, cross-functional QFD committee).

Year	1	2	3	4	5
Stage	**Introduction**	**Promotion**		**Implementation**	
Objectives	Introduction of management by policy and quality circles Establishment of quality assurance system	Full promotion of hoshin management concept (through understanding of law of priorities)	Full promotion of the concept of daily routine work Full implementation of quality assurance concepts	Introduction of quality function deployment	Full implementation of cross-functional management
New Organization	Established CWQM office	Quality control committee organized by division or plant	Established CWQM management committee at headquarters Established quality assurance committee	Established 5 cross-functional committees	Development of cost deployment, technology deployment, and reliability deployment at the cross-functional level

Vital Actions

Hoshin Management

Definition and implementation of the first medium-term plan

- Introduced
  - Review of current practice
  - Established HM manual
- Identification of vital few problems and solution
  - Policy deployment practices
  - Self-evaluation of policy achievement
  - Improving the process of defining the president's policies
  - Defining standards to establish "control item"
  - Experimenting with HM in each major function
  - Defining other standards
  - Defining control procedures for "control items"

Definition and implementation of the second medium-term plan

- Full implementation of hoshin management
  - Defining rules for the medium-term policies of divisions
  - Estabishing the "policy" for each main function
  - Examining management's tasks and top management's long-term policies

President's diagnosis (X2)	Diagnoses by the president and by the department managers	Standardizing the diagnoses

Evaluation and Dissemination of CWQM Activities

Development of improvement awareness, of problem-solving capabilities, and strengthening of the above

- CWQM education at all levels
- Training of quality circle leaders, through expert support
- Presentations of improvement cases (twice a year)
- Education in statistical quality control
- Suggestions system reorganization
- Training of middle management (3-year plan)
- Improving/analyzing project registration system
- Strengthening the training of circle leaders
- Refresher course on statistical tools from in-house instructors

Research and Development

New product development

- Introducing the product planning committee
- Identifying key design problems and their solution
- Strengthening preproduction capability
- Introducing design review and FMEA
- Use of design of experiments
- Analyzing factors in the lack of success
- Introducing FTA
- Improving standard tables
- Reorganizing the new product development system
  - Improving the new product development system
  - Developing ways of using a new product by analyzing needs (QFD)
  - Improving the internal quality information system
  - Improving the system for gathering market information

Figure 24-1. CWQM Implementation

<table>
<tr><th>Year</th><th>1</th><th>2</th><th>3</th><th>4</th><th>5</th></tr>
<tr><th>Stage</th><th>Introduction</th><th colspan="2">Promotion</th><th colspan="2">Implementation</th></tr>
<tr><td></td><td colspan="5">Quality Assurance

Development of New Materials in Cooperation with Suppliers
- Development of new materials to satisfy customer needs
- Stricter quality assurance clauses

Introduction and use of quality function deployment
- Preparing the market-share map
- Studying new quality characteristics
- Gathering market information
- Initial applications of quality function deployment
- Review of quality function deployment procedures

Improvement of purchase methods and new equipment
- Defining plans for the installation of new equipment
- Checking the operations defined earlier

Complete in-process control
- Improvement by process analysis
- Introduction of quality assurance tables
- Development of the day-by-day control concept through the QA and QC process sheet
- Defining process control standards

Improvement of technical service through the development of a new system of production plant tools
- Initiating new relations with suppliers
- Improving methods for evaluating quality
- Feedback information for new product design</td></tr>
<tr><td>Results</td><td>Introduction of quality circles in the main plants
Introduction of a quality assurance system for the main products</td><td>Comment or diagnosis from the top:
“all control systems are organized to promote CWQM”</td><td>Quality level of principal products comparable to that of the most competitive products
Quality assurance system well organized by products</td><td>First application of QFD
Optimal levels of intensive training reached
Increase in productive capability based on the concept of companywide quality control</td><td>Full implementation of QFD</td></tr>
</table>

- Introduce hoshin management gradually, prefacing it with an experimental phase during which "control point" standards can be redefined. During all phases, perform the president's diagnosis to check for consistency and progress of CWQM application.
- Fully train middle managers, emphasizing field activities (and in particular, improvement activities).
- With CWQM, the multiyear plan for the development of new products must be the result of an intense exchange among all unit of a company. The application of advanced techniques such as FMEA, FTA, the design of experiments, and multi- varied analysis (see Chapter 13) allow the early detection of two crucial aspects of research and development:
  1. the allocation of resources for the development of products and technology
  2. the identification of technological bottlenecks in the development of new products
- Because all units of a company are involved in quality assurance, each unit should carry out both QC and QA functions, from relations with suppliers to the operational realization of quality assurance, according to the customer's demands. In the multiyear development plan for quality assurance, the following important points can be noted:
  1. the development of new materials, in cooperation with the supplier of raw material
  2. the introduction of quality function deployment, and full use thereof
  3. the improvement of purchase methods as a result of new relationships with suppliers
  4. total in-process control

- Finally, checking the results provides the feedback necessary to measure the degree to which the multiyear plan is being carried out and to adjust company policies accordingly.

In Table 24-1 we show a few basic steps undertaken in the CWQM introduction among Deming Prize winners.

Problems in CWQM Introduction in Japan

Despite the perception in the West that CWQM is second nature to Japanese companies, numerous problems were encountered during its introduction in that country. Professor Mizuno, who for 40 years has assisted many Japanese companies in introducing CWQM, mentions the following problems as among the most frequently encountered:

- Uninterested top management
- Middle management's failure to recognize its role in CWQM

Table 24-1. CWQM Introduction in Some Deming Prize Winners

Name	Introduction of Quality Control	Adoption of CWQM	Initiation of President's Diagnosis	Receipt of Deming Prize
Nippondenso	1949	1956	1960	1961
Sumitomo Electric Ind.	1949	1956	1960	1962
Toyota	1949	1961	1962	1965
Matsushita (Electric Comp. Division)	1949	1964	1965	1966
Bridgestone Tire	1950	1964	1965	1968
Tejin	1954	1959	1959	1961
Komatsu	1961	1963	1963	1964

- Unclear CWQM targets
- Lack of product quality policies
- Failure to clarify scope of CWQM activities
- Lack of clear-cut program for CWQM implementation
- Too much stress on theory and too little effort to learn the methodology
- Ritualized CWQM activities with little or no meaningful content
- Assumption that CWQM is limited to quality circles
- General lack of interest
- Problems in the CWQM headquarters
- Incomplete understanding of what to achieve with CWQM
- Lack of well-defined and uniform CWQM terminology

In small and medium-sized companies, the most common problems are the following:

- establishing and spreading policies and goals
- spreading the awareness of the QC concept among management
- carrying out training, and follow-up
- implementing the president's diagnosis
- identifying control points and check points

Responsibility for the difficulties encountered belongs entirely to management, which alone can remove them. The companies that successfully introduced CWQM share the following features:

- The policies of top management are well defined and effectively deployed throughout the company.
- Policies are aimed at revealing problems and establishing priorities.

- The limits of responsibility and authority are clearly defined.
- There are no administrative or psychological barriers within the company, whether vertical or horizontal.
- Problems are dealt with so that their causes can be prevented, not so that results can be influenced.
- The PDCA cycle "runs" smoothly.
- Actions are carried out on the basis of careful analysis of statistical data.

Some Considerations on CWQM in Japan

(By Ryuichi Kobayashi, Deming Prize Winner, 1987)

Introduction

In these paragraphs the development and implementation of CWQM activities in Japanese industry are explained.

As is well known, two great teachers in this field were Professor Shigeru Mizuno, from the Tokyo Institute of Technology, and Kaoru Ishikawa, from Tokyo University. I had the good fortune to personally observe how these men guide many Japanese businesses in CWQM introduction during the difficult postwar period.

In a private letter to Professor Mizuno, I once wrote that I expected European and American experts, not Japanese ones, to succeed in systematizing and building the theoretical structure of CWQM. I believed this in light of the fact that customarily, in Japan, the formulation and description of CWQM activities appear in the form of articles, according to tradition in Japanese technical literature.

A few years ago, Professor Mizuno made a donation to the Japan Society for Quality Control, so that it could begin systematizing the theoretical structure of CWQM in Japan. Research on this subject is carried out by a research committee, under the guidance of Kenichiro Imai. The results of the study will soon appear in Japanese, and they will show the stages of CWQM activities, and the explanation of CWQM technical tools used in CWQM.

The above-mentioned research, however, is not exactly what I mean as an explanation of CWQM activities. I believe that it is more important to specify the goal, the fundamental principles, the basic technology, and underlying CWQM activities in Japan.

The Goal of CWQM

The goal of quality control in Japan is the achievement of customer satisfaction, that is, the appropriateness of the product or service to the use that the customer will make of it. As Professor Mizuno used to say, quality is the customer's profit. The immediate goal of QC, therefore, is not the company's profit, as is usually thought. Quality control allows line workers and technicians to be proud of what they produce. Additionally, quality control results, without a doubt, in higher levels of customer satisfaction. On the basis of what I said above, the consumer will be grateful for the efforts of the producer, and will be satisfied with what he has bought. In Japan we use the expression *kokoro ga tsu-jiru,* which means, "the producer and the consumer have a good relationship."

Producers do not obtain their profits in a direct way. They must first of all have good relations with their customers. Success in business can be simplified according to the following flowchart:

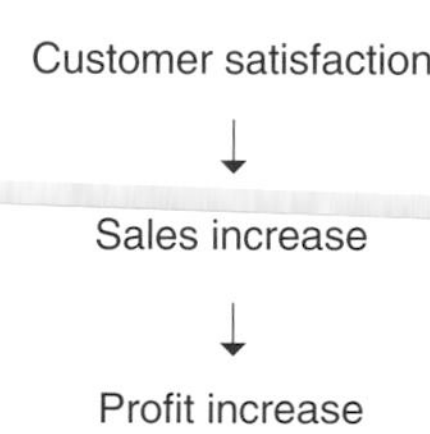

The main goal is customer satisfaction, or in other words, quality. Profit is the final result.

The Three Basic Principles of CWQM

CWQM presents the following three basic principles:

1. Great management effort should be placed on the initial stages of design and production, so that defects can be prevented from the start.
2. In the setting up of any activity, priority stages should be identified. These stages should be managed with a wider use of resources, such as time, money, and personnel. The policy of resource allocation is an essential component.
3. Plans must be made to deal with quality problems. Such plans should be made considering all resources — not only the time schedule, but also production equipment, technical information, and cooperation among departments. The results of activities carried out within quality control should be compared with the original plan. If there are great differences, their causes should be carefully studied through use of the PDCA cycle.

Anyone can understand these three guiding principles. Yet, in almost all companies, they are not applied in an effective manner. Training activities in these three principles are very important for CWQM, in all companies. Executives, managers, technical employees, and operators, should all keep understand the importance of these three guiding principles to the achievement of excellence.

The Three Methodologies Used in CWQM

Appropriate goals should emerge through kaizen activities, yet they cannot be carried out by technicians or by operational employees who are not acquainted with improvement methodologies. There is a need, therefore, for training in kaizen methods for all employees. This is the key to effective CWQM activities in every company.

Japanese managers are willing to invest broadly in this field. They do not calculate the returns gained directly through such training activities. They look far enough ahead to know that training represents a long-term profit for their companies. Training will result from the bottom line over a long period. three kinds of techniques are used in CWQM activities.

1. Managers study the critical aspects of their job, check them periodically, and keep them in mind. If something appears amiss, they take appropriate measures. A record of all such analyses and actions is made. The PDCA cycle is always important. The efficiency of such a cycle is measured by the degree to which responsibilities are clearly defined, by the time spent for control, and by the results obtained. Managers then ask themselves three questions:
   - Who is responsible for this part of the process?
   - With what frequency should it be checked?
   - Where are the results of this part of the process?
2. Statistical methods are used in CWQM activities. Data are the real key to kaizen, beyond what they represent in themselves. Observing production processes is very important for kaizen. All technicians and direct operators should learn statistics as if it were a technology. Real data provide the truth.
3. A systematic approach is important in CWQM activities, and this implies standardization (*hyojunka*). Each system of knowledge for the solution of problems must be expressed and written in a way that is clear and understandable to everyone

within the company. A technique that is inside one person's memory cannot be used by anyone else, and is of no use to the company.

Promotion of CWQM Activities

Some companies have their own CWQM training programs. These might include lessons for newly hired employees, training courses for technicians, talks on CWQM by experts (*shidou-kai,* in Japanese), top management QC diagnoses, or QC diagnoses by outside consultants. A few companies send their employees to outside CWQM training courses.

CWQM training for newly hired employees. An example is the new-hire training at New Japan Steel (formerly Yahata Steel Company). Its training course is aimed each year at 150 engineers and 150 office workers. There are 40 hours of lessons for the newly hired employees, followed by another 40 hours the year after they join the company.

Periodic seminars on CWQM. At Bridgestone a seminar takes place, lasting four months, with eight-hour lesson cycles every day. Employees attend one week of lessons once a month. They work for three weeks in their departments, and for one week they attend the seminar on CWQM. During the course, they must study a real kaizen problem. They may consult a tutor to help resolve their kaizen problems. Each year 100 technicians follow this training program.

CWQM research/guidance meeting. In Japan, some companies hold research/guidance meetings every month or two. They are attended by top executives, QC consultants, academics, managers and technicians. The executives express their ideas and opinions, and listen to those of others. Discussions are based on facts and data, the aim being to seek proper solutions for each difficult problem within the company. On-site observation and correct analysis of data enables the company to find solutions.

The president's diagnosis. A brief report is prepared, explaining the main elements of a department's work. In reading it, the president can understand the department's current status and problems: Is there unnecessary equipment that leads to financial losses? Are the managers able, through PDCA cycles, to carry out their functions with regard to the most important management problems?

The most important quality-related problems within a department must be pointed out and discussed. The president's leadership role in this regard is critical.

Diagnoses by QC consultants or academics. Sometimes diagnoses are carried out by consultants or academics. Such diagnoses are later submitted to the president for comment.

Features of CWQM in Japan

People think and act in essentially the same way all over the world. However, Eastern countries do differ from Western ones in some respects. So are there differences between the Eastern countries themselves.

The research and development pertaining to CWQM in Japan is basically different from those in other countries. Some approaches are very successful in Japan, but fail to produce the same results elsewhere. Japanese success is not a model for all other countries, but it can represent a useful reference model for development. With this in mind, consider the following points:

1. In the East there is a tendency to reflect. We Japanese consider that a man with a noble character will change or modify his opinion if he discovers that he is mistaken. In discussing CWQM activities, we can thus agree to recognize our mistakes.
2. QC consultants in Japan do not carry out analyses; nor do they submit proposals concerning kaizen. They suggest ways in which a kaizen group, con-

sisting of company members, can analyze data or make proposals to top management.

3. The Deming Prize has been very useful in stimulating CWQM activities in Japan. In order to be awarded the prize, all employees must carefully study how to increase the company's quality level. This represents a strong motivational factor in relation to CWQM. In general, a consumer tends to trust products by companies that have won the Deming Prize.
4. There are two main organizations that promote CWQM in Japan: the Union of Japanese Scientists and Engineers (JUSE), and the Japanese Standards Association (JSA). These two associations cooperate to promote CWQM.
5. In order to promote kaizen in an effective way, companies must develop excellent kaizen problem analysts. Intensive education and training of many technicians can guarantee experts for kaizen activities. If companies are able to develop these abilities, their progress will be faster.
6. We must carefully observe every phenomenon taking place within departments. A small change in the sound of a machine or in the features of a particular material can be a sign of a source of defects. Careful observation can tell us the real reason for product defects. A technician's ability to discover the causes of defects is a key to effective CWQM activities. I believe this is the main path to excellence.

CHAPTER TWENTY-FIVE

Quality Improvement Programs: The Entry Point for CWQM

Introduction

One important problem in introducing companywide quality management in a Western company is that of defining an "entry point." In this chapter I wish to present what I consider the best entry point, according to the experiences gathered in my consulting practice. As Chapter 26 demonstrates, this program represents the first in a series of phases that will involve a company for a few years.

The entry point is the "quality improvement program," which we first began applying to companies in 1981. The strategy we followed was suggested to me by Dr. Juran, and that was to speak to companies through the language of money rather than quality. In other words, begin introducing CWQM with an application that brings about important economic advantages in the short term (four to six months).

To inform Italian companies about the results obtained with this program, in March 1984 we organized the First National Galgano Convention, on the subject of the quality improvement program. Nine companies contributed their testimony to this gathering, with six presentations by quality circles and three projects by management groups.

In 1985 we organized another national convention, this time on "The Strategy of Quality — A Challenge to Company Management." During this convention, seven CEOs presented their testimony on current applications of total quality within their companies. During this gathering, Galgano presented four research papers, the most demanding of which examined Italy's main 1,600 manufacturing companies.

Another Galgano convention, held in 1986, focused on the theme of "Quality Circles in Services," and was attended by nine companies, each with a circle.

The Basic Features of the Program

The quality improvement program represents the tool by which improvement activities take shape within a company, with participation of a large number of people. Through this program, moreover, concrete results can be obtained rather quickly.

Often this program initially involves only one sector, but the first results obtained often prompt management to extend improvement programs to the entire company, and toward the total application of CWQM.

The program detailed in this chapter follows the general outline of a Galgano & Associati project that has been successfully tested in 200 manufacturing and service companies. It is adjusted, of course, to the specific reality of the company. The program is characterized by two main features:

1. the project concept
2. the industrialization of project production

The Project Concept

The basic building block of the quality improvement program is the *project*. The definition of a project is brief but clear: a problem for which a solution has been planned. A project presupposes

- a specific theme
- a goal to achieve
- one or more people to accomplish it
- a deadline for accomplishing it

The most effective way to improve quality concretely is to carry out projects. Management awareness of this fact is crucial to the program's success.

The small-step improvement approach that characterizes this program is an aggregate of many small projects carried out month after month and year after year. A single project is not in itself always innovative. The innovation of CWQM is that projects become highly organized and involve all people within the company, from executives, to middle management, to line workers and office operations personnel.

The Industrialization of Project Production

If the project forms the foundation of the program, the program's logic is the following:

1. *Premises:*
   - The company can improve quality by carrying out projects.
   - The company wants to improve quality considerably.
2. *Consequences:*
   - The company must complete a large number of projects each year.

Since the company must "produce" a great number of projects, a brilliant solution is to "industrialize" the production of such projects. The concept of industrialization is central to the quality improvement program. To achieve this industrialization a company must follow these guidelines in setting up the program:

- commitment and full involvement by management
- potential involvement of all employees in projects

- use of simple yet powerful tools in the search for improvement
- adherence to a few procedural formalities
- wide use of awards for employees
- constant promotion of the concepts of quality and continuous improvement

The third item (use of tools) is particularly important because it is not easy to find concrete solutions to problems in a relatively short time. If solutions are not found, project-driven work usually ends quickly, for lack of motivation. In project-driven work, the seven statistical tools and PDCA are applied extensively.

Structure of a Quality Improvement Program

From a practical viewpoint, the quality improvement program is divided into two subprograms:

- the program involving managers (*managers program*)
- the program involving operational employees (*quality circles program*)

Because these two subprograms speak to different needs for "industrialization" of the improvement process, both in number of people involved and in professional activities of the people involved, they take different shapes. Table 25-1 shows the main differences between the two programs.

In addition to representing a highly organized way of obtaining the company's top priority (continuous quality improvement in order to achieve maximum customer satisfaction) the program structure promotes the achievement of two fundamental goals of the company:

1. Concerning management: It generates problem-solving abilities, which are then used in the individual improvement activities. This individual work is the most important aspect of improvement

Table 25-1. Main Differences Between Managers Program and Quality Circle Program

Aspects of the Program	Project Teams at the Management Level	Quality Circles
Participation	Nonvoluntary	Voluntary
Choice of Theme	Guided by management	Usually autonomous
Team Composition	Defined project by project	Stable over time
Origin of participants	From different departments linked with competency related to the problem	From the same work area
Type of problems dealt with	Medium to large	Small to medium
Intervention by management	Direct/guided process	Indirect/promotional and support
Running of the program	Simple	Complex

activities carried out within the company, and is coordinated with the application of CWQM.

2. Concerning operational employees (line workers and office staff): It contributes in a concrete way to the people-building process, that is, to the management of human resources through professional growth and training. It also promotes integration of people with their workplaces, and thus with the company.

Committees are formed to head the preparation and implementation of the program, which is carried out according to a sequence of clearly defined steps. The unique character of the program owes largely to the innovation of quality circles, or more specifically, employee participation. This feature satisfies two needs:

- It tests the program in small steps, with practical problems being studied before circle activities are extended.
- It brings employees into direct contact with project work concerning concrete problems that involve

their job. This yields maximum advantage both in terms of motivation and in terms of greater integration within the workplace and the department.

Program Guidelines

Carry out the program according to the following guidelines:

Give great importance to training activities. The quality improvement program is the first step in introducing CWQM into the company, and as such requires a considerable change in management attitudes and criteria. Careful preparation is therefore necessary, through preliminary actions aimed at training and sensitizing executives and managers to CWQM, so that they become aware of the new values underlying the program and their role in it.

Initiate the managers program first. The application of CWQM presupposes a top-down process, and activities carried out at the level of top and middle management are at the heart of company improvements. The first step, therefore, is to train managers and supervisors. Not only does this approach enable managers to provide an example for operational employees, but it enables them to contribute effectively to the quality circles program, in which they play an essential role.

Begin the circles program as soon as possible. Because the circles program requires careful testing, through the start-up of a number of circles during a rather prolonged period, a company should not postpone this stage in the program for too long. Under normal circumstances, it can be started seven to eight months after the start of the managers program, although its preparation can begin even sooner.

The managers program presupposes continuity and further developments. The managers program, with its initial projects, is the vehicle by which improvement activities within the company begin to take shape according to CWQM logic. The program presupposes, therefore, continuity and evolution toward the management criteria put forward by the new model.

Once the managers program is well established and the first circles experiment widen the quality circles program. Six to eight months after the start-up of the first experimental circles, it is possible to evaluate the results of the experiment. The managers program is also sufficiently well tested. At this point one can gradually extend the number of circles and, thus, the employees involved in these activities.

Program Stages

The program implementation can be divided into four stages:

- preliminary stage
- preparatory stage
- execution stage
- evaluation stage

Figure 25-1 shows a general outline of the program as it evolves through these four stages.

Preliminary Stage

The preliminary stage consists in creating an awareness among executives and upper management of the new CWQM approach, and reviewing and discussing the program.

Preparatory Stage

The preparatory stage involves preparing managers involved in running improvement projects, preparing quality circle leaders, and planning the introduction of circles. Its main features are the following:

- *Managers program*
    1. Making middle management aware of CWQM, and training them in the use of the PDCA method

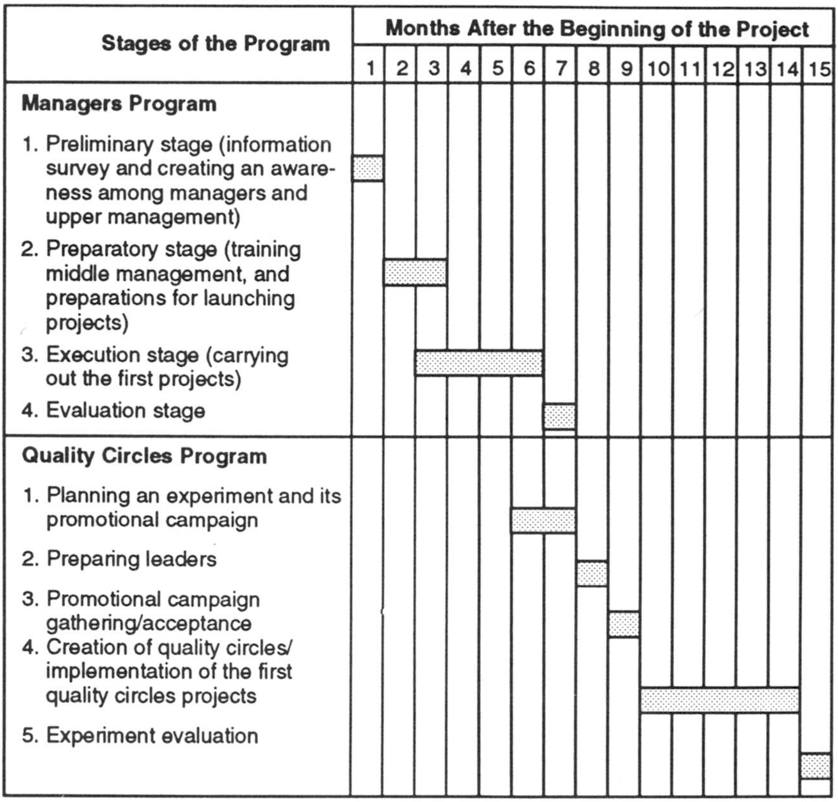

Stages of the Program	1	2	3	4	5	6	7	8	9	10	11	12	13	14	15
	Months After the Beginning of the Project														
Managers Program															
1. Preliminary stage (information survey and creating an awareness among managers and upper management)	■														
2. Preparatory stage (training middle management, and preparations for launching projects)		■	■												
3. Execution stage (carrying out the first projects)			■	■	■	■									
4. Evaluation stage							■								
Quality Circles Program															
1. Planning an experiment and its promotional campaign						■	■								
2. Preparing leaders								■							
3. Promotional campaign gathering/acceptance									■						
4. Creation of quality circles/ implementation of the first quality circles projects										■	■	■	■	■	
5. Experiment evaluation															■

Figure 25-1. General Schedule for the Program

and the seven statistical tools during a four-to five-day seminar.

2. Definition by management of the themes for specific projects, and formation of project groups, with the names of participants.

- *Circles program*

1. Training of the first facilitator.
2. Preparation of circle leaders. This is carried out through a seminar. Leaders must be able to teach the seven tools, and to guide circle activities.

3. Planning the quality circles experiment. This is carried out by an ad hoc committee. During this stage the following are set:
   - policies concerning circles activities
   - an operational schedule
   - organizational aspects
4. Planning the promotional campaign for quality circles, for the purpose of preparing the ground for the experiment and obtaining the necessary support.

The promotional campaign is particularly important, because it is necessary to create a favorable climate for the development of quality circles in the units involved in the initiative.

Execution Stage

The execution stage includes the start-up of the managers program and the initial phase of the quality circles experiment. Its main features are the following:

- *Managers program*
  1. Implementation of the first projects by managers, divided into groups of five to seven people, through the use of the seven tools and the PDCA method. Usually these projects are scheduled to last about 12 to 15 weeks.
  2. Preparation and presentation of projects to management.

- *Circles program*
  1. Informing trade unions of the purposes of the project, and informing all company structures of the operational details of program implementation.
  2. Carrying out a promotional campaign.
  3. Gathering the support of operational employees for quality circles.

4. Composition of the first four to six quality circles.
5. Beginning circle activities, with the training of members by leaders, while at the same time initiating improvement projects.
6. Carrying out projects over a three- to five-month period.
7. Official presentation of results to management.

Evaluation Stage

The evaluation stage involves evaluation of the managers program and the quality circles experiment, the setting of guidelines for broadening the experiment, and the definition of further initiatives in the introduction of CWQM. Its main features are the following:

- *Managers program*
  1. Evaluating the results obtained by the first managers' projects.
  2. Defining the criteria for pursuing improvement activities at the managers' level.
- *Circles program*
  1. Evaluating the results obtained through the first circles activities.
  2. Review of experiences gathered, and setting of possible modifications to the functioning of circles.
  3. Decisions concerning widening the quality circles program.

Extending the program

Once total involvement by a company's management has been achieved through a first cycle of projects (a cycle that basically acts as an experiment), the company can define projects to be assigned to managers with greater precision. The stages of this process are shown in Figure 25-2.

Organizational Aspects

Committees and Work Teams

To carry out the program, the company must create committees and work teams:

- *Executive committee for the quality improvement program:* This is made up of the principal managers of the company, and its task is that of guiding and coordinating all activities concerning the program.
- *A work team for developing the program:* Its task is to plan all operational details concerning the program, and oversee the activities of project groups during the program's initial stages.
- *A work team to prepare the promotional campaign for the circles:* Its task is to prepare a promotional campaign aimed at informing and sensitizing all of the employees involved in the program.

Specific Roles (Coordinator/Facilitator)

The program requires a coordinator, or facilitator, who works on a part-time basis to directly and concretely assist and support the development of the program. This support is in addition to that given by the management structure as a whole.

The role of facilitator comprises the following specific tasks:

- coordinating all organizational aspects of the program
- promoting the goals and meaning of the program (especially for the circles program)
- directly supporting project groups and circles, with particular reference to training

The facilitator is the reference point for training employees in the use of the tools and techniques necessary for efficient implementation of projects.

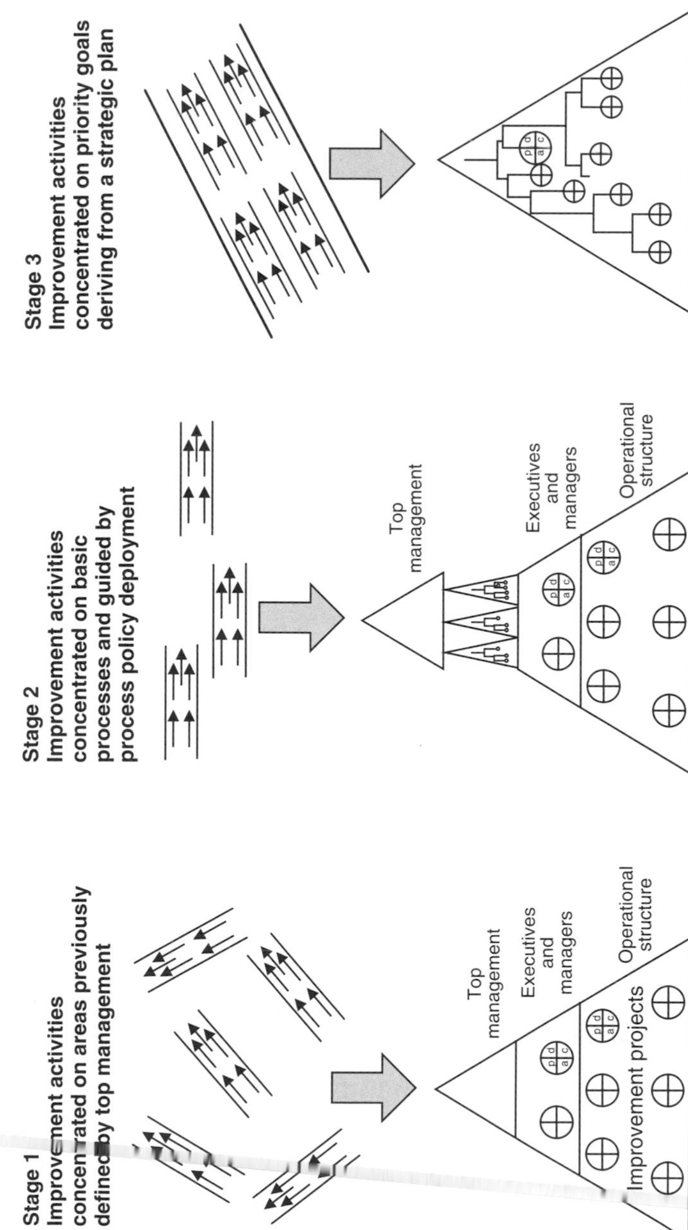

Figure 25-2. Gradual Focusing of Project Groups

CHAPTER TWENTY-SIX

The Introduction of CWQM in Europe

Introduction

The introduction of companywide quality management in Western companies, which began in 1980, was initially not very successful. A distorted interpretation of the meaning of CWQM, together with a low level of commitment by company management, led to the implementation of programs that yielded limited results. Such programs shared the following features:

- general, not clearly defined
- too philosophical or too technical
- not considered priority
- excessively aimed at the rank and file (quality circles)
- not managed by either top managers or line workers
- not clearly focused
- not integrated into the company's management systems

During the past four to five years, making good use of past mistakes, Western companies have achieved a new awareness.

Thus a second generation of CWQM program has arisen, with the following features:

- the genuine leadership by top management
- based on an internally designed reference model
- developed through a multiyear plan
- backed by multiyear and annual policies
- gradual change in the managerial system
- hoshin management as the basic management tool
- the market-in culture
- stressing process management and the mechanism of daily routine work
- quality function deployment as a basic tool for the development of new products and services
- the use of advanced tools (including visual control systems for the development of improvement, the seven management tools, the X matrix, and principal component analysis).

The results obtained by second-generation CWQM programs in the West are now on a par with those obtained in Japan about 20 years ago. Of course, Japanese companies in this respect today.

For example, Toyota won a Deming Prize in 1965, and had thus already reached a high level of excellence. American and European automobile manufacturing companies began total quality programs only 20 years later.

Galgano & Associati introduced the new program in Italy and into some European companies, with interesting results. The turning point occurred when we were able to develop a reference model to expand a multiyear plan for introducing CWQM.

The Reference Model for Introducing CWQM

We have seen that the quality improvement program is an excellent entry point for CWQM, yet it represents only an initial stage in this introduction. The experience gathered in the Western world by CWQM experts during the past 10 years allows us to proceed with greater assurance in the introduction of CWQM, by applying the processes described in Part 4.

The main problem in introducing CWQM in a Western company lies not so much in *what* to do as in *how* to do it. This problem becomes particularly difficult for large companies, where American organizational techniques have created the deepest trenches, and where any change requires greater efforts. The know-how in need of being developed concerns

- the rate at which the existing managerial system should be changed
- over how long a period, and with what stages
- which techniques and which sequence to adopt
- how and where to test the new techniques
- how to make the company's top and middle management aware of the necessary changes.

It is a question of building a customized model for the particular company involved. In doing this one needs to keep in mind the culture of that particular company, its organizational level, its technology, its business areas, and its market relations. The full application of CWQM is analogous to scaling a mountain peak, such as Everest. The plan to reach it not only describes the path to follow, but it also spells out:

- what base camps to set up, and where to set them up
- what installations to use in the different camps
- what equipment and what techniques to use in proceeding from one base camp to another
- what diet to follow, and what clothes to wear from one camp to the next
- what physical exercise to engage in at different altitudes

Applying CWQM involves similar factors, and, as have said, requires building a model. Galgano & Associati derived the idea and general outline of its model from Philips, one of the first Western multinational companies to apply the new approach to quality. The structure of the Philips model is based on the evolution of the main company subsystems from the traditional approach to excellence, and is divided into seven stages (see Figure 26-1).

The evolution is defined by seven subsystems, representing the main aspects to monitor and develop. In the Philips diagram, such subsystems are the following:

1. cultural features
2. quality-related activities
3. procedures
4. results
5. relations with customers

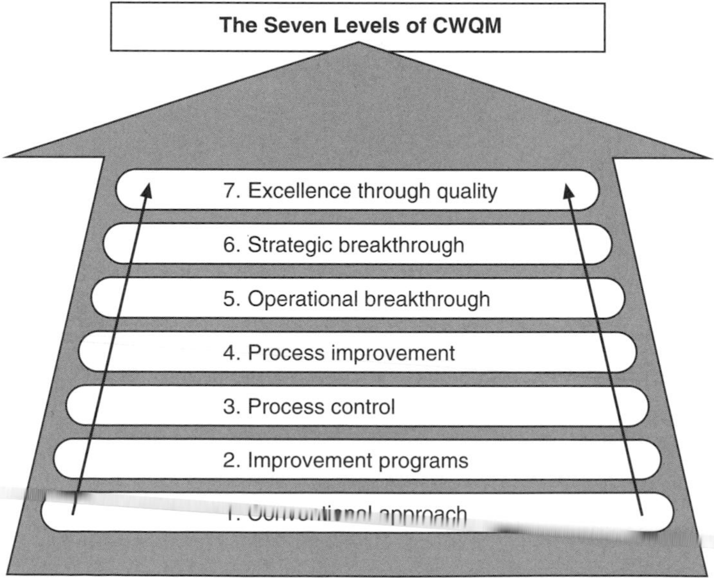

Figure 26-1. The Structure of the Reference Model

6. relations with suppliers
7. the role of management

The intersection of stages and subsystems forms a grid that, if adapted to the particular company under scrutiny, constitutes a reference model for the development of CWQM within that company (see Figure 26-2)

Taking this structure as a point of departure, Galgano & Associati developed an approach and a procedure for planning a customized model for the company. It is a question of designing the grid, and, in it, the evolution of the internal management system, keeping in mind the premises, the culture of quality, and CWQM processes, and establishing the necessary stages and schedules. As an example, we show a few components of the grid, pertaining to the "cultural and organizational features" subsystem.

- *Second Stage (improvement programs)*
  1. understanding the need for continuous improvement as a strategic factor
  2. education and training aimed at CWQM
  3. awareness that quality does not derive from the techniques used but by whom and how they are used
  4. aiming at customer satisfaction (external and internal)
  5. launching the company's quality improvement program
  6. awareness that quality is important and should constantly be improved

- *Third Stage (process control)*
  1. understanding the importance of carefully managing processes
  2. approach by special and common causes
  3. preventing defects through process control

CWQM Growth Phases	Cultural and Organizational Characteristics	Main Quality Activities	Basic Procedures	Product Development/ Industrialization	Relations with Customers	Relations with Suppliers	Role of Management	Results
1. Conventional Approach	Emphasis on product quality Quality as a technical problem	Tests (AQL) Redrafts Certificates	Inspection/ certification procedures Quality assurance manuals	Quality is not a planning priority Quality equals technical performance	Minimal acceptable quality is decided or agreed upon	Prices are purchased Suppliers are mistrusted	Quality is not seen as a top management problem	High cost of "nonquality" AQL protection
2. Introduction of Improvement Programs	Awareness of the importance of quality, and of the need to continuously improve it	Training Improvement programs	Procedures for managing improvement programs	Quality is important Technical — technological approach	Customer satisfaction is a "must" Internal supplier/ customer links	Conviction that trusting suppliers might be useful	CWQM promotion, commitment, and budget	Small reductions of nonquality costs Some product improvements
3. Process Control	Product/ service quality is seen and managed as a result of process quality	Analysis and management of process capabilities	Organization for the management and improvement of process capabilities	Quality equals conformity to purpose Emphasis on organization FMEA	Customer satisfaction through internal process management Quality assurance through protection of process capabilities	Self-certification is encouraged Total cost vendor rating	Issuing quality related policies Management by process	Reduction of below-standard elements "Cleaning up" processes (problem reduction)
4. Process Improvement	Improvements planned and managed by the line	Concentration on improving priority processes	Management of improvement programs by improvement areas (priority deployment)	Quality planned according to customer's needs Quality deployment DOE	Improvement of processes related to customer satisfaction	Linking up with the most capable suppliers Emphasis on improvement capability	Managing supplier/ customer links through daily routine work	General quality cost reduction, inspection ones in particular

5. Operational Breakthrough	Definite performance improvement through orientation of CWQM programs towards operational priorities	Important improvement programs guided by the business plan Deployment activities	Procedures for the deployment of business plan and "catchball" goals	Quality as starting point Cost and start-up time reductions	Concentration on basic customer satisfaction processes, under the guidance of top management	Comakership with main suppliers Important improvements in the materials supplied	Management by policy	Improvement of the company's competitive position through key process improvements
6. Strategic Breakthrough	Seeking excellence through market-in	Improvements focused on the processes most closely linked with the market Hoshin management	Procedures/ linking systems between market and internal processes	Planning positive quality Total product/ process deployment	Market-in culture Independent ability to react to change	Partnership agreements regarding the business of excellence	Market priority management	Leadership through process quality
7. Excellence Through Quality	Excellence earned every day on the market through quality	Process for maintaining continued excellence	Market monitoring procedures in real time	Automatic continuous improvements Product development as the essence of CWQM	The company for the customer in real time Emphasis on positive quality	Long-term agreements for continued excellence together	Management guided by the market	Continued leadership through continued customer satisfaction

Figure 26-2. Reference Grid

4. controlling processes rather than output
5. processes equal cross-functional links (suppliers-customers)
6. overseeing (process capabilities)
7. each function isolates and supervises the dispersion of its processes (including offices)
8. product or service quality is the result of process quality

- *Fourth Stage (process improvement)*
  1. ability to concentrate improvement activities on priorities
  2. management of improvement programs by the line (daily routine work)
  3. planning improvements along basic processes
  4. improvement in the dispersion of all operational processes
  5. developing a high number of improvement projects
  6. strong involvement by the entire structure
  7. total quality equals quality, costs, service, morale, safety

- *Fifth Stage (operational breakthrough)*
  1. important improvements in basic business processes
  2. improvement plans directly connected with business goals (deployment) in each company sector
  3. capability to find improvement opportunities and to plan them
  4. hoshin management
  5. applying quality function deployment

The basic advantage obtained by use of the grid is guidance in the introduction of CWQM through assurance of consistency among subsystems, and control of their advancement in a coherent fashion (see Figure 26-3).

Depending on the company's features, the number of levels in the grid varies between 4 and 7 (to be developed over a period of four to eight years), and the number of subsystems varies between 6 and 12, grouped into three categories:

1. company culture, organization, and management
2. CWQM organization, methodologies, and tools
3. main operational processes (customer and supplier relations, new product/service development, production, etc.

It is essential that the grid be prepared by the company's managers themselves, as it must have a "custom fit." According to our experience, its construction enables managers to become acutely aware of the changes that must be carried out and the direction to follow to apply CWQM.

For large and medium-large companies, the use of a grid model is possibly essential. In general, with appropriate modifications, the model can also be used in companies with fewer than

Stages \ Subsystems	1	2	3	...	...	...	...	n
1								
2								
3								
...								
...								
...								
m								

Figure 26-3. Ideal Advancement Front Along the Grid

500 employees, although often it might be convenient to follow a less global approach. In these companies, change is obtained more easily, and full adoption of the new approach more immediate than in a larger company. It is therefore better to avoid excessive formalities, which might lead to bureaucratization.

The Multiyear Plan for Introducing CWQM

Preparing a multiyear plan for the introduction of CWQM is one aspect of the second-generation programs. Based on the Galgano & Associati approach, the plan results from the blending of three basic elements:

- the reference model developed by the company itself (the grid)
- the company's strategic long-term plan
- the identification of critical company processes according to top managers assessments

Figure 26-4 shows a diagram of the processes involved in defining the plan. The company's strategic plan provides the company's strategic and operational goals to be considered in formulating the plan; thus it establishes "how much" and "when." Assessment of a company's main priorities suggests the priority areas for intervention, thus "where." The reference model also establishes "how" to proceed, in terms of cultural, organizational, and technical change.

The blending of these three elements allows us to draw up a multiyear plan, which should be more detailed during the first two years and more general during the ensuing years. The program should be organized into stages calling for:

- general progress of the development front of the multiyear plan, by the definition of "general" goals and programs in the whole company
- management projects to prepare the contents of the next stage

Figure 26-4. Planning the CWQM Program

- pilot areas for experimenting with advanced techniques and methodologies, to be applied later on a companywide basis
- a consistent development of management/information/quality assurance systems and of CWQM organization (committees, responsibilities, roles)

Figure 26-5 provides an outline of the support that can be relied upon in the preparation of this plan. The elements to define are:

- general goals
- cultural/organizational/technological goals, etc.
- actions

Each stage must call for specific goals and actions:

- four kinds of goals (the latter three are based on the reference and self-evaluation model)
  1. quantitative
  2. cultural

3. technical
4. organizational

- three types of actions
  1. for the development of a general program (general projects)
  2. for the development of "pilot areas"
  3. for management projects

Once the multiyear plan is established, it is possible to define the first annual plan in its details. Figure 26-6 provides an example of this.

Pilot areas are areas of the company (office, department, unit) in which one immediately tests a particular methodology of CWQM. Since methodologies are many, only the most appropriate in terms of areas of intervention and organizational state should be chosen.

The pilot area logic answers two needs that must be satisfied if a CWQM program is to succeed:

1. The need to quickly obtain tangible results, both so that the people involved can be motivated and

Year	Quantitative Goals	Cultural/Organizational/ Technological Goals	Actions
X			General actions Pilot areas Management projects
X+1			General actions Pilot areas Management projects
X+2			General actions Pilot areas Management projects
X+3			General actions Pilot areas Management projects

Figure 26-5. The Multiyear Plan

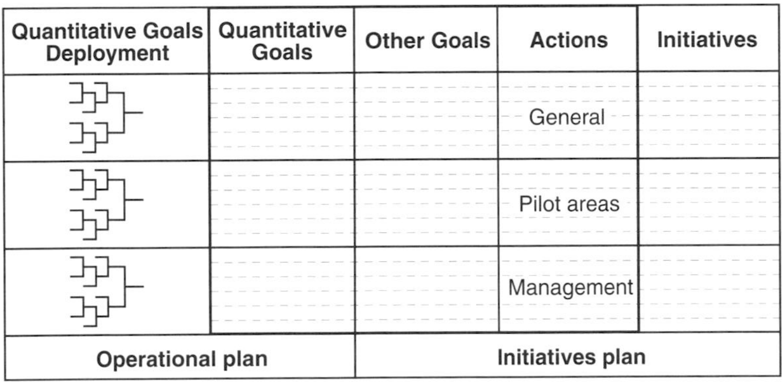

Quantitative Goals Deployment	Quantitative Goals	Other Goals	Actions	Initiatives
			General	
			Pilot areas	
			Management	
Operational plan		Initiatives plan		

Figure 26-6. The Yearly Plan

so that management is guaranteed that the path undertaken is the good one

2. The need to experiment and gain experience with the most effective methodologies so that they can be disseminated throughout the company in the fastest and most effective way.

Therefore, the following points apply in the planning stages of the CWQM program:

- Pilot areas are established according to
  1. critical processes or urgent goals
  2. the experiences necessary for the development of later-stage activities

- Pilot areas are planned in terms of
  1. size and length of time
  2. goals
  3. resources to involve
  4. necessary training
  5. responsibilities

Introducing CWQM in Small to Medium-sized Companies

We have seen that the introduction of CWQM in small to medium-size companies in Japan is carried out in a much less formal way than in medium-large and large companies. In Italy, too, the problem presented itself in the same way. The method and time of introduction vary from company to company. A considerable influence derives from the size, product sector, product variety, and features of the market served by the company.

Here we describe a standard model, giving general guidelines for introducing CWQM into a small or medium-sized company. The process is divided into stages, which are not to be understood in a strictly sequential sense, as some stages can partially overlap. The sequence will also vary according to factors in the company involved. The stages are the following:

1. study of CWQM contents, and evaluation of the situation
2. sensitization of management
3. involvement of personnel in improvement
4. introduction of process control
5. customer satisfaction and new products
6. application of hoshin management

The diagram in Figure 26-7 shows a hypothesis of the program.

Here we show some clarifications concerning the various stages.

Stage 1: Study of CWQM Contents, and Evaluation of the Situation

This stage comprises two steps:

1. A study of the contents of CWQM by the company's top management: Such study can consist in attending a seminar or visiting a company already

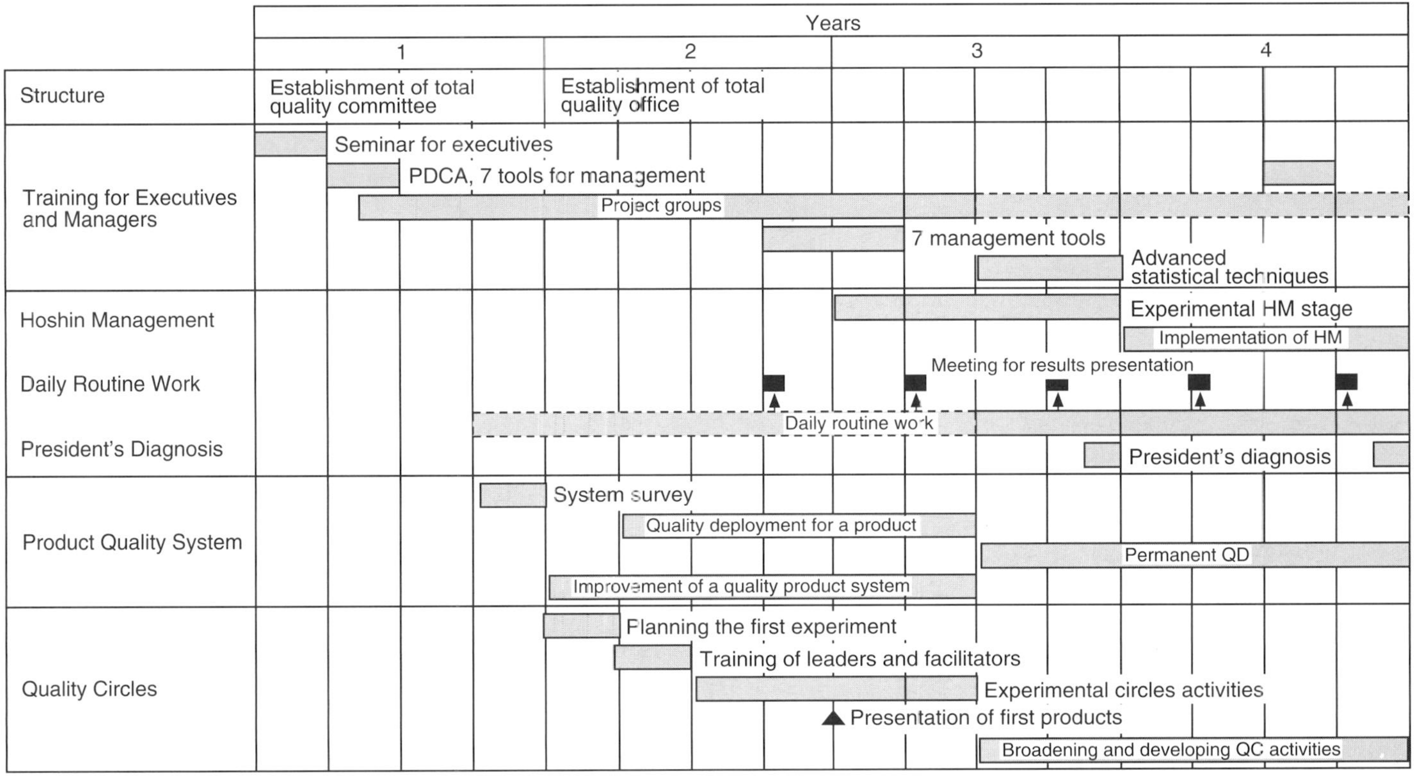

Years: 1, 2, 3, 4

Structure
- Establishment of total quality committee
- Establishment of total quality office

Training for Executives and Managers
- Seminar for executives
- PDCA, 7 tools for management
- Project groups
- 7 management tools
- Advanced statistical techniques

Hoshin Management
- Experimental HM stage
- Implementation of HM

Daily Routine Work
- Meeting for results presentation
- Daily routine work

President's Diagnosis
- President's diagnosis

Product Quality System
- System survey
- Quality deployment for a product
- Permanent QD
- Improvement of a quality product system

Quality Circles
- Planning the first experiment
- Training of leaders and facilitators
- Experimental circles activities
- Presentation of first products
- Broadening and developing QC activities

Figure 26-7. Hypothesis for the Development of a CWQM Program Over Time

involved in CWQM. It might also be useful to study the concepts of the reference model and the multiyear plan.

2. A diagnosis of the product or service quality system's weak points, in order to define intervention priorities. In particular, the following must be shown:
   - customer complaints and claims
   - rates of process and product defects

This evaluation can be conducted by an outside expert, or be obtained through an assessment by the company's top executives.

An important choice concerns the decision to introduce total quality without the assistance of outside resources, or with the support of a consultant. In the former case, one of the company's executives should study the most appropriate approaches for introducing total quality into the company. In the latter case, it is possible to gather two or more companies together so as to reduce the related costs. In fact, a number of training activities can be carried out by bringing together managers from several companies.

Stage 2: Sensitizing of Management

All employees who occupy a role of responsibility within the company must attend a seminar on CWQM, as well as on statistical tools for problem solving. Through such a seminar people are made aware both of the new approach and of the role to assign to all employees in order to improve quality. During this stage a deeper knowledge is acquired concerning the most effective techniques and tools for achieving improvements.

Stage 3: Involvement of Employees in Improvement

This stage involves starting up the company's quality improvement program, involving both managers and operational employees.

Managers. During this stage employees first become involved in the so-called improvement projects. Top management chooses a few important themes, and groups are formed with four to seven people. Such groups, with CWQM methods, carry out the projects assigned to them. Themes are chosen so that a project can be completed in three to four months, at most.

Upon completion of a project, it is customary to organize an official presentation of projects to top management, for the purpose of describing the results obtained. Once the first projects are complete, top management assigns others. As a rule, except for periods in which a company's management is particularly busy, an attempt is made to always have projects active.

Operational employees. After completion of the initial projects, top management is already in a position to evaluate whether operational employees, both in departments and offices, should become involved. Quality circles can then be introduced into the company. The company will have to choose a person to carry out the role of circles facilitator or coordinator. This person will be in charge of preparing circle leaders and training circle members in the use of the seven statistical tools for problem solving. In this endeavor, training packages can be very useful.

To motivate employees to join circles in large numbers, the company should wage a promotional campaign.

Stage 4: Introduction of Process Control

During this stage the company tackles its main processes, so as to better control them. The aim is to reduce the variability of the processes themselves and to standardize conditions (daily routine work). The goal of DRW is to minimize the time spent by both managers and operators on process maintenance, both at the department level and in offices, so that they can devote more time to improvement. Whenever necessary, a quality manual is prepared, based on standard rules, and certification procedures take place.

Stage 5: Customer Satisfaction and New Products

This stage involves perfecting the methods for defining those products or service features that most contribute to customer satisfaction. An initial trial with quality function deployment also takes place.

At the same time, quality control is applied to new product development and planning. The goal is to improve the quality and reliability of new products introduced in the market, and to minimize their development time. Executives and managers are taught the Seven management tools so that they can better define problems and carry out QFD projects.

Stage 6: Application of Hoshin Management

Through implementation of the stages just described, the main problems have been dealt with, employees have become familiar with the application of PDCA in its work, internal cooperation has improved considerably, and a quality system has been developed. Now, the company is ready to take the most important step, that is, the application of hoshin management.

Through this new management system the chief executive officer establishes each year two or three main priority goals, which become reference points for all employees. Through hoshin management, an attempt is made to achieve breakthroughs, that is, major improvements in the strategic areas specified by top management.

Bibliography

Chapter 1

Corvin, D. Edwards. "The Meaning of Quality." *Quality Progress*. October 1968.

European Organization for Quality. *Glossary*. 1989.

Garvin, David A. Chaps. 3, 4, and 5 in *Managing Quality*. New York: The Free Press, 1988.

Gruppo Galgano. "131 parole chiave per capire la Qualità Totale." Supplement to no. 246 of *Espansione,* October 1990.

Morgan, Leonard A. "The Importance of Quality." In *Perceived Quality,* edited by Jacob Jacoby and Jerry Olson. Lexington, Mass.: Lexington Books, 1985.

Chapter 2

Bloch, Philippe, Ralph Hababou, and Dominique Xardel. *Service Compris*. Paris: L'Expansion-Hachette Editions, 1986.

Deming, W. Edwards. *Quality, Productivity and Competitive Position*. Cambridge, Mass.: MIT Press, 1982.

Ernst & Young Quality Improvement Consulting Group. *Total Quality*. Homewood, Ill.: Dow Jones-Irwin, 1990.

Feigenbaum, Armand V. *Total Quality Control*. New York: McGraw-Hill Books, 1983.

Hasegawa, Keitaro. *Japanese-Style Management.* Tokyo: Kodansha International, 1986.

Hirimoto, Toshiro. "Another Hidden Hedge — Japanese Management Accounting." *Harvard Business Review,* July-August 1988.

Ishikawa, Kaoru. *What Is Total Quality Control? The Japanese Way.* Englewood Cliffs, N.J.: Prentice-Hall, 1985.

Iwata, Ryushi. *Japanese-Style Management: Its Foundations and Prospects.* Tokyo: Asian Productivity Organization, 1982.

Kano, Noriaki. "Quality & Economy. More Emphasis on the Role of Quality on Sales rather on Cost." In *Proceedings of the European Organization for Quality Control, 30th Conference, Stockholm, 1986.*

Karatsu, Hajime. "How to Cope with the Gray Part of Management." In *Proceedings of the International Conference on Quality Control, Tokyo, 1987.*

Karatsu, Hajime. *TQC Wisdom of Japan, Managing for TQC.* Cambridge, Mass.: Productivity Press, 1988.

Kobayashi, Kaoru. *Japan: The Most Misunderstood Country.* Tokyo: Japan Times, 1984.

Kono, Toyohiro. *Strategy and Structure of Japanese Enterprises.* London: Macmillan & Co., 1984.

Kume, Hitoshi. "Business Management and Quality Cost: the Japanese View." *Quality Progress,* May 1985.

Kume, Hitoshi. "Business Management and Quality Economy." In *Proceedings of the European Organization for Quality Control, 30th Conference, Stockholm, 1986.*

Laboucheix, Vincent., ed. *Traité de la Qualité Totale.* Paris: Bordas, 1990.

Mann, Nancy R. *The Keys to Excellence.* Los Angeles: Prestwick Books, 1985.

Monden, Yasuhiro, Rinya Shibakawa, Satoru Takayanagi, and Teruya Nagao. *Innovations in Management.* Atlanta: Industrial Engineering and Management Press, 1985.

Morishima, Michio. *Why Has Japan "Succeeded"? Western Technology and the Japanese Ethos.* Cambridge, Mass.: Cambridge Corporation, 1982.

Nakatani, Iwao. *The Japanese Firm in Transition.* Tokyo: Asian Productivity Organization, 1987.

Nemoto, Masao. *Total Quality Control for Management.* Englewood Cliffs, N.J.: Prentice-Hall, 1987.

Oakland, John S. *Total Quality Management.* Oxford: Heinemann Professional Publishing, 1989.

Oess, Attila. *Total Quality Management.* Wiesbaden: Gabler, 1989.

Ohmae, Kenichi. *The Mind of the Strategist.* New York: McGraw-Hill Books, 1982.

Ozawa, Masayoshi. *Total Quality Control and Management.* Tokyo: JUSE Press, 1988.

Perigord, Michel. *Achieving Total Quality.* Cambridge, Mass.: Productivity Press, 1990.

Ricci, Aldo. *Qualità Totale per l'azienda.* Milan: Etas Libri, 1990.

Scherkenbach, William W. *The Deming Route to Quality and Productivity: Road Maps and Roadblocks.* Washington, D.C.: CEE Press Books,1986.

Schrage, Michael. "A Japanese Giant Rethinks Globalization: An Interview with Yoshihisa Tabuchi." *Harvard Business Review,* July-August 1989.

Shibagaki, Kazuo, Trevor Malcolm, and Abo Tetsuo, eds. *Japanese and European Management.* Tokyo: University of Tokyo Press, 1989.

Stora, Gilbert, and Jean Montaigne. *La Qualité Totale dans l'Entreprise.* Paris: Les Editions d'Organisation, 1987.

Vogel, Ezra F. *Japan as No. 1.* Tokyo: Charles E. Tuttle Co., 1981.

Wilkinson, Endymion. *Misunderstanding: Europe versus Japan.* Tokyo: Chuokron-Sha, 1981.

Zink, Klaus J., ed. *Qualitat als Managementaufgabe.* Landsberg/Lech: Verlag Modern Industrie, 1989.

Chapter 3

Box, George E.P., et al. "Quality Practices in Japan." *Quality Progress,* March 1988.

Caplan, Frank. *The Quality System.* Radnor, PA.: Chilton Book Company, 1990.

Dale, Barrie, and Jim Plunkett. *Managing Quality.* Hemel Hempstead: Philip Allan, 1990.

Feigenbaum, Armand V. *Total Quality Control.* New York: McGraw-Hill, 1983.

Harada, Akira. "Features of Quality Control and TQC Activities in Japan." In *Proceedings of the 44th Annual Quality Congress, San Francisco, 1990* (American Society for Quality Control).

Kawai, Ryoichi. "Total Quality Control at Komatsu Ltd." In *Proceedings of the European Organization for Quality Control, 30th Congress, Stockholm, 1986.*

Ozawa, Masayoshi. *Total Quality Control and Management.* Tokyo: JUSE Press, 1988.

Tsuda, Yoshikazu, and Myron Tribus. "Managing for Quality: Does Culture Make a Difference?" *Quality Progress,* November 1985.

Walsh, Loren M., Ralph Wurster, and Raymond J. Kimber. *Quality Management Handbook.* New York: Dekker, 1986.

Chapter 4

American Society for Quality Control, American Marketing Association. *Customer Satisfaction Measurement Conference, Chicago, 1989.*

American Society for Quality Control, American Marketing Association. *2nd Annual Customer Satisfaction and Quality Measurement Conference, Arlington, Virginia, 1990.*

Desatnick, Robert L. *Managing to Keep the Customer.* San Francisco: Jossey-Bass, 1987.

Hutchens, Spencer, Jr. "What Customers Want: Results of ASQC/Gallup Survey." *Quality Progress,* February 1989.

Muroi, Akira. "Customer's Needs: How to Identify and How to Utilize Resultant Information." In *Proceedings of the International Conference on Quality Control, Tokyo, 1987.*

Schonberger, Richard J. *Building a Chain of Customers.* New York: Free Press, 1990.

Chapter 5

Abe, Yoshio. *People-Oriented Management.* Tokyo: Diamond, 1987.

Bundy, Rebecca, and Robert Thurston. "Transforming Supervisors into Coaches and Advisors." *Journal for Quality and Participation,* June 1990.

Dreyfack, Raymond. *Making It in Management. The Japanese Way.* Rockville Centre, N.Y.: Farnworth Publishing Co., 1982.

Inohara, Ideo. "Human Resources Development in Japan Companies." Tokyo: Asian Productivity Organization, 1990.

Ishikawa, Kaoru. Chap. 7 in *What Is Total Quality Control? The Japanese Way.* Englewood Cliffs, N.J.: Prentice-Hall, 1985.

Itami, Hiroyuki. "Mobilizing Invisible Assets." Cambridge, Mass.: Harvard Business School Press, 1987.

The Cambridge Corporation, "Japanese Management and Employee Benefit Programs." Tokyo, 1982.

Japan External Trade Organization (JETRO), "Japanese Corporate Personnel Management." Tokyo, 1982.

Kondo, Yoshio. "Human Motivation and Achievement of Work — A Report of Motivation Study Group." In *Proceedings of the 30th Congress of the European Organization for Quality Control, Stockholm, 1986.*

Michel, Robert, Bernard Racine, and Craig Bowers. "A Worker's Mind Is a Terrible Thing to Waste." *Quality Progress,* October 1990.

Nakatani, Iwao. *Japanese-Style Management.* Tokyo: Kodansha International, 1988.

Oakland, John S. *Total Quality Management.* Oxford: Heinemann, 1989.

Yamashita, Toshihiko. Chap. 4 in *The Panasonic Way — From a Chief Executive Desk.* Tokyo: Kodansha International, 1989.

Warren, Jim. "We Have Found the Enemy, It Is Us." In *Proceedings of the 43rd Annual Quality Congress, Toronto, May 1990* (American Society for Quality Control).

Chapter 6

Brown, John, and James Bossert. "Supplier Certification: A Formula for Improvement." In *Proceedings of the 44th Annual Quality Congress, San Francisco, 1990* (American Society for Quality Control).

Gordon, Niall. "Supplier Quality Partnership Program." In *Proceedings of the 44th Annual Quality Congress, San Francisco, 1990* (American Society for Quality Control).

Hopkins, Carlton L. "Vendor Quality Improvement — The FPL Approach." In *Proceedings of the 44th Annual Quality Congress, San Francisco, 1990* (American Society for Quality Control).

Ishikawa, Kaoru. Chap. 9 in *What Is Total Quality Control? The Japanese Way.* Englewood Cliffs, N.J.: Prentice-Hall, 1985.

Itoh, Yasuro. "Upbringing of Components Suppliers Surrounding Toyota." In *Proceedings of the International Conference on Quality Control, Tokyo, 1978.*

Merli, Giorgio. *Co-makership: The New Supply Strategy for Managers.* Cambridge, Mass.: Productivity Press, 1991.

Mizuno, Shigeru. Chap. 12 in *Company-Wide Total Quality Control.* Tokyo: Asian Productivity Organization, 1989.

Chapter 7

Ashby, Ross W. *Introduzione alla cibernetica.* Milan: Giulio Einaudi, 1971.

Bachler, Helmut. "Business Process Quality Management in IBM Switzerland." In *Proceedings of the Conference of the European Foundation for Quality Management, Montreux, October 1989.*

Besterfield, Dale H. *Quality Control.* Englewood Cliffs, N.J.: Prentice Hall, 1990.

Ford Motor Company. *Continuing Process Control.* Statistical Methods Office, 1984.

Grant, Eugene L., and Richard S. Leavenworth. *Statistical Quality Control.* New York: McGraw-Hill, 1988.

Juran, Joseph M., and Frank M. Gryna. Chapters 16 and 17 in *Juran's Quality Control Handbook,* 4th ed. New York: McGraw-Hill, 1988.

Munechika, Masahiko. "Studies on Process Capability in Machining Processes." In *Proceedings of the International Conference on Quality Control, Tokyo, 1987.*

Ottand, Ellis R., and Edward G. Schilling. *Process Quality Control.* New York: McGraw-Hill, 1990.

IBM Quality Institute. *Process Control, Capability and Improvement.* 1985.

Takahashi, Takenori. "Process Control in Service Industry." In *Proceedings of the 44th Annual Quality Congress, San Francisco, 1990* (American Society for Quality Control).

Von Rutte, Wolf. "Selection of Business Processes and their Critical Success Factors (CSF)." In *Proceedings of the Conference of the European Foundation for Quality Management, Montreux, October 1989.*

Chapter 8

Ishikawa, Kaoru. Chap. 5 in *What Is Total Quality Control? The Japanese Way.* Englewood Cliffs, N.J.: Prentice-Hall, 1985.

Mattana, Giovanni. *Qualità, affidabilità, certificazione.* Milan: Franco Angeli, 1990.

Mizuno, Shigeru. Chap. 1, 2 in *Company-Wide Total Quality Control.* Tokyo: Asian Productivity Organization, 1989.

Nayatani, Yoshinobu. *TQC in Japan.* Tokyo: JUSE Seminar, 1988.

Sasaki, Naoto, and David Hutchins., eds. *The Japanese Approach to Product Quality.* Oxford: Pergamon Press, 1984.

Chapter 9

Abegglen, James C., and George Stalk, Jr. *Kaisha: The Japanese Corporation.* New York: Basic Books, 1985.

Chalmers, Stuart W. "Western Application of Kaizen." In *Seminar and Plant Tour to Study Productivity of Japanese Industry.* Tokyo: The Cambridge Corporation, June-July, 1987.

Harrington, James H. *The Improvement Process.* New York: McGraw-Hill, 1986.

Harrington, James H. *Excellence — The IBM Way.* Milwaukee: ASQC Quality Press, 1988.

Imai, Masaaki. *Kaizen.* New York: Random House, 1986.

Japan Management Association. "Continuous Improvement at Canon." *Total Quality Management,* November 1988.

Juran, Joseph M. *Managerial Breakthrough.* New York: McGraw-Hill, 1964.

Juran, Joseph M., and Frank M. Gryna. Chap. 22 in *Juran's Quality Control Handbook,* 4th ed. New York: McGraw-Hill, 1988.

Chapter 10

Andreasen, Mogens Myrup, and Lars Hein. *Integrated Product Development.* Berlin: IPS Publications Springer-Verlag, 1987.

"Designing Quality Process." *TQM Magazine,* April 1990.

Ishikawa, Kaoru. Chap. 4 in *What Is Total Quality Control? The Japanese Way.* Englewood Cliffs, N.J.: Prentice Hall, 1985.

Makino, Noburo. *Decline and Prosperity: Corporate Innovation in Japan.* Tokyo: Kodansha International, 1987.

Mizuno, Shigeru. Chap. 11 in *Company-Wide Total Quality Control.* Tokyo: Asian Productivity Organization, 1989.

Mizuno, Shigeru, and Norikazu Mizuno. "Total Quality Activities and Their System." In *Proceedings of the International Conference on Quality Control, Tokyo, 1987.*

Moritani, Masanori. *Japanese Technology.* Tokyo: Simul Press, 1982.

Moritani, Masanori. *Advanced Technology and the Japanese Contribution.* Tokyo: Nomura Securities Co., 1983.

"A Survey on Japanese Technology." *The Economist,* December 1989.

Takeuchi, Hirokata, and Ikujiro Nonaka. "The New Product Development Game." *Harvard Business Review,* January-February 1986.

Tatsuno, Sheridan M. Chap. 6 in *Created in Japan.* New York: Harper & Row, 1990.

Chapter 11

The Cambridge Corporation. "QC Circle Activities of the Tochigi Plant – Nissan Motor Co., Ltd." In *Seminar and Plant Tour to Study Productivity of Japanese Industry.* Tokyo, June 1986.

The Cambridge Corporation. "QC Circle Activities in Nissan Motor – Nissan MotorCo., Ltd." In *Seminar and Plant Tour to Study Productivity of Japanese Industry.* Tokyo, June-July 1987.

The Cambridge Corporation, Seminar and Plant Tour to Study Productivity of Japanese Industry. June 1982; June 1986; June-July 1987; February 1988.

The Cambridge Corporation. "TQC Activities at Fuji Photo Film Co., Ltd." In *Seminar and Plant Tour to Study Productivity of Japanese Industry.* Tokyo, February 1988.

The Cambridge Corporation. "TQC Promotion of Tokyo Juki Industrial Co., Ltd." In *Seminar and Plant Tour to Study Productivity of Japanese Industry.* Tokyo, June 1986.

"TQC and QC Circle Activities at Ricoh," In The Cambridge Corporation, *Seminar and Plant Tour to Study Productivity of Japanese Industry,* Tokyo, February 1988.

Japan Human Relations Associations. *The Idea Book*. Cambridge, Mass.: Productivity Press, 1988.

Mizuno, Shigeru. *Company-Wide Total Quality Control*. Tokyo: Asian Productivity Organization, 1989.

Chapter 12

Galgano, Alberto. *I Sette Strumenti della Qualità Totale*. Milan: Il Sole 24 Ore Libri, 1992.

Gitlow, Howard, Shelly Gitlow, Alan Oppenheim, and Rosa Oppenheim. *Tools and Methods for the Improvement of Quality*. Homewood, Ill.: R.D. Irwin, 1988.

Iizuka, Yoshinori. "Key Points for Success in Problem Solving." In *Proceedings of the 44th Annual Quality Congress, San Francisco, May 1990* (American Society for Quality Control).

Ishikawa, Kaoru. *Guide to Quality Control*. Tokyo: Asian Productivity Organization, 1976.

Kume, Hitoshi. "Statistical Methods for Quality Improvement." Tokyo: Association for Overseas Technical Scholarship, 1988.

Popplewell, Barry, Lonni Rodgers, and Jan De Vries. *Top Tools — Teamwork on Problems*. Eindhoven: Philips International Corporate Quality Bureau, 1990.

Chapter 13

Barker, Thomas B. *Quality by Experimental Design*. New York: Marcel Dekker, 1985.

Bhote, Keki R. "DOE — The High Road to Quality." *Management Review*, January 1988.

Davies, Owen L. *Design and Analysis of Industrial Experiments*. New York: Hafner, 1971.

Grant, Eugene L., and Richard S. Leavenworth. *Statistical Quality Control*. Tokyo: McGraw-Hill (International Student Edition), 1980.

Hunter, Box. *Statistics for Experiment*. New York: Wiley, 1978.

Kobayashi, Ryuichi. "QC-Game, A Powerful Tool of Statistical Quality Control Education." *Proceedings of the International Conference on Quality Control, Tokyo, 1987.*

Ross, Phillip J. *Taguchi Techniques for Quality Engineering.* New York: McGraw-Hill, 1988.

Shainin, Dorian, and Peter Shainin. "Analysis of Experiments." In *Proceedings of the 44th Annual Quality Congress, San Francisco, May 14-16, 1990* (American Society for Quality Control).

Chapter 14

Brassard, Michel. "The Memory Jogger Plus — Featuring the Seven Management and Planning Tools." Methuen, Mass.: GOAL/QPC, 1989.

Galgano, Alberto. *I Nuovi Sette Strumenti Manageriali.* Milan: Il Sole 24 Ore, 1993.

Mitonneau, Henri. *Changer le management de la Qualité: sept nouveaux outils.* Paris: Afnor Gestion, 1989.

Mizuno, Shigeru, ed. *Managing for Quality Improvement: The 7 New Tools.* Cambridge, Mass.: Productivity Press, 1988.

Natayani, Yoshinobu. "The 7 Management Tools and Their Applications." In *Proceedings of the International Conference on Quality Control, Tokyo, 1987.*

Union of Japanese Scientists and Engineers (JUSE). "Seven Management Tools for QC." In *Reports of Statistical Application Research,* special edition, vol. 33, no. 2, Tokyo: June 1986.

Chapter 15

Adams, Robert M., and Mark D. Gavoor. "Quality Function Deployment: Its Promise and Reality." In *Proceedings of the 44th Annual Quality Congress, San Francisco, May 14-16, 1990* (American Society for Quality Control).

Akao, Yoji. *Quality Function Deployment: Integrating Customer Requirements into Product Design.* Cambridge, Mass.: Productivity Press, 1990.

Akao, Yoji, Tadashi Ohfuji, and Tomoyoshi Naoi. "Surveys and Reviews on Quality Function Deployment in Japan." In *Proceedings of the International Congress on Quality Control, Tokyo, 1987.*

Bersbach, Peter L., and Philip R. Wahl. "QFD on a Defense Contract." In *Proceedings of the 44th Annual Quality Congress, San Francisco, May 14-16, 1990* (American Society for Quality Control).

Hauser, John R., and Don Clausing. "The House of Quality." *Harvard Business Review*, May-June, 1986.

Kogure, Masao, and Yoji Akao. "Quality Function Deployment and Company-Wide Quality Control." *Quality Progress*, October, 1985.

Kymal, Chad A., Michael J. Ryan, and Claes G. Fornell. "Getting More Out of QFD by Integrating It with Corporate Strategy."

Proceedings of the 44th Annual Quality Congress, San Francisco, May 14-16, 1990 (American Society for Quality Control).

Proceedings of the 1st Symposium on Quality Function Deployment, Novi, Michigan, June 19-20, 1989.

Proceedings of the 2nd Symposium on Quality Function Deployment, Novi, Michigan, June 18-19, 1990.

Sullivan, L.P. "Quality Function Deployment." *Quality Progress*, June 1986.

Yoshizawa, Tadashi, and Hisakazu Shindo. "Quality Deployment in Software Product Development." *Proceedings of the International Congress on Quality Control, Tokyo, 1987.*

Yoshizawa, Tadashi, Yoji Akao, Michiteru Ono, and Hisakazu Sindou. "Recent Aspects of QFD in the Japanese Software Industry." In *Proceedings of the 44th Annual Quality Congress, San Francisco, May 14-16, 1990* (American Society for Quality Control).

Zucchelli, Francesco. "Total Quality and Quality Function Deployment." *European Quality Management Forum*, October 19, 1989.

Chapter 16

Fukuda, Ryuji. "Introduction to CEDAC." *Quality Progress,* November 1981.

Fukuda, Ryuji. *Managerial Engineering.* Stamford, Ct.: Productivity Press, 1983.

Fukuda, Ryuji. *CEDAC: A Tool for Continuous Systematic Improvement.* Cambridge, Mass.: Productivity Press, 1989.

Galgano & Associati. *La gestione del miglioramento: il sistema CEDAC* (seminar materials).

Chapter 17

Imai, Masaaki. Chap. 5 in *Kaizen.* New York: Random House, 1986.

Ishikawa, Kaoru. Chap. 6 in *What Is Total Quality Control? The Japanese Way.* Englewood Cliffs, N.J.: Prentice-Hall, 1985.

Miyauchi, Ichiro. "Il CWQC." Papers from the Galgano & Associati seminar, Milan, November, 1987.

Chapter 18

Akao, Yoji. *Hoshin Kanri.* Cambridge, Mass.: Productivity Press, 1991.

Amon, V., and Mogollon-Seemer, M.T. "The Deming Prize Process at FPL." In *Proceedings of the 44th Annual Quality Congress, San Francisco, May 14-16, 1990* (American Society for Quality Control).

The Cambridge Corporation, "Policy Deployment at the Production Headquarters of Kobayashi Kose Ltd." (1986 Seminar and Plant Tour).

Galgano, Alberto. "Policy Deployment and Quality Deployment in Italy." In *Proceedings of the 44th Annual Quality Congress, San Francisco, May 14-16, 1990* (American Society for Quality Control).

Imai, Masaaki. Chap. 5 in *Kaizen.* New York: Random House, 1986.

King, Bob. *Hoshin Planning, the Developmental Approach.* Methuen, Mass.: GOAL/QPC, 1989.

Kogure, Masao. "Some Fundamental Problems on *Hoshin-Kanri* in Japanese TQC." In *Proceedings of the 44th Annual Quality Congress, San Francisco, May 14-16, 1990* (American Society for Quality Control).

Koura, Kozo. "System of Management by Policy." In *Proceedings of the International Congress on Quality Control, Tokyo, 1987.*

Koura, Kozo. "Survey and Research in Japan Concerning Policy Management." In *Proceedings of the 44th Annual Quality Congress, San Francisco, May 14-16, 1990* (American Society for Quality Control).

Mizuno, Shigeru. Chap. 6 in *Company-Wide Total Quality Control.* Tokyo: Asian Productivity Organization, 1989.

Motumo, Baba. "La Direzione per Politiche nel quadro del Company-Wide Quality Control." Documents from the Galgano & Associati Seminar, Milan, May 27, 1987.

Chapter 19

Berger, Roger W., and Thomas Hart. *Statistical Process Control — A Guide for Implementation.* Milwaukee: ASQC Quality Press, 1986.

Brunetti, Wayne. "Il successo di Qualità Totale premiato con il prestigioso premio Deming — Il caso Florida Power and Light." Documents from a Galgano & Associati Seminar, Milan, February 1, 1990.

Caplette, Michele, and David Saunders. "Becoming the Internal Vendor of Choice through Systematic Segmentation and Research." In *Proceedings of the 44th Annual Quality Congress, San Francisco, May 1990* (American Society for Quality Control).

Deming, Edwards W. Chap. 10 in *Out of the Crisis.* Cambridge, Mass.: MIT-CAES, 1986.

Kamio, Makoto. "Some Topics on Daily Improvement Activity." In *Proceedings of the 44th Annual Quality Congress, San Francisco, May 1990* (American Society for Quality Control).

Lynch, Barbara F. "How to Write a Quality Procedure." In *Proceedings of the 43rd Annual Quality Congress, Toronto, May 1989* (American Society for Quality Control).

Sterett, Kent. "L'applicazione della Qualità Totale in una grande azienda americana: la Florida Power and Light." Documents from a Galgano & Associati Seminar, Milan, May 29-30, 1989.

Chapter 20

Galgano, Alberto. "Quality Circles Movement in the Italian Manufacturing and Service Industries." In *Proceedings of the 44th QC Circle Convention, Tokyo, October 24-26, 1990* (JUSE, QC Circle Headquarters).

QC Circle Headquarters. *General Principles of the QC Circles.* Tokyo: JUSE, 1980.

QC Circle Headquarters. *How to Operate QC Circle Activities.* Tokyo: JUSE, 1985.

Imaizumi, Masumasa. "History of QC Circles." In *Proceedings of the International QC Circle Convention, Tokyo, 1981.*

Ishikawa, Kaoru. *Quality Control Circles at Work — Cases from Japan's Manufacturing and Services.* Tokyo: Asian Productivity Organization, 1984.

Izui, Tsutomu. "Factors to Activate QC Circle Activities and Communication Structure." In *Proceedings of the 44th Annual Quality Congress, San Francisco, May 1990* (American Society for Quality Control).

Union of Japanese Scientists and Engineers. *Reports of QC Circle Activities 1989.* Tokyo: JUSE. (Contains presentations of numerous quality circle projects from top Japanese companies. A report is prepared each year on the occasion of visits by the leaders of circles in Europe and the USA.)

Lawler, Edward, III, and Susan A. Mohrman. "Quality Circles After the Fad." *Harvard Business Review,* January-February, 1985.

Merli, Giorgio. *I Circoli della Qualità.* Rome: Edizioni Lavoro, 1986.

Nicoletti, Bernardo. *I Circoli della Qualità.* Milan: Franco Angeli, 1986.

Shea, Gregory P. "Quality Circles: The Danger of Bottled Change." *Sloan Management Review,* Spring 1986.

Tsuge, Takayuki. "QC Circles Activities at Nippondenso." In *Proceedings of the International Quality Control Circles Congress, Seoul, 1982.*

Chapter 21

Abe, Yoshio. *People-Oriented Management.* Tokyo: Diamond, 1987.

Inohara, Ideo. Chap. 6 in *Human Resources Development in Japanese Companies.* Tokyo: Asian Productivity Organization, 1990.

Kondo, Yoshio. "Improvement of Productivity versus Humanity." *Proceedings of the International Congress on Quality Control.* Tokyo: 1987.

Miyauchi, Ichiro. "Education and Training for TQC." In *International Seminar for Senior Management.* Tokyo: JUSE, 1989.

Union of Japanese Scientists and Engineers (JUSE)."Education and Training, Foreman and QC Circle Leaders in Japan." In *Reports of Statistical Application Research,* Special Edition, Vol. 21, No. 4, December 1974.

Tsuda, Yoshikazu. "Management Through Company-Wide Quality Control — Management Tools and Management Training Method Using Those Tools." In *Proceedings of the European Organization for Quality Control — World Quality Congress, Brighton, U.K., 1984.*

Chapter 22

Arter, Dennis A. "Evaluate Standards and Improve Performance with a Quality Audit." *Quality Progress,* September 1989.

Ishikawa, Kaoru. Chap. 7 in *What Is Total Quality Control? The Japanese Way.* Englewood Cliffs, N.J.: Prentice-Hall, 1985.

Mizuno, Shigeru. Chap. 14 in *Company-Wide Total Quality Control.* Tokyo: Asian Productivity Organization, 1989.

Shimoyamada, Kaoru. "The President's Audit: QC Audit at Komatsu." *Quality Progress,* January 1987.

Chapter 23

Dorski, Lawrence R. "Management Commitment to Japanese Apple Pie." *Quality Progress,* February 1984.

Holder, Robert, and Richard McKinney. "Leadership from Depth." *Journal for Quality and Participation,* September 1990.

Ishikawa, Kaoru. Chap. 7 in *What Is Total Quality Control? The Japanese Way.* Englewood Cliffs, N.J.: Prentice-Hall, 1985.

Juran, Joseph M. "Upper Management and Quality." In Juran, Joseph M., and Frank Gryna, *Juran's Quality Control Handbook.* New York: McGraw-Hill, 1988.

Juran, Joseph M. *Juran on Leadership for Quality.* New York: Free Press, 1989.

Karatsu, Hajime. Chap. 2 in *TQC Wisdom of Japan.* Cambridge, Mass.: Productivity Press, 1988.

Kobayashi, Koji. "Quality Management at NEC Corporation." *Quality Progress,* April 1986.

Mizuno, Shigeru. Chap. 2 in *Company-Wide Total Quality Control.* Tokyo: Asian Productivity Press, 1984.

Mozer, Clark. "TQC: a Route to the Deming Prize." *Quality Progress,* September 1984.

Nemoto, Masao. Chap. 4 in *Total Quality Control for Management.* Englewood Cliffs, N.J.: Prentice-Hall, 1987.

Chapter 24

The Cambridge Corporation. "Quality Control Activities at Matsushita Electric Ind." In *The Cambridge Report n. 1,* Tokyo, February 1982.

Itoh, Tokuhei. "Implementation of TQC at Shimizu Plant." In *Seminar and Plant Tour to Study Productivity of Japanese Industry.* Tokyo: The Cambridge Corporation, 1982.

Karatsu, Hajime. "Quality Control — The Japanese Approach." In *The Cambridge Report n. 1.* Tokyo: The Cambridge Corporation, February 1982.

Kobayashi, Yotaro. "CWQC in Fuji-Xerox Co. Ltd." In *The Cambridge Report n. 1.* Tokyo: The Cambridge Corporation, February 1982.

Koshiyama, Kinpei. "TQC at Shimizu." In *Seminar and Plant Tour to Study Productivity of Japanese Industry.* Tokyo: The Cambridge Corporation, 1982.

Miyauchi, Ichiro. "Company-Wide Quality Control Implementation." Paper for a Galgano & Associati Seminar, *Company-Wide Quality Control in Production,* Milan, July 4-5, 1984.

Mizuno, Shigeru. "The CWQC Introduction and Promotion." In *Proceedings of the International Congress on Quality Control, Tokyo, 1987.*

Chapter 25

Churchill, Larry. "Using Multidisciplinary Teams to Enhance Business Performance." In *Proceedings of the Convention of the European Foundation for Quality Management, London, October 1990.*

Galgano & Associati. "Il programma aziendale di Miglioramento della Qualità [A Company Program for Quality Improvement]." In *Proceedings of the Galgano National Convention, March 1984.*

Galgano & Associati. "La strategia della Qualita nelle prime 1.600 aziende industriali italiane; La Qualita nelle piccole e medie aziende delle province di Bergamo e Ancona; Lo sviluppo dei Circoli delle Qualita in Italia; La Formazione per la Qualita nelle grandi aziende italiane [Quality Strategy in the principal 1600 maufacturing companies in Italy; Quality in small- and mid-size companies in the provinces of Bergamo and Ancona; The Development of Quality circles in Italy; Quality Training in Italy's large companies]." Research papers presented at the Galgano National Convention, Milan, May 1985.

Miyaguchi, Ichiro. "Company-Wide Quality Control Implementation." Documents from a Galgano & Associati Seminar, *Company-Wide Quality Control in Production, Milan, July 4-5, 1984.*

Mizuno, Shigeru. "The CWQC Introduction and Promotion." In *Proceedings of the International Congress on Quality Control, Tokyo, 1987.*

Chapter 26

Anderson, Douglas N., and George D. Murphy. "Quality, a Positive Business Strategy." In *Proceedings of the 34th Annual Convention of the European Organization for Quality, Dublin, 1990.*

Proceedings of the European Quality Management Forum, Montreux, October 19, 1989.

Blauw, Jan Nico. "A Strategy for the Implementation of Company-Wide Quality Control." In *Proceedings of the 34th Annual Convention of the European Organization for Quality, Dublin, 1990.*

Brown, Mark Graham, and Ray Svenson. "What 'Doing' Total Quality Management Really Means." *Journal for Quality and Participation,* September 1990.

Cullen, Joe, and Jack Hollingum. *Implementing Total Quality.* Bedford, U.K.: IFS Ltd., 1987.

Denecker, Peter. "TQC, A Decade of Experience." In *Proceedings of the Convention of the European Foundation for Quality Management, London, October 1990.*

Dillon, Linda S. "Can Japanese Methods Be Applied in the Western Workplace?" *Quality Progress,* October 1990.

Hutchins, David. "Total Quality — a Strategy that Works Outside Japan." In *Proceedings of the 34th Annual Convention of the European Organization for Quality, Dublin, 1990.*

Ishikawa, Kaoru. "How to Apply Company-Wide Quality Control in Foreign Countries." In The Cambridge Corporation, *Seminar and Plant Tour to Study Productivity of Japanese Industry,* Tokyo, June 1986.

Jablonski, Joseph R. *Implementing Total Quality Management — Competing in the 1990s.* Albuquerque: Technical Management Consortium, 1990.

Philips International B.V. *Managerial Guide to Breakthrough in CWQC.* Eindhoven: Corporate Quality Bureau, 1987.

Merli, Giorgio. "The Evolution of Quality Improvement Programmes in Western Europe." In *Proceedings of the European Quality Management Forum (EQMF), October 19, 1989.*

Pascale, Richard Tanner. *Managing on the Edge.* New York: Simon & Schuster, 1990.

Sullivan, Lawrence P. "The Seven Stages in CWQC." *Quality Progress,* May 1986.

About the Author

Alberto Galgano has been chairman of the Galgano & Associates Consulting Group since 1962. The group, comprising six companies with more than 120 consultants, offers an extensive range of advisory services to management. Before forming his own firm, Mr. Galgano held managerial positions in two major Italian industrial groups for more than six years.

Highly regarded throughout Europe, Mr. Galgano served for four years as president of the *Fédération Européenne des Associations de Conseil en Organisation,* (FEACO) a continental organization of consulting firms. He is also past president of the Italian Association of Management Consulting Firms (AICOD), president of ASSOQUALITY (the quality organization supported by Assolombarda), and vice president of the Italian Federation of National Associations for Companies in the Tertiary Sector (FONTI).

Mr. Galgano was awarded a chemical engineering degree in 1952 by the Politechnico di Milano. He is the author of nine books on quality and management-related subjects. *Companywide Quality Management* is his first book available in English.

OTHER BOOKS FROM PRODUCTIVITY PRESS

Productivity Press publishes and distributes materials on continuous improvement in productivity, quality, and the creative involvement of all employees. Many of our products are direct source materials from Japan that have been translated into English for the first time and are available exclusively from Productivity. Supplemental products and services include membership groups, conferences, seminars, in-house training and consulting, audio-visual training programs, and industrial study missions. Call toll-free 1-800-394-6868 for our free catalog.

Achieving Total Quality Management
A Program for Action

Michel Perigord

This is an outstanding book on total quality management (TQM) — a compact guide to the concepts, methods, and techniques involved in achieving total quality. It shows you how to make TQM a companywide strategy, not just in technical areas, but in marketing and administration as well. Written in an accessible, instructive style by a top European quality expert, it is methodical, logical, and thorough.

ISBN 0-915299-60-7 / 392 pages / $49.95 / Order ACHTQM-B142

The Benchmarking Management Guide

American Productivity & Quality Center

If you're planning, organizing, or actually undertaking a benchmarking program, you need the most authoritative source of information to help you get started and to manage the process all the way through. Written expressly for managers of benchmarking projects by the APQC's renowned International Benchmarking Clearinghouse, this guide provides exclusive information from members who have already paved the way. It includes information on training courses and ways to apply Baldrige, Deming, and ISO 9000 criteria for internal assessment, and has a complete bibliography of benchmarking literature.

ISBN 1-56327-045-5 / 260 pages / $39.95 / Order BMG-B142

The Benchmarking Workbook
Adapting Best Practices for Performance Improvement

Gregory H. Watson

Managers today need benchmarking to anticipate trends and maintain competitive advantage. This practical workbook shows you how to do your own benchmarking study. Watson's discussion includes a case study that takes you through each step of the benchmarking process, raises thought-provoking questions, and provides examples of how to use forms for a benchmarking study.
ISBN 1-56327-033-1 / 169 pages / $29.95 / Order BENCHW-B142

Better Makes Us Best

Dr. John Psarouthakis

A perfect way to introduce the concept of total employee involvement to your workforce. Here's a short, simple, yet very powerful guide to improvement for any business or individual. The secret is making incremental progress toward clear goals. Working this way, people feel more satisfied and productive, and their work measurably improves. That makes the critical difference in everything from the quality of a corporate culture to the bottom line.
ISBN 0-915299-56-9 / 95 pages / $19.95 / Order BMUB-B142

Caught in the Middle
A Leadership Guide for Partnership in the Workplace

Rick Maurer

Managers today are caught between old skills and new expectations. You're expected not only to improve quality and services, but also to get staff more involved. This stimulating book provides the inspiration and know-how to achieve these goals as it brings to light the rewards of establishing a real partnership with your staff. Includes self-assessment questionnaires.
ISBN 1-56327-004-8 / 258 pages / $29.95 / Order CAUGHT-B142

Continuous Improvement in Operations
A Systematic Approach to Waste Reduction

Alan Robinson (ed.)

Here in one place is the world's most advanced thinking on Just-in-Time, Kaizen, Total Employee Involvement and Total Productive Maintenance. This handy book brings you a compendium of materials from our best-selling classics by world-famous manufacturing experts. The excerpts you'll read offer wisdom and experience that is unique to the developer of each approach. The authoritative introduction integrates the developments of these manufacturing gurus within a twofold theme — the elimination of invisible waste and the creation of a work environment that welcomes and implements employees' ideas.
ISBN 0-915299-51-8 / 406 pages / $34.95 / Order ROB2C-B142

Cycle Time Management
The Fast Track to Time-Based Productivity Improvement

Patrick Northey and Nigel Southway

As much as 90 percent of the operational activities in a traditional plant are nonessential or pure waste. This book presents a proven methodology for eliminating this waste within 24 to 30 months by measuring productivity in terms of time instead of revenue or people. CTM is a cohesive management strategy that integrates just-in-time (JIT) production, computer integrated manufacturing (CIM), and total quality control (TQC). From this succinct, highly-focused book, you'll learn what CTM is, how to implement it, and how to manage it.
ISBN 1-56327-015-3 / 200 pages / $29.95 / Order CYCLE-B142

Handbook for Productivity Measurement and Improvement

William F. Christopher and Carl G. Thor, eds.

An unparalleled resource! In over 100 chapters, nearly 80 front-runners in the quality movement reveal the evolving theory and specific practices of world-class organizations. Spanning a wide variety of industries and business sectors, they discuss quality and productivity in manufacturing, service industries, profit centers, administration, nonprofit and government institutions, health care and education. Contributors include Robert C. Camp, Peter F. Drucker, Jay W. Forrester, Joseph M. Juran, Robert S. Kaplan, John W. Kendrick, Yasuhiro Monden, and Lester C. Thurow. Comprehensive in scope and organized for easy reference, this compendium belongs in every company and academic institution concerned with business and industrial viability.
ISBN 1-56327-007-2 / 1344 pages / $90.00 / Order HPM-B142

Handbook of Quality Tools
The Japanese Approach

Tetsuichi Asaka and Kazuo Ozeki (eds.)

The Japanese have stunned the world by their ability to produce top quality products at competitive prices. This comprehensive teaching manual, which includes the 7 traditional and 5 newer QC tools, explains each tool, why it's useful, and how to construct and use it. Information is presented in easy-to-grasp language, with step-by-step instructions, illustrations, and examples of each tool.

ISBN 0-915299-45-3 / 315 pages / $65.00 / Order HQT-B142

Hoshin Kanri
Policy Deployment for Successful TQM

Yoji Akao (ed.)

Hoshin kanri, the Japanese term for policy deployment, is an approach to strategic planning and quality improvement that has become a pillar of Total Quality Management (TQM) for a growing number of U.S. firms. This book is a compilation of examples of policy deployment that demonstrates how company vision is converted into individual responsibility. It includes practical guidelines, 150 charts and diagrams, and five case studies that illustrate the procedures of hoshin kanri. The six steps to advanced process planning are reviewed and include a five-year vision, one-year plan, deployment to departments, execution, monthly audit, and annual audit.

ISBN 0-915299-57-7 / 241 pages / $65.00 / Order HOSHIN-B142

Measuring, Managing, and Maximizing Performance

Will Kaydos

You do not need to be an exceptionally skilled technician or inspirational leader to improve your company's quality and productivity. In non-technical, jargon-free, practical terms this book details the entire process of improving performance, from why and how the improvement process work to what must be done to begin and to sustain continuous improvement of performance. Special emphasis is given to the role that performance measurement plays in identifying problems and opportunities.

ISBN 0-915299-98-4 / 284 pages / $39.95 / Order MMMP-B142

TQM for Technical Groups
Total Quality Principles for Product Development

Kiyoshi Uchimaru, Susumu Okamoto, and Bunteru Kurahara

Achieving total quality in product design and development is a daunting but essential goal for technical personnel. This unprecedented and highly practical book was written especially for technical groups working to achieve total quality in product development. Originally published by JUSE, the Union of Japanese Scientists and Engineers, the book includes an important case study of NEC IC Microcomputer Systems, winner of the Deming Prize. A separate section of the book addresses all the changes required in corporate management to institute TQM at the product design level. Step-by-step instructions, with specific examples of each, show you how to plan, implement, and sustain an effective TQM program.
ISBN 1-56327-005-6 / 258 pages / $60.00 / Order TQMTG-B142

Vision Management
Translating Strategy into Action

SANNO Management Development Research Center (ed.)

For over ten years, managers of Japan's top companies have gathered at SANNO University to brainstorm about innovative corporate management methods. This book is based on the proven methodology that evolved from their ideas. It describes how the intangible aspects of vision-based strategy can be integrated into a concrete implementation model and clarifies the relationship among vision, strategy, objectives, goals, and day-to-day activities.
ISBN 0-915299-80-1 / 272 pages / $29.95 / Order VISM-B142

Workplace Management

Taiichi Ohno

An in-depth view of how one of this century's leading industrial thinkers approaches problem solving and continuous improvement. Gleaned from Ohno's forty years of experimentation and innovation at Toyota, where he created Just-In-Time (JIT), this book explains the concepts Ohno considered most important to successful top management, with an emphasis on quality.
ISBN 0-915299-19-4 / 165 pages / $39.95 / Order WPM-B142

TO ORDER: Write, phone, or fax Productivity Press, Dept. BK, P.O. Box 13390, Portland, OR 97213, phone 1-800-394-6868, fax 1-800-394-6286. Send check or charge to your credit card (American Express, Visa, MasterCard accepted).

U.S. ORDERS: Add $5 shipping for first book, $2 each additional for UPS surface delivery. We offer attractive quantity discounts for bulk purchases of individual titles; call for more information.

INTERNATIONAL ORDERS: Write, phone, or fax for quote and indicate shipping method desired. For international callers, telephone number is 503-235-0600 and fax number is 503-235-0909. Prepayment in U.S. dollars must accompany your order (checks must be drawn on U.S. banks). When quote is returned with payment, your order will be shipped promptly by the method requested.

NOTE: Price are in U.S. dollars and are subject to change without notice.